Marvin B. Sussman
Jane F. Gilgun
Editors

The Methods and Methodologies of Qualitative Family Research

T his volume is a stimulating and multi-faceted study of qualitative research about families. Through the contributors' thoughtful reflections on their methodologies, one is drawn compellingly into the creative process of qualitative research–the journeys researchers take with their work and the ways they are affected, often deeply, by their travels. The writers also illustrate beautifully how qualitative analysis of nontraditional data, such as folktales and letters, yields rich insights into families. This book is an exciting introduction for anyone embarking on qualitative family research, and for researchers already working in the field, it offers new directions and fresh ideas.

Elizabeth Church, PhD
Associate Professor, University Counselling Centre, Memorial University of Newfoundland, St. John's, Newfoundland, Canada

When faced with the task of coming up with "a quotable review, or blurb, that consists of a paragraph or two and includes a few catchy and poignant statements about the book's highlights, strengths, benefits, and its intended audience" I intended to do my usual skimming of the book for particular portions of interest and whipping out my review in a couple of hours. As I got into the book, I decided to set aside chapters that were particularly interesting to file for later reference. Before I realized what was happening, my entire morning was gone, I had nearly every chapter of the book in my "to file" stack, I had set aside two chapters as required readings for a class I am teaching this semester, and I was contemplating new ways to approach the analysis of step-mother interviews that I had recently been involved in collecting.

The Methods and Methodologies of Qualitative Family Research is fascinating reading that provides wonderful examples of feminist qualitative research. The chapters are engaging in the stories that they tell, but they also provide access to the "jargon" of qualitative research in an informative but easily assimilated manner. The "how to" aspects of these chapters are exceptional. A classic example is Walker's study of women's letters and her companion piece about how she did the study (her dissertation). What a wonderful source of information to be able to provide a graduate student who is contemplating conducting a qualitative study!

A final note. During my term as editor of *Journal of Marriage and the Family*, I encouraged the submission of qualitative research only to have manuscripts rejected because, "Although we need to publish more qualitative family research THIS is NOT a good example." These kinds of responses were from the qualitative reviewers. The reviewers who were primarily quantitative researchers were much more caustic. In a few instances I kept with the piece through revision after revision, much as did the editors of this book. I think the final product was worth the extra time and energy spent, and this book is an excellent example of similar efforts. The book will be especially inspiring to novice qualitative researchers. I also firmly believe that the more good qualitative research is published, the more good qualitative research will be available for publishing. Models of excellent qualitative family research are needed, and this book provides them.

Marilyn Coleman, EdD
Professor of Human Development and Family Studies
University of Missouri-Columbia

This volume is an intriguing collection of research reports and essays that provides a rich interplay of qualitative studies and reflections on the research process. The focus on showcasing methods and methodologies is the theme that weaves together topics as diverse as Bahamian family life, generative fathering, and the effects of research on the researchers. Each chapter makes a unique contribution to a book that is not only stimulating and provocative in itself, but also a valuable resource for anyone teaching a qualitative research course. It is unusual when a book is able to satisfy the needs and interest of both novice and experienced researchers. This book offers that potential as it documents the state-of-the-art in qualitative family research and suggests the vast array of possibilities for thinking about and doing innovative research.

Kristine M. Baber, PhD
Associate Professor,
Department of Family Studies
University of New Hampshire

Qualitative research has always been informed by various theoretical and methodological traditions. This volume testifies to this diversity. It makes qualitative approaches more explicit in methodological essays and research reports, addresses the uses and generation of theory; links between practice, education, and research; maximizing rigor; and ethical issues.

Doctoral students and experienced family researchers will benefit from discussions that describe the pragmatic considerations and intellectual skills involved in designing and conducting qualitative studies. Contributors' personal reflections provide a glimpse into the many challenges and demands that confront the qualitative researcher. Finally, the research reports contribute to the understanding of contemporary families.

Lee SmithBattle, RN, DNSc
Assistant Professor, School of Nursing
Saint Louis University
St. Louis, MO

The Haworth Press, Inc.

The Methods
and Methodologies
of Qualitative
Family Research

The Methods
and Methodologies
of Qualitative
Family Research

Marvin B. Sussman
Jane F. Gilgun
Editors

The Haworth Press, Inc.
New York · London

The Methods and Methodologies of Qualitative Family Research has also been published as *Marriage & Family Review,* Volume 24, Numbers 1/2 and 3/4 1996.

The development, preparation, and publication of this work has been undertaken with great care. However, the publisher, employees, editors, and agents of The Haworth Press and all imprints of The Haworth Press, Inc., including the Haworth Medical Press and Pharmaceutical Products Press, are not responsible for any errors contained herein or for consequences that may ensue from use of materials or information contained in this work. Opinions expressed by the author(s) are not necessarily those of The Haworth Press, Inc.

Cover design by Monica L. Seifert

The Haworth Press, Inc., 10 Alice Street, Binghamton, NY 13904-1580 USA

Library of Congress Cataloging-in-Publication Data

The methods and methodologies of qualitative family research / Marvin B. Sussman, Jane F. Gilgun, editors.
     p. cm.
    Also published as Marriage & family review, v. 24, nos. 1/2, 3/4 1996.
    Includes bibliographical references and index.
    ISBN 0-7890-0015-6 (alk. paper)–ISBN 0-7890-0305-8 (alk. paper)
    1. Family–Research. 2. Family–Research–Methodology. I. Sussman, Marvin B. II. Gilgun, Jane Frances. III. Title: Marriage & family review.
HQ10.M49 1997
306.85'07'2–dc21   96-51967
                                                             CIP

INDEXING & ABSTRACTING

Contributions to this publication are selectively indexed or abstracted in print, electronic, online, or CD-ROM version(s) of the reference tools and information services listed below. This list is current as of the copyright date of this publication. See the end of this section for additional notes.

- *Abstracts in Social Gerontology: Current Literature on Aging,* National Council on the Aging, Library, 409 Third Street SW, 2nd Floor, Washington, DC 20024

- *Abstracts of Research in Pastoral Care & Counseling,* Loyola College, 7135 Minstrel Way, Suite 101, Columbia, MD 21045

- *Academic Abstracts/CD-ROM,* EBSCO Publishing Editorial Department, P.O. Box 590, Ipswich, MA 01938-0590

- *Academic Search: database of 2,000 selected academic serials, updated monthly,* EBSCO Publishing, 83 Pine Street, Peabody, MA 01960

- *AGRICOLA Database,* National Agricultural Library, 10301 Baltimore Boulevard, Room 002, Beltsville, MD 20705

- *Applied Social Sciences Index & Abstracts (ASSIA) (Online: ASSI via Data-Star) (CDRom: ASSIA Plus),* Bowker-Saur Limited, Maypole House, Maypole Road, East Grinstead, West Sussex RH19 1HH, England

- *CNPIEC Reference Guide: Chinese National Directory of Foreign Periodicals,* P.O. Box 88, Beijing, People's Republic of China

- *Current Contents: Clinical Medicine/Life Sciences (CC:CM/LS) (weekly Table of Contents Service), and Social Science Citation Index. Articles also searchable through Social SciSearch, ISI's online database and in ISI's Research Alert current awareness service,* Institute for Scientific Information, 3501 Market Street, Philadelphia, PA 19104-3302 (USA)

- *Expanded Academic Index,* Information Access Company, 362 Lakeside Drive, Forest City, CA 94404

(continued)

- *Family Life Educator "Abstracts Section,"* ETR Associates, P.O. Box 1830, Santa Cruz, CA 95061-1830

- *Family Studies Database (online and CD/ROM)*, National Information Services Corporation, 306 East Baltimore Pike, 2nd Floor, Media, PA 19063

- *Family Violence & Sexual Assault Bulletin,* Family Violence & Sexual Assault Institute, 1211 East South East Loop, Suite 130, Tyler, TX 75701

- *Guide to Social Science & Religion in Periodical Literature,* National Periodical Library, P.O. Box 3278, Clearwater, FL 34630

- *IBZ International Bibliography of Periodical Literature*, Zeller Verlag GmbH & Co., P.O.B. 1949, d-49009 Osnabruck, Germany

- *Index to Periodical Articles Related to Law,* University of Texas, 727 East 26th Street, Austin, TX 78705

- *INTERNET ACCESS (& additional networks) Bulletin Board for Libraries ("BUBL"), coverage of information resources on INTERNET, JANET, and other networks.*
  - JANET X.29: UK.AC.BATH.BUBL or 00006012101300
  - TELNET: BUBL.BATH.AC.UK or 138.38.32.45 login 'bubl'
  - Gopher: BUBL.BATH.AC.UK (138.32.32.45). Port 7070
  - World Wide Web: http: / / www.bubl.bath.ac.uk./BUBL/ home.html
  - NISSWAIS: telnetniss.ac.uk (for the NISS gateway)
  The Andersonian Library, Curran Building, 101 St. James Road, Glasgow G4 ONS, Scotland

- *MasterFILE: updated database from EBSCO Publishing,* 83 Pine Street, Peabody, MA 01960

- *PASCAL International Bibliography T205: Sciences de l'information Documentation,* INIST/CNRS-Service Gestion des Documents Primaires, 2, allee du Parc de Brabois, F-54514 Vandoeuvre-les-Nancy, Cedex, France

- *Periodical Abstracts, Research I (general & basic reference indexing & abstracting data-base from University Microfilms International (UMI), 300 North Zeeb Road, P.O. Box 1346, Ann Arbor, MI 48106-1346),* UMI Data Courier, P.O. Box 32770, Louisville, KY 40232-2770

(continued)

- *Periodical Abstracts, Research II (broad coverage indexing & abstracting data-base from University Microfilms International (UMI), 300 North Zeeb Road, P.O. Box 1346, Ann Arbor, MI 48106-1346),* UMI Data Courier, P.O. Box 32770, Louisville, KY 40232-2770

- *Population Index,* Princeton University Office Population, 21 Prospect Avenue, Princeton, NJ 08544-2091

- *Psychological Abstracts (PsycINFO),* American Psychological Association, P.O. Box 91600, Washington, DC 20090-1600

- *Sage Family Studies Abstracts (SFSA),* Sage Publications, Inc., 2455 Teller Road, Newbury Park, CA 91320

- *Social Planning/Policy & Development Abstracts (SOPODA),* Sociological Abstracts, Inc., P.O. Box 22206, San Diego, CA 92192-0206

- *Social Science Source: coverage of 400 journals in the social sciences area, updated monthly,* EBSCO Publishing, 83 Pine Street, Peabody, MA 01960

- *Social Sciences Index (from Volume 1 & continuing),* The H.W. Wilson Company, 950 University Avenue, Bronx, NY 10452

- *Social Work Abstracts,* National Association of Social Workers, 750 First Street NW, 8th Floor, Washington, DC 20002

- *Sociological Abstracts (SA),* Sociological Abstracts, Inc., P.O. Box 22206, San Diego, CA 92192-0206

- *Special Educational Needs Abstracts,* Carfax Information Systems, P.O. Box 25, Abingdon, Oxfordshire OX14 3UE, United Kingdom

- *Studies on Women Abstracts,* Carfax Publishing Company, P.O. Box 25, Abingdon, Oxfordshire OX14 3UE, United Kingdom

- *Violence and Abuse Abstracts: A Review of Current Literature on Interpersonal Violence (VAA),* Sage Publications, Inc., 2455 Teller Road, Newbury Park, CA 91320

(continued)

SPECIAL BIBLIOGRAPHIC NOTES

related to special journal issues (separates)
and indexing/abstracting

☐ indexing/abstracting services in this list will also cover material in any "separate" that is co-published simultaneously with Haworth's special thematic journal issue or DocuSerial. Indexing/abstracting usually covers material at the article/chapter level.

☐ monographic co-editions are intended for either non-subscribers or libraries which intend to purchase a second copy for their circulating collections.

☐ monographic co-editions are reported to all jobbers/wholesalers/approval plans. The source journal is listed as the "series" to assist the prevention of duplicate purchasing in the same manner utilized for books-in-series.

☐ to facilitate user/access services all indexing/abstracting services are encouraged to utilize the co-indexing entry note indicated at the bottom of the first page of each article/chapter/contribution.

☐ this is intended to assist a library user of any reference tool (whether print, electronic, online, or CD-ROM) to locate the monographic version if the library has purchased this version but not a subscription to the source journal.

☐ individual articles/chapters in any Haworth publication are also available through the Haworth Document Delivery Services (HDDS).

ABOUT THE EDITORS

Marvin B. Sussman, PhD, is UNIDEL Professor of Human Behavior Emeritus at the College of Human Resources, University of Delaware; and Member of the CORE Faculty, Union Graduate School, Union Institute, Cincinnati, Ohio. A member of many professional organizations, he was awarded the 1980 Ernest W. Burgess Award of the National Council on Family Relations. In 1983, he was elected to the prestigious Academy of Groves for scholarly contributions to the field, as well as awarded a life-long membership for services to the Groves Conference on Marriage and the Family in 1984. Dr. Sussman received the Distinguished Family Award of the Society for the Study of Social Problems (1985) and the Lee Founders Award (1992), SSSP's highest Professional Award. Also in 1992 he was the recipient of the State of Delaware Gerontological Society Award for contributions to research and education in the family and aging fields. Dr. Sussman has published over 250 articles and books on family, community, rehabilitation, organizations, health and aging.

Jane F. Gilgun, PhD, LICSW, is Associate Professor, School of Social Work, University of Minnesota, Twin Cities. A social work practitioner with Rhode Island Child Welfare Services for more than a decade before she returned to graduate school for her PhD, Gilgun has bachelor's and master's degrees in English literature (from The Catholic University of America, Washington, DC, and the University of Rhode Island, Kingston, respectively), a licentiate in family studies and human sexuality from the University of Louvain, Belgium, a master's degree in social service administration from the University of Chicago, and a PhD in family studies from Syracuse University. As an antidote to all this education, Gilgun revels in her immersion in data, grounding not only her theory but herself in the concerns of other human beings. She has assumed leadership roles in the development of qualitative family research, chairing the Qualitative Family Research Network of the National Council on Family Relations during the early 1990s; editing *Qualitative Family Research*, the newsletter of the Network; and editing with Kerry Daly and Gerry Handel *Qualitative Methods in Family Research* (Sage, 1992), a text now in its fourth printing. She has published substantive and methodological articles in the major journals of her field, such as *Social Work, Families in Society, Journal of Social Service Research,* and *Journal of Marriage and the Family.* She has served on the Reuben Hill Award Committee of the National Council on Family Relations three different times over the past decade and has yet to see a qualitative piece receive the award.

The Methods and Methodologies of Qualitative Family Research

CONTENTS

PART III: ESSAYS ON METHODOLOGIES

The Methods
and Methodologies
of Qualitative
Family Research

Preface:
A Look at the Mosaic
of Qualitative Family Research

Michael Quinn Patton

As I was reading the contributions in this collection, a former student sent me the following story, which she had received by e-mail.

> Once upon a time, not so very long ago, a group of statisticians and a group of qualitative researchers found themselves together on a train traveling to the same professional meeting. The quals, all of whom had tickets, observed that the quants had only one ticket for their whole group.
>
> "How can you all travel on one ticket?" asked a qual.
>
> "We have our methods," replied a quant.
>
> Later, when the conductor came to punch tickets, all the quants slipped quickly behind the door of the toilet. When the conductor knocked on the door, the head quant slipped their one ticket under the door, thoroughly fooling the conductor.
>
> On their return from the conference, the two groups again found themselves on the same train. The qualitative researchers, having learned from the quants, had schemed to share a single ticket. They were chagrined, therefore, to learn that, this time, the statisticians had boarded with no tickets.

Michael Quinn Patton is affiliated with Union Graduate School, 3228 46th Avenue S., Minneapolis, MN 55406.

[Haworth co-indexing entry note]: "Preface: A Look at the Mosaic of Qualitative Family Research." Patton, Michael Quinn. Co-published simultaneously in *Marriage & Family Review* (The Haworth Press, Inc.) Vol. 24, No. 1/2, 1996, pp. xv-xxi; and: *The Methods and Methodologies of Qualitative Family Research* (ed: Marvin B. Sussman, and Jane F. Gilgun) The Haworth Press, Inc., 1996, pp. xvii-xxiii. Single or multiple copies of this article are available for a fee from The Haworth Document Delivery Service [1-800-342-9678, 9:00 a.m. - 5:00 p.m. (EST). E-mail address: getinfo@haworth.com].

"We know how you traveled together with one ticket," revealed a qual, "but how can you possibly get away with no tickets?"

"We have new methods," replied a quant.

Later, when the conductor approached, all the quals crowded into the toilet. The head statistician followed them and knocked authoritatively on the toilet door. The quals slipped their one and only ticket under the door. The head quant took the ticket and joined the other quants in a different toilet. The quals were subsequently discovered without tickets, publicly humiliated, and tossed off the train at its next stop.

METHODOLOGICAL RESPECTABILITY

This story offers a remnant of what was once a great paradigms debate (Patton, 1986, 1990). That debate has run out of intellectual steam and is now relegated to comedy on the Internet. As Tom Cook (the Cook of Campbell & Cook, 1979, the Bible of quasi-experimentation) pronounced in his keynote address to the 1995 International Evaluation Conference in Vancouver: "Qualitative researchers have won the qualitative-quantitative debate."

Won in what sense?

Won acceptance.

The validity of quantitative methods was never in doubt. Now, qualitative methods have ascended to a level of parallel respectability. That ascendance has not been without struggle, as several of the authors in this volume attest, but the victory has been won on its merits, on the basis of grounded theoretical insights and significant intellectual contributions, as the scholarship in this collection bears witness.

In recent years, the contributions of qualitative methods have been acknowledged by distinguished methodological scholars like Donald Campbell and Lee J. Cronbach. Ernest House (1977: 18), in describing the role of "qualitative argument" in evaluation research, observed that "when two of the leading scholars of measurement and experimental design, Cronbach and Campbell, strongly support qualitative studies, that is strong endorsement indeed" (p. 18). In my own work I have found increased interest in and acceptance of qualitative methods in particular and multiple methods in general.

This volume, *The Methods and Methodologies of Qualitative Family Research,* pulls together in one place a diverse set of contributions that attests to the rich mosaic that qualitative inquiry has become. Qualitative research never has been, and is not now, a singular approach. Nor does it permit only exploratory research and tentative conclusions. This volume is evidence of how qualitative research can and does contribute across all fronts of inquiry into families, informing both practice and theory, and involving both small case studies conducted by lone researchers as well as large, multi-site, multi-method team approaches.

A LOOK AT THE MOSAIC

The data reported in this volume include letters, journals, clinical case notes, official files, oral histories, biographies, tales passed on from one generation to another, interviews, ethnographies, field observations, and personal reflections. Such is the variety of qualitative inquiry. Topics include fathering, mothering, relations with children, couples decision-making, interactions between family therapists and clients, elderly in long-term care, women's work, women's lives over time, welfare, families in poverty, money and families, grieving, the experiences of adolescent African-American females, and the social psychology of families. Qualitative researchers herein reflect on learning qualitative methods, teaching qualitative methods, gathering qualitative data, reporting qualitative findings, and the effects of qualitative inquiry on researchers. Here are a few of the items that stood out to me and, despite my having been involved with these issues a long time, made this volume fresh and exciting for me:

- The women in Joyce Walker's study committed to work with her in reviewing and confirming interpretations and themes so as to capture "the words and music of our correspondence." Here was a genuine collaboration. And I loved the challenge of one participant: "Why call us a cohort? There must be something better–a group, maybe?" Took me back to the time I . . .
- The intergenerational wisdom passed on in Bahamian sayings about black crabs, lizards, goats, roosters, fish, and guinep trees makes dramatic the connection between family lore and place (Hamon). Perhaps the paucity of animal and plant life in cities contributes to the distance between generations in urban settings. A different, but no less deep, form of wisdom is recorded from 74-year-old Ana: an elder role model (Kivnick & Jernstedt).
- The chasm between the official file and the journal of a woman on welfare is the magnitude of a social Grand Canyon (Holbrook).
- The social and economic struggles of women born early in this century inspire with their revelations of what it took to sustain and survive (Meadows).

INSIDE QUALITATIVE INQUIRY

While, as illustrated above, this volume offers an array of stimulating perspectives on diverse aspects of family life, the greatest contribution, in my opinion, will be the reflections offered about how to conduct qualitative inquiry and the struggles attendant therein. The authors manifest a palpable commitment to rigor that is the hallmark of intellectual inquiry. Rettig and colleagues take us inside the rigors of pattern matching and analytic induction. Hanawalt struggles with using historical data to construct composite cases true to the times. Every study in this volume sheds light on the challenges of being true to the data and conscientious about supporting conclusions. We are treated to Handel's reflections on ground-breaking qualitative family research conducted 35 years ago. Having this pioneer's thoughts alongside the confessions of fresh doctoral students honors both.

If students learn nothing else from this volume, they will learn that qualitative inquiry is a highly personal undertaking. All the researchers and practitioners here end up reporting stories of personal engagement and change whether that was their intention or not, and often it was not. The abstract jargon of "reflexivity" can disguise the fact that qualitative researchers must inevitably engage the issue of how studying the world affects those doing the studying, and how those effects, in turn, enter into interpretations and conclusions. Dollahite and colleagues ponder the issue of reflexivity as they consider their research as an intervention with the fathers they interviewed, and their own roles as scholar-practitioners. Franklin gives special emphasis to reflexivity in teaching qualitative methods because, she observes, "I believe from my own experience that this style of writing is most difficult to teach students." Olsen lives reflexivity and thereby struggles with being true to the voices of adolescent African-American females as she considers how her perspective is affected by "the privilege of my skin color and my experiences as a white person." Gale and colleagues take us inside the world of reflective practice, and the attendant challenges to long-held beliefs; as one team member explained:

> After 20 years of clinical experience, I felt quite able to target segments of change and comment on them without having to review text [session transcripts]. However, this came to be one of the greatest and most humbling changes in my beliefs about "seeing" and interpreting clinical work [because] . . . what I "saw" on video and what I "saw" in the transcriptions were not the same.

Here is reflective practice at its best, and we, as readers, are taken inside the experience. Let me share some other highlights that gave me the feeling of being brought inside the research and the researchers' experiences.

- Goldstein and colleagues, in a multi-site study, struggled with how to incorporate an "ecological perspective" across levels of analysis (microsystem, mesosystem, exosystem, and macrosystem) in order to ground insights about families in context as they studied service use among ethnically diverse low-income families. They also struggled with issues of reciprocity, ethics, collaboration, authenticity of transcription, and credibility. How to empathically help a mother get assistance for her daughter, who had been sexually assaulted at school, while maintaining researcher neutrality, provides a particularly moving and enlightening focus for these oft-times seemingly academic issues of methodological rigor.
- Farnsworth draws poignantly on her own experience as a bereaved mother to connect with others likewise bereaved. Together they delve into what it means to lose a child. The sterile language of methodology cannot do justice to such highly personal inquiry.
- Hall and Zvonkovic courageously explore the discomforting emotions that their mixed-gender team experienced in reflecting on how their study of couple decision-making affected them personally.
- Singh's account of how her study of money and family affected her marriage goes to the heart of the personal nature of qualitative inquiry: "I did not want to reflect on money in my marriage. It was dangerous territory for it threatened to unmask some of the troubling compromises in my marriage. . . . " Yet studying others inevitably led to personal reflection and, ultimately, connection: "Questions of power were troubling in a personal sense because they shone the torchlight on the power games in my own two marriages." Here is the courage to look outward at the world and follow the path of inquiry back home.
- Joyce Walker shares her uncertainties about whether what she was doing was *really* research—*really* scholarly—and whether it would be acceptable to those who sat in judgment of her work. Along the way she found that her experiences had "changed forever the way I understand and value research work."

CUTTING EDGE INQUIRY: OF ROOTS, STEMS, AND BOUQUETS

The methodological past of qualitative inquiry was dominated by debate about validity and comparisons to quantitative approaches. That is now behind us. The methodological present acknowledges the value of different methods for different kinds of questions, and judges designs on the appropriateness of the match, i.e., the extent to which a particular method fits a specific problem.

The methodological future of qualitative inquiry will involve exploring new applications, attending to nuances in designs, delving into ethical and reflexive dilemmas, increasing triangulation to correct for fallibilities, deepening the connection between theory and practice, enhancing the skills and understandings of qualitative researchers, and developing standards of rigor and excellence unique to qualitative/naturalistic approaches. This volume points in all these directions. Our understanding of families can only benefit from such approaches, dedicated as they are to thick description, depth, and detail; and grounded as they are in systems thinking, holistic formulations, attention to context, cultural sensitivity, and nonlinear dynamics. This volume foreshadows a future in which a thousand methodological flowers bloom, not just the varieties of old, but new hybrids, born of cross-fertilization, and nurtured by a new generation of caring methodological florists. Yet, though the promise be great, every bulb will not a flower yield and weeds inevitably appear in every garden. How to distinguish qualitative weeds from flowers among the thousand promised blooms may be our greatest challenge. The editors of this volume have gifted us with a marvelously variant bouquet, but not every bloom will please every eye. Understanding what pleases, and what does not, is one worthy use of this display. In so judging, we could do worse than heed Shakespeare's wisdom:

> The summer's flower is to summer sweet,
> Though to itself it only live and die,
> But if that flower with base infection meet,
> The basest weed outbraves his dignity:
>> For sweetest things turned sourest by their deeds:
>> Lilies that fester smell far worse than weeds.

–Sonnet XCIV

Inspect each flower. Judge each, if judgment be your inclination, being sure along the way to be explicit about your criteria for judgment. But, in the end, look at the whole bouquet. As so often revealed in qualitative analysis, the whole is greater than the sum of parts. This volume, *as a whole,* reveals more about the present and future of both qualitative inquiry and family research than does any particular contribution.

REFERENCES

Cook, T. D., & Campbell, D. T. (1979). *Quasi-experimentation: Design and analysis issues for field settings.* Chicago: Rand-McNally.

House, E. R. (1977). "The logic of evaluative argument." *CSE monograph lines in evaluation 7.* Los Angeles: UCLA Center for the Study of Education.

Patton, M. Q. (1990). *Qualitative evaluation and research methods.* Newbury Park, CA: Sage.

Patton, M. Q. (1986). *Utilization-focused evaluation.* Newbury Park, CA: Sage.

Introduction:
Showcasing Qualitative Family Research

Jane F. Gilgun
Marvin B. Sussman

KEYWORDS. Methodology, Chicago School of Sociology, Family research, Qualitative family research

This collection showcases the methods and methodologies of qualitative family research. The purpose of the volume is to demonstrate how emerging and established methodologies can advance understanding of families and contribute to social change. This volume contains two types of articles: research reports and essays on methodologies. In our call for abstracts, we solicited these two types of papers. The research reports provide examples of qualitative family research, of which there are still too few. The essays are of two types: discussions of how the authors learned to become qualitative and reflections on methodologies and their purposes. As a whole, the papers in this collection represent well the depth and breadth of both thinking about and doing qualitative family research.

The push toward applying qualitative methodologies to studies of families is coming from graduate students and their methodologically-oriented professors. So new are many of these methodologies to research on families that we, as co-editors of the publication, made provisions to encourage

Jane F. Gilgun is Associate Professor, School of Social Work, University of Minnesota, Minneapolis, MN 55455. Marvin B. Sussman is UNIDEL Professor of Human Behavior, Emeritus, University of Delaware, Newark, DE 19716 and Core Faculty, Union Graduate School, Union Institute, Cleveland, OH.

[Haworth co-indexing entry note]: "Introduction: Showcasing Qualitative Family Research." Gilgun, Jane F., and Marvin B. Sussman. Co-published simultaneously in *Marriage & Family Review* (The Haworth Press, Inc.) Vol. 24, No. 1/2, 1996, pp. 1-7; and: *The Methods and Methodologies of Qualitative Family Research* (ed: Marvin B. Sussman, and Jane F. Gilgun) The Haworth Press, Inc., 1996, pp. 1-7. Single or multiple copies of this article are available for a fee from The Haworth Document Delivery Service [1-800-342-9678, 9:00 a.m. - 5:00 p.m. (EST). E-mail address: getinfo@haworth.com].

1

and support new researchers. For instance, in our call for abstracts, we extended a special invitation to graduate students to submit abstracts of their dissertations. We received a hearty response: six of the articles in the volume are from dissertation research. We wanted to emulate the tradition of the Chicago School of Sociology, whose professors facilitated the publication of their students' research (Bulmer, 1984).

A PEER, BLIND TWO-STAGE REVIEW PROCESS

Provisions in the review process also were intended to be responsive to graduate students, as well as to other new qualitative researchers. The review process was two-staged and composed of peer, blind reviews. Blind, peer reviews are important because they facilitate the career advancement of new academics more than invited publications. The two-stage process was a means of providing intensive feedback to prospective authors, who often had little experience in writing up qualitative research. At each stage of the process, the reviewers, who were consulting editors, did not know the identities of authors.

The process was as follows. We first issued a call for abstracts. Consulting editors reviewed the abstracts and gave detailed feedback. We invited many but not all authors who submitted abstracts to submit papers. When we received the papers, the consulting editors again did a blind review. On the basis of this review, we gave detailed analyses to each author, accepted some papers for publication, requested revisions with no guarantee of acceptance to others, and did not accept still others. The third stage was the reading of the revised papers, which the consulting editors did with grace. At this point, we again gave detailed feedback to some authors, accepted some papers, requested yet more revisions for some papers, and did not accept others. This process began with the call for abstracts in November 1993 and ended with the final acceptance of a paper in February 1996.

The papers accepted through this review process covered many major issues in contemporary qualitative family research. We especially tried to include papers on poor families and families of color, of which there are several in this volume. There were, however, other topics we wanted covered. We therefore invited the submission of five papers that now are part of this collection: Holbrook, Franklin, Gale et al., Hanawalt, and Handel. Though invited, each of these papers was peer, blind reviewed and underwent the same scrutiny as other papers in this publication. We solicited still other papers, but authors were not able to respond to our requests. These papers were on topics such as lesbian and gay families, Southeast

Asian refugee families, and philosophy of science. Though these papers would have added additional diversity, as Michael Patton pointed out in the preface, this volume succeeds in portraying the mosaic that is qualitative family research.

DEFINITIONS OF METHODOLOGY

For this collection, *methodologies* stem from and are embedded in epistemologies (principles for developing and evaluating knowledge), ontologies (aspects of human experience that count as foundational), and ethics (principles for guiding the conduct of knowledge so that harm does not come to the researcher or the researched). Methodologies, then, not only guide what phenomena we research but are composed of principles underlying procedures of research. Examples of methodologies are postmodernism, feminist methodologies, positivism, post-positivism, critical theory, grounded theory (which could also be a set of procedures), life histories, interpretivism, and hermeneutics. Some methodologies have more explicit epistemologies, ontologies, and ethics than others. Case studies and life histories, for instance, can be considered closer to sets of procedures than to methodologies. Yet case studies can be done with a variety of methodologies, such as feminist post-modernist, positivist, and hermeneutic. Choice of methodology stems from the nature of the research inquiry, e.g., research question. Often methodologies are implicit, as are epistemologies, and ontologies.

DEFINITION OF METHODS

Methods, in this volume, are the research procedures stemming from the methodology and the nature of the research inquiry. Methods include procedures of data collection, such as participant observation, in-depth interviewing, and document analysis; procedures of data analysis; descriptions of reflexivity; descriptions of persons researched; procedures to safeguard the well-being of researched and researcher; and procedures for interpretation. For example, when a researcher wants to understand how individuals experience a state of being or actions in historical context, interpretive, phenomenological, and/or hermeneutic types of methodologies would be appropriate. The method of data collection would include, minimally, in-depth interviewing and document analysis. Observation might also be appropriate.

Following Guba (1990), we did not view the term *qualitative* as a methodological-level term. This term only has methodological meaning in the context of the epistemologies, ontologies, and ethical principles in which it is embedded. Therefore, qualitative methods—usually meaning the procedures of data collection of participant observation, document analysis, and in-depth interviewing—can be embedded in positivistic, interpretive, or critical methodologies. Much of the graduate training available in the United States until recently has been in positivistic methodologies, although these methodologies often were not named. Students appear to have been socialized to think that this was the only way to do research. In many instances, the interpretive nature of qualitative methods also has not been delineated. We intend this volume to clarify some methodological issues of qualitative family research.

MAY SOUND HARDER THAN IT IS

We were concerned that the demands we were placing on researchers for this publication would discourage many. For example, the requirement to make methodologies explicit might have appeared too daunting. We told potential contributors that almost all of us are beginners at making methodologies explicit. We will be learning together. Furthermore, much of what will help us create more explicit methodologies is present in contemporary methodological discussions. In our 1993 call for abstracts, we recommended a brief set of readings to help clarify the then contemporary methodological issues in qualitative family research. These readings are Allen and Baber (1992), Gilgun, Daly, and Handel (1992), LaRossa and Reitzes (1993), Morgaine (1992), Osmond (1987), Rosenblatt and Fischer (1993), and Thompson (1992).

In creating the articles for this volume, we all did the best we could. We hope that we will see ourselves as learning together and working together to take another step into a new era of methodological pluralism in family research, theory, practice, and policy.

THE CENTRALITY OF CONSULTING EDITORS

Consulting editors were essential to this volume. They put in a lot of time, first to review abstracts and then to review the completed papers. As mentioned earlier, authors often rewrote their papers more than once and the consulting editors, therefore, reviewed the papers more than once.

Each of the consulting editors was responsive, conscientious, and insightful. Given the breadth of the methodologies we want to include in this volume, we sought consulting editors from many different disciplines, such as nursing, social work, sociology, counseling, and family studies. All of them are scholars of breadth and distinction. The consulting editors are listed below. We want to give special thanks to Dr. Linda Jones and Dr. Kim Gottfried-Strom, both on the faculty of the School of Social Work, University of Minnesota, Twin Cities. At a crucial point when the pressure of deadlines was heavy, Linda and Kim did reviews that greatly facilitated getting this collection to the publisher.

REFERENCES

Allen, Katherine R., & Kristine M. Baber (1992). Ethical and epistemological tensions in applying a postmodern perspective in feminist research. *Psychology of Women Quarterly, 16*, 1-15.

Bulmer, Martin (1984). *The Chicago School of Sociology.* Chicago: University of Chicago Press.

Gilgun, Jane F., Kerry Daly, & Gerald Handel (1992). *Qualitative methods in family research.* Beverly Hills, CA: Sage.

Guba, Egon G. (1990). The alternative paradigm dialog. In Egon G. Guba (Ed.), *The paradigm dialog* (pp. 17-27). Beverly Hills, CA: Sage.

LaRossa, Ralph and Donald C. Reitzes (1993). Symbolic interactionism and family studies. In Pauline G. Boss, William J. Doherty, Ralph LaRossa, Walter K. Schumm, & Suzanne K. Steinmetz (Eds). *Sourcebook of family theories and methods: A contextual approach* (pp. 135-163). New York: Plenum.

Morgaine, Carol A. (1992). Alternative paradigms for helping families change themselves. *Family Relations, 41*, 12-17.

Osmond, Marie Withers (1987). Radical-critical theories. In Marvin B. Sussman & Suzanne K. Steinmetz (Eds.), *Handbook of marriage and the family* (pp. 103-124). New York: Plenum.

Reinharz, Shulamit (1992). *Feminist methods in social research.* New York: Oxford University.

Rosenblatt, Paul & Lucy Rose Fischer (1993). Qualitative family research. In Pauline G. Boss, William J. Doherty, Ralph LaRossa, Walter K. Schumm, & Suzanne K. Steinmetz (Eds). *Sourcebook of family theories and methods: A contextual approach* (pp. 167-177). New York: Plenum.

Thompson, Linda (1992). Feminist methodology for family studies. *Journal of Marriage and the Family, 54*, 3-18.

THE CONSULTING EDITORS

Susan Murphy
School of Nursing
San Jose State University
Los Altos, CA 94024

Lynn Meadows
Family Medicine
University of Alberta
Edmonton, Alberta
Canada T6G 2G3

Scott P. Sells
School of Social Work
UNV–Las Vegas
Las Vegas, NV 89154-5032

Ed Sherman
School of Social Welfare
State University of New York at Albany
Albany, NY 12222

Jetse Sprey
Professor Emeritus
Sociology
Case Western Reserve University
Cleveland, OH 44120-3456

Linda Wark
Human and Family Resources
Northern Illinois University
DeKalb, IL 60115

Kathleen Wells
Case Western Reserve University
10900 Euclid Ave.
Cleveland, OH 44120-3456

PART I: RESEARCH REPORTS

Letters in the Attic:
Private Reflections of Women, Wives, and Mothers

Joyce A. Walker

SUMMARY. This article reports on an hermeneutic interpretive study of letters 18 women wrote to each other annually for 25 years, from 1968 to 1993. Six themes related to personal success and achievement emerged from readings and systematic study of this set of more than 250 letters. The stories in these letters connect the private and public worlds; they communicate the events experienced, things hoped for, and things not done. *[Article copies available for a fee from The Haworth Document Delivery Service: 1-800-342-9678. E-mail address: getinfo@haworth.com]*

KEYWORDS. Hermeneutics, Interpretive research, Document analysis, Women's lives

Joyce A. Walker is Professor and Extension Educator, 4-H Youth Development Center, 340 Coffey Hall, University of Minnesota, Twin Cities, St. Paul, MN 55108. This article is developed from the author's (1993) dissertation.

[Haworth co-indexing entry note]: "Letters in the Attic: Private Reflections of Women, Wives, and Mothers." Walker, Joyce A. Co-published simultaneously in *Marriage & Family Review* (The Haworth Press, Inc.) Vol. 24, No. 1/2, 1996, pp. 9-40; and: *The Methods and Methodologies of Qualitative Family Research* (ed: Marvin B. Sussman, and Jane F. Gilgun) The Haworth Press, Inc., 1996, pp. 9-40. Single or multiple copies of this article are available for a fee from The Haworth Document Delivery Service [1-800-342-9678, 9:00 a.m. - 5:00 p.m. (EST). E-mail address: getinfo@haworth.com].

We needed more time. I am eternally grateful to Leah [not her real name] for organizing the whole thing down to the tiniest perfect detail and to Joyce [my real name] for giving us the purpose for the meeting. I would have had a hard time justifying the time and expense for just a frivolous reunion with friends, and yes, I should work on this issue in therapy but I can't justify the time and expense. I loved our reunion–the memories have propelled me through this horrible winter–and I want to do another one anytime, anywhere, with all of us there. (Eve 1994)

The reunion was risky business, flying across the country to spend four days in New Mexico with women I'd corresponded with but hadn't seen for 30 years. It turned out to be a splendid, inspirational event. For me, it was tangible affirmation of my research, a face-to-face confirmation of my themes and observations. As a group, the women offered hearty endorsement of the final manuscript. And they shared stories about how their decision to come to Taos grew out of their engagement in the research process that had generated powerful personal reflection in their lives.

The purpose of this paper is twofold: (1) to report on the themes and observations from a hermeneutic interpretive research study of more than 250 personal letters written and exchanged by 18 women between 1968 and 1993, and (2) to discuss methodological strategies that enhance research designed to make meaning and gain understanding from written text. It begins with a discussion of the understandings gleaned from my study which focuses on the mid-life perspectives of educated women reflecting on personal success and achievement within the context of marriage, motherhood, career, and personal life. The article concludes with a discussion of three strategies–consent, collaboration, and confirmation–that can promote a thorough, systematic interpretation of narrative text that is firmly grounded in the lived experiences and understandings of the women whose stories are mined for meaning.

Although this study is grounded in the shared ideas, thoughts, and reflections of 18 women, it informs the research base of marriage and family studies. These women define themselves first and foremost as wives and mothers. Until their children were grown, their central commitment was to child-rearing. Their letters describe their perceived lack of preparation for parenting despite their education and relatively secure marriages during their younger years. Likewise, their letters reveal a struggle to define themselves as successful based upon their roles as wives and mothers in a world that increasingly undervalues accomplishments of the private life and holds high the publicly acclaimed values of positional power, public visibility, high salary, and independence. Half of the women's first marriages end in divorce, and they expose their disbelief and even shame in their inability to avoid the ultimate failure, the collapse of a marriage. Through it all, these women strengthen their friendship and use each other as benchmarks against which to assess their own achievements. In some ways, their correspondence is a proxy for the support others experience from extended families. Certainly for this group of eighteen, deeply embedded in family life, relationships outside the family that listen but do not judge play a critically important role through the years.

This study explicates six themes that required resolution before the women really experienced a personal sense of achievement and success in the private as well as the public arena. These themes are relevant to family study. Issues of caring, connection, space, and place are fundamental. While marriage and family were given top priority, these women needed caring connections and personal space linked to their personal identities apart from their roles as wives and mothers. Old friends were enormously valued as were spaces and places that gave time to be thoughtful and alone. Balance is an issue, not surprisingly, but for this group it is less one of family vs. work and more one of attention to self vs. relationships. The women are challenged by the loud and powerful voices of their society giving prescriptions and public benchmarks for the perfect marriage, the ideal child, the model mother, the successful career person, and the ideal family. These women are both intelligent and fully functioning pleasers, women caught between the 1950s model of their mothers and the evolving notion of modern womanhood in the 1960s, 1970s, and 1980s.

THE LETTERS IN CONTEXT

Several points of context are important. First, a body of private and potentially important texts exists that is only accessible to researchers with a personal connection to the source. They are best studied using qualitative methods. My collection of letters is an example. This private, often intimate, correspondence was available to me because I am one of the letter writers. Other collections of letters exist. Recently I learned of a grandmother who saved hundreds of letters written by her husband, her son, and her grandson during their military service on the front lines in three different wars. Journal entries of women and men as well as letters written as sweethearts, partners, and parents capture ideas and feelings that inform our understandings in a way selective recollections cannot.

Second, studies of small, relatively homogeneous groups have significant value even when the observations cannot be used to generalize a finding or predict future trends. Intact texts written by or about specific groups are potentially very useful in theory-building and the grounding of research hypothesis. Any study of a single text is informative; cumulatively, hermeneutic studies on common topics or groups can provide rich perspectives and insights that inform researchers and help in the framing of questions. The search is not for a right answer, but for more enlightened, critical questions. This power to inform the questions, the search, suggests that interpretive study of existing text has particular use for therapists and clinicians, those for whom the right question at the right time is an art. Understandings from these studies, if used judiciously, can also illuminate other similar situations.

Third, the people studied or those close to the written text have a stake in the findings. If they are invited to participate in important yet manageable ways in research processes, they can offer valuable perspectives and can bring clarity to the search for meaning. They have the potential to become excellent collaborators. Sixteen of the women in my study were actively involved in the work from beginning to end. In cases where the authors of the text are not available, people who know them may also provide assistance in the interpretive process. Following the death of one of the women in my study, her brother-in-law wrote to express what the letters meant to Pat over the years. He also sent what he believed to be her last message. His letter adds an important dimension to the study.

Fourth, in the absence of a prescriptive formula or conventional process for interpretive text analysis, the qualitative researcher designs methods that are sensitive to the texts and respectful of the people involved. These methods have a better than average chance to expand understanding and are academically defensible to a group of scholarly peers. As I discuss my study of women's letters, I focus attention on my processes for involving the women as my guides and "validity checks."

Fifth, the frame or perspective taken on an interpretive study is important to establish and to acknowledge. Although letters in my collection are written by 18 different women from the time they were about age 26 until age 51, I decided early on to treat the letters as a set of intact work, not as the individual stories of 18 individual women. When I came upon a first edition of Edna St. Vincent Millay's (1934) poems entitled *Wine From These Grapes* (1934) in a New Orleans used book store, I had my metaphor–I was studying wine, not grapes. The collection of letters approached in total offered insights far more complex than the contributions of any single woman.

Moreover, I became clear that the letters in total presented a unique challenge: I held the answers in hand, but I had to discover the question to which the letters were an answer. It was only after many readings of the text, many conversations with the letter writers and other women, and analysis of coded text that I concluded that these letters were responding to a basic question, "What does it mean to be a successful woman in the second half of the 20th century?" Jill put her finger on this issue in 1984:

> I have also wondered why more of the women in our group are not better off (or am I reading these letters wrong?). Here we are–some of the "best" [our university] had to offer. Broke our backs being top dogs on campus–beaten badly by the real world.

> I thought [our university] had produced in us the next LEADERS OF THE FREE WORLD–well, at least a few corporate VP's, maybe a President. One of us was certainly going to turn the educational establishment on its ear–is no one even in politics???? (Jill 1984)

THE WOMEN

Reflections spanning a quarter century are captured in this rare correspondence. Five years after their college graduation, the women established a tradition of composing a personal letter of thoughts and life event stories that was sent each February to a designated "annual editor." The editor assembled the letters, photocopied 17 sets, and mailed a packet of all the letters to each woman. The letters were filled with revelations about themselves, their feelings and ideas; certainly, their children, spouses, and other family members were often mentioned. However varied the topics, the consistent theme laced through the letters over the years was the personal search to identify, measure, or understand what it means to be a successful woman.

Born in the 1940s, teenagers in the 1950s, and college students in the 1960s, these women met in Mortar Board, a collegiate honor society that recognized the leadership, service, and academic achievement of women at a midsized midwestern public university. At graduation, these talented women had great expectations for future achievement despite the contradictory messages of society in 1963: be an outstanding partner, mother, professional, and community leader. Be a nurturer, a supporter, a person who puts the needs of others first, but by all means do something significant, make a difference. They floundered when their vague, socially acceptable aspirations failed to meet their public and private definitions of success. Their annual correspondence became a forum to share and compare the experience of being wives and mothers, women prepared for careers but who elected family life as a priority. Over time, the women created their own internal definitions of success reflective of their experiences and the lives they were composing. Their ideas and struggles, shared in thoughtful, often hilarious personal disclosures, raise provocative questions for women desirous of having it all—a relationship, a child, a family, a career, and a personal life.

Today these friends, spread across the United States, reside in urban, suburban, and rural communities in 14 different states. Seventeen of the 18 are living and took part in the study. I am the author of the study, and I am also one of the correspondents. I know these women to be self-reflective, articulate witnesses to their time and their life experiences. As authors of the text, they most intimately understand the intent and context of the narratives. All agreed to help formulate the coding categories, to review and comment on draft findings, and to confirm the final findings and implications.

WORKING WITH THE TEXT

Six assumptions, like foundation stones, set the boundaries of the work. First, understanding the past lived experience of women is a relevant way to gain knowledge for the future. Second, understanding the experiences and reflections of a small group of relatively homogeneous women has value. Third, self-reflection is a legitimate way to make meaning out of experience. Fourth, the women have shared and reported the truth about themselves as they understood it at the time. Fifth, my own experience as a member of the group increases my understandings of intersubjective meanings in the correspondence and interview text. And sixth, it was important to leave my own letters in the text base; to remove them would alter the text in a fundamental way.

Interpretation of intact text requires a deconstruction of the text for coding and thematic analysis, and a simultaneous persistent and precise attention to the totality of the text for context and understanding. I found that the use of a computer-assisted text management software package allowed me to move between coded and categorized sets of text separated out from the whole and back to text passages integrated into the whole by letter writer, year, and sequence. This capacity to move around in the voluminous text with ease (once thematically organized and coded line by line) gave me confidence to focus on construction of a system and a strategy for making meaning out of the words and ideas in the letters.

I used The Ethnograph (Seidel 1988) software package because I was familiar with it and because it did everything I required. I never felt I pushed the package to its limits in my coding or analysis. The idea is to be able to mark and label text passages so they can be moved around, grouped with other passages of text, and read in context with other words as well as in their original context. All this marking and labeling is contingent on the identification of descriptive, relevant coding categories at the beginning of the analysis, a task that comes from the integration of reading text, reading related literature, and grappling with the totality of the texts in question.

THEMES CENTRAL TO SUCCESS

Six themes emerge as touchstones upon which the women came to build their internal definitions of success and achievement. The themes represent challenges to be reconciled in life before the women were able to feel genuinely successful in their relationships, work, and personal lives. The themes are figurative units of measurement for the women. Without satisfaction in these fundamentally important areas, success can feel false or hollow. Bateson (1989) noted, "Friends guide and learn from each other, especially in unexplored terrain" (p. 103). The letters are a vehicle for the women to share ideas, learn strategies that have worked, and compare their decisions with women they see as peers, educated women successful in college with whom they have a shared past. These themes were present in the writing of all the women, and they persisted over time. For these women, it was essential to:

1. Value connection and the continuity of relationships
2. Balance care and responsibility for self and others
3. Work passionately to make a difference
4. Abandon the dream and the presumptive search for closure
5. Establish personal space and models of success
6. Embrace the wisdom of the defining moments in life

These are not the only themes in the letters, but they are strong, clear ideas that directly relate to the concept of success for these women. A common feature of these six themes is that they represent powerful challenges that few if any of the women anticipated or were prepared for when they left the shelter of college to take on the world.

These themes all have a connection to personal achievement and societal definitions of success. As the women worked to achieve a sense of success and personal achievement, they began by aspiring to society's definition of what a successful woman does. This view is constructed based on growing up in the 1940s and 1950s and coming to young adulthood in the early 1960s. The external messages were often perplexing because they were contradictory: be an outstanding partner, mother, professional, and community leader but be a nurturer, a supporter, a person who puts the needs of others first. Setting priorities was confusing. They started out achieving three of the four pretty handily, but then motherhood threw things out of kilter. Care of children proved very time and energy consuming, and the professional or career aspect became increasingly difficult to maintain with pressure to put the spouse first in regard to paid work priorities.

Over time, the women began to move toward their own definitions of success supported by their experiences and the lives they are composing. They worked their way through uncharted waters using spouses and peers as their primary guides and role models. They ended up feeling satisfied that they made a difference doing what had significant meaning to them, and they measured their success in personal terms rather than in the acquisition of dollars or positional power.

This personalized definition of success works because the base line measure against which it was tested is the integrity of oneself and the survival of family relationships. Not every family survived the 24 years intact, but issues like leaving a marriage with dignity, providing emotional and physical support to children as they moved toward adulthood, maintaining open channels of communications with family members, and acting responsibly in relationships appear to be important. If the base line measure of success was to be tested against accomplishments in the areas of career advancement, financial self sufficiency, professional recognition, or the size of one's retirement package, feelings of achievement would not have been felt until much later in life–well into the late forties if at all.

The six themes emerge as the touchstones upon which the women built their definitions of success. This is never stated directly, but the themes occur over and over as the challenges with which the women struggled. The themes are figurative units of measurement for the women that mark or indicate achievement. Without satisfaction in these fundamentally important areas, there was no real sense of success. The themes were not clearly delineated or articulated as standards of success by society, so the letters became a vehicle for the women to share ideas, learn strategies that worked, and compare their own status to the lives of the other "sure to be successful" women who appeared to be dealing with the same basic set of issues.

Relationships: Connection, Continuity, Care, and Responsibility

The first two themes center on relationships. The women express great value in connection and the continuity of relationships with family, colleagues, and friends; special attention is given to women friends. They also describe an unrelenting struggle to balance issues of care and responsibility in these relationships.

Connection and Continuity

Connection between friends and the importance of continuity in relationships is spoken of often. Eve (1985) wrote, "My old friends are still my best friends." Friends from the past have shared experiences. They understand in a special, personal way because they know where you have come from and what you have been. Old friends know each other as individuals with their own names apart from an identity as someone's wife or someone's mother. Clare (1987) said, "My friends are simply wonderful. I am grateful for their humor and understanding. I couldn't exist without them." When Ruth (1985) asked, "What part do your friends play?" Eve responded, "That's easy; they're everything."

The caring connection between the women has a competitive edge. The women never spoke of competing *against* each other, but they acknowledge that they measure themselves against the successes, interests, and activities of the other women. Nan (1988) says, "I feel fortunate to have been part of this chain of connections and remembrances and sharing. I'm impressed with our honesty. Is it because we write? How would it be in person?" May writes,

> My family proceeds normally. All of you who have children permanently on the honor roll, presidents of their classes, training for the Olympics, etc., and husbands who understand all about foreplay and a woman's deep personal need, whether she's salaried or not, for a housekeeper, need to know that your families are not normal. They are at the upper and insufferable end of the bell-shaped curve. (May 1987)

Letter writing is itself an act of connection. The women were often harsh judges of their own successes and failures. A pattern of disconnecting in difficult times became clear for at least 1/3 of the group. When these women felt they were not measuring up to the friendly competition, particularly in terms of being model wives and mothers, they stopped writing. In the midst of divorce or family troubles, women stop writing for a year or two, maybe more. The urge of reconnect was also powerful. One woman began to write again after an absence of eleven years. When she wrote again, the subjects of success and comparisons were couched with humorous or self-effacing language. But the bond–power of the connection–

seemed stronger than the competition, and the letter writing continues today.

> The circumstances of my life have changed rather drastically over the past year, and were revving up to change two winters ago when the MB letter came around. I was so filled with confusion and distress and fear that I couldn't bring myself to write in the face of Ruth's prize-winning kids and marriage, etc., etc., even Nel's courage. (May 1989)

> I did not write last year because I was not personally up to writing. After all these years of being faithful to this newsletter and really wanting to hear what you have to say, I am still intimidated. I still often feel like a country mouse among her "sister" city cousins. Part of my problem is a built-in abhorrence of Christmas letters in which every one is doing so damn well. Maybe some people do live Barbie Doll lives. I am not one of them. Yet, many of you write of real concerns, and I am constantly amazed at how much I care about you when I never knew you really till our correspondence started, so many years ago. (Rene 1991)

The women who shared deep personal losses do so after the turmoil associated with the events passed. It is difficult to write about crisis in the midst of it, but the time for reconnection brings relief. Following divorces, May and Dot re-engage:

> So I guess the reason I didn't write was because I had so much to say, and I wanted to say it in a way it wouldn't be misunderstood—I wanted to control everyone's reactions, make them understand it was painful but wonderful, etc., and it was such a daunting task I simply avoided writing at all. (May 1989)

> Where have I been for three plus years? In the throes of personal crisis, where else! Growth for me, the end of my marriage—all the relief and pain that goes with that process. I lingered long on the edges—for a while I thought I could keep it all together and make it work. Then I had to let go and take the step. (Dot 1982)

Care and Responsibility

The second theme is the unrelenting struggle to balance issues of care and responsibility. Who comes first, me or the rest of them? Am I giving all I can? Am I giving enough? Have I gotten lost along the way? Over 25 years, the letters describe the initial submersion of self in family and others, the dissatisfaction, the rebellion, and the gradual recapturing of personal identity through work. Care of self and others, responsibility to family and community, work at home or work in the community, time for self and spouse–some version of these themes came up every year.

> I am confused a lot about things I would think an adult should be sure. The concept of responsibility is often the conundrum for me–to whom? to self? to mate? to children? to other commitments? (Kate 1982)

The balance theme divides roughly into three periods. In the Younger Years (1969-1975), the pull is to balance care for and responsibility to self with the new roles of wife and mother. In the Middle Years (1976-1986), the balance is one of personal pursuit of work and career juxtaposed against family and community expectations. In the Later Years of the correspondence (1987-1992), the issues center on personal searching, self-discovery, and satisfaction with identity.

Eve's story illustrates the Younger Years. The last to have a child, her description of the changes wrought by motherhood captured the tension between the joy of having a child and the setting aside of self that accompanied the birth.

> The mothering on the other hand has not been so easy. I am feeding her pureed Adelle Davis,[1] but there are times when I feel like substituting ground glass and cat hairs, and I crave sleep like a drunk craves hootch.

> I was amazed and depressed to discover that I had become very set in my ways and [daughter] was a definite intrusion. . . . I suspect that this abrupt ending of the old life and creation of a totally new life is easier to take at 25 than at 35. She came just at the time when I finally admitted (even out loud) that I hate everything associated with housewifery. I daydream about those carefree days of standing nine hours behind a perfume counter fending off insults from obnoxious cruise-shippers or those wonderful years of cooking three meals a day in the hot galley of a 50 foot boat for six hostile strangers.

> On the plus side, [daughter] has indeed filled the empty place in me and she has put me back on the track in several areas where I'd gone astray. I still think the world is headed for bad times but instead of just wanting to escape to a place where we can survive if the crunch

comes, I think more and more about getting into the fight to reverse America's trend toward self-destruction.

I'm already aware of her little eyes watching me, and I desperately want to become a good model for her. These new responsibilities have got me growing again but not without a certain amount of creaking and groaning. (Eve 1978)

The balance issues of the Middle Years focus on what Kate calls a "personal pursuit of some substance," the drive to move out into the workplace. All but one of the women who gave birth or decided to raise a child left the full-time paid workforce at least temporarily. All of the women (except Pat who had multiple sclerosis and was confined to a nursing home) were mothers—biologically, as stepmothers or as adoptive mothers. After approximately ten years of giving top priority to mothering, homemaking, and community service, the women began to actively reconnect and explore their own development. This does not happen suddenly or without considerable guilt and questioning.

Through the ups and downs of recent years I was not able to deny that my family is my priority. The family's strength must now be supportive of me and my growth as it has been for [husband] and the children. (Kate 1982)

The Middle Years were also the time for divorce, and the lack of preparation to be self-sufficient and to take on the responsibility of financial and family matters came as a shock to the eight women divorced between 1976 and 1986. Most had only the most remote contingency plans to deal with the unexpected. They never seriously considered they would not have choices.

I continue to grapple with the issues of financial independence, marriage, career development and the like. . . . Why aren't we, many of us, highly paid, highly visible executives and vice presidents? Because we were programmed differently, and have been living with the conflict all our adult lives between wanting to achieve individually and wanting to nurture and support others. And, proportionately to choosing nurturing instead of achieving, we've lost the ambition and motivation we had as undergraduates. (Leah 1987)

I'm nearing the end of full time mothering, leery of full time work if I even knew what I wanted to do. I realize I *never* thought in terms of a career–only interim jobs until marriage, kids, etc. Finding my niche now is not easy; my inability to move out decisively somewhere gets to me. (Dot 1976)

Even Jill, who started her own business, admitted that she never actually thought she would have to depend on herself for support.

I've always been well cared for. Now it's me alone–and I have a few people now that *I* must take care of. You never know. It's so different not having anyone to answer to. Like a ball with no floor to bounce on–free fall. (Jill 1984)

In the Later Years, the struggles for balance become intimate and personal, focusing on husband-wife time and intimacy, adult child-parent caregiving, and individual self-discovery and time for self. There is more peace and self-acceptance in the later years and less negative judging of self. Adversities such as loss, death, illness, and poor health impact on relationships and present special challenges emotionally and spiritually. Professional competence and recognition, family solidarity and survival, individual "blooming," a maturing faith, and the support of longtime friendships give life a full, rewarding quality.

I'm confused by the fact that I turn 45 next month, and my mission in life remains undisclosed. I have a strong feeling that I'm just preparing for some main event, that I'm in a holding pattern waiting for the way to show itself. It doesn't really interfere with my day to day happiness, but it does keep me from feeling "at home" in my house and in my head. Anybody know what I'm talking about? (Eve 1988)

I even feel that I'll begin writing fiction again one day. Not this week, maybe not this year–maybe not fiction. But I can't seem to let go of the idea that writing is what I'm supposed to do, that a writer is who I am, and I tried hard for a few years to give up that vision, that image of myself, because I wasn't doing it, but the yearning wouldn't quit. (May 1989)

Over the years, I've given attention to either family or job and not a whole lot to me. My therapy now is focusing on that need for nurturing that suddenly seems very important. I also tend to be future-oriented, which means I sometimes miss the specialness of today. . . . I know I want to learn to savor today before it's gone and I'm one day older. (Nel 1991)

The discovery that relationships can be vital and resilient after 25 or more years of marriage is invigorating. The concept of partnerships is more balanced, and sharing in married life has a new reality. Expectations are more realistic, and the insistent pleasers have become women who like to be pleased.

> My most salient observation about our 17 year-old marriage is that, in spite of ongoing efforts, trying to nurture our own relationship is difficult. The demands of career, community and child-centered activities leave us little time and less energy. We are conscious of the need and do have occasional weekends away together but I crave more unscheduled hours and time together. (Nan 1981)

> What has been a struggle for [husband] and me is just time together. We always made time for the children but have come late to understand the need to nurture each other–not just relieve or support the other so that more can be accomplished. Also, we have both lacked in taking time for self. (Kate 1988)

> We continue to fight awfully once a month. Our desire for intimacy of thoughts and body and willingness to nurture seem more balanced and equal. We will be married 25 years in June. (Kate 1990)

The knowledge that the pain of severed relationships can heal and be replaced by companionship, love, intimacy, understanding and support from another partner likewise is assuring.

Passions Around Work and Dreams

Issues of making a difference in the world and discovering the potential for contributions beyond marriage and family dominate the next two themes. Both are linked to an understanding of what success and achievement mean to these women.

Work to Make a Difference

The third theme refers to the passion of the women to make a difference through paid and unpaid work. Community involvement is an intentional decision as is the move back into the workforce after years dedicated to child-rearing. Because most of the women do not reenter the workforce in fields related to their education, they make strategic decisions to work in fields that contribute to the private and public life.

The most important thing, I feel, is to be involved–both in family and other things–politics, advanced education, volunteer work, community life–and contributing to something beyond or outside oneself. (Nel 1977)

If I began my volunteer career for personal reasons, I finish this stint an advocate for volunteerism as excellent force for positive change and essential to our democracy. I am also convinced that volunteer work and work-for-pay can be equally important and honorable and that one is not exclusive of the other. (Kate 1980)

I have so much responsibility now and a job which requires about all the energy I have. My life is hardly my own, but I love what I do and the people I do it with. Now this is the strange part–Bette do you agree?–I like the kids the best. I hope I never get too old or tired to teach (at least for a long time). (Rene 1986)

Abandon the Dream

The fourth theme is the abandonment of the dream. In 1991, over mid-morning coffee at an up-scale cafe near her office, I asked Kate, "What do you know now that you wish you'd known in 1963?" She only paused a moment before she replied, "I wish someone had told me you never get there." From the prescriptive formula of education, job, marriage and motherhood, the question changes from "Am I getting where I am supposed to be going?" to "Is this getting me where I want to go?" Early on, getting there is part of the definition of success for the women, but because "where" is never really clear, each presumed step in the right direction ends up feeling incomplete. In 1963, college graduation was a rather universally acclaimed benchmark of success intended to insure that one would find fulfilling work and be a competent (even inspired) wife and mother. Most of the women accepted the assumption that a job, a husband, and a child followed by a house and a steady income were the ultimate achievement.

Overall, the 18 women moved into the life of the dream with happy anticipation. Their joy in their relationships was an extension of courtship, the time when they were sought after and treated as valuable acquisitions at the very center of the dating rituals (Heilbrun 1989). In the dream, it is implied that the woman remains at the center of family life, beloved of her children, a treasure to her husband, and an asset to her community. The romance continues and the love grows strong, the one certain force under-girding the marriage.

This stereotypical ideal reinforces a belief that within the dream there is "a place" at which one arrives, a level of accomplishment and harmony that is a reward unto itself. But this ideal is grounded in the much discussed experience of courtship, not in the lived experience of real women. Clare, for instance, found that,

> Looking back on any assumptions I might have had about marriage and my life thereafter—most of them have gone out the window. However, they have been replaced with a rich fabric of a life with [husband] I never would have anticipated and two beautiful sons. (Clare 1980)

By putting the husband at the center and making him in fact the goal (all the while believing she was at the center and charting the mutual path), a woman appeared to be fulfilling, with great competence, the dictums of the dream. While life and the pattern of daily events became increasingly characterized by disruption and discontinuity, the myth never acknowledged this and so it was easy for the women to attribute their failure to "get there" to their own shortcomings.

> Yipes! What made it [the divorce] so slow? I never planned for it, never dreamed of it, and with my decisions, others had to come along. (Dot 1982)

> I feel like we grew up in a pre-Judy Blume world of happy endings and Doris Day, and problems were hidden or brushed over, or worse, made people that had them feel like second class citizens! But having problems is what life's all about, and how much better we can deal with our own when we learn about wonderful human beings from our past who are out there struggling too—and doing okay, by God. (Leah 1984)

> It [Betty Friedan's *The Feminine Mystique*] really caused me to start seriously thinking about my future; when you spend the bulk of your time being a mother and housewife you do tend to define yourself in terms of other people. (Nan 1972)

Gradually the assumption that there was "somewhere to get" began to unravel. While all of the women acted on the pattern of the dream, some of them did express apprehensions along the way. They write of not trusting their situation or the course of events in which they find themselves.

I never got comfortable [with the role of non-working wife]–deep in my heart (because of my childhood?) I didn't trust life. I knew that the world didn't give a damn about me–that life was demanding and full of both pleasant and unpleasant surprises. (Jill 1987)

To maintain a discipline, a structure, if you will, in every aspect of life is a goal. Compartmentalizing is my way of coping, but it isn't easy. Sometimes I wish I were more oriental. . . . Most of my life is lovely, but part of me is cynical and mistrusting. (Clare 1987)

By the mid 1970s, more of the women were openly acknowledging that the great American stereotype was not working out as they had expected.

I loved being married, found it deeply satisfying, and sorely miss the closeness we had. I hope I have an opportunity to work at a marriage again, but I know I would do some things differently. I would not submerge my own identity as much in a husband's, and I would not limit myself by doing things with him or not at all. I would not take our relationship for granted. Marriage, I suspect, needs constant attention and nurturing to stay alive and growing. I would also, I hope, be able to accept him as he is, and not try to mold him into an image of what I thought a husband should be. (Leah 1980)

You asked for thoughts of the past ten years and for a look ahead to this decade: Personally, the past ten years have been a roller coaster–marriage, babies, illness, understanding, biting my lip and looking forever like I knew what I was doing and always flexibility. (Clare 1980)

The discrepancy between how we view ourselves and how the outer world sees us can be so great–and so incapacitating. (Nan 1988)

The aspect that startled both the women divorcing and those reading their letters was the surprising energy and sense of rebirth that accompanied the end of the marriages. Words like rebirth, rediscovery, and finding myself were used. They recognized how much of themselves they had set aside–how far out of balance the balancing act had become. The unexpected "coming alive again" feeling really surprised them. They came to a more complete understanding of their own needs and desires, and they grew.

I even "date" a bit, which may sound absurd at the ripe old age of 35–and yet, I feel very "alive" and "young" and am becoming–

more and more–open to these and other new experiences, which were not part of any "plan" I ever had! (Nel 1977)

I have to say I keep waking up and feeling good. I really am scared about going it alone, but each day seems to work itself out, and the feeling of being caught in an undertow is gone. I am happy. (Dot 1982)

The good news is that this seemingly catastrophic upheaval has forced a rather retiring homebody to do some incredible learning and growing. I have had experiences I would never have believed myself capable of two years ago. (Leah 1980)

Our divorce will be final May 9. I am still happier than I have been since I can remember, off the booze and the food, ironically, I guess, becoming again the woman I was when we got married–fun, independent, optimistic, joyous. (May 1989)

Little by little, I am reclaiming my life with such happiness. (Clare 1992)

I've been divorced now for nearly nine months, and I believe the oddest thing about it is that I don't feel that different. I've certainly done some grieving, yet often I've grieved more for what might have been than for what actually was. For the most part, I'm feeling an inner calm, a sense that my life is unrolling as it should. Faith, maybe. (May 1990)

The Wisdom of Personal Discovery

Personal discovery sums up the last two themes. Slowly each of the eighteen peel away the expectations of others and discover some core truths about themselves. They demonstrated a great need for personal space and for models of success as women. As they lived through life's tragedies and joys, they came face to face with new understandings about life as they knew it and as they once thought it would be. They moved forward when they accepted the truths they knew in their souls.

Personal Space and Models of Success

The women sought models of success and they valued personal space. This is the fifth theme. The two common strategies employed by the women in their search for personal space and for models of female success are reading books and creating private places to retreat. Reading has long been an established, acceptable way to achieve private space–a room of one's own–and to cavort privately and freely with role models, problem solvers, teachers, and lovers. Books provided the role models, the most accessible, articulated female achievement models in their time, stories of women experiencing adventure and romance and success. They discovered models who were strong and others who were pitiful. In the act of reading, they also found private personal space as they no doubt did in the act of writing letters. In the act of creating personal places for themselves, they became models of success for each other, carving out time and space to attend to their interests and needs. By middle age, most found ways to achieve actual private personal space over and beyond the mental privacy between the book covers. The recognition that women have a need for personal space, whether a room, a place, an activity, or an escape, is not an old or widely accepted idea. When Woolf (1929) suggested that a woman writer required a room of her own, the idea was dismissed by most as the ultimate in feminist hutzpah. The home and hearth were the female domain, no single place hers alone yet all places her responsibility, to be assembled and maintained for the comfort of her husband, children, and larger family. The pantry, the sewing room, the garden were spaces for women–spaces to carry out women's work in the service of other family members. By contrast, May, a writer, shared her thoughts as she tried to visualize working at home, and she ended up visualizing the space in which she will write:

> When I think about working at home, I find myself thinking about the accoutrements of work, not the work itself . . . When I talk to anyone about the money, I kind of skate over it in my mind, because it's scary, it sounds low, it sounds like I can't make enough to eat on, much less live on, so I go back to the calendar, the chair–a rolling one, with arms and comfortable seat–the lights, and how important it will be for me to claim that room and the computer as mine, my work place, my work things, to keep it serious, to not let it be family property like the sewing machine or the TV room. (May 1991)

The women describe the pursuit of space and place in terms of seeking a refuge, a retreat from the affairs of daily living; escaping to a new environment that promotes their preferred way to life; or creating a home, a spot that is safe and certain. One group of women worked very hard to keep a balance in life, to integrate their personal space and place into their daily living. They tended to find peace in a room or a spot that surrounded them or to which they had ready access. Another group plunged into life with little constraint or few boundaries on a daily basis and then sought peace and replenishing by stepping out of the mainstream into a space or place quite different from the rhythm of daily living. In both cases, the women talked about these renewing places as if they were part of it, an extension of it, linked by tradition, history, or an intentional decision.

> Last spring we had the chance to purchase a wonderful home built in 1865, its original elegance now gone somewhat tawdry. We'd hardly thought about moving and to buy was an impetuous decision of the heart–certainly not the mind. (Kate 1978)

> Five years ago [husband] built us a passive solar home in the woods in this small mountain community. We think we've found nirvana. (Lyn 1988)

> As you would guess, [the college campus] offers an academic, intellectual and cultural environment–for work and play–and a place of physical beauty which brings both joy and stimulation. (Nel 1977)

> I am also looking for a little house to buy, not a condominium, in spite of what well-meaning friends say. Not yet. I like trees and privacy and air around me. (May 1989)

The positive characteristics of personal space and place were commonly metaphors for home. A good place is one that is safe and secure, where one is nurtured and protected. A good place has walls to hang the things that are mine–a base or central space to which I return. It has a sense of permanency; it will be there for me. This good place shows the work of my hands both inside and in the gardens surrounding it.

> I know life is a compromise, but how do you know when you're making the best one you can? Finding a permanent place is a top priority for me now; I'm ready to settle. (Eve 1978)

> [Husband] is determined to retire very early and become a career traveler. I'm in favor of that, but I think I'll always want a home base–walls on which to hang the needlework and weaving we've collected, filing cabinets in which to keep my annual Mortar Board letters. (Leah 1989)

> A very important ingredient, I believe, was that the unit was very safe and secure, a place where I felt nurtured and protected. (Nel 1989)

The Wisdom of Life's Defining Moments

The sixth and last theme addresses the power of defining moments in life—moments of truth—and the courage of the women who accepted the challenge to learn from these moments of clarity and understanding. The epistemology of their knowing rests not in some expert truth or some rational argument, but in the confident knowledge of personal truth, an expression of their own considered judgment. Both the women and the psychological literature in general suggest that defining moments of pain, suffering, and disequilibrium are pivotal for personal growth. In the letters there were also moments of great affirmation and exhilaration that cannot be ignored as markers of growth. These moments may not have the power of traumatic events that literally shake one's foundations, but they built confidence, promoted significant personal learning, and brought the women face to face with who they are (not who others think they are).

As they shared personal experiences that were powerful and important in their life and growth, the women acknowledged the fairly commonplace nature of experiences like death, disappointment, divorce, job loss, moves, fear, and illness in the larger scheme of human living.

> Another year and a couple of giant steps backward. Leah thinks there might be some enrichment in these downside trips so I won't spare you the details. (Eve 1984)

Through these experiences the women appeared to get in touch with their real wisdom. In the midst of weighing painful choices and making difficult decisions related to experiences of loss and personal searching, the women exhibited strength and wisdom in ways that they did not expect. They seemed quite aware that their experiences are unique to them but also common to humanity.

The defining moments were the points after crisis when one sees the way, knows what has to be done. At these moments, priorities became more clear and the power to act was present. The process of negotiating difficulties and coming to resolution through personal modes of knowing generated considerable growth and confidence. When called upon to be strong, these women responded with caring and ethical, intentional strength that they had not previously named, acknowledged, or perhaps known existed. Their actions under duress allowed them to define them-selves (often to their own amazement) as competent and wise.

> As many (or all) of you know, I have been anorexic for a long time. . . . Finally . . . I entered [an] Eating Disorders Unit (weighing 67

pounds) much closer to death than life, both physically and emotionally. I left there four months later, 40 pounds heavier, and changed in
more ways than I would have thought possible. I could write a book
on those four months, for it "transformed" me in a way I would
never have thought possible. (Nel 1989)

Where they were rewarded as young women for being cooperative,
having orthodox ideas, not disputing authority, striving for perfection, and
behaving discreetly, they now felt achievement when they attended to their
own needs as well as others, acted on their own considered judgment, and
courageously determined to make a difference. These defining moments
brought to the surface the discrepancies between what these women anticipated in life and the unavoidable realities of living.

We have just learned [my 14 year old step-son's] 18 month old
remission is over; the cancer has returned in his bone marrow. What
this means is that [his] chances for a cure have diminished considerably, though there is still hope. But only a small percentage of the
kids who relapse hold a second remission, if they attain one, for very
long. Faced with such a grim prospect for 1985, it is difficult to
imagine our lives will have room for anything but dealing with this
crisis. Already I look with nostalgia on the months when we could
tell ourselves [he] would be among the 50 percent who recover, and
we lived our lives almost normally. (Leah 1985)

I wish I could tell you about triumphs with my work, but since [he]
died I've ground to a terrible halt and can't seem to get going again.
(Leah 1986)

The essential theme is the discovery that they cannot ignore what they
found to be true, and they cannot live life in basic conflict with their
deepest held personal beliefs. It is a sense that the "real me" was encountering the "real world" and growing because of it.

Much of this past year I have been forced to learn about letting go–of
people, mostly. My son, now 13, has been living at a boys' ranch
since February, where he is a ward of the county court. Our decision
to place him there, as you can imagine, came after months of trying
other options, agonizing, and especially (fairly new for me) prayer.
What it came down to was that we couldn't give him what he needs
right now, couldn't even identify what his needs were, and couldn't
continue to live in a constant state of anxiety, fear, and emotional

pain. I believe we did the right thing and I still cry often. It was the hardest thing I've done in my life. (May 1986)

I'm sending you all my cards so you can send me your friends (or enemies—I'm not particular) who are moving to [East] – or anywhere for that matter . . . and you can help me support myself and the three children [husband] and I had. Well, we had four, but [daughter] was killed in a traffic accident 15 years ago, when she was 13 months old. She was killed just before [husband] got his PhD. . . . I didn't feel like writing then, either. Then, in great sorrow, depression and anxiety, [we] moved [East] to start over. [He] had a post doc for 2 1/2 years, we bought our first home—had [a son and a daughter] and [he] became a professor. . . . There is a memorial garden there now for [him]. It was dedicated to his honor last month—and he was just awarded the rank of full professor—posthumously. He was killed by a drunk driver at 8 am November 2, 1982, Election Day. He was on his way to teach. I had just left him to go work at the polls. So. It can happen twice—what next? (Jill 1984)

CONSENT, COLLABORATION, AND CONFIRMATION

The fact that 17 of the 18 correspondents are alive and continue to write each year afforded me the opportunity to involve them actively as participants in the study. With their consent, they had a role at every step of the process. They helped assure that the set of letters was complete. They consented to exploratory interviews in order to surface critical ideas and themes. They reviewed written drafts and identified missing ideas. And finally, they confirmed the authenticity of the final paper in a telephone interview after a final reading as well as at the 1993 Taos reunion. This interpretive work is theirs as well as mine. As Bateson (1989) writes of her friends and collaborators,

> For a long time, I was puzzled about how to think about my relationship with the women who worked with me on this book. . . . Sometimes I refer to Joan, Ellen, Johnetta, and Alice as "the women I have been working with"—as collaborators—and yet this belies the playfulness of many of our conversations. The words used by social scientists for those they involve in their research feel wrong to me, even though as an anthropologist I believe that the people we call "informants" are our truest colleagues. These women are not "interviewees," not "subjects" in an experiment, not "respondents" to a

questionnaire. There is symmetry in our mutual recognition but there is asymmetry in that I am the one who goes off and weaves our separate skeins of memory into a single fabric. (p. 101)

Participant Confirmation

Participant confirmation is a process by which the authors of the text endorse the researcher's interpretation of words and events as an authentic, reasonable understanding of the text as they themselves know it. Participant confirmation is the final stamp of approval, the critical appraisal by the authors of the text that gives validation to the interpretation (Carr and Kemmis 1986). The confirmation process with the letters established that the authors endorsed the interpretation given to the letters and the creation of the six themes as authentic, contextual, and connected. This is a methodologically sound and ethically responsible approach since all but one of the letter writers is living. The process does make the women the authoritative speakers of their own experience as well as the authoritative judges of my interpretation of their words and meanings.[2]

The process of participant confirmation was driven not only by a desire for validation, but by a felt obligation on my part to create a process that did not undermine the on-going letter-writing and that tapped into the energy and thoughtfulness of the women in the group. I wrote to each of the women in 1991 that I was considering a study of the letters and asked for her opinion of this idea as well as for their participation:

> I read with some sadness Mary McCarthy's New York Times obituary this year. It said that she had written The Group without the consent of her friends, and that she betrayed secrets and mean-heartedly characterized her Smith College women so that they despised her and her work. How terrible! This is not what I want. I want to consider us—our lives and our times, our choices and our growth—so that we further document our lives and relationships and contribute knowledge about women to be useful to our granddaughters. . . . I am absolutely clear that I do not want to jeopardize confidentiality or future correspondence.

When each woman agreed to have her letters included in the study, she also agreed to review the draft of the themes of the study (a task estimated to take 45 minutes but which took much longer) and to take part in a telephone interview to discuss her reactions to the interpretation. The goal was not to seek agreement on every point; rather, it was to identify interpretations or understandings that clearly lacked authenticity, meaning, or relevance to the authors of the letters.

There was 100% participation in the confirmation process, and the women unanimously confirmed the interpretations and themes. (No name identifiers were used on this commentary in order to assure confidentiality within the group.) Every one endorsed the interpretations and indicated that the themes and implications captured the words and music of our correspondence or were at least a reasonable interpretation of our letters.

> And the other thing I want to tell you is that I enjoyed it so much more this way than I did the other way, and I loved getting those letters. The way you put this thing together is incredibly fascinating. I just couldn't stop reading it. . . .

> It's right on target. I didn't feel you stretched it, trying to make the letters fit some theory.[3]

Minor Modifications

The women identified two points that invite comment, two points where I failed to speak strongly enough or to listen carefully enough to their shades of meaning. These have to do with (a) the special difficulties women have succeeding in a man's world, and (b) the assumption that the women have rejected an external definition of success for themselves in favor of an internal one. These points were only specifically mentioned by two women, but I think they are important because they feel accurate. They identify and address ideas that I originally glossed over or minimized. Perhaps I said what I hoped was real–or real for some of us–or nearly real–but I did not hit the points with adequate power.

One woman argued forcefully that, for the women of our generation, I minimized the real difficulty of succeeding as a woman in a man's world. In her opinion, it's not terribly different today than it was in the years when we were growing to maturity. She pointed out that it was and still is very difficult for women who have devoted significant segments of their lives– ten or more years–to child-raising and community work to gain real financial independence, the kind that gives one powerful choices and options.

> The economic realities of this time make it extraordinarily difficult to "succeed" in a man's world. While women are contributing and frankly making the world a better place, it is still a man's world. Coalition building is one answer. Other answers do not come easily. I have seen unbelievable bravery among women who have chosen to divorce or are thrown aside.

I suspect that if I had written those words in my draft, other women would have agreed with them. It brought to mind Jill's related observation in her 1987 letter:

> I worked on [my career] to make our lives more secure, to take pressure off [husband] so we could enjoy life more—never dreaming that I would be required to carry it all myself. I was ready and able. As I look back I marvel at all this. . . . No hard decisions were forced on me out of necessity—some women have to rush into marriage in order to survive. . . . And I understand what people mean when they say "Well, she's been lucky." They're wrong, of course. There was no damn luck involved; just hard work and a life of planning and preparing. Like most men do. I am writing this because I want to know—is this so unique? (Jill 1987)

I noted this observation, but it did not change any of my basic themes.

The other disagreement with the draft had to do with my statement that the women had moved from an external standard or measure of success to an internal, more personal one. One woman said, "I'm just not sure I'm there. Am I the only one?" Surely she isn't. I only have to search myself to know that. While I still believe that the pattern in the letters argues for a move from external standards of success to internal ones, few of us are 100% there. We were, in the main, high achieving, obedient pleasers. At times we struggled with addiction, compulsion, depression, sadness, and despair related to our own unrealistic expectations as well as those we believed others held for us. It will take many of us many years to do a 180-degree turn!

In response to this commentary, I modified my earlier fairly definitive statements that the women had come, after thirty years, to find internal definitions for success. I focused on the difficulty of defining women's success in what can be viewed as a man's world, and yet I did not give up my understanding that the women had come a long way toward creating their own internal definitions of success based upon their experiences to deal with their issues of caring and connection, balance, working to make a difference, abandoning the dream, making space, and learning their own wisdom from joy and tragedy.

Important Participant Insights

The participant confirmation process generated some very provocative and important insights. While many observations and comments were interesting and helpful, three particular issues are explored in greater depth because they were mentioned by several different women. These points do not run counter to any of the ideas presented in the original findings; therefore, they are included as enhancements to the findings rather than modifications. The first has to do with the challenge of straddling two worlds, the second with the issue of truthfulness in the letters, and the third with the perspectives of the occasional contributors to the correspondence.

Straddling Two Worlds

> I wonder—maybe you say this—if we weren't particularly stressed as women teetering on this fulcrum between traditional women's roles and values and the newer attitudes influencing women's behavior that were coming into the fore just as we left school. In a way we lived with a foot firmly planted on each side, for we WERE mothers and nurturers first, most of us, but still we all developed an identity as a worker and professional person of some sort or another.

The letters show that this tension between mother and career woman felt precarious, was precarious, for the women. One remarked that her favorite part of the draft document was the section that discusses women's challenge to balance the public and private life.

Issues of Truthfulness

The second issue is one of truthfulness. No one suggests that what is written in the letters is untrue, but the question of what is intentionally omitted was raised in the telephone interviews. While several of the women made it clear that they never consciously censored their contributions, at least three talked about how they carefully considered what they wrote either to protect themselves or others who read the letters.

> A confession . . . I have always been very careful not to say very much in the letters. I have been guarded, but that is because I am a private person and do not want my "soul" revealed.

Another woman said she was honestly surprised to see the extent of her sharing in the draft; she had not consciously intended to share very personal matters. Certainly the early letters were originally more superficial in their sharing; the emphasis on feelings, struggles, and personal revelations began in the late 1970s as has been noted. Also, the revelations were cumulative. The accumulated contributions of individual women frequently revealed far more about them than any individual contribution offered in any single year.

Thoughts of Occasional Contributors

Three women who participated intermittently in the correspondence over the years discussed why they had not written with greater regularity Their reasons included (a) feelings their life was on a different track, (b) feelings of intimidation, and (c) feelings of disappointment in the life stories and achievements described in the letters. One said she was glad to receive and read the annual packet of letters, and even though she wrote letters of response, she seldom mailed them. She wrote, "I suspect that one of the reasons my MB letters often ended in the desk drawer was that my life seemed so far removed from you all when you started marrying and having families." Another wrote, "You know . . . I think a lot of times I just felt real intimidated. I mean everybody else was publishing or travel-ing around the world or you know, joining the Weathermen—something so exciting. And my life, and my little research, and my little kids—who were wonderful—seemed kinda boring." The notion of disappointment is not new, but because it comes from one who watched from a distance, it is helpful.

> I expected more of us: the academic/leadership women of one of the finest public universities. And when I saw you all evolving unpro-testingly into your mother's roles, I was disappointed and angry. I loved my independent life—and recognized later in the letters of the divorcees that they were discovering its joys as well. And I thought I recognized it in the letters of the still married in their search for "personal" time and need for independence.

Then she added:

> Our lives are surely not over by a long shot, so political, legal, medi-cal, social, educational contributions of the group are still to come.

What Women Need to Know

The ultimate confirmation by the women came during our reunion in August, 1993. Until this time, the participants had been dealing one-on-one with me, the researcher. At the Taos gathering, the women had an opportunity to talk to each other about the significance of their correspon-dence, the meaning of their shared confidences, and the understanding each had about the messages in the letters. Around the fireplace in the evenings, the talk was of the present and the future, not so much on the past. They affirmed the themes fundamental to their feelings of success and achievement, and they took their understandings a step further to formulate some messages for their daughters and granddaughters. They framed the question slightly differently: What do women need to know to feel successful and competent in undertaking the important challenges and decisions of adult life?

First and foremost, women of all ages must recognize how subtle and deep is the expectation in our society that females are the primary nurturers. Whether a woman accepts that role or not, it is important to explore the assumptions about women's roles that have been directly and obliquely reinforced by parents, teachers, peers, and society. The women in this study to a large degree minimized the importance of the mother-nurturer role in college and in the several years that followed. They thought they could do it all–independent woman, career success, wife, mother, community leader–and simultaneously and successfully at that. It didn't turn out that way, and many felt questionable success on most fronts until well into middle age.

Second, women can examine the reasons they fail to feel successful and actively reframe these notions to their advantage. Because they commonly place high value on personal attachments, on relationships past and present, women often have a difficult time claiming credit for what goes well. If my marital relationship is wonderfully rewarding, can I take the credit? If my child succeeds in school, how much of the success is mine? Because there are no generally accepted benchmarks or standards for what it means to be a successful woman, one never knows how to measure success from an external perspective. Is a successful woman slim? Beautiful? Fit? Intelligent? Compliant? Powerful? Compassionate? Passionate? A board president? A law partner? A medical technician? A child care provider? All of these things? Perhaps none of them. And finally, because the work of "making and mending the social fabric" (Gilligan et al. 1990, p. 300) and rearing and teaching the children is routinely trivialized in our society, it takes considerable self-assurance to proclaim oneself a noteworthy success in these arenas.

Third, women must consider ways to establish their own markers of success and then work to meet their established standard. Consider negotiating markers or goals with parents, partners or friends and then celebrating the achievement or dissecting the failure. People need clear measures of success in order to know when they have succeeded. For a long time, the Mortar Board women used each other as yardsticks by which to measure their ideas and actions. Other people use mentors, role models, or a collage of models of success melded to fit their special needs.

Fourth, the women grew in their feelings of success as they became more intentional about their actions. To the extent they did things because it was the thing to do, because it fulfilled someone else's expectations, or because there was no competing alternative, they did not necessarily make bad choices, but they did not feel particularly successful. When they began to make intentional choices, they felt powerful and more often than not, successful. Young women must consider the value of acting strategically, deliberately, and intentionally as opposed to going along, not rocking the boat, being part of the team, or not being selfish.

Fifth, the letters in the attic are concrete testimony to the tenacious and rewarding quality of women's friendships. The friendships of girls cannot be fairly labeled as substitutes for independence or crutches against loneliness. Based upon the experience of these women, such friendships are important, worthy of attention, and valuable for the continuity they provide in a modern life often characterized by discontinuity and uncertainty. This suggests that young women examine their friendships and consider making a deliberate commitment to maintaining them despite the considerable pull to put all available energy into a career, a partnership, or a family. It takes time and determination to nurture a friendship, especially at a distance. But as this study has pointed out, friendship has the potential to provide markers of success, affirmation for achievement, support for times of trial, and continuity in a world that often seems fragmented.

Sixth, the letters of the women affirm the value of the private life. This is not to say it is a preferred or even compelling mode for young women today. It does attest to the compatibility of the private life with attachments and relationships. It suggests that young women intentionally consider the role of a partnership, children, and a family in their life plan. If these are valued goals, then thought must be given as to how and when to make the choices that will be required. Talk to other women who have made deliberate choices. Consider the trade-offs and the options. Plan ahead. The goal is to have the confidence and understanding to say about any choice or lifestyle, "I know who I am and why I do what I do."

Seventh, an education remains a powerful advantage for women in contemporary American society. This is most dramatic for the women who relied upon their credentials for employment and economic self-sufficiency following divorce. While formal education guarantees nothing, it opens doors of association, of credentials, and of credibility. Perhaps it is less an issue of "certification" than one of benchmark setting: I have passed the strenuous test once, and I can do it again. Many of the Mortar Board women describe how they relied on their college success as a symbol of their capacity when faced with adversity later in life. Perhaps the test need not be in higher education, but it should be somewhere. Young women gain strength when they know they have faced challenges and succeeded.

> For if the world we give our children is different from the one we envisioned for them, then we need to discover the moments when we, weary, distracted, and intimidated, sold out. . . . As we study the forms of our own experience we are not searching only for evidence of the external forces that have diminished us; instead, we are recovering our own possibilities, ways of knowing and being in the world that we remember and imagine and must draw into language that can span the chasm that presently separates what we know as our public and private worlds. (Grumet 1988, p. 532)

The stories in the letters connect the private and public worlds and communicate the things experienced, the things hoped for, and the things undone in life. Thus the understandings and meanings from these women's lives may help provide the daughters coming after them with more brightly lit paths to follow and more clearly illuminated questions to ask about their own futures.

NOTES

1. The 1960s health food writer who urged diligent mothers to prepare nutritional baby food at home in kitchen blenders.

2. For an informative discussion of research ethics and the involvement of women in studies done of them, see Daphne Patai's article "Is Ethical Research Possible?" in Sherna Berger Gluck and Daphne Patai, *Women's Words: The Feminist Practice of Oral History* (New York: Routledge), 1991.

3. In the participant confirmation section, I did not attach any names to the responses and comments in order to protect the confidentiality of those commenting.

REFERENCES

Bateson, M. C. (1989). *Composing a life.* New York: Plume.

Carr, W., & Kemmis, S. (1986). *Becoming critical: Education, knowledge and action research.* London: Falmer Press.

Gilligan, C., Lyons, N., Hanmer, T. (Eds.). (1990). *Making Connections: The Relational Worlds of Adolescent Girls at Emma Willard School.* Cambridge: Harvard University Press.

Gluck, S. B., & Patai, D. (Eds.). (1991). *Women's words: The feminist practice of oral history.* London: Routledge.

Grumet, M. R. (1988). Women and teaching: Homeless at home. In W. F. Pinar (Ed.). *Contemporary curriculum discourses* (pp. 531-539). Scottsdale: Gornuoh Scarisbrick

Heilbrun, C. G. (1989). *Writing a woman's life*. London. Women'o Pruss Ltd

St. Vincent Millay, E. (1934). *Wine from these grapes.* New York: Harper & Brothers.

Seidel, J. (1988). *The Ethnograph 3.0: A user's guide.* Littleton, CO: Qualis Research Associates.

Walker, J. (1993). Women's voices, women's lives: Understandings from women's twenty-four year correspondence (Doctoral Dissertation, University of Minnesota, 1993). *Dissertation Abstracts International, 54 (03A)*, 1124.

Woolf, V. (1929). *A room of one's own.* New York: Harcourt, Brace.

OTHER REFERENCES RELEVANT TO THIS ARTICLE

Beauman, N. (1983). *A very great profession: The woman's novel 1914-1939.* London: Virago Press.

Brown, M. M. (1989). What are the qualities of good research? In F. H. Hultgren & D. L. Coomer (Eds.). *Alternative modes of inquiry.* Washington, DC: American Home Economics Association, Teacher Education Section.

Gadamer, H. G. (1981). *Reason in the age of science.* (FG. Lawrence, Trans.). Cambridge: MIT Press.

Heilbrun, C. G. (1990). *Hamlet's mother and other women.* New York: Ballantine.

Lather, P. (1986). Research as praxis. *Harvard Educational Review, 56*, 257-277.

Madison, G. B. (1988). *The hermeneutics of postmodernity: Figures and themes.* Bloomington: Indiana University Press.

Pinar, W. F. (1988). Whole, bright deep with understanding: Issues in qualitative research and autobiographical method. In WF. Pinar (Ed.). *Contemporary curriculum discourses* (pp. 134-153). Scottsdale, AZ: Gorsuch Scarisbrick.

Reinharz, S. (1992). *Feminist methods in social research.* New York: Oxford University Press.

Document Analysis:
The Contrast Between Official
Case Records and the Journal
of a Woman on Welfare

Terry L. Holbrook

SUMMARY. This article contrasts the journal writings of Dorothy Thompson, a woman on welfare, with the official agency case records and an oral tradition handed down by successive caseworkers. The record and oral tradition portray Dorothy as an undeserving, offensive, neglectful mother while Dorothy's journal reveals a strong-willed and valiant woman struggling with circumstances she cannot understand. The clash between the official ideologies contained in the case record and Dorothy's lived experience is startling and very much to the detriment of Dorothy and her family. The power is in the social welfare system and not with Dorothy, and her life becomes a documented tragedy, though her humanity endures and makes her story bearable and sometimes uplifting. *[Article copies available for a fee from The Haworth Document Delivery Service: 1-800-342-9678. E-mail address: getinfo@haworth.com]*

KEYWORDS. Self appraised, Social welfare, Journaling, Bureaucracy, Story

Terry L. Holbrook is Director of Social Work, Finger Lakes Development Center, Newark, NY. Address correspondence to the author at 4056 Allen's Hill Road, Holcomb, NY 14469.

[Haworth co-indexing entry note]: "Document Analysis: The Contrast Between Official Case Records and the Journal of a Woman on Welfare." Holbrook, Terry L. Co-published simultaneously in *Marriage & Family Review* (The Haworth Press, Inc.) Vol. 24, No. 1/2, 1996, pp. 41-56; and: *The Methods and Methodologies of Qualitative Family Research* (ed: Marvin B. Sussman, and Jane F. Gilgun) The Haworth Press, Inc., 1996, pp. 41-56. Single or multiple copies of this article are available for a fee from The Haworth Document Delivery Service [1-800-342-9678, 9:00 a.m. - 5:00 p.m. (EST). E-mail address: getinfo@haworth.com].

41

Personal document analysis has a long but rather obscure history in social science research. Thomas and Znaniecki (1918-20) were among the first researchers to use this qualitative research strategy. Personal documents are defined by Bogdan and Taylor (1975) as "any first person account of whole or part of his or her life or an individual reflection on a specific topic or event" (p. 96). Personal documents can include autobiographies, diaries, letters, journals, oral histories, recorded verbatim, or other material authored by a single person. Personal documents can be solicited or unsolicited, limited or complete, edited or unedited. The documenter can be known or unknown to the researcher, an historical figure or an ordinary citizen. The documenter can be randomly selected or deliberately chosen to illustrate a typical problem or category of persons (Holbrook, 1986).

This article is excerpted from my unpublished book *Deadwood: Thirty Years on the Welfare Dole* (Holbrook, 1994), where I compared the personal journal of a welfare mother and her official case record. A related article recently was published (Holbrook, 1995). The book began in 1969 as a by-product of a professional relationship between myself, a welfare caseworker, and Dorothy Thompson, a pseudonym for my collaborator and a mother on welfare. At the time, I knew nothing of personal documents or social science. I do not recall exactly when Dorothy and I first talked about collaborating on a book. However, each time I stopped by to visit, she would hand me another yellow tablet crammed with her thoughts and feelings. I was deeply moved by Dorothy's monumental effort to communicate and felt her story deserved to be told.

A SINGLE CASE "TOO SUBJECTIVE AND SOFT"

Sadly, there was not much interest among my colleagues in what one welfare mother had to say. Unless I had several journals to compare, permitting computerized content analysis, I was told there was not much social science could do with the material. The documents were simply "too subjective and too soft." Fortunately, recent challenges to the alleged "objectivity and hardness" of social scientific facts has led some researchers to attempt to reintroduce the single subject's voice into the research knowledge/power equation, unencumbered by methodological assumptions (Hartman, 1992). As a result, numerous diaries and journals written by slave women in the antebellum South and pioneer women in the West have demonstrated interest in personal document research (Alexander, 1984; Jacobs, 1987; Exley, 1985). I still am not convinced that everyone will be interested in Dorothy's views, but from my point of view her story cuts to the heart of prevalent attitudes toward poor women and their children.

GENERAL RESEARCH PRINCIPLES

Although there is a variety of ways to approach personal documents, researchers observe the following general principles:

1. maintain the integrity of the documents.
2. provide contextual descriptions to evoke the natural setting in which the documents were written.
3. insure that the documenter's voice is not overwhelmed or distorted by the researcher's voice and descriptions.

POWER AND PERSPECTIVE

By comparing Dorothy's journal with her official welfare case record, Dorothy and I discovered we were able to reveal a number of hidden assumptions about welfare casework, professional authority, and the management of social conflict at the interpersonal level. We were also able to uncover a pattern of gender discrimination within welfare agencies. Men managed these agencies, but other women, possibly as a condition of their employment, perpetrated the gender discrimination. By situating both documents in a socio-historical context, it was also possible to demonstrate the political to personal linkages between welfare state policies and mothers on welfare.

Juxtaposing the various perspectives on a single life reveals the socially constructive power of welfare caseworkers to define, prescribe, and control the behavior of welfare mothers as well as their power to resist. By going from person to problem definition, individual situation to collective stereotypes, it was possible to describe how we manage to distort the real lives of welfare recipients by simply refusing to allow them to speak, or speaking on their behalf. Confidentiality laws not only protect the privacy of families, but protect the actions of social service agencies from public scrutiny.

In this article, I hope to be able to demonstrate the significant contributions personal document research can make to knowledge, practice, and values. Dorothy Thompson, a mother of 12 children, agreed to share her welfare case history as well as her personal journal, with the hope others can learn from it. Dorothy's reasons are best said by her:

> Sure hope this book of mine (well, part of it will be mine) is going to help people instead of causing more heartbreak. If anyone realizes what family it is written about . . . I hope and pray it does not bring

more hurt to my children than they have already lived. Maybe I am making a wrong decision in continuing on with this book. I care for my children and I hope they all know that. Maybe I can help other mothers from making stupid mistakes I did while raising my children. Looking back, I tried too hard to keep them in decent clothing, and accepted too many second-hand clothes so that it was hard to keep apartment clean, because by the time I moved all boxes of clothes, I was too tired to finish housework with everything else I had to do. Social workers, authorities and neighbors had no understanding or feelings about how tiring everything was for me.

In the following pages, I will contrast Dorothy's perspectives with viewpoints and portraits contained in her agency case record. I begin with my introduction to Dorothy and her family through agency oral tradition and case records.

MY PREPARATION FOR WORK IN SOCIAL WELFARE

When I accepted the job of welfare examiner, my knowledge of poverty was limited. I had no personal or professional experience to rely on; I knew what I had read or had been told. My father worked for General Motors and my mother worked part-time at the post office. Although I was the oldest of six children, there always seemed to be enough money to go around. My father believed strongly in the work ethic, and I had uncritically absorbed that ethic. I was the first of my family to attend college. The job as a welfare examiner was my first full-time position.

It was the late sixties. The U.S. was embroiled in the Vietnam War. There was student unrest, civil disobedience, race riots, and political assassinations. There were rumblings of a feminist movement. The War on Poverty had been declared but there were signs that the War had been lost. Rural America watched and waited for the rest of the country to settle down and for common sense to prevail.

The agency had a staff of seven public assistance caseworkers and three child protective workers. My supervisor had worked in county welfare since the days the money was kept in a drawer and passed out and recorded in a ledger by hand. As far as the agency was concerned, my college degree qualified me for the position, and my supervisor would teach me what I needed to know. Like most U.S. citizens, I believed that poverty was probably the result of some combination of individual misfortune and the lack of opportunity. My job was to provide temporary assistance until those in my caseload got back on their feet.

THE THOMPSONS: "DEADWOOD" BY AGENCY STANDARDS

A senior case worker introduced me to the Thompsons. This staff person had worked with the family and long ago declared them "deadwood," cases that always had been and always will be impossible to do anything with. "Deadwood" was in every caseload, the staff person explained, and my caseload was no exception. If I could deal with dirt, odors, and attitudes offensive to middle-class sensibilities and not betray my offense to the recipient, then I had passed my first test by fire. I would probably make it as a caseworker, though there was no hope that anyone could ever change the families and their situations.

According to the senior staff person, Dorothy Thompson and her family had been a burden to the taxpayers of this rural county since 1948, when she and her husband signed their first application for medical assistance to pay for the birth of their fourth child. They had had a child each year since Mr. Thompson's discharge from the service and their marriage in 1945. At the time of application for welfare, Mr. Thompson had been fired from his job for drinking. The family had no savings and could not pay for the cost of hospitalization. They were then both 23 years old. According to my co-workers, this was just the beginning of a pattern of public assistance that had cost the county thousands of dollars, with no end in sight. Without conscience or consideration, the Thompsons, already indebted to the largess of the taxpayers, had repaid taxpayers by having more children than they could support. The only positive thing that the senior staff person could say was that the family was still intact. The rest was in the case record, which I could read at my leisure. Thus did my co-worker inform me of the Thompson situation.

THE CASE RECORD SUMMARY

When I read the case record, the transfer note helped me become more acquainted with the family's case history:

> This has always been a problem case created mainly due to the father's drinking problems. Mr. Thompson has not lived at home for a few years and has been ordered not to. Mrs. Thompson has given birth to 12 children. She is a very poor housekeeper. Her house is always dirty and no doubt has done much to affect the children psychologically. Mrs. Thompson has been approached many times by various workers as to cleaning up her home but each time she

claims she will try to but no improvement seems to be accomplished. Mrs. Thompson has at times trouble managing her money but in recent months, she has been doing quite well with some guidance from this worker. Mrs. Thompson seems to be a woman who has given up on ever being anything more than a public charge and seems satisfied living in a dirty home.

SHOCKED BUT DETERMINED TO MAKE A DIFFERENCE

I was appropriately shocked, but armed with the idealism of youth, I was determined to make a difference. Over the next several months, I spent hours talking with Dorothy, trying to understand what I could do to help. I found the afternoons not long enough, or the interruptions too numerous and sustained to do much of anything but listen. One afternoon, I suggested that she keep a journal of her thoughts, feelings, and the daily events of her life. Each week I would pick up the entries, and we would discuss them on my next visit. I left welfare casework after two long years. Twelve years later, Dorothy was still writing. Dorothy's journal gave an account of her life very different from the case record and the impressions of a succession of caseworkers who had come and gone over the course of her "career" on welfare. The discrepancy between Dorothy's journal and her case record led me to wonder why no one had asked for her opinion before, and if they did, why it had made no difference.

DOROTHY'S VIEW ON HELPING OTHERS

To make an understatement, Dorothy's inner life was not represented in her case record. Contrast the portrait of Dorothy I received with an excerpt from her journal, where she expressed her hope to help others.

> Sure wish I could think of something I could do to help other people, or maybe just someone. David [one of her sons] says I should be a little greedy so people don't keep using me. He may be right, but I am just not that way.

In another part of her journal, Dorothy elaborated on why helping others was important to her.

> Have to do something to change each day so I don't just exist. Help someone who feels left out of things as I do. But main idea is, how?

Without making person feel like they are being moved around like checkers on a checker board. Just be a friend who stops in and says hello once in a while is the best way, I guess.

This woman was feeling dehumanized and was searching for meaning in her life. Helping others was her way of feeling her life had meaning.

Elaboration on feeling dehumanized and an indirect assertion of her worth are contained in the following excerpt.

If people that have most everything money can buy could only see that people lacking money to buy what they want don't lack feelings and sometimes have more talent and intelligence than children, or even adults, who are born with a silver spoon in their mouths.

The intelligence and command of language that emanate from Dorothy's writings suggest that she may have been thinking–or hoping–deep inside herself that she has "talent and intelligence." It's doubtful, given her life as I knew it, that anyone ever assured her of her worth and that she ever had opportunity to test out how talented and intelligent she was. Of course, our joint effort to tell her story affirms her worth, talent, and intelligence.

PORTRAIT OF A FAMILY

The case record documents how caseworkers perceived Dorothy and her family. Given the difficulty of her life circumstances, the attitudes of caseworkers could only have driven Dorothy to a desperate search for meaning. The narrative portion of the case record began with the family's application for assistance in May of 1949. Mr. Thompson was working but was spending his income on alcohol and not on his family. They had four children, four years old and younger. Thus is the family as presented in the case record:

The baby Susan, now seven months old, only weighs twelve pounds. Her little legs are terribly thin, no color in face, and very peaked. Worker talked with County health officer. He said that this baby was ailing from malnutrition. The baby had been brought in office three times by County nurse and mother. He had given it shots, vitamins and a great deal of medication. These calls had not been paid for and they had just scratched them off the books. He said the child will need considerable care and it was he who suggested they apply for medical care.

Poor Mrs. Thompson's face is all pitted with scabby sores. When worker asked how she was, she replied that she had gotten her strength back since baby was born. She said her teeth bother her a lot.

The family lives in the lower part of a large house belonging to husband's employer. The house is terribly run down and applicant said her husband is no man to make repairs and she can't do it and have money to pay for cost they just have to remain broken [sic].

Worker has noticed while passing very white washing on the line and commented to applicant as to this. She said that her husband complained because she took all of afternoon to wash but when she did do things she always did them thoroughly. The house is not tidy, but she has four babies, little furniture, and no help from husband, so what could one expect.

John is a boozer and seldom has a full week's pay. Now, Mrs. Thompson goes each Friday and collects husband's pay. She gives husband $5.00 and spends all she can for groceries and other bills for if she still has money in the home, she states husband will demand it. She states he is mean when drinking.

Worker stopped in the home on 7/22/49. Mrs. Thompson said that they were fine and proudly displayed Susan, the baby, who now looks greatly improved and just like a normal baby. Case closed.

The caseworker's narrative reflects the rules for obtaining welfare by establishing a rationale and context for assistance created out of the circumstances of Dorothy's and John's life. The malnourished baby, the medical needs of the boys and Dorothy, the living arrangements, her husband's drinking and his "meanness," the resultant lack of income, all this is social evidence of the need for public assistance.

FACTS: WHAT'S THERE AND WHAT'S NOT

The caseworkers' narrative reflects more than just the facts of the case and is as significant for what facts the narrator leaves out as well as what is left in. In between Dorothy's telling of her story and the caseworker's listening, both Dorothy and worker are attempting to understand the unfolding of events. However, each is concerned for different purposes: the caseworker from the point of view of justifying assistance and from Dorothy's point of view of needing it. Both Dorothy and the caseworker are relying on the wider culture's social conventions, language forms, and commonly shared meanings to create a plausible scenario, a mutually understood biography composed of past and present experiences.

In the first case record entry above, all ends well. Although the narrative does not say it, Dorothy is home, where she belongs. John is working but drinking excessively. Dorothy is doing the best she can for her children and herself, with little help from her husband. Dorothy is not asking for cash assistance but seeking medical care for the children. Her domestic labors, washing, housecleaning, and money management are initially acceptable. Upon a return visit, everything appears to be "normal." John's "meanness and boozing" are excused, Dorothy's living arrangements and the child's malnourishment are ignored or used as evidence of need. The story has a happy ending when assistance is provided and the case is closed after only three months.

EXTREME NEED TWO YEARS LATER

Two years after the initial application, the case was reopened. John was not bringing money into the home, and the children were in dire need of medical care. The same caseworker was not as supportive or optimistic as she was earlier.

3/10/50: The case was re-opened. Health officer called early on the morning of March 9th, stating he had been called to the Thompson home due to Allen, son, having had convulsions and another child with running ears. He was informed to send bill to the County.

John has been employed for over two years, earning an average of $40.00 per week. He works on the garbage wagon. He is a habitual drinker and often does not show up for work. Mrs. Thompson said that her husband got drunk Friday night and has not returned to the job. He states he was fired but no one has told him so, except the last time this occurred, the boss told him the next time he drank and didn't show up he was through.

The family lives in a house belonging to employer. Applicant not a good housekeeper but she has little to do with, so perhaps this is partly the trouble. Worker recommends this case be opened for Medical Care only.

Medical care, however, was not enough. With no money, the family needed heat for the home, and food. In desperation, Dorothy called for help.

3/20/50: Client called this morning. She stated that husband returned to work this morning. They were all out of food and had no fuel. Would we purchase these items?

John was no longer a carefree "boozer" but a habitual drinker. The caseworker gave Dorothy the benefit of the doubt regarding her housekeeping, but instead of saying for the record that she discouraged Dorothy and John from seeking anymore assistance, she recommended that they receive coal for their furnace. The caseworker wrote in the Thompson record:

> Worker gave her little encouragement. It was talked over with Commissioner, who approved one (1) ton of Chestnut coal to be purchased. We did this because of the fact that three of the children are ill.

LET THEM EAT COAL

The worker knew she did not have authority to grant the request for coal and that the commissioner would be reading the record in order to make his decision. By this time, the Thompson family was well-known to the community and there was little community support to lend a "helping hand" to a large, poor family where the husband's alcoholism destroyed any opportunity for income. Dorothy was probably stigmatized for the size of her family. Why did she have all those kids with a drunken husband and no money? This may have been the prevailing opinion about Dorothy.

It seemed the more knowledge the community had of the Thompson family, the less compassion there was toward them, to the point where they received coal but no food. The commissioner had to appear "tough" if he were to be reappointed, but not so tough as to allow a family to freeze to death. The problem of how much carrot and how much stick applies to welfare administrators as well as policy makers.

ON-GOING TRAVAIL

In the fall of 1950, Dorothy separated from her husband John for the first time and moved to an adjacent county to be near her parents. Her father, a grocer and meat cutter, purchased a house for Dorothy and the children, and the family applied for public assistance. Records for this six year period were sketchy. Dorothy eventually reunited with her husband. She once again became pregnant and gave birth to twins. John subsequently fell off the wagon and ended up in a state hospital for treatment of his alcoholism. The following is a verbatim report from his treating psychiatrist to the county court:

5/27/54: It may be noted that Mr. Thompson has been considered to be Without Mental Disorder, by the Qualified Psychiatrist, acting in this case. It has been further evaluated that Mr. Thompson will, in all probability, continue the pattern of his present and past behavior upon his return to the community. For this reason it is felt that some definite means might be taken whereby community supervision can be maintained over this man's earnings, to the point that his family will have the benefit of his earnings, rather than permit them to be spent on whiskey or other alcoholic beverages. Should there be no community supervision in this case, it is felt that there will be numerous recurrences of the present situation, possibly with danger to his wife or family, and certainly with a burden being placed upon the Welfare Department for the maintenance of the family. Further consideration should also be given the guidance of the children in the family since, should the present situation continue, there is no question but what personality behavior will be noted in the children in the near future, of some abnormal type.

Despite the clear recommendations in this report, the agency did nothing. John was destroying the family with his drinking. Allowing individuals the right to self-destruct is one thing, but allowing men to "destroy" their families is another.

John was the rightful head of the Thompson family, and the legal system supported his authority over and above the welfare of Dorothy and the children. Although there was plenty of evidence that John was not supporting his family, as long as he was in the home, Dorothy and the children were dependent on his income, regardless of whether he gave any of it to Dorothy or not. The court could threaten John with jail time, but the law could not force John to become a good provider or father. Dorothy found herself with more children than she could support and with little choice but to pin her hopes once again on John. After all, he was their father.

FAMILY COURT RESPONDS

A year later Dorothy gave birth to yet another child. Mr. Thompson's pattern of drinking and non-support continued. Finally Family Court responded by offering Mr. Thompson the choice of moving out of town or going to jail. By this time, Dorothy's family had given up on her. Pregnant again and without the support of her family, Dorothy followed her husband back across the county line. Predictably, in 1956, the Thompsons applied for medical assistance to help with the cost of the pregnancy. Mr. Thompson earned $1.35/hour and his wages were garnished.

DOROTHY'S APPRAISAL OF HER SITUATION

Dorothy's appraisal of her own life was in stark contrast to the case record. Implicit in her account is a portrait of a young woman who was trying her best to live up to social expectations for women and mothers. Raised in a well-off blue-collar family with clear roles designated along the lines of gender, she was unprepared to deal with an alcoholic husband. It's clear that no one else, including her family of origin, was able to help her cope with an impossible situation. This is Dorothy's view of her life at that time:

> It is said that you shouldn't live in the past. I wonder if this is true. There was a part of my past life that is the way I wanted it for my children, but things didn't work out that way. No one I was near was interested in my opinion, from the day John and I were married. When I first met him, there wasn't any great moment. It was just, oh I don't know . . . He was alone and asks my girlfriend if we would like a sandwich or something at the bus terminal before the bus came. That day I never thought anything would come of meeting him again. Just young people exchanging addresses for something to say to each other. I admit he was a neat, good-looking soldier. That proves my mother's point that you can't tell a book by its cover. You should take the time to get to know a person. That wasn't possible, as he was in the service and we just corresponded until he stopped writing because of lots of reasons. One was, he was in the brig and didn't have honesty enough to get someone to let me know why he didn't write after I had sent some money and package of food to him.
>
> Trying to please my husband in anything I did for him was a lost cause. He didn't even want me to talk to his own girl cousin next door to us. Was going next door to another neighbor's but her life was just about like mine, well a little. Her husband was good to her. She had friends and relatives come to her house. When John wasn't around, his cousins used to come to talk to me. I really tried to be happy and was for a while. Then he just seemed to be telling me something was wrong in the way I acted. Work and drink, go out with old friends. I sat home most of the time. Laughed and talked with neighbors mostly but it got so he didn't even want me to do that. His mother and he complained no matter how hard I tried to please

them. Didn't have a washing machine for a while and I washed railroad clothes by hand. Wasn't brought up that way, but that doesn't matter if just once someone would say I was doing anything right. He never talked much except when complaining about my work not being done the way his mother did it. We had to leave that house because he lost job on railroad and no one rented a house then unless working for railroad.

The power of gender is vastly underrated. What was it that convinced Dorothy it was her responsibility to please John or his mother, to hand wash his clothes, or have his children, one after another, even though her own health was being badly compromised, to make excuses for him, to take his criticism, to put up with his drinking and irresponsibility?

Feminists have railed against subservient, self-sacrificing, submissive behavior such as this, while understanding how women have been socialized to behave in just these ways. Others would blame Dorothy for "enabling" John's alcoholism by giving him the support he needed to continue his self-destructive addiction. The failure to understand how much Dorothy's identity was tied to her role as mother and wife and how that identity, responsibility, and sacrifice was reinforced by everyone around her is precisely the power of gender socialization. Dorothy had no apparent choices except to be dependent on her husband.

SECOND-CLASS CITIZENS

Though tied to a non-functioning husband, she could not ignore the contradictions, inequities, and unfairness in her life. What Dorothy resented most was the way she and her children were treated as second-class citizens in the welfare system. She wrote in her journal:

> One week from today, I have to re-certify over to the County Building. Just think I am finished with one episode with them, and then I have to go over and answer silly questions that they know already the answers to. Between landlady not wanting my youngest son to have a friend stay over night, and welfare having to know everything about my son's wages and job . . . he won't tell them what his wages are. I've never seen such a mess of not understanding other humans' feelings like the county people have turned into. It never was such a 'cold fish' arrangement as it is now. And some young snot who doesn't even know why, giving you remarks before she knows your situation and what kind of person you are, makes me mad.

The excessive rationality ("answering silly questions"), the coldness, and commitment to education and credentials over life experience ("young snot") all contributed to the chasm between Dorothy's experiences and the offerings of the welfare system. Dorothy, like many of us when confronted with cold-heartedness, felt powerless and did not protest, except in her journal.

DOROTHY CONVICTED OF CHILD NEGLECT

On the surface these differences in perception may not seem shocking, unusual, or important, but in 1972 Dorothy was convicted of child neglect. Three of her children were placed in foster homes, based on evidence from her case record. Her conviction stemmed on a complex web of assumptions, prejudices, and lack of understanding.

The contrasts between the official record and Dorothy's personal diary disclose that official reality as documented in the welfare case record is a complex social construction, made up of conflicting facts, opinions, and conjecture by ordinary men and women whose job is to make this conflict appear conforming and harmonious. By tacitly agreeing to avoid the obvious, the professionals in Dorothy's case engaged in a conspiracy of silence regarding the undeniable evidence in the case record that poverty and the debilitating effects of her marriage, not inadequate mothering, resulted in the Thompson children's neglect.

This resulted, not from a willful conspiracy among cynical professionals, but by the mutual acceptance of taken-for-granted assumptions by the trial participants about the causes of poverty, child abuse and neglect, and individual responsibility. Dorothy's 30 years of welfare assistance, the professionals' working knowledge of each other's roles, their naive faith in the accuracy of the case record, combined to create a situation in which conviction was virtually assured. Contrasting Dorothy's journal and case record, however, showed how official reality is created out of a historical process of negotiation between Dorothy and her caseworkers, with the outcome depending more on the power to define reality and write in the case record than any ability to record "objective" facts.

DISCUSSION

The subtle but pervasive use of official power in the case record to define needs and problems, control resources, reward compliance and punish assertiveness contrast sharply with Dorothy's description of shame, self-doubt, and defeat in her journal. Dorothy's case record and journal clearly show how the control inherent in welfare dependency is reinforced over time by the psychological pain of being blamed repeatedly. Apart from the use of case records as a means of individual control over dependent women's lives, professional power and influence extends well beyond the welfare agency to the actual formation of social welfare policy itself. Case records and the statistics extracted from them frequently are the only source of information we have on which the effectiveness of welfare programs can be evaluated, or the impact of policy decisions can be determined. When a president declares that the only way to reduce poverty is to reduce the attractiveness and welfare benefit levels to women, case records are the only evidence we have to evaluate the results of those reductions.

I suggest that what researchers and judges are willing to accept as evidence and the way they define the problem determine what we can do about it. With much of this so-called scientific knowledge of professionals based on case-record data, the circle of self-fulfilling prophecy is made complete from insidious prejudice to case record, to science and legitimation, to professionals teaching other professionals, or from belief to knowledge. When Dorothy's case record is shorn of its bureaucratically assigned meanings and professional mystification, it reveals the officially sanctioned and documented efforts of welfare bureaucracy to assign blame for family failures to women.

Ironically, this punishing role has been given to female caseworkers whose job it is to visit the homes of poor women and insure their compliance with normative values by threat of removal of the children. What better disguise to enforce the status quo of male and class privilege and dominance than to hire women to deliver this message? Since social work has been one of the few historical employment opportunities open to professional women, it again illustrates the power of patriarchal institutions to engage in sexual discrimination, pitting women against each other, without any apparent agent or willful intent. Personal document research not only challenges social science as usual, but, by allowing the individual's voice to be heard, reveals other equally powerful social, psychological, economic, and gender-related forces as they are enacted in individual lives.

I believe that Dorothy was a survivor, and her drive to write a journal and have it published stemmed as much from a desire to help others as to document her suffering. Survivors of Nazi concentration (death) camps had an intense determination to document in writing the atrocities they experienced. Dorothy never experienced death camps, but her suffering was no less real. Des Pres (1976) described survivors as

> anyone who manages to stay alive in body and spirit enduring dread and hopelessness without the loss or will to carry on in human ways.

I see Dorothy this way. In her journal, she bore witness to what she endured for 30 years, circumstances she was not able to alter. She wanted to tell others in her own voice, in her own time, and in her own words what really had happened to her and her family.

REFERENCES

Alexander, M. (1984). *Speaking for ourselves: women of the South.* New York, NY: Pantheon.

Bogdan, R., & Taylor, S. (1975). *An introduction to qualitative research methods.* NY: John Wiley.

Des Pres, T. (1976). *The survivors.* NY: Oxford University Press.

Exley, P. J. (Ed.). (1985). *Texas tears and Texas sunshine: Voices of frontier women.* University Station: Texas A & M University Press.

Hartman, A. (1992). [Editorial]. In search of subjugated knowledge. *Social Work, 37,* 483-484.

Holbrook, T. (1986). Current renewed interest in personal document research. *Social Casework, 67* (7), 403-410.

Holbrook, T. (1994). *Deadwood: thirty years on the welfare dole.* Unpublished manuscript.

Holbrook, T. (1995). Finding subjugated knowledge: Personal document research. *Social* Work, *40,* 746-752.

Jacobs, H. (1987). *Life of a slave girl.* Cambridge, MA: Harvard University Press.

Thomas, W.I., and Znaniecki, F. (1918-1920). *The Polish peasant in Europe and America.* (5 vols.). Boston: Badger.

Bahamian Family Life
as Depicted by Wives' Tales
and Other Old Sayings

Raeann R. Hamon

SUMMARY. Proverbs, stories, and wives' tales have been used to teach, entertain, and impart important cultural information for generations. For this paper, two colleagues and I conducted ethnographic interviews with native Bahamians, primarily those residing on the family islands of Eleuthera and Harbour Island. We asked 56 informants, teenagers to octogenarians, to recall old sayings or tales which have been passed on to them over the years. Several hundred such sayings were recorded verbatim on tapes and in fieldnotes. Transcripts were analyzed to learn how Bahamian family life is depicted in wives' tales, proverbs, and other old sayings. *[Article copies available for a fee from The Haworth Document Delivery Service: 1-800-342-9678. E-mail address: getinfo@haworth.com]*

KEYWORDS. Bahamians, Ethnographic interviews, Family life, Stories, Sayings

Raeann R. Hamon is Associate Professor, Family Studies and Gerontology, Messiah College, Grantham, PA 17027.

The author wishes to acknowledge Stephen Cobb and Jennifer Bailey for their assistance with data collection.

A version of this paper was presented at the 56th Annual Conference of the National Council on Family Relations, November 11, 1994.

[Haworth co-indexing entry note]: "Bahamian Family Life as Depicted by Wives' Tales and Other Old Sayings." Hamon, Raeann R. Co-published simultaneously in *Marriage & Family Review* (The Haworth Press, Inc.) Vol. 24, No. 1/2, 1996, pp. 57-87; and: *The Methods and Methodologies of Qualitative Family Research* (ed: Marvin B. Sussman, and Jane F. Gilgun) The Haworth Press, Inc., 1996, pp. 57-87. Single or multiple copies of this article are available for a fee from The Haworth Document Delivery Service [1-800-342-9678, 9:00 a.m. - 5:00 p.m. (EST). E-mail address: getinfo@ haworth.com].

57

Folklore serves a multitude of functions: it is used to teach valued attitudes and behaviors, maintain conformity to accepted cultural norms, entertain or amuse, promote group solidarity, and validate and strengthen traditions and rituals (Bascom, 1965). Proverbs, stories, and wives' tales are an integral part of culture, especially for those societies enriched by oral traditions. For black Bahamians, the telling of stories originated with African slaves. Their folklore is descriptive and falls somewhere between science and superstition, between the real and unreal (Burroughs, 1993). Not only do these sayings and oral tales communicate life as it is seen and known, but they also function to impart wisdom and pleasure to subsequent generations. Most importantly, folklore is an artistic reflection of how participants of culture perceive, interpret, understand, and enjoy the world in which they live (Haviland, 1993).

MacIntyre (1984) asserts that humans are "story-telling animal[s]." "It is through hearing stories . . . that children learn or mislearn both what a child and what a parent is, what the cast of characters may be in the drama into which they have been born and what the ways of the world are" (p. 216). Stone (1988), too, believes "the family is our first culture, and like all cultures, it wants to make known its norms and mores. It does so through daily life, but it also does so through family stories which underscore, in a way invariably clear to its members, the essentials, like the unspoken and unadmitted family policy on marriage or illness" (p. 7).

For scientists and other persons interested in cross-cultural understandings, wives' tales and proverbs offer an abundant store of cultural information. According to Seitel (1976), proverbs in particular are important to folklorists in that "by pushing around these small and apparently simply constructed items, one can discover principles which give order to a wider range of phenomena" (p. 140). Proverbs, rarely more than one sentence in length, reflect "a summary of the wisdom of collective experience" (Hasan-Rokem, 1992, p. 128). They are frequently employed during circumstances characterized by conflict and skepticism, when invoking collective authority transforms the difficulty from a personal to a conceptual level, preserving traditional values of the community (Hasan-Rokem, 1992).

Sharing folklore in the form of wives' tales and proverbs appears to be diminishing among residents of the family islands of Eleuthera and Harbor Island in the Bahamas. Now rare, it once was usual for mothers to tell their children stories at night while they sat "spinning for straws" [doing straw work] or when communities would sit around fires outside at night and tell tales. The telling of tales does not seem to be as deliberate or as prominent as it once was.

Expediency seems to be one reason for the change. A nurse and her brother agreed that "sometimes we're getting so lazy" that it is much quicker to just tell the child what to do and not to do rather than relate some instructive tale or story. As one informant said:

> Whereas now I think it's, . . . if you go outside and you don't watch where you're walking, or if you don't have on any shoes, . . . you could get stuck with a nail or something. . . . Most people tend to just tell their kids that. . . . Whereas back then they would probably say, 'Away know, I have this fellow . . . who lived by my father, and this that and the next, and he ran outside and he didn't have any shoes on and his father told him. . . .' And then it was up to you . . . back then it was up to you to think of the moral of the story. . . . Now it's, 'don't go outside without any shoes.'

These informants believe that the same instructive functions are being accomplished, but many people today are using simpler, easier and quicker methods.

Advances in technology also seem to contribute to the reduction of deliberate tale-telling. Children are frequently more interested in videos, televisions, and stereo systems than in listening to their parents or grand-parents relate old stories. Perhaps video or computer programs need to be the new avenues which allow children to learn about and record their own family and community information in order to maintain and promote cultural knowledge.

Despite the notion that folklore is not transferred from generation to generation to the degree that it once was, most of the people we inter-viewed provided a least a few proverbs and tales, supporting Ben-Amos'(1992) notion that "storytelling and folktales may change, but they do not go away" (p. 117). While several lucid, elderly adults were the most helpful informants, people of all ages contributed to the store of tales collected by the author and her colleagues. Recognizing that tales provide rich and meaningful insights about family life from the insider's perspec-tive, this paper asks the question, "What do old tales or sayings reveal about Bahamian family life?"

METHOD

During several research trips lasting a minimum of two weeks over a four-year period, two colleagues and I conducted ethnographic interviews (Spradley, 1979; 1980) with native Bahamians, primarily those residing on the islands of Eleuthera and Harbour Island. Ethnographic methodologies place the utmost importance on understanding belief and behavior from indigenous perspectives.

Fifty-six informants, teenagers to octogenarians, provided wives' tales, old sayings or proverbs, and stories. Most are residents of Eleuthera, with a few living in Harbour Island, both family islands of the Bahamas. Eleuthera, which means "freedom," is 110 miles long and is less than two miles wide. It is speckled with small settlements and has 10,600 inhabitants (Glass, 1992). Harbour Island is located off the northeastern tip of Eleuthera and is about three miles wide with a population of 1000 (Whittier, 1991). Residents of these two islands are descendants of the Eleutherian Adventurers, British Loyalists from the United States, and the Loyalists' African slaves. All but two of the 30 respondents providing the sayings and tales specific to family life used for this analysis are Bahamians of African descent. The exceptions are women who married black Bahamian men and have lived in the Bahamas for more than 10 years; one is white and from the United States and the other is from South America.

Most make their living via fishing, farming, or other small businesses (e.g., grocery store, small shop). A large number of young people leave the islands to find employment. Most residents make do with small homes and very modest incomes.

We asked informants to recall old sayings or tales which have been passed on to them over the years. Participants were also asked to relate the meanings, uses, and purposes of the sayings, as well as any personal experiences they might have had with any of the tales. Most interviews occurred in homes or on porches of the informants or at local hang-outs and generally took more than one hour. Several older informants were interviewed on multiple occasions. Several hundred sayings and stories were recorded verbatim on tapes and in field notes. All tapes were transcribed verbatim.

For this paper, I examined more than 350 wives' tales and proverbs we collected. Lengthy stories were eliminated for later analysis. During the first level of analysis, I identified those tales and sayings having to do with family life. In the second stage of analysis, I created eight relevant domains of family life: marriage, pregnancy, parent-child relations, work, finances, well-being, death, and visitors and friends.

In a third step of analysis, I attempted to categorize how my Bahamian informants classify the tales and how the sayings are related to each other. In choosing terms, I primarily used categorizations or groupings reflective of informants, although in some cases, the specific terms used were mine. For instance, "pregnancy" is one of the domains about which there are many sayings within the culture scene of family life. Within the domain of "pregnancy," there are five categories of tales or sayings. These groupings disclose pregnancy of oneself or another ("signs"), describe behaviors indicative of a pregnant state ("peculiar habits"), offer prescriptive advice ("prescriptions"), acknowledge unique abilities or privileges of pregnant women ("special powers"), and foretell the child's gender or appearance ("predictions"). "If a man has a toothache, his wife or girlfriend is pregnant" is an example of a wives' tale that is included in the "signs" category.

RESULTS

About 200 wives' tales and proverbs offered information relative to eight domains of Bahamian family life: marriage, pregnancy, parent-child relationships, work, financial matters, well-being, death, and visitors/friends. Taxonomies are in the Appendix.

Marriage

Morsels of wisdom concerning marriage inform recipients about ways to prevent marriage; signs of an upcoming wedding or marital hardship; prescriptions for marital preparedness, success and commitment; appropriate husband-wife relations; and how to identify and describe bad marital outcomes. Bahamians desiring marital success and happiness can take heed of the instruction and experience found in the sayings.

A few wives' tales share secrets about how to prevent someone from getting married. For instance, "if you sweep a lady that isn't married, she will never get married." Or "if you see someone you like [and] you eat out of a pot in front of him, [he] won't get married."

As with most family processes, signs are available for the marriage event, offering information about the likelihood of its success. Weddings can be foretold in dreams: "If you dream you're going to a funeral, you're going to a wedding." Some signs about the success of the marital relationship were completely based upon chance and were unavoidable. Several informants reported that old folks said it's bad luck to have rain when you get married. An elderly man said

> if it rain[s] on your wedding day, you and your husband don't pull too good . . . cat and dog you know. Fight, fight, fight. But they say if it's a pleasant day, sunny day, said a chance everything going smooth.

A middle-aged woman confirmed the truth of this sign in the following:

> I've seen . . . these tales come from things that they have observed over the years. So, if you were supposed to get married and it rains a lot, I guess you still have to get married, but everybody would be more sad than happy because they would feel that the marriage wouldn't work out, because if you have a bad day, usually you don't have a happy marriage, either the spouse dies or the marriage doesn't work out.

Another woman summed it up: "When it rain to weddings, it's hard luck."

Old sayings frequently offer prescriptions for desirable or appropriate behavior. Relative to marriage, they offer all sorts of advice. First, there is a certain need for formal acknowledgement of relationships as evidenced in "The old people say, when a man shack up in the house with a woman unmarried, they call that driving without a license."

Second, preparedness for married life is emphasized. One never-married male informant in his sixties offered the following:

> Here is advice for the young man. Old people say, before a bird lays, she builds a nest to lay her eggs and adds her young ones in. The young man should learn from the bird. Today they go, get wives and children, and have no house to put them in. Don't let the bird be wiser than you.

Third, several of the tales had to do with things that should be done in order to ensure the success of the marriage union. One woman told how her mother advised her to wear her engagement ring only on her right hand, as this is supposed to bring good luck to the marriage relationship. The same woman informed me of a custom that could help to foster a happy marriage:

> In days gone by, . . . the night before the wedding, people would go into whatever house the bride and groom were supposed to live in, and clean it up and make up the beds and stuff like that, and they always said whoever makes up your bed should be a married person that's living happily. You should never allow a married person to make up your bed if the marriage isn't working well–separated from your husband. They can do other things, but the person who was to actually make up the bed that you were to lay on should be a happily married person.

Successful marriages also need parental involvement and approval. An often-cited saying suggested this:

If you get in with a boy, if [his] parents don't like you, you might as well leave it right there. Because it's never going work.

An even stronger message is evidenced in the following: "If the man's parents don't attend to your wedding, it's a curse."

Once married, women should also use precautions to avoid marital unhappiness. For instance, "when washing [clothes] and your stomach get[s] wet, you are going to have a drunken husband." So too, anytime the table is set for a meal, be certain that the blade of the knife is not pointing up or "you and your husband going to fuss."

Fourth, a few sayings speak to fidelity. A Harbour Island mother-in-law told her young, businessman son-in-law:

Don't let another woman climb your guinep tree, or your guineps will go sour. [Likewise,] never let another woman touch your pepper tree.

Maintaining relationships appears to be of greater concern for women than for men. There are prescriptions, such as, "Be careful about the gifts you give to your special someone." Another saying is the following.

They say if you're in love with a man, a woman should never give their boyfriends or their fiances or their husbands pens or socks. They say if you give them a pen, they will write your love away, and if you give them socks they will walk your love away.

A woman might also consider putting various ingredients in the food of her man so as to ensure his faithfulness. As one young man said

If you have a girlfriend and she wants to keep you, she will do something to your food. She may make coocoo soup.

An older woman suggested

if you want to make sure your man stays with you, take the left foot of his socks and boil it and drink the water.

Despite the concern for fidelity and "keeping" your man, there are also prescriptions for having a good time without one's spouse. This includes the possibility of extramarital affairs. One saying points out, "You don't take sand to the beach—you meet it there." An informant explained that this means if you have a wife, and you want to go out on the town, you don't take her with you. You find a girl where you going.

This applies to wives who want to go out.

Struggles over control or power are evident in a number of the sayings. An elderly male informant related the following:

A woman told her husband, 'You wore the pants for 50 years. Now you are sick and disabled. You cannot get around. I wear the pants.' The man resent that. He said, 'You wear the pants, but I control the zipper.'

The same informant shared the saying

She is playing snake in the grass, but the grass she is hiding in, I put it there.

He said the meaning is that after living with his wife for so long, the husband knows what she is up to. During a lengthy discussion of wives' tales with two married female informants, one woman related that during the '60s and '70s, in particular, many believed that "the man is the captain of his ship." The two women shared their observation that with the advent of more women working outside the home for wages, women are gaining more power in their families, although the evidence still is not compelling.

When people make poor marital choices (e.g., when a woman picked a husband that didn't like to work or was a womanizer) one might say things like, "She's picked a needle with no eye," "I made my bed hard," and "Oil and water don't mix together." This tension between the sexes was revealed by an old, never-married Bahamian male who laughed heartily as he relayed the following sexist saying:

God made the world and he rested. God made man and he rested. Then God made woman. Since then, God and man never rested.

Pregnancy

The most frequently cited wives' tales and sayings had to do with pregnancy. If a green lizard has jumped on someone, if a tree is not producing fruit, or if there are questions about the gender of a fetus, these have implications for pregnancy.

Certain events or signs were indicative of pregnancy. For example:

If you see a spider and it drops on you, either you or someone you know is pregnant.

If a man has a toothache, his wife or girlfriend is expecting.

If there is a lizard in your house or on your doorpost, or a bird tries to get in your window, someone you know is pregnant.

If you're out in the yard and one of these little green lizards be out in the garden, if they jump on you, in a couple of weeks, you'll pop right out.

Dreams were revealing too. "If you dream about crabs or fish, someone in your family is pregnant. It could even be you!" If you just see a fish in your dreams, it is probably family or friends. If you're catching a fish in your dreams, it is someone close to you. Several informants told me of this belief and reported it to be "true," providing their own stories of proof. One woman verified her confidence in these signs in the following account. Before school started in September, she had recurring dreams about fish. Her sister's daughter was living with her at the time, and, although she did not readily admit that she was with child, it soon became evident. As the same informant said, "If you knead bread, it will rise." In other words, there is no hiding pregnancy; the truth will be revealed. Another woman who dreamed about a man bringing her a big basket of fish, swore that this particular tale "is true."

Pregnant women are known to have peculiar habits, as these sayings show:

You can tell a pregnant woman by she's spitting a lot.

Sometimes pregnant women eat ashes when they're pregnant. Eat young fruits . . . Get salt and dip the tambran in the salt. Some will eat ashes plain, and some will dip the tambran in the ashes.

Some sayings prescribed appropriate behavior for pregnant women. A multitude of informants offered the following warnings:

Pregnant women [especially those in their first trimester] should not look at anything peculiar or pitiful while they are pregnant. If they see someone that looks funny or pitiful, they should look the other way. If they would feel sorry or pity the person or creature, their child will look the same as that they just pitied.

You don't look at anything ugly because it might cause your child to be deformed. No ugly animals or anybody that got killed or they don't allow you to look at dead people when you're pregnant. If you look at them you have to laugh. You don't look at them. You can go to funerals, but you can't look at the person even if it's your mother or father, you're not allowed to look at them unless you look at them and smile, but not to be sad or anything.

Two women who were sharing tales with the researcher related a case where a child was born with a deformed arm. Many people thought that the child was born such because the mother pitied a goat during her pregnancy. These two, however, suspected that it was more likely that the child was born with the defect because his father was drinking alcohol. So, while the prescription is taken very seriously and has been confirmed by some individuals, some doubts about its total accuracy exist.

Another popular saying warned of the consequences of not fulfilling the wishes of pregnant women. It says

If a pregnant woman craves something which she does not get and then touches or scratches herself, she will mark her baby at the same spot.

The birthmark will be in the shape of the desired item and located on the area which she scratched. To rid the baby of the birthmark, advised an old woman,

use a little spittle and wipe it first thing in the morning before you eat anything. After [you] do it for the first nine days . . . eventually it will go away on its own time.

Many tales warned about other possible dangers that can befall newborns. Pregnant women are advised

never to tell exactly when you're going to have the baby because you never know when you might have a secret enemy or something like that. You always keep the exact month to yourself. You just tell the nurse or the doctor, but not everybody.

Other precautions included a variety of instructions, which probably evoke a great deal of anxiety in pregnant women:

Tie something around your waist because there's a danger of bumping your stomach to the washing board.

Don't do a lot of sewing because if you do a lot of sewing, it must cause the umbilical cord to be wrapped around the baby's neck.

Be careful not to fall.

Don't overreach . . . because that too may hurt the baby's neck.

No lifting because you might endanger the pregnancy.

Men and other family members make sure that pregnant women do not do these things. Reportedly, someone would be ready to assist a pregnant woman, if asked. Sitting with legs crossed is prohibited by at least two sayings. If pregnant women do so, they are likely to be in labor a long time or have a baby which is "born with a cord around the neck."

Pregnant women are perceived to have special powers related to fertility:

When a pregnant woman . . . plants the seed, the vine will bear big, big fruit.

If you have an avocado tree or a tangerine tree and it don't bear, let a pregnant lady spike it with a nail and then she'll shoot fruit.

A man in his late seventies told of a coconut tree which would not bear fruit. He asked a woman pregnant with her first child to "spike it." The tree became productive in its next season.

Some wives' tales have predictive value. For instance, some suggest that it is possible to determine the gender of the child the woman is carrying. One man reported that if parents' heads are westward at the time of conception, the baby will be a boy. If parents' heads are eastward, the baby will be a girl. When a woman is carrying an unborn child, according to one man, it is possible to tell if it is a boy or a girl. When one says 'Stand and walk to me,' if she steps first with her left foot, it is a boy. If she steps with her right foot, she is carrying a girl. A very old woman says that "the mark of the beast" is telling. A broad mark from the navel down and a tiny mark on top of the navel indicates that the baby is a boy. If a woman has a tiny mark underneath her navel and broad one on top, the baby she is carrying is a girl.

Predictions about the newborn are also made, depending on a number of circumstances. A baby born "when the moon is full" will have a huge head. If a woman "always have stomach burn" during her pregnancy, the "baby's head is going to be full of hair when it is born." If the "child looks like the husband . . . [the mother/wife] really like[s] him."

Parent-Child Relationships

Although there are several sayings relative to things one should or should not do as parents, the importance of discipline, and similarity of parents and their children, most of the proverbs and tales in the domain of parent-child relations had to do with instilling virtues in children. Important relational and character-building information is relayed in these simple lessons.

Prescriptive tales gave advice for how to raise children. One young woman reported that parents could stunt their children's growth by cutting their hair prematurely:

> That's why people don't cut the children's hair while they are just around seven months. They wait until they turn two, because they say that it [child] wouldn't be able to talk or walk or anything like that.

Prescriptions are also given to children. For instance, "don't cross hands on top of your head or you're mourning your mommy and daddy away."

Intergenerational transmission of characteristics or predispositions, as well as the effects that parents have on their children are acknowledged. "Kicking cow brings kicking calf" means that children will learn to be like their parents. "The father eats the sour grapes, the teeth of the children are set on edge," suggests that the children pay the price of their parents' transgressions.

A number of tales and proverbs offer advice about the importance of disciplining children while they are young. The following is an example:

> Bend the tree while it is young; when it gets old, it cannot bend.

A man in his seventies explained that

> If crab don't walk, he won't get fed. If he walk too much, he get put in the pot.

To him, this meant that children can have some freedom to explore, but if they wander too far they can get in trouble. "Foolishness is bound in the heart of a child, but the rod of correction drives it far from him" was interpreted for the researcher to mean that if parents correct children's foolishness, they will not keep doing it. "Everywhere a puppy go, he carry his tail" acknowledges that rude and ill-behaved children carry their bad ways everywhere they go.

Parental authority and power are also evident. "If you don't like my way, loosen your donkey from my gate" suggests that if children do not like their parents' rules, they should find a place of their own. Such sayings are tempered by others such as "If you powerful, be merciful." In other words, those in positions of authority need to be merciful to those under them because some day those in authority may need the other.

Parental or elder instruction to younger generations is frequently transmitted via parables, tales, or stories. One woman said that her grandmother would tell her, "Don't you mind the weather. Keep your legs together." Two different men related the same object lesson told to them by their father. Each child was asked to bring the parent a stick. One by one, the father would break each individual stick across his knee. Then, he asked each of the children to bring him another stick. This time, he put the sticks together and tied them in a bundle. He asked each child to try to break the stick. When each was unsuccessful, he instructed that "As long as you stick together, no one can break you. If you go off on your own, however, they can break you."

Other tales also highlight the importance of family unity and pride. Parents often told their children, "As long as you keep together, no one can destroy you." "Death before dishonor" advised children to die before they dishonor their families.

Some sayings are meant to teach children the value of sharing:

> If you have a dollar, share it, 25 cents each. Let a dollar be for all. Everybody will not have like, all the same time. Share, everyone will have alike.

"Put meat with bone" also instructed to share the best that you have. Individual character is emphasized and advice is freely given:

> A fool's way in his eyes seem right. But a wise man will take counsel and a word to the wise is sufficient.

Some sayings teach that people get what they deserve:

> Every dog will have its day.

> Tit for tat, butter for fat. Kill my dog, I'll kill your cat.

The importance of goodness is emphasized in "Beauty without virtue is a rose without fragrance" and "You can catch more flies with two drops of honey than with a barrel of vinegar." Values of persistence and patience are also revealed. "One man with courage makes a majority." "Patience is bitter, but its fruit sweet." Discretion and personal restraint are encouraged in "Shut mouth catch no flies." Children are encouraged to avoid procrastination, "The longest journey is begun with the first step" and to keep themselves occupied, "A watched kettle takes longer to boil."

Though sayings having to do with work are fewest in number, those that exist are helpful about developing skills, directing energies, and doing business. Advice is given relative to work or occupations, with emphasis being placed upon persistence and skill development:

> Fowl don't find worms everywhere she scratch.

> Setting hen gets very little corn.

> Son, it takes more than one iron to iron your clothes.

An elder Bahamian man interpreted these to mean that young people need to develop more than one skill or trade since the ability to do a variety of things is crucial for accomplishment and island survival. Other sayings related to work include:

> A mother's lesson: Give a man a fish. Don't give a man a fish. Teach him how to fish, to catch a fish, and he can take it from there.

> When a man know thing, it's half done.

The way in which people performed their work was important:

> He that soweth sparingly, shall also reap sparingly.

> Too many chiefs, not enough Indians.

Knowing when efforts are futile appeared important: "Never fertilize a dead stump."

An elder man shared several parables told to him by his supplier during his early years of operating a dry goods store:

> You cannot do business from an empty wagon.

> Put some clean water in the dirty water and it will not smell.

Thus, this man learned to keep his store well-stocked and to mix some new items in with the old, existing items so as to freshen the store.

Finances

In the area of finances, signs indicative of receiving or losing money are central as are prescriptions for saving money and making do with the little that one has.

There are many signs or indicators of wealth or lack thereof. Body itches and twitches could bring you money, although interpretations of itches vary somewhat:

> If your right hand itches, somebody's going to give you money. If your left hand itches, you're going to have to pay somebody money.

In contrast

> If your left hand itches, there's money. If your right hand itches, you're going to shake a stranger's hand or give all the money away.

> When the palm of you hand is itching a lot and you're scratching it, they say it's going to be getting you some money. Or if you rub it on the side of your pants, you be getting some money.

> If your eye twitches, you'll receive some money.

> When you scratch your head, you're going to get some money.

> If an M is on your hand, you will get money. If there is a W on the palm of your hand, you will have to work.

Several other people told us of money bats. When these money bats fly into your house, they could bring you money.

Dreams, too, are revealing:

> They say if you dream about green plants, like fruits or green corn or green plants, that's prosperity.

> If you dream about waste matter, that indicates money.

Sayings offer advice about money management. Saving money is salient in a number of different sayings, such as "Go to the ant, thou sluggard. Consider her ways and be wise." The informant said this means that people should save for days when other resources are gone. Providing for old age is important: "While young, learn to save. When you are old, no one will have to pass the hat around for your benefit." One middle-aged woman related an "olden day" parable: "Always look out for rainy days." As a child, she thought that somehow she needed to be watching for rain, saving 50 cents from each dollar so she could buy a hat or raincoat for when it rains. Later she realized that rainy days were emergencies.

Similarly, "If you can't ride the cow, they say jump on the horse's back" instructs people to make do with what they have. If there is no Wesson oil, use lard. If you can't get sweetened milk to put on your bread, use butter or jam, or whatever you can get and be satisfied with it. Some days there might be cold soda to drink. Other days there might not be anything but crystal water. People need to take the good, smooth days and make the best of the tough ones.

Well-Being

There are a number of sayings about signs which are indicative of fortune or misfortune. These signs can come in the form of dreams, involuntary muscle contractions or intentional behaviors. Informants are replete with prescriptions for optimizing one's well-being while functioning at home, in the bush, or in the graveyard.

Sayings reveal signs about well-being. Real-life events or dreams could be omens of misfortune. "If your left eye twitches, you're going to have some unexpected sorrow. You're going to cry." If a black cat crosses the street in front of you or if someone breaks a mirror, bad luck will follow, seven years of bad luck in the latter instance. On "hard luck day," Black Friday, people are particularly susceptible to bad luck. "If you are thinking of something that you want, and you see a green lizard, that means disappointment."

Certain signs positively affect well-being. For instance, if person A is talking to person B about person C and person C calls or passes by during that conversation, person C will live a long life. It is also a good luck sign when a black bee flies around one's person.

Dreams could offer good or bad signs. If people dream of "calm, clear waters, they will have victory." Dreams of paper money, sugar apples, or walking in a corn field mean blessings or good luck. On the other hand, dreams of silver money or sucking sugar cane bring disappointment. Dreams of eggs mean that it is likely that the dreamer will get in a row. Dreams of fire predict fights or confusion, but if one throws salt into the fire in the morning, the dream's effects can be negated. Dreams about snakes mean enemies are lurking around and someone may be coming to hurt you. Dreams about killing snakes symbolize conquering one's enemies.

There are certain prescriptions about behaviors to be avoided if one is to be fortunate. One elderly woman said, "When I was a child, my mother always used to say, 'never take that broom and sweep out after sunset. Leave that until morning . . . sweep the dirt in the corner [because] when you sweep that out, you sweep out all your luck.' " People should avoid sitting in doorways, because there they will "pick up the aches and pains of everybody who walks through the door." If someone is lying down and someone jumps over his/her body, this will stop the person from using the toilet ever again, unless the jumped person jumps over the original jumper, but in the opposite direction.

Although people frequently went into the bush to look for black crabs when the moon was dark, they were warned "not to stay in the bush too long, because it isn't good." They "might hear different sounds in the bush, like people telling you things." One woman related an incident a number of years ago when she heard an elderly neighbor woman calling her for help from the bush behind her house. When she reached the elderly woman, the old lady was bloody and bruised and reported that she heard this voice which kept luring her further and further into the bush. The old woman had merely gone to her farm to cut some corn for harvest for the church.

Graveyards are particularly ominous. Some parents warned their children not to walk in the graveyard at night or they were likely to see ghosts that look like white people walking in garments. Small children were to stay at the gate of the graveyard because otherwise they "will see the people who died some day when [they] are sleeping, [they] will see them in shadows . . . that same person that died will be haunting [them] at night." If such misfortune should occur, parents could "tie a black cord around [the child's] hands at night to keep the spirits away." Cemeteries are particularly dangerous for those who have certain injuries. If a person had

> an abrasion on the lower or upper foot and there is a funeral, do not enter the graveyard. Go only as far as the gate. If you enter the graveyard with an open wound and graveyard dirt gets into the wound, you will have problems.

One young woman in her twenties went so far to say that

> if you walk through water that is in the graveyard, your foot will rot off.

Death

Signs are part of the tales and sayings having to do with death. A number of events or dreams reveal when death will occur and who will die. Certain signs make people aware of an impending death. A retired school teacher said

> I've heard, when I was little, that if a bird flew and hit your window and if it fell dead, someone in the family would die. Bees and birds that fly into a house, as well as scratchy feet, are foretelling of death in the family. Every time you see a hole in the grave, someone else is going to die. When it rains on the first day of the year, it is going to be a rich burial ground; there will be a lot of deaths that year. When it rains the day someone dies, it is believed that the deceased is washing his/her tracks from the earth. When a person shudders involuntarily, someone is walking on his/her grave.

A middle-aged woman told of a particular sign and her own experience of it:

> If a big dark mark comes on your skin and you can't figure out where it comes from, they say somebody you know very close is going to die. And as the person gets sicker and sicker, as it becomes closer to their death, the spot will fade away. I've proven the wonder of the dark spot [also called 'spirit pinch']. I had one before my brother-in-law died. And honestly I didn't get a bruise or anything. I couldn't figure it out. But I heard people say that if you have these dark marks, watch and it's going to be somebody died that's very close to you. And it happened just like they said. The sicker he got the more the spot faded away . . . after he died it went completely. I'm serious . . . that mark on my upper thigh.

An elder man told a story of a woman who had swarms of black flies on her veil on the day of her wedding. The bride died within six months of her wedding day. Flies on wedding veils are bad signs.

Dreams can be premonitions of death. Dreams about a crowd of people, rough seas or a boat going out to sea, a boat on land, pork or pork product, red meat, airplanes, digging sweet potatoes, black crabs, processions, playing an organ at church, or a wedding all mean death. Dreams can foretell who will die. Thus,

> If you dream about a white man dying, a colored man is going to die.

> If you dream that you see a dead or sick woman, it is going to be a man. If it is a sick or dead man, it is going to be a woman.

Dreams about teeth mean that a family member will die:

When you dream that your teeth are dropping out, someone in your family will die. If they are your front teeth, it will be a close relative. If back teeth, it will be a far relative.

Certain behaviors are to be avoided, for instance:

If you dig a hole in the ground and you don't cover back the hole . . . they say you're digging a hole for one of your relatives to die in.

If someone is ill and another person keeps crying and crying for weeks and weeks, they say it won't be long before the ill person dies. When a person who "has the feeling" is asked "to carry [a sick relative or other person] to Nassau" for treatment, he/she should refuse to do so. It is possible for people to sense that they "don't have no luck" and in such cases, should seek others to assist in transporting the ill person for medical treatment. Otherwise the person might die.

Another woman related a wives' tale told to her by her mother when she was a younger woman: when a woman is menstruating she should not view a dead body or she will bleed to death. Having taken her mother's advice to heart, this woman went to her uncle's viewing, but sat in the far rear of the church, so as not to view the body. The members of her family who were uninformed could not understand why she refused to come forward. When her uncle, a medical doctor, came back to investigate her reasons for refusing, she confided in him and told him of her condition. Despite her real fears and reluctance and the chiding of her informed female relatives, he led her up to view her uncle's body. Although she still believed that she might "overflow" and die, she soon learned that nothing would happen to her.

Empathy for the sorrowful is encouraged:

And the old folks tell us, we see one cry, we all must cry because we all are human beings and . . . because all of us going to die some day.

Some practices surrounding death in the distant past differ from contemporary practices. In the old days when someone died, everyone "closed the house up very early" and brought their children inside because they were afraid of the return of the dead. The fears of yesteryear seem to have dispelled somewhat, since children of today are not afraid to view bodies up close. Wakes, where people stay up all night to sing, pray and eat, are also quite common, suggesting that people are not as afraid anymore. However, "when people die bad, they haunt you." There are a number of things that the living can do to keep bad spirits away: "put black under and around your head and bed when you go to sleep at night;" Write "10 X 10" on a door with black crayon; turn hats upside down; "wear your clothes inside out; talk to Jesus;" and turn your left shoe upside down by your bed.

Visitors and Friends

Some sayings assist in predicting when one will receive company at home and some of the qualities associated with the impending visitors. They also include instructions about fostering and valuing interpersonal relationships. Spiders, roosters, twitching eyes, ringing ears, bridges, birds, and rotten eggs are all used to make a point.

Different signs predict visitors. An older woman said that when she was a little girl, they didn't have glass window panes, only shutters to close window openings. When the little wooden shutters were open, so were the windows. She learned that

> if a bird flew straight through, came through one window and went through the other, you would have a visitor. If a spider comes in your house and it has seven legs, you're going to have a man visitor. If it has eight legs, the family will have a woman visitor. If a spider is carrying a white pillow or something underneath him, there will definitely be a visitor. If a spider tries to crawl on you, there is someone strange coming to your house. If a small child spontaneously picks up a broom and starts to sweep, the family is sure to have a visitor. A twitching left eye or ringing ears means that you're going to see a stranger or someone you haven't seen in a long time. If a big fly is coming out of your doorway or if a rooster is crowing at the front of your door, a stranger is coming in your house.

Only one saying seems to offer any rules about visiting. It indicates that "house guests and fish get bad after a couple of days," a saying well-known cross-culturally.

The value of friendship. "Never throw away the old kettle until you are sure the new one hold water" warns people to be careful about discarding old friends, especially when they are uncertain what the new one will be like. "Never burn the bridges behind you. You never know when you will turn back to use them" suggests that people should never discard a friend, since they may need the friendship some day. "You never miss the water until the well go dry" suggests that sometimes people do not appreciate people or things until they are gone. "If you don't stink for me, I will not rotten for you," "Water will find its level," "bird of one feather, all flock together," and "two clean sheep cannot dirty one another" talk about reciprocity, equality, and likeness in friendship relationships.

There are occasions when people desire to terminate their relationships. If persons do not want individuals to return, a proverb instructs them to throw a rotten egg behind the unwanted persons as they go away. The undesirable party is not likely to reappear.

DISCUSSION

Although the sharing of folklore via wives' tales and proverbs appears to be diminishing among residents of Eleuthera and Harbour Island, some transmission of information in this form still occurs. Old people play a special role in conveying important cultural knowledge; elders are "irreplaceable storehouses of information about the past" (Goody, 1992, p. 16). Frequent reference to what "the old people say . . . " constantly reiterates the value of old people and the importance of collective authority in promoting desirable behavior and in preserving history and traditions (Hasan-Rokem, 1992).

Women more than men are the tellers of parables and wives' tales related to Bahamian family life. Although there were a few notable male informants, women were usually most informed about collective wisdom and traditions having to do with family life, supporting Ben-Amos' (1992) notion that women's tales often differ from men's tales. Thematic spheres of pregnancy and childbearing appear to be articulated best by women, supporting more traditional differentiation of roles by gender. Future research might more explicitly explore gender differences in folklore. Are women and men narrators of different types of stories and tales? Are males or females more likely to be the recipients of certain tales or parables? My sense is that women are more likely to be tellers and receivers of tales relative to the family.

Old sayings are frequently communicated in the course of everyday activities and events, especially when the mode of speech is prescriptive (Hasan-Rokem, 1992). One young woman, who is a first-year college student, said that she has learned such things from her parents over the years as the various subjects come up.

In contemporary Eleuthera and Harbour Island, persons most likely to be recipients of morsels of instruction and wisdom offered via wives' tales and proverbs are young people who spend time with elderly members of the community. Many people, who have developed an appreciation for the tales of old, are fearful of what will happen to that aspect of their culture when the current generation of elderly dies. Even though his own grandparents who were a major source of family tales were gone, one man in his thirties believes "that sort of upbringing and that sort of family spirit and all of that stuff is part of us now." Those bits of folklore that have been transferred are important to many informants, although most agree that the old people possess the greatest number of sayings.

Anthropological interpretations encourage us to consider how these tales serve as a mirror of culture, a way of creating, being in, and seeing the world (Ben-Amos, 1992). The tales of Eleuthera and Harbor Island are replete with symbols and values particular to island culture. Sayings about black crabs, boats, lizards, goats, roosters, guinep trees, calm seas, beaches, and fish have special significance because these things are meaningful and part of everyday life. The fact that "The last one there is a rotten egg and everyone must be included" was not told to me by Bahamians, while "If you can't ride the cow, jump on the horse's back" was, is significant. The American saying encourages speed, swiftness, and competition, qualities not of particular value in the family islands. The latter saying is Bahamian, however, and encourages people to make do with what they have when necessary. It has special significance when considered within the islands' context, since imported products are crucial and not always readily forthcoming. Future research might make a more deliberate effort to uncover specific cultural values (McAdoo & Rukuni, 1993) and symbols located within and promoted by various types of folklore.

Some of the folklore examined here also has a religious element. The people of the Bahamas consider themselves Christian. Some of the tales reflect Biblical influence. Since many of these families had regular times each day when they read and discussed scripture, and talked, it is reasonable to see how Christian teachings could become part of their folklore. For instance, discouraging parents from cutting their children's hair until two years of age in order not to stunt their growth resembles stories of Samson. The saying that "the father eats sour grapes, the teeth of the children are set on edge" parallels the Christian notion that children pay for the transgressions of their parents.

Just as Christianity is influential in the lives of Bahamians, so is voodoo. Concerns about being "fixed" by the living or haunted by the dead permeate some tales. Prohibitions about being in the bush for too long and walking in the graveyard are outgrowths of fear of bad spirits. Practices such as tying black cord around a child's wrist, turning hats upside down, turning left shoes upside down next to one's bed, and putting black around one's head at night keep bad spirits away reveal real concerns with the spirit world. By not telling anyone the due date of her child's birth, the pregnant woman prevents her child from being "crossed." One middle-aged female informant told me that, to this day, when she bathes she washes her pubic area first in order to prevent anyone from doing voodoo to her. Her mother-in-law, who was also a mid-wife, informed her of this precautionary practice.

Personal experience is important in verifying or refuting wives' tales. One woman said that although she heard some things so many times, she did not fully believe some of them until she experienced them. She said that "as unusual, as unbelievable as it [her "spirit pinch" incident] sounds, it happened to me!" "Proof" exists for other tales as well. There was an unfruitful coconut tree that began bearing after a pregnant woman spiked it. Many people were foretold of a pregnancy, a death or a wedding in their dreams and several children are known to have been "marked" by their mothers' unmet desires during pregnancy.

Some other tales are less believable because their predictions have not materialized. Although she adamantly believes in the viability of a number of other tales, the woman who survived looking at her uncle's corpse while menstruating is no longer convinced of the truthfulness of that particular belief. She now goes to viewings and walks through graveyards while menstruating and "nothing happens." Similarly, several people mentioned that they have yet to see any bats carrying money.

Knowing a people's stories, tales, and sayings is very revealing. While descriptive studies which use domain and taxonomic analyses such as this one can be informative, future research might address how folklore shapes cultural meanings and family life over time. Such an analysis would be possible if researchers spent considerable time with few families, learning how wives' tales, proverbs and stories are embedded in the family's world view, daily activities, family relationships, and larger culture. Comparative analyses that examine differences and similarities in folklore between two cultures might also prove helpful. The beauty of qualitative methodologies in family research is that there are a number of ways to become familiar with families, understand their experience, and develop and revise hypotheses about their lives (Gilgun, 1992). The study of wives' tales and parables is just one means of qualitatively examining family life.

REFERENCES

Bascom, W. R. (1965). Four functions of folklore. In A. Dundes (Ed.), *The study of folklore* (pp. 279-298). Englewood Cliffs, N J: Prentice-Hall.

Ben-Amos, D. (1992). Folktale. In R. Bauman (Ed.), *Folklore, cultural performances, and popular entertainment: A communications-centered handbook* (pp. 101-118). New York: Oxford University.

Burroughs, S. (1993, October). Personal interview. Governor's Harbor, Eleuthera, Bahamas.

Gilgun, J. F. (1992). Definitions, methodologies, and methods in qualitative family research. In J. F. Gilgun, K. Daly & G. Handel (Eds.), *Qualitative methods in family research* (pp. 22-39). Newbury Park, CA: Sage.

Glass, I. (1992). *Fodor's 92: The Bahamas.* New York: Fodor's Travel Publications.

Goody, J. (1992). Oral culture. In R. Bauman (Ed.), *Folklore, cultural performances, and popular entertainment: A communications-centered handbook* (pp. 12-20). New York: Oxford University.

Hasan-Rokem, G. (1992). Proverbs. In R. Bauman (Ed.), *Folklore, cultural performances, and popular entertainment: A communications-centered handbook* (pp. 128-133). New York: Oxford University.

Haviland, W. A. (1993). *Cultural anthropology.* Orlando: Harcourt Brace Jovanovich.

MacIntyre, A. (1984). *After virtue* (2nd ed.). Notre Dame, IN: University of Notre Dame.

McAdoo, H., & Rukuni, M. (1993). A preliminary study of family values of the women of Zimbabwe. *Journal of Black Psychology, 19,* 48-62.

Seitel, P. (1976). Proverbs: A social use of metaphor. In D. Ben-Amos (Ed.), *Folklore genre* (pp. 125-143). Austin, TX: University of Texas.

Spradley, J. P. (1979). *The ethnographic interview.* Fort Worth, TX: Holt, Rinehart & Winston.

Spradley, J. P. (1980). *Participant observation.* Fort Worth, TX: Holt, Rinehart & Winston.

Stone, E. (1988). *Black sheep and kissing cousins: How our family stories shape us.* New York: Penguin.

Whittier, S. (Ed.). (1991). *Insight guides: Bahamas.* Singapore: APA Publications.

APPENDIX

M **A** **R** **R** **I** **A** **G** **E**	Prevent Marriage	Sweep an unmarried lady Eat out of a pot in front of someone you like	
	Signs	Dream about a funeral → will attend a wedding Bad luck to have rain on wedding day	
	Prescriptions	Make it legal	Shack up unmarried = driving without a license
		Prepare	Wisdom from birds: Build a nest first
		Ensure success	Wear engagement ring on right hand Only happily married should make up bed for newly married Woman should avoid getting stomach wet when washing clothes → drunken husband Involve parents and seek their approval Groom's parents must attend wedding or it is a curse When setting table be sure knife blade is not pointing up. Wife and husband will fuss.
		Commitment/ Fidelity vs. Infidelity	Don't let another woman climb guinep tree → sour Never let another woman touch pepper tree Never give husband pens or socks → will walk or write love away Put special things in husband's food to keep him Boil husband's left sock in water and drink it to keep him Don't take sand to the beach, meet it there
	Husband/Wife Relations/Power	The man is the captain of his ship Old, frail man tells wife "You wear the pants, but I control the zipper" She is playing snake in the grass, but the grass she is hiding in, I put it there. God made world and rested. God made man and rested. Since God made woman, God and man never rested.	
	Bad Outcomes	She's picked a needle with no eye I made my bed hard. Oil and water don't mix together	

P	Signs	A spider drops on you A man has a toothache → girlfriend or wife pregnant A lizard in house or on doorpost A bird tries to get in window A green lizard jumps on you A dream about crabs or fish		
	Peculiar Habits	Spitting a lot Eating ashes Eating young fruits		
R **E** **G**	Prescriptions	Do not look at anything pitiful and feel sorry → deformed child Do not look at dead person and be sad Give a pregnant woman what she craves or the baby will be "marked" If baby is marked, wipe with spittle before eating for first nine mornings Never tell exact due date → someone could "cross" baby Avoid bumping stomach on washboard Don't do too much sewing → umbilical cord wrapped around baby's neck Be careful not to fall Don't overreach → hurt baby's neck Do not lift Do not sit with legs crossed → long labor or baby born with cord around neck		
N	Special Powers	Plant seeds → vines bear big fruit Spike unproductive trees → fruitful		
A **N** **C** **Y**	Predictions	Gender of Child		At time of conception, if parents' heads are westward → baby boy, eastward → baby girl If galloping on right side → girl If galloping on left side → boy If takes first step on right foot → girl If takes first step on left foot → boy
			"Mark of the Beast"	Broad mark from navel down/tiny mark on top of navel → boy Tiny mark under navel/broad mark on top → girl
		Child's Appearance		Baby born during full moon → huge head If woman "always have stomach burn" during pregnancy → full head of hair on newborn If child looks like husband, mother really likes him

P A R E N T - C H I L D R E L A T I O N S	Prescriptions	Don't cut child's hair before 2 years → stunt growth Don't cross hands on top of head → mourn mommy and daddy away	
	Intergenerational Transmission	Father eats sour grapes → teeth of children are set on edge Kicking cow brings kicking calf	
	Discipline	Bend tree while it's young, when old, it cannot bend If crab don't walk, he don't get fed. If he walks too much he gets put in the pot. Foolishness is bound in heart of child, but rod of correction drives it far from him Everywhere a puppy goes, he carries his tail	
	Parental Authority/Power	If you don't like my way, loosen your donkey from my gate If you be powerful, be merciful	
	Parental Instruction to Children	Unity	Object lesson: Individual sticks can be broken; a bundle of sticks tied together cannot be broken Death before dishonor
		Sharing	If you have a dollar share it Put meat with bone
		Character	A fool's way in his eyes seems right, but a wise man will take counsel Every dog will have its day Tit for tat, butter for fat. Kill my dog, I'll kill your cat Beauty without virtue is a rose without fragrance Don't you mind the weather, keep your legs together You can catch more flies with two drops of honey than with a barrel of vinegar One man with courage makes a majority Patience is bitter, but its fruit sweet Shut mouth catches no flies The longest journey is begun with the first step A watched kettle takes longer to boil

W **O** **R** **K**	Skill Development	Fowl don't find worms everywhere she scratches Setting hen gets very little corn It takes more than one iron to iron your clothes A Mother's lesson: Rather than give a man a fish, show him how to fish When a man know thing, it's half done In olden days, white man grabbed pen, ink, and paper. Black man wanted hoe, shovel and ax	
	Directing Energies	He that soweth sparingly, shall also reap sparingly Too many chiefs, not enough Indians Never fertilize a dead stump	
	For the Business Person	You cannot do business from an empty wagon Put some clean water in with the dirty and it will not smell	
F **I** **N** **A** **N** **C** **E** **S**	Signs	When palm of hand really itches → will receive money If rub itchy hand on side of pants → will get money Right hand itches → will receive money Right hand itches → give money away If eye twitches → will receive money When scratch head → will get money M on palm of hand → will get money W on palm of hand → will have to work Money bat flies into house → will get money Dream about green plants, like fruits or green corn or green plants → prosperity Dream about waste matters indicates money	
	Prescriptions/ Advice	Saving	Go to the ant, thou sluggard. Consider her ways and be wise. While young, learn to save so when old no one will have to pass hat around for your benefit Always look out for rainy days
		Make Do	If you can't ride the cow, jump on the horse's back

				Left eye twitches → unexpected sorrow Black cat crosses in front of you Break mirror → 7 years bad luck Black Friday → susceptible to bad luck If see green lizard when thinking of something you want → disappointment
W		Misfortune		
E	Signs		Dreams	Silver money → disappointment Sucking sugar cane → disappointment Snakes → enemies lurking Eggs → get in a row Fire → fight or confusion → throw salt in fire to offset it
L				If people are talking about you and you call or pass by → long life Black bee flying around
L		Good Fortune		
-			Dreams	Calm, clear, waters → victory Paper money or sugar apples → blessings Walking in a corn field Killing snakes → conquering enemies
B		Home		Never sweep after sunset → sweep luck away Avoid sitting in doorway → pick up aches and pains of all who walk through door If jump over someone lying down, jump back over them the other way
E	Prescriptions	Bush		Remember that the bush has ears Do not stay in bush too long → might hear people telling you things
I				
N		Graveyard		Don't walk in graveyard at night → see ghosts that look like white people walking in garments Small children should stay at gate of graveyard → haunted by dead Tie black cord around children to keep spirits away Do not enter graveyard with abrasion on foot → problems
G				
	Greetings/ Blessings			May your best years in the past be your worst in the future May your joys be as deep as the ocean and your problems be as light as its foam

D **E** **A** **T** **H**	Signs	Bird hits window and falls dead → someone in family will die Scratchy feet → death in family See hole in grave Rain on first day of year → rich burial ground (lots of deaths that year) When it rains the day someone dies, person is washing his/her tracks from the earth When you shudder involuntarily, someone is walking on your grave "Spirit pinch" (unexplained dark mark on body) Wedding veil covered with black flies		
		Dreams	Crowd of people Rough seas or boat going out to sea Boat on land Pork or pork products Red meat Airplanes Digging sweet potatoes Black crabs Playing organ at church Processions Wedding	
			Foretell Who Will Die	Dream of white man dying → black man Dream of sick or dead man → woman Potatoes → family member Front teeth dropping out → close relative Back teeth falling out → distant relative
	Prescriptions	Fill in any holes you dig or you are digging a hole for relatives to die in Avoid crying and crying while someone is ill or ill person will soon die If "have the feelin'" and are asked to transport sick relative to Nassau for medical treatment, refuse → sick person might die Do not view dead body when menstruating → bleed to death When we see one cry, we must all cry, because we are all human beings and all will die some day		
	Practices	Close house up early and bring children inside due to fear of dead When people die bad, they haunt you		
			Keep Bad Spirits Away	Put black under and around head and bed when sleep at night Write "10 × 10" on door with black crayon Turn hats upside down Turn left shoe upside down by bed Wear clothes inside out Talk to Jesus

V
I
S
I
T
O
R
S
	Signs	Bird flies in one window and out another → visitor
		Find spider in house and it has 7 legs → man visitor
		Find spider in house and it has 8 legs → woman visitor
		If spider is carrying white pillow under him → visitor
		If spider tries to crawl on you → strange visitor
		If small child spontaneously picks up broom and starts to
		  sweep → visitor
		Twitching left eye or ringing ears → will see someone haven't
		  seen in long time or stranger
		Big fly coming out of your doorway → stranger
		Rooster crowing at front door → stranger

	Rules	House guests and fish get bad after a couple of days

&	Value	Never throw away the old kettle until you are sure the new one
		  holds water
		Never burn bridges behind you. You never know when you will
		  turn back to use them.
		You never miss the water until the well runs dry

F **R** **I** **E** **N** **D** **S**	Reciprocity	If you don't stink for me, I will not rotten for you Water will find its level Birds of one feather, all flock together Two clean sheep cannot dirty one another
	Terminate Relationship	Throw rotten egg behind person you dislike as they leave, if you don't want them to return

Egalitarianism and Oppression in Marriage: The Effects of Research on Researchers

Leslie D. Hall
Anisa M. Zvonkovic

SUMMARY. In this paper, we explored the effects of doing research on seven researchers engaged in a study of couple decision-making. While not focused on oppression of women in marital decision-making, our interviews revealed a great deal of it. The seven members of our research team were affected, with age, marital status, and prior attitudes accounting for much of the variation in how deeply researchers were affected. This study explores these issues and makes practical and theoretical points about their importance. *[Article copies available for a fee from The Haworth Document Delivery Service: 1-800-342-9678. E-mail address: getinfo@haworth.com]*

KEYWORDS. Marital relationships, Oppression, Researchers, Interviews

---

Leslie D. Hall is Instructor, and Anisa M. Zvonkovic is Associate Professor, Department of Human Development and Family Sciences, Oregon State University, Corvallis, OR 97331.

The authors thank the research team for their participation, and Leslie Richards, Mina Carson, Jane Gilgun, and two anonymous reviewers for their helpful comments.

[Haworth co-indexing entry note]: "Egalitarianism and Oppression in Marriage: The Effects of Research on Researchers." Hall, Leslie D., and Anisa M. Zvonkovic. Co-published simultaneously in *Marriage & Family Review* (The Haworth Press, Inc.) Vol. 24, No. 1/2, 1996, pp. 89-104; and: *The Methods and Methodologies of Qualitative Family Research* (ed: Marvin B. Sussman, and Jane F. Gilgun) The Haworth Press, Inc., 1996, pp. 89-104. Single or multiple copies of this article are available for a fee from The Haworth Document Delivery Service [1-800-342-9678, 9:00 a.m. - 5:00 p.m. (EST). E-mail address: getinfo@haworth.com].

This paper considers how the process of being involved in research affects researchers personally. In a study of how married couples made work and family decisions, seven members of a research team were intensively involved in conceptualizing the study, talking to the respondents over the telephone, transcribing the qualitative interviews, and analyzing the data (Zvonkovic, Schmiege, & Hall, 1994). Our involvement in the research and our statuses in academe and in family life were related to how the research affected us.

In this paper, two members of the original research team explore how each of the seven researchers responded to the data of the research. We sought to emulate the high standards set by Fonow and Cook (1991) when they defined reflexivity as a critical examination of research processes that includes both reflection and analytic thinking. Reflexivity offers opportunities to examine and explain ourselves and our behaviors and how these influence research processes (Whitchurch & Constantine, 1993). While most discussions of reflexivity focus on how researcher's values and perspectives are related to research processes (e.g., Lather, 1988; Smith, 1987), we are more in the tradition represented by the recent feminist volume edited by Sollie and Leslie (1994).

In this volume, feminist researchers presented reflexive accounts of their experiences with research projects. Allen (1994), for example, reflected on her years of scholarship and the changes she had experienced as her feminism deepened, her life changed, and her reflexivity increased. In the same volume, Walker (1994) described a research project in which she tried to work in a feminist way with the co-principal investigator, graduate students, and the clerical assistant. She "was determined to break down the hierarchy of the research process by involving members of the staff as much as possible in research decisions" (p. 90). Her chapter addressed how graduate students may be involved in research in ways different from faculty principal investigators. While this chapter presented valuable insights into how a feminist researcher sought to be more egalitarian on a research team, differences within members of a research team, such as the differences that might exist among different graduate students, were not systematically considered.

Investigations of an entire research team from each team member's viewpoint may be a logical outcome of contemporary interest in reflexivity and research. Social scientists traditionally were trained to believe that scientists are objective and, thus, that change of personal beliefs when doing research is not a proper topic to explore (Baber & Allen, 1992; Stacey, 1988). Furthermore, if participating in research projects did result in personal change among scientists, scientific objectivity could be suspect. Social scientists today are more articulate than formerly about the reflexive nature of research processes. Emerging are views that examining the extent to which participating in research affects researchers is part of research processes and that research findings may resonate with the personal experiences of researchers.

GENDERED OPPRESSION IN MARRIAGE

When we began our study of marital decision-making in the areas of family and work, we were not searching for insight into marital oppression, nor were we setting out to examine the effect of research on researchers. Nonetheless, marital oppression was present in our interviews, as were individual personal responses of each member of the research team. In retrospect, we aren't surprised because possibilities and actualities of marital oppression in decision-making are consistent with theories of gender. Feminists have long been critical of marriages structured by gendered expectations and behaviors because women usually are in a subordinate position, at great cost to them (Allen, 1994; Berk, 1985; Hochschild, 1989; Osmond & Thorne, 1993). Men and women traditionally construct gender in unconscious but important ways, placing more value on men's paid work than in women's contribution to marriage and family (Hochschild, 1989; Thompson & Walker, 1989; West & Zimmerman, 1987). In this way, gender is created, maintained, or reconstructed through decisions couples make and their reflections on the meaning of those decisions.

METHOD

Who the researchers are as individual human beings is important to research, but this is rarely discussed (Allen & Walker, 1992). Many feminist qualitative approaches, however, emphasize acknowledging researchers' perspectives. Thus, as feminist researchers, we believe it important to describe the situations of the seven researchers in our project.

The research team included an assistant professor, three graduate students, and three undergraduate students who designed the study, conducted the telephone interviews, and transcribed the interviews. The three undergraduate students did most of the telephone interviews, while one graduate student transcribed all interviews. The professor and three graduate students repeatedly read the transcripts, individually coded the material for themes, and as a group discussed the material to achieve consensus. The views that emerged bespoke a wide range of perspectives and provided insight into how each team member constructed gender.

All seven researchers were women, four married, three never married. One of the presently married researchers became engaged to be married during the time she was doing telephone interviews. All of the researchers were students or faculty at the time of the telephone interviews in the original study, but some had graduated by the time our study of our own reflexivity occurred. Three of the team were mothers of young children. Most team members defined themselves as heterosexual, although some avoided so exclusive a term. Not all of the seven women were in partnered relationships. Six of team members were white and one was bi-racial, ranging in age from early twenties to early forties. Concerning family background, the educational level of parents is quite varied, with some research team members having parents with high school diplomas and others having parents with graduate degrees.

The following were the team members, whose names have been changed. Gabriella, 34, is married, has two young children, and works. Iva, 39 is working. Although she is not married and does not have children, she intends to help care for her parents in the future. Quinci, 33, is single, works, and is a student. Randi, 23, is working and recently married. Sarah, 40, is married, has children, works, and is a student. Trina, 35, is married, working, and has a child. Yvonne, 24, is single, helps raise a relative's children, and is in school. Team members, therefore, lived during different socio-historical eras, had a range of family and personal histories, and were in a variety of phases of the life cycle. The authors believe the diversity of the team's life experiences has been helpful to the validity of the qualitative analysis, in that team members have been able to check each others' subjective impressions of the interviews. At the same time, on the whole, the researchers were similar in their discomfort with strictly traditional values (i.e., that women and men are inherently different, women should stay home and care for children, and men should be economic providers). The research team members varied on how committed they were to feminism; the professor and graduate students were strongly committed, the undergraduates less so.

The present article is based upon interviews we conducted with other members of the research team. Guided by a set of questions available in the Appendix, the interviews became conversations. Data were collected by typing conversations almost verbatim via the use of a laptop computer.

Data Analysis

We did a standard analysis of the transcripts of our interviews, reading and re-reading the transcripts, spending hours discussing the meanings we were finding, and conducting on-going discussions with the other members of the team. In reflecting upon the questions we asked in the guided conversations, we note that we could have probed more, but we were concerned with causing or exacerbating negative feelings. This was, in part, because we would see the researchers in our daily life on campus and at professional meetings and because researchers had personal relationships with each other. Our experience highlights the importance of acknowledging and respecting personal boundaries in reflexive research. This research is limited by our own imperfections, as we "felt our way" amidst these parameters (Gilgun, 1992).

FINDINGS

Diversity in how researchers viewed the effects of their participation in research was apparent. Part of this diversity seemed to occur as results of (a) the variety of levels of involvement in the project; (b) the congruence/incongruence between ideology and life experience in marriage and the content of the interviews; (c) researchers' awareness of power, gender, and oppression in marriage; and (d) the emotions evoked via the research process and what researchers did with their emotions. Members of the research team felt that participating in the research project had affected their views to differing degrees, but all identified difficulty with separating out the effects of the research from other experiences.

Involvement in Project

Those members of the research team who invested the most hours in a concentrated time period were the most affected by the research. The experience of participating seemed more vivid for them, and they recalled more easily what respondents said verbatim along with the emotional tones they used. These women also expressed more emotional reactions to the process, as we will discuss later.

During data gathering, these members of the research team worked at least 10 hours a week. One researcher did no interviews but transcribed all of the interview tapes in an intense three-month-long period. The length of time that a member of the research team was involved in the project did not seem to make a difference in how intensely the research affected them. Across the seven women, intensity, independent of marital status, age, and length of time in the project, appeared to be a key factor in the effects of the research on researchers.

Congruence Between Ideology and Experience in Marriage

Researchers had thought about egalitarianism in their marriages or potential marriages prior to being involved in the research process, but

exposure to research interviews that actualized the challenges of egalitarianism seemed to provoke clarity and solidification to the researchers'
points. For some of the married researchers, the stories of marriages to
which they were exposed in the research provided more evidence that
marriage can be an oppressive institution, reinforcing their own experiences in their marriages and their observations that practice in marriage is
often inconsistent with preferences. By turning oppression into an institutional problem—rather than a personal problem—it is possible that the married members of the research team could be less likely to agitate for
change in their own marriages.

After exposure to intimate decisions of married partners through the
interviews, researchers who were not married and who had strong egalitarian ideologies doubted they would find a marital partner who would
behave consistently with their researchers' ideologies.

When we discussed the patterns of their own marriages and what they
preferred, researchers had many reflexive observations. Gabriella, for
example, preferred to be in an egalitarian marriage, but said she probably
is in a transitional or near-peer marriage; that is, her husband contributes a
moderate amount to the marriage and she expects he will contribute more
in the future. As Schwartz (1994) found in her study of marital relationships, Gabriella believed her marriage was more egalitarian before their
children were born. She and her marital partner continued to have egalitarian ideologies once they had children, but the egalitarianism became
more difficult to actualize. Yet, she saw her marriage as more egalitarian
than those of most of the couples in the study.

Trina reflected on her own marriage through doing the research, seeing
things she found positive and negative compared to others' marriages. She
had an egalitarian ideology and wanted to be in an egalitarian marriage,
but she characterized her husband as more transitional or traditional in
ideology. In addition, she experienced her marriage in practice as reflecting his ideology. She said

> I am well aware that the more education the woman has, or at least
> having a job, or bringing money in from outside, means she has
> more power in the relationship.

She was painfully aware that her husband had a stable job in which he
earned more money than the jobs for which she qualified. Her linking of
women's economic contribution to their families with their power in their
families provided a justification for her husband's power in her marriage.
In her own marriage, Trina identified this problem:

I'm going to lose my job. I'm really worried about not having a job. I get bullied by my husband anyway. . . . I don't know if it's the research or money coming in. Regardless of whether it changes the dynamics, it makes me feel like I have a right to complain about something.

This justification, that earning income was related to having a voice in the marriage, was uncomfortable for her and incongruent with her ideology.

Iva and Quinci said they would insist on egalitarian marriages if they were to marry, while Randi and Sarah said their marriages were egalitarian. Three of these women noted that such marriages, in view of the sample of marriages with which they became familiar, apparently were rare. Yvonne, helping raise a relative's children, did not talk about her attitudes about marriage, although she said she planned to marry in the future. Ideology and practice in marriage were not salient to her.

Some researchers felt the research affected their future plans. Quinci and Iva both felt that the research experience helped to solidify doubts that they would marry. Iva said:

It would be hard at this point to get married. I'm so independent. I would have trouble adjusting. I wouldn't be willing to do what most men expect you to do. It'd take an extraordinary person and I don't meet too many of them; and they're married.

Quinci remarked

Doing this research makes me really wonder if I want to get married; not if I could tolerate marriage, but if I could find it a satisfying enough of an experience that I would want to continue doing it.

Doing research on marital decision-making, thus, was provocative personally for the researchers, leading to deepened reflections on their present and future situations.

Power, Gender, and Oppression in Marriage

All members of the research team had thought deeply about respondents' lives and had much to say about how power was distributed in the marriages of the couples they had studied. Gabriella, in perhaps the most extreme statement concerning a changed perspective, asserted that through the research she came to regard

> Every decision and everything I do I see as a power issue. . . . when you think about it in terms of power, you tend to deal with it differently.

Gabriella is steeped in the literature on feminist and qualitative issues. Thus, it is not surprising that power became foremost in her mind. Respondents who were not surrounded continually by gendered perspectives, including power in gendered relationships, were less likely to see decision-making as an issue of power (Zvonkovic et al., in press). Like Gabriella, Quinci was also engrossed in gender issues. She too focused on power:

> I've learned a lot about power that women don't have, the powerlessness of women in society. Everyone goes into a relationship with a set of rules or expectations. If you play football, you know the rules. In a relationship, one of those rules is he has more power because he's a man, because he makes more money, mainly just because he's a man. There were a few couples where the wife makes more money and he has more power. She felt uncomfortable making more money. She tried to give him more power in other areas. It made him feel less right, responsible, controlling, less a man. So I believe men have more power because they have a penis [laughter] because they're men; not money, job, or being able to command respect.

Quinci, going further, stated

> It's very disconcerting, it's just marriage sucks for women and it did for the women in this study. They're struggling every day and their husbands were completely oblivious to their wives' multiple roles. Husbands didn't consider their wives' lives if they made a specific work and family decision. When wives made decisions they first thought of 'how is this going to change my husband's life?'

This response of wives' thinking of the spouse, often first, when husbands did not do so, felt oppressive to some research team members. Thompson (1991) presented an argument that women may not see this situation as unfair, for a variety of reasons.

Both Quinci and Sarah highlighted examples of couples who made family moves because of the husband's job. As Sarah put it,

> Her job is 'scramble to find another one' after they've moved; she gets to pack up the kids and the house. Even when the wives stay

home, her community of colleagues changes dramatically, whereas he steps into a new community of colleagues.

Some members of the research team took home the changed perspective they had acquired from the study. Iva said

I went home one year at Christmas and was vacuuming. My mother said 'Thank you for helping me.' I said 'It's not your job. It's everyone's.' She understood that I got a different perception of housework, it's everybody's.

Trina also compared information from the respondents to her own experiences in her marriage. She was aware of the differences in power between herself and her husband and the differences between his liberal ideology and non-egalitarian behavior:

I think the only thing that has changed in my family life is the awareness of the power difference between men and women; he's more powerful. My husband, politically and in all aspects of his life, is liberal, but I would consider our marriage more traditional. . . . It would have been nice to interview someone who didn't do joint decisions like we don't.

Both Trina and Gabriella, who are parents of young children, noted a heightened awareness of power without a change in behavior. Involvement in the research seemed to have sensitized them to the oppressive nature of marriage for many women in the study.

These team members articulated justifications for the non-egalitarian practices of their own marriages, justifications which they presented at the same time that they criticized the oppressive marriages of the women in the original study. For example, Trina admired a couple who told her they "calendared," sitting down weekly to arrange family work, leisure activities, and child care needs. Trina said, "My husband and I would probably benefit from that structure of sitting down weekly with calendars." She does not feel she and her husband are as organized as some respondents.

Gabriella mentioned justifications or excuses for oppressive behavior, issues discussed by Thompson (1991). She identified excuses for leaving the paid workforce, particularly made by wives in original study. Gabriella connected the justifications and excuses for male power made by respondents to her own life, now seeing every conflict as a power issue, wanting to "bargain rather than accept" her partner's preferences. This recognition that justifications function in her life to uphold oppressive patterns is not necessarily comfortable. When researchers heard different justifications to support patriarchal patterns, the patriarchal underpinning of the decisions became evident. An event or experience that figured in one couple's decision regarding work and family may not be seen as outstanding or unique by that couple.

This does not mean, however, that in the lives of the members of the research team, idiosyncratic justifications for patriarchal decision-making patterns necessarily were recognized, or that such justifications did not prevail. If research team members did come to recognize excuses, this could be a benefit of meta-perspectives arising from respondents' stories.

Recognition of justifications as non-idiosyncratic could be transforming in the relationships of the research team members, particularly around the ideal of egalitarian marriage. If married team members agitated to change their marital practices, perhaps this meta-perspective heightened their vigilance, a pattern Blaisure and Allen (1995) noted in their research on marriage. If they did not agitate to change, they may stay in positions similar to those of Hochschild's (1989) respondents, unwilling to risk losing the marriage by working for relationships that fit their own ideologies.

Emotions

Clearly, some of the research team had more emotions evoked by the research process than others. By and large, in people's answers, one could see how the interview touched a nerve. It was not so much the respondent's situation that affected researchers, as how what the respondent said reverberated with the researchers' life experiences. Gabriella said

> Some of the men made me really angry: the men who had a mixed message, when you read deeper they didn't believe their wives had a right to work. . . . Women, I identified with more positively, trying to be good in all their roles, . . . I could even empathize with women staying home when their children were young. I could connect with what they were saying, frustrated because they didn't see any other way to deal with their lives. With them, what got to me was the solution was right for them. That was hard for me to deal with.

As stated earlier, Gabriella faced a dilemma in her own life concerning inconsistency between egalitarian ideology and non-egalitarian practice. When in the research she dealt with interviews where the women practiced non-egalitarian behaviors, she sometimes lacked empathy. Sometimes she felt frustrated, as when women were comfortable with this solution. Other researchers had similar responses.

Another source of discomfort for some team members was hearing remarks that were very similar to their marital patterns. For example, Trina recalled

> I remember this guy who didn't mind her having a job as long as she got the housework and dishes done. I can still hear his voice. My marriage comes very close to that perception.

The marriage of the couple she described might be defined as transitional (Hochschild, 1989).

Quinci, not married, did not find any respondents who resonated with her:

> I don't think I heard any women who were outspokenly feminist. Deep inside they were. They believed in equality in every way, but didn't speak it or demand it. I would demand it; maybe not equity, but consensus, taking turns. I would not put up with it [inequality]. I wouldn't have let it go.

Quinci and Trina had strong emotional reactions to the respondents. Quinci said

> It could be that I have an even less positive view of marriage now, of marital relationships. I just am really angry at men for not realizing what their role is in an equal relationship, since they so many times would say this is an equal relationship and it's not. . . . I found it hard to sympathize with husbands who didn't participate in family life. I sympathized with a lot of the women who were struggling with what almost seemed like 'how do I get my husband to do more without pissing him off, without making him angry when he thinks he's doing enough, how do I make him see all I do?'

The graduate students in particular seemed sensitive to issues of fairness. All of them described emotional reactions to particular couples who "weren't fair to each other." Iva said

> The woman that got so much out of her job, and her husband didn't see it as a job. Or the woman who had to make her job fit, and sacrifice a lot, and he had to sacrifice a little bit of his life. He didn't understand.

The two other graduate students also brought up this latter couple, in which the husband reported he had "sacrificed" for the work decision, because he had reduced his "athletic endeavors." The wife reported that she could only seek a job with limited hours and that she had to arrange for child care.

Some researchers wondered why people who were in a marriage, generally assumed to be a loving relationship, treated each other unfairly. Sarah found herself trying to figure out "why women put up with this and why men act this way toward the person they have pledged to love the rest of their lives." Iva similarly wondered how the marriages of the people she was reading about could work, when "They don't seem to listen to each other."

What researchers did with their emotions varied. It was evident that the research team provided a forum for discussing and venting emotions. All of the researchers talked about how sharing with other researchers made it easier to process comments from respondents. Trina noted that the undergraduate researchers often worked together at the telephone lab and that

> Sometimes we laughed about something we had said . . . I shared with them more because they were doing it at the same time.

Some members of the research team discussed with other people their emotional reactions to the issues raised from collecting data. Among the researchers who were married or engaged, there seemed to be a difference in who shared these issues with their intimate partners. The women who were in self-described egalitarian partnerships tended to bring these disturbing issues home and discuss them with their intimate partners, whereas the women who were not in such relationships did not.

The women who did not discuss these issues with their partners were nevertheless affected, probably more so. To whom they chose to talk was illuminating. Sarah commented that the research had influenced her to think "even more minutely" about power. She noted that people can easily espouse equality, "but if you hang out in their house for a day, the power differential is there, usually by gender."

Gabriella, who had earlier stated that she saw everything as a power issue, remarked that issues of power and fairness came up when she was talking to her woman friends and in her classes. Because she did not talk to her husband about these issues, she found the research did not affect him at all. However, when Gabriella talked with her friends, they also shared their stories of oppression in marriage. This further angered her and sensitized her to stories both of respondents and others.

Randi, engaged at the time, now in a new egalitarian marriage, recalled one frustrating interview after which she talked with the principal investigator of the research and with her fiance so that "it didn't torment me for years." Sarah, in an egalitarian marriage, stated she talked with her husband about the research in addition to the research team. She said

> He doesn't feel like I'm male-bashing to discuss these issues. He doesn't understand why men don't share either. There is nothing that really changed [in our family life], the way we did things.

Quinci did not mention talking with anyone except the research team and said this decision may affect her later. She found it harder to deal with the emotions provoked because she lived alone. She said

> Maybe the emotions will all come out in a relationship. I'll give it to him. He'll wonder where it's all coming from. I'll say, 'I did this research project two years ago.' Maybe it's buried somewhere. I have a lot of anger and disappointment in men.

Quinci was disappointed in marriage as an option before the research, but was angrier and more deeply disappointed after reading the transcripts repeatedly.

DISCUSSION

Among the members of the research team, there was variability in how the research affected us. This variability was important and could be partially explained by different life contexts. Researchers found it hard to separate out the extent to which the research affected them from other life experiences they had had, particularly related to the congruence, or lack thereof, of their desired type of relationship and their life experience. This is natural considering that Stacey (1988) described on-going processes of reflexive research as "excruciatingly self-conscious."

The student researchers and the faculty member have self-selected into the field of family studies, into these particular programs, and into being more active in the field through research. Others with less intense involvement in family studies might have different experiences in research. Nevertheless, researchers reflected extensively on the meaning of the information they had gathered. In efforts to understand the respondents, the researchers experienced a variety of discomforting emotions. The researchers were also sensitized to issues of egalitarianism, power, fairness, and how married couples constructed gender, which often served to oppress women.

Because of the teams' familiarity with the literature and being outside of the respondents' relationships, hidden power issues were salient for them. In addition, hearing over and over about decisions which benefitted men affected the team. Team members saw patterns that reflected patriarchy. Researchers described discomfort when respondents' voices were different from their own voices. Researchers also experienced discomfort when respondents' voices were quite similar to their marital partners, echoing a situation that was distressing for them. Other members of the research team were unsettled by the fact that there were no respondents whose voices sounded similar to their own. Lastly, there was discomfort and frustration when a clash existed between researchers' egalitarian ideologies and respondents' non-egalitarian practices, but the researchers realized that the decisions might be right for the respondents. The research team could understand where the respondents stood given their particular gendered approaches to work/family decision-making. The researchers continually attempted to be reflexive to help guard against the reification about which Lather (1988) warned. It is standard practice for qualitative researchers to keep fieldnotes, which usually become reflexive journals. Perhaps this practice could extend to survey researchers and other types of researchers as well. In this way, reflexive comments could be recorded and then examined more thoroughly later.

In the present study, we focused on reflexivity in research processes. Such a focus takes us away from the assumption that science in general, and social science in particular, is objective (Baber & Allen, 1992). More than two years after the telephone interviews, research team members were still processing how they viewed marriage as an institution, husbands as a category, and their own marriages or future plans for marriage.

Understanding that these types of personal effects may occur is important for researchers. We believe our research findings on these effects and our suggestions for being prepared for such effects can make a contribution to scholarship. We do not disassociate the scholarly and personal. This research, therefore, may contribute insight to the personal lives of scholars. Research can affect researchers positively and negatively, hopefully in therapeutic and preventive ways. Findings about personal effects may parallel some of the personal effects clinicians experience when doing therapy (Whitaker & Ryan, 1989). The challenge ahead is to use these effects to spark the creation of new knowledge. We encourage more researchers to explore their personal journeys in research and to attend to the often unanticipated journeys that may be embarked upon by students.

REFERENCES

Allen, K. R. (1994). Feminist reflections on lifelong single women. In D. L. Sollie & L. A. Leslie (Eds.), *Gender, families, and close relationships: Feminist research journeys* (pp. 97-119). Thousand Oaks, CA: Sage.

Allen, K. R., & Walker, A. J. (1992). A feminist analysis of interviews with elderly mothers and their daughters. In J. F. Gilgun, K. Daly, & G. Handel (Eds.), *Qualitative Methods in Family Research* (pp. 198-214). Newbury Park, CA: Sage.

Baber, K. M., & Allen, K. R. (1992). *Women and family: Feminist reconstructions.* New York: Guilford.

Berk, S. F. (1985). *The gender factory: The apportionment of work in American households.* New York: Plenum.

Blaisure, K. R., & Allen, K. R. (1995). Feminists and the ideology and practice of marital equality. *Journal of Marriage and the Family, 57,* 5-19.

Fonow, M. M., & Cook, J. A. (1991). Back to the future: A look at the second wave of feminist epistemology and methodology. In M. M. Fonow & J. A. Cook (Eds.), *Beyond methodology: Feminist scholarship as lived research* (pp. 1-15). Bloomington, IN: Indiana University Press.

Gilgun, J. F. (1992). Definitions, methodologies, and methods in qualitative family research. In J. F. Gilgun, K. Daly, & G. Handel (Eds.), *Qualitative Methods in Family Research* (pp. 22-42). Newbury Park, CA: Sage.

Hochschild, A. R. (1989). *The second shift.* New York: Avon.

Lather, P. (1988). Feminist perspectives on empowering research methodologies. *Women's Studies International Forum, 11,* 569-581.

Osmond, M. W., & Thorne, B. (1993). Feminist theories: The social construction of gender in families and society. In P. G. Boss, W. J. Doherty, R. LaRossa, W. R. Schumm, & S. K. Steinmetz (Eds.), *Sourcebook of family theories and methods: A contextual approach* (pp. 325-352). New York: Plenum.

Schwartz, P. (1994). *Peer marriage: How love between equals really works.* New York: The Free Press.

Smith, D. E. (1987). Women's perspective as a radical critique of sociology. In S. Harding (Ed.), *Feminism and Methodology* (pp. 84-96). Bloomington, IN: Indiana University Press.

Sollie, D. A., & Leslie, L. A. (Eds.). (1994). *Gender, families, and close relationships: Feminist research journeys.* Thousand Oaks, CA: Sage.

Stacey, J. (1988). Can there be a feminist ethnography? *Women's Studies International Forum, 11,* 21-27.

Stacey, J. (1990). *Brave new families: Stories of domestic upheaval in late twentieth century America.* New York: Basic Books.

Thompson, L., (1991). Family work: Women's sense of fairness. *Journal of Family Issues, 12,* 181-196.

Thompson, L., & Walker, A. J. (1989). Gender in families: Women and men in marriage, work, and parenthood. *Journal of Marriage and the Family, 51,* 845-871.

Walker, A. J. (1994). You can't be a woman in your mother's house: Adult daughters and their mothers. In D. L. Sollie & L. A. Leslie (Eds.), *Gender, families, and close relationships: Feminist research journeys* (pp. 74-96). Thousand Oaks, CA: Sage.

West, C., & Zimmerman, D. H (1987), Doing gender. *Gender & Society, 1,* 125-151.

Whitaker, C., & Ryan, M. O. (1989). *Midnight musings of a family therapist.* New York: Norton.

Whitchurch, G. G., & Constantine, L. L. (1993). Systems theory. In P. G. Boss, W. J. Doherty, R. LaRossa, W. R. Schumm, & S. K. Steinmetz (Eds.), *Sourcebook of family theories and methods: A contextual approach* (pp. 325-352). New York: Plenum.

Zvonkovic, A. M., Greaves, K. M., Schmiege, C. J., & Hall, L. D. (in press). The marital construction of gender through work and family decisions: A qualitative analysis. *Journal of Marriage and the Family.*

Zvonkovic, A. M., Schmiege, C. J., & Hall, L. D. (1994). Influence strategies used when couples make work-family decisions and their importance for marital satisfaction. *Family Relations, 43,* 182-188.

APPENDIX

Conversation Guides
1. How has participating in this research affected your future plans?
   a. Has it affected your marriage or family life in positive or negative ways?
   b. Has it affected your views of power in marriage relationships?
2. How did you respond emotionally to couples?
   a. Were there types of respondents toward whom it was hard to be neutral, because you empathized, were angry, and so on?
      i. Who were they?
      ii. How did you feel and why?
      iii. What about them made you feel that way?
      Was there a resonance or dissonance of their voices and yours?
      iv. What did you do with the emotions?
      Did you take them home and talk them over?
      Did they change your family life?

African-American Adolescent Women: Perceptions of Gender, Race, and Class

Charlotte Schoup Olsen

SUMMARY. This is a reflexive account of a study of the perceptions of young women of African-American descent on gender, race, and class. These abstractions come to life as these young women provide concrete instances of how these stratifications systems affect their everyday lives. The young informants clearly perceive the challenges that these systems represent. In reporting the results of this study, the researcher is reflexive on two counts. First, she reflects upon the implications of her European-American heritage for the quality of her interviews and analysis. Second, she discusses the challenges of writing qualitative research reports. Not only was she inexperienced in how to write reports based on qualitative data, but she also felt constrained by the length restrictions from telling the whole story. *[Article copies available for a fee from The Haworth Document Delivery Service: 1-800-342-9678. E-mail address: getinfo@haworth.com]*

KEYWORDS. Feminist research, African-American adolescent women, Qualitative research, Qualitative interviewing, Cross-cultural interviewing

---

Charlotte Shoup Olsen is Assistant Professor/Extension Educator, School of Family Studies and Human Services, 343 Justin Hall, Kansas State University, Manhattan, KS 66506.

The author would like to thank the anonymous reviewers for their help on earlier drafts of this article.

This article is based on the author's (1993) dissertation.

[Haworth co-indexing entry note]: "African-American Adolescent Women: Perceptions of Gender, Race, and Class." Olsen, Charlotte Schoup. Co-published simultaneously in *Marriage & Family Review* (The Haworth Press, Inc.) Vol. 24, No. 1/2, 1996, pp. 105-121; and: *The Methods and Methodologies of Qualitative Family Research* (ed: Marvin B. Sussman, and Jane F. Gilgun) The Haworth Press, Inc., 1996, pp. 105-121. Single or multiple copies of this article are available for a fee from The Haworth Document Delivery Service [1-800-342-9678, 9:00 a.m. - 5:00 p.m. (EST). E-mail address: getinfo@ haworth.com].

The social and historical dynamics of race, class, and gender are key to our experiences in families and in the larger society (Zinn & Eitzen, 1987). Yet research that focuses specifically on African-American adolescent young women, especially those not designated as having problems, is not easily available (Butler, 1990). These young women have stories to tell, stories that are unique to them and unlike the stories of their white female counterparts and African-American adolescent males.

As a European-American woman, I began to appreciate the uniqueness of young African-American women in my first job out of college, being a summer counselor in a New England camp for teenagers from a Harlem community center. Over the years, as I continued to work with young women of color, I realized that qualitative methods are well-suited to gathering and telling their stories. I wanted to capture their perspectives on race, class, and gender in terms of how these statuses relate to their perceptions of their places in American society. I felt more or less prepared for this phenomological study through nearly 10 years of observations and informal discussions with African-American adolescent young women, starting with the camp experience, continuing in an Upward Bound high school program, and then in a college Student Support Services project. These latter two projects provided academic support to families with limited resources and parents who had not graduated from college. I used these undocumented observations and conversations to conceptualize questions and conduct interviews.

DOING RESEARCH ACROSS CULTURES

A major task throughout the research process was addressing the cross-cultural nature of the research design; that is, I was white and my informants were black. Using the guiding principles of cross-cultural feminist scholarship as defined by Reinharz (1992), I started with an intensive self-analysis, asking myself questions raised by other researchers (Gorelick, 1991; McIntosh, 1989; Reinharz, 1992; Smith, 1994). As a member of the dominant racial group, I was aware of my ignorance related to other racial groups. In addition, I was a generation or more older than the young women I intended to interview.

The following gives a picture of my on-going self-reflections. I saw myself as having the effrontery to study the lives of African-Americans. I asked myself how I could collect information in ways that facilitate an in-depth understanding of these young women within the context of their family lives. How could I identify my personal assumptions constructed by the privilege of my skin color and my experiences as a white person?

For instance, did I view the researched population as victims in our society? How would any assumptions I have affect my interpretations of their responses? Would differences in age and thus the effects of history influence research processes?

As I struggled with these questions, I began to believe the most trustworthy analysis results from the researcher being in the same critical plane as the researched, thereby allowing not just the content, but the entire research process to be scrutinized (Gorelick, 1991; Harding, 1987; Mies, 1983). Yet, the inherent structures of inequality between the researched and the researcher create paradoxical power relationships. Being older and white compounded these power dynamics. Nonetheless, I was invested on a personal level to strive for egalitarian, reciprocal interview relationships and to show respect and regard for the knowledge being shared (Oakley, 1981). While I continually reflected upon these issues, I also had confidence in my ability to establish rapport because of my long-term involvement and success in cross-cultural settings and relationships.

My self-reflections were also stimulated by my review of the theoretical and research literature generated by African-American scholars. Not only did I gain insight into the experiences of well-functioning individuals and families, but I developed a deep scholarly appreciation of the complexities of studying the interplay of gender, race, and class. (See Olsen [1993] for details.) While I had been aware of the numerous scholars who brought attention to the historical marginalization of women and girls in social science research, through this literature review, I came to know and appreciate the work of African-American feminist scholars who demonstrated that women and girls of color are marginalized even within feminist research (Butler, 1990; Dill, 1983; Giddings, 1984; Higginbotham, 1981, 1992; Hooks, 1981, 1984, 1989, 1990; Ladner, 1972, 1987; Lorde, 1984; McAdoo, 1988; Scott, 1991; Scott-Jones & Clark, 1986; Smith, 1983). In my reporting of my research, I did not want to join those who marginalize women of color.

THE INFORMANTS

The young women in my study were volunteers between 14 years to 18 years old and were in good academic standing in public schools. Their families represented diverse economic, social, and educational backgrounds. Principals in two midwestern schools identified samples of young women with these qualities, and I contacted the parents of every third young woman on the lists the principals provided. A few other informants were recruited from Upward Bound students at a midwestern

University. Dealing with the parents was the toughest part of the research for me. I felt as if I were intruding into these families, and, as Daly (1992) indicated, imposing upon protected family boundaries. My age, race, and gender also concerned me as possible barriers. Yet, the parents and their daughters were overwhelmingly receptive. Of the families contacted, only two refused permission for their daughters' participation.

Although the interview was structured like an informal conversation, I had an interview guide with such general questions as, "What are your greatest concerns?" "What do you expect to do in the future?" and "Are things better or worse for you than for your mother?" I conducted one interview per informant, with an average interview time of 50 minutes. The interviews were tape-recorded and transcribed verbatim. The research procedures were approved by the institutional review board of my university.

DATA ANALYSIS

In seeking to understand my findings, I looked for "chunks of meaning" as suggested by Marshall (1981) and Hewitt (1988). I used the grounded theory tradition of Glaser and Strauss (1967), seeking first to identify themes and concepts and create categories of meaning. I analyzed the data using a four-stage constant comparative method: (1) comparing the incidents applicable to each category; (2) integrating categories and their properties; (3) delimiting the theory; and (4) writing the theory. Delimiting and writing the theory were the hardest. In a qualitative study of this nature, the findings are best reported in the words of the respondents, yet there were more than 500 pages of transcripts in this study. I struggled and continue to struggle with such questions as how to summarize dimensions of the findings without marginalizing individual voices.

IN THEIR OWN WORDS

From the moment I began to write up my results, I struggled with how to do so succinctly, while preserving the richness and intensity of these young women's experiences. I was so touched, so moved by their words, their hopes, their dreams, their sadness I wanted all who read their words to understand them as I did. Yet, like all researchers who write for journals, I was limited to a finite number of pages. My inexperience in the analysis, interpretation, and the writing of qualitative data also were challenges to rendering my insights into succinct form. I decided I would minimize the extensive literature review I did, discuss frankly my frustrations with length, and then give as much space as I could to the young women.

Gender

These young women saw male domination and advantages related to gender as major issues, often potential obstacles for the achievement of their own life goals. Studies abound to testify to how gender organizes lives. Some, as pointed out by Ferree (1990), focus on how gender creates "oppositional categories with unequal social value" (p. 869), with the male gender more valued than the female. School environments, families, and other social institutions routinely reinforce the higher social worth of males (Lightfoot, 1980; Okin, 1989). Some of the young women in my study heard these messages loudly and clearly, and they were concerned about and preparing to cope with these portrayals of the meanings of gender:

> I think females, we have to take a little bit more. Men, you know, they I don't know how to say this, but men, like they get things served to them on a platter. We have to work for it.

> There are a lot of areas where men are dominant, but I don't think that should be necessarily so. I think everything should be equal. I know that it probably is not going to work. Like it is how society portrays them, like in advertising. You know, like car sales. You wouldn't think it was an ad for a car the way you see a woman sitting out in a bathing suit. I mean stuff like that, women being used. It just seems to me that men have the upper hand.

> You know you see it on TV a lot. Men think they are the superior ones, and the dominant ones and all that stuff. I don't know. I think it is kind of stupid.

Despite the advantages they saw in being male and the frequent disparagement of the female gender role, none of the young women said they wanted to be boys:

> If I woke up this morning and I was a boy, I'd be scared. I think it's better to be a woman because if you have a head on you, you know

not to do stuff, but boys might have a good schooling, but it's always their peers pressuring them. They like go with the flow or whatever, but a girl will just sit and think about it. I'm happy to be a girl.

You see a male and there is a way a male is supposed to be. A male is stereotyped to be macho, but I feel as though a male is not necessarily like a woman, but has a lot of characteristics like feelings and not always being macho and being soft-hearted, but there is so much stereotyping and so much said out loud, and they are afraid to show it.

Gender and Family Life

In thinking about the future, the young women had a range of expectations. Some had definite plans about the distribution of work in the families they would create, while others showed ambivalence about how equality would play out in marriage and family life. The following quote represents a stance of equality voiced by some of these young women:

I think about getting married and before we start thinking about getting married, we are going to set down together to set the rules, and we are going to be equal. Equal. Fifty-fifty.

Still others wanted to remain staunchly independent:

I want to be dependent on no one. I want to be what I want to be and he needs to be what he wants to be. I want to be independent.

Yet, many voiced expectations or longing for dependency, not commenting on possible dissonance with the goal of equality:

Men believed in taking care of their wives, but not so much now. They don't believe in taking care of her.

Others thought they might want to take care of a man:

The woman, you know, should take care of the house, be a housewife when she comes home [from work] and takes care of her husband. A rough day and you give him a back rub.

Intermixed with this range of expectations about taking care and being taken care of was a strong desire for at least some help around the house.

I feel that they [house chores] should be shared to make you a real rounded person.

I don't know about all the other families around here, but my family is going to be like a traditional family. I want a traditional family where I get home from work, cook dinner, clean up the kids, but I also want my husband to help.

I feel that everybody is equal so women should be able to do whatever they want to do and whatever they put their minds to do, and men, whatever, they want to do, should be able to, too . . . I don't think the man should do it [housecleaning and changing the diapers], but he should learn just in case his wife is at work. He should know how to do it.

The '60s were pretty nice in a way, though, but that was too stereotyped. The wife stayed home, took care of the children, cooked for your husband when he came home. I don't see that but I think the male part in the '60s was more efficient because at least he supported the family and the black community and I don't see much of that.

These young women were struggling to fit their thinking about the equality of the genders with what they expected in marriage. Their perceptions appear to have been shaped by deeply-entrenched norms of gender-linked roles in contemporary U.S. society. In addition, at least one young woman was concerned about African-American men's abilities to support their families.

Race and Racism

The young women in this study reported many instances of discrimination and prejudice. Sometimes, when they were not sure of the meanings of the behaviors of others, they checked their perceptions with others. Overall, the portrait that emerged from my interviews is that of young, advantaged African-American women confronted repeatedly with instances of racism, whether at school or in other public places.

When we came to our summer program, there were a whole lot of blacks in our group and when we went to play putt putt, or whatever, when we went anywhere people looked at us. You know like they had never seen black people before and we got pretty upset because you know they didn't have to treat us like that. It's just that they stared at us and they made us think that we were outcasts or whatever. We didn't belong there.

If a whole bunch of black people hang together, principals like to say we have a gang. We like live around each other, so we always are around each other. They want to call it a gang.

You are always going to find somebody who might not necessarily be racist, but it just might happen. They might not know they're doing it, but it's going to happen to you sometime.

One young woman stated that racism no longer existed and a small proportion of the 31 informants thought they had never experienced racism personally. One of these girls described a type of experience that made her uncomfortable, though she didn't describe it as racist:

Like in classes, we're watching a movie and they start a racist move [in the movie] and then I'm the only black in there. I might feel like I'm on the spot, but, other than that, no, I have not really experienced racism.

Most of the young women attached the meaning of racism to behaviors they had encountered from others, witnessed on television, or observed in society in general. Each story was unique. Here are samples of other stories that showed the discrimination to which these young women were subjected.

The audiences were pretty good where our school group went to perform. There was only one place that we went that I really felt bad about because two of the [white] guys did solo and the crowd was really appreciative and clapped and everything, and then I did mine and there was no sound. There was no sound, nothing. I don't know if I was the only one that noticed, but they didn't say anything about it. I told my mom, and she said, 'Well, some people are like that.'

My friends and I will go to the mall and we'll go in a store and there will be like maybe a group of white girls going in the store, too, but the people, they won't say anything to them at all, but they'll come over to us and start bugging us. Do we need any help and follow us around the store while we look at every single thing. It's not in all stores, but a few and sometimes they do that and it just like makes us mad.

They [store clerks] tell me different things like I can go home now and there is still some people when you go to pay for something, they don't want to touch your hand so they put it [money] down.

We have been friends since third grade and people tend to look at her more because she has long hair and lighter complexion skin and stuff. I never really wished for lighter skin even though I know people are more attracted to that. I have some light complexion skin friends that would rather be dark, and it is just sometimes, the lighter skinned black people in the consolidated school district were treated better than the dark skin people.

Despite these experiences of prejudice and discrimination, most of the young women were steadfast in their racial pride:

I am proud that I am black. It is different. To me, it is good. I am liking how blacks are starting to move up in the world. I like seeing blacks. Like when I went to Georgia, I saw blacks carrying brief-cases, and I never really had seen that before.

These young women, then, are sorting the racial meanings of the behaviors of others, behaviors that cause them concern. Combined with their struggle to understand the implications of gender, their experiences of racism and race-related behaviors of others creates problematic situations for them. These girls are young, and, therefore, how their interpretations of racial and gendered meanings will affect them over their lifetimes is not known. What is clear is that these young people are grappling daily with stresses engendered by race and sex stratification systems.

Race and Gender: The Double Whammy

Many of the young women clearly saw challenges and pitfalls in being black and female, both groups that historically have held subordinate social locations in U.S. society. One young woman called it a double whammy. Others talked about being at the bottom of the social echelon:

I'm a black female and black females are the lowest. The black female has a hard time, for one, because she's black, two, because she's a female, and I think it would take more for me to strive to get what I want than if I was a white female or black male.

One young woman named the biggest challenges of being a black woman were getting a job and finding a husband of African-American descent. She talked about African-American women going to college in larger numbers than men, affecting how the women and men get along and creating a scarcity of desirable and favorable mates. A great deal of research suggests that hui concern is reality-based. Finding husbands can be problematic for many African-American women (South, 1993).

For many girls, employment in the adult world was the overriding concern. Several compared themselves to white women. The following is an example.

> Getting a job would probably be my biggest challenge as a black female. It seems like they always underestimate us. They probably don't feel that we can do it. They know we went through college or whatever, but they feel that we still can't meet the needs that they have. I will have to work harder to prove a point.

Besides employment, the second major concern of the girls was living with the expectations of others. One young woman succinctly stated that her biggest challenge was "to voice my opinions and to be taken seriously." Like other adolescents described in such studies as Brown and Gilligan (1992), this young woman was struggling not to be silenced by social expectations related to age, gender, and race. Another informant appeared to be struggling against the stereotype that adolescent African-American girls are likely to have out-of-wedlock babies. For her, avoiding pregnancy was one of her biggest challenges:

> To stay out of statistics, being pregnant before I have done something. Like the most sensible talk I have heard about not getting pregnancy is from my grandfather. My mother says, 'I don't regret having you, but it's just like it's not something you want to do to start a family so early.' I sat down and I had a talk with my grandfather. I guess she had told him about some feelings I was having for the guy I settled down with for a year. He [grandfather] said I had a lot going for me and I was bound for great things, but why make a clone of myself before I have done anything? It was, like, it really sunk in. I will clone myself after I have done everything, instead of cloning myself now while I am still young.

In this case, the expectations of her family fit well with her own ambitions. The fears her family expressed, however, not only were conditioned by her mother's own experience of adolescent motherhood, but possibly also by a society-wide stereotype of African-American female adolescents: young, black, and pregnant.

Socio-Economics, Gender, and Race

When the young women talked about gender and race issues, they personalized their answers more readily than when talking about socioeconomic status. They attached personal meanings to behaviors they experienced as related to being young women and African-American, but they frequently generalized their answers to the total society when talking about socioeconomic status. Of course, many of these young women were not poor, though they had insight about poverty and showed empathy for those who were poor. A few discussed their personal experiences with poverty. Their perspectives supported Hooks' (1984) view that class is more than disposable income; it involves behaviors, judgments of others about personal worth, and basic assumptions about one's place in the world.

> I feel that the poor do want to get better, but they are not getting too far because if they get up they are going to get stepped on and be right back down. I think that most poor people are still poor because every time they take an inch they get pushed back down two inches.

This young woman appears to be responding to a major theme about the poor: that they are satisfied with their lot and want to live off taxpayers' money.

Others thought of poverty as part of a class struggle. The following is a representative quote.

> I think they take more from the poor than they do from the rich. That's why the poor don't really go nowhere because the rich already have it all and they are not giving any.

Often the young women strongly defended poor people against prevalent stereotypes:

> People lose out on opportunities because they are in certain classes. People have a lot of potential. There are a lot of students that I have known in what you would call the lower class and a lot of people I have known and they have so much potential. But because they are in a lower class, they're not well-dressed. The girls don't have earrings to match every outfit or shoes to match, and then they would be discriminated against. People would say they are not worth it.

Two girls talked about personal experiences with rich kids at school, bragging and flashing their money. One young woman talked about feeling put down by a rich peer at her church. Others noted socioeconomic class differences in peer relationships. The following is an example.

> A lot of us blacks live in one part of town and I know there are some blacks that live in the other part of town, but I heard all of those say that being she lives down here, we thought we'd be with you, and they have another set of friends who are rich, but it seems that they think we have more fun because we don't have a lot of money. We just go out and spend it and waste it, but we're always together.

My sense is that these young women were strongly affected by the stigma of being black and poor, even though they themselves were not poor. They identified with and had strong feelings about what they perceived to be unfair portrayals of poor people.

Comparisons with Mothers

When the young women talked about the differences between themselves and their mothers, most said their lives were better than their mothers' in terms of income and social class. They expressed a great deal of admiration for their mothers' grit in doing well despite great odds. As one young woman said:

> I admire my mother because I have seen where she used to live and she used to live in the projects. When I was younger, we used to go over there, but I never really thought about it. So, one day it clicked in my mind. This is where poor people live!

This young person did not identify herself as poor and one day realized that her mother had grown up poor.

Sympathy for the hardships their mothers experienced also pervaded the accounts. Some of the mothers grew up in the South and migrated north and west while teenagers and young adults. Their daughters often had a deep understanding of their mothers' experiences. This is what a young woman said:

> My mom grew up with her grandparents because her mother had a lot of other kids, so my grandparents and her grandparents were farmers. They were sharecroppers and she didn't have a lot of opportunities like I do. They were very, very strict with her. She didn't have the freedom I have and missed out on a lot of good times in her life. She had to take care of the kids and go out and work on the farm. She had to get up real early in the morning and walk to school.

In addition, the informants in this study believed they would have more choices than their mothers about whether or not they would be employed outside of the home when they married. They realized that their own mothers and grandmothers were forced by economic pressures to have paid employment. These assumptions are supported by the research of Herring and Wilson-Sadberry (1993), who found that economic pressures were much stronger in the past in determining the labor force participation of African-American women.

Families of Origin

Most of the girls experienced their families as supportive and providing guidance, regardless of their family's income. There were comments like, "my parents do everything in their power to make us happy." Given the challenges posed by being African-American and being female, their families may be key to whether or not they achieve their vocational and personal goals. On the whole, these young women experienced their families as supportive and providing models of behavior that they wanted to emulate. One young woman said:

> We all help each other. That's why I have to share my room since my sister came back. My younger sister is eight and a half and she's going to summer school and we all try to help her. I do pretty good in school, but my brother is not as good and I try to help him out. Since my older sister goes to summer school, I stay and watch my nephew. The most important thing is staying with my family.

Religious practices were an important component of family supportiveness for some young women:

> My mom prays and we get together at night before we go to sleep. Some people think it is kind of corny, but we say prayers before we go to bed at night. I think it is part of the reason I have done so well.

Parents as devoted and wanting the best for them came through powerfully in some interviews. The following is an example.

> My mother is a fine lady. She done raised six kids and raised us pretty well without a father. She's like a father and mother to us and she wants us to achieve what she didn't achieve. She didn't finish high school. She wants us to finish high school and college to make something out of ourselves.

Fathers often were confidants and sources of inspiration.

> I am really close to my dad and he is really a nice person for some-
> one to talk to. He doesn't always listen, but I am pretty sure he
> understands me. He thinks he knows me like a book, but we are just
> exactly alike. And I know him like a book.

These quotes provide a picture of the family experiences of well-functioning African-American adolescent women. Assumptions about young
African-Americans can be distortions of the actualities. These young
women experienced love and support in their families of origin, and their
families of origin no doubt have given them what they have needed and
will need to deal with the daily challenges posed by inequalities linked to
race and sex-stratified systems.

DISCUSSION

The purpose of this study was to broaden the information base on
African-American adolescent young women by analyzing their insights
and opinions to determine their perceived social location. Why is it important to know about their perceptions about gender, race, and class as it
relates to their social location? First, gender, race, and class are powerful
constructs in determining a person's social location and quality of life
(Dill, 1983; Higginbotham, 1992). Second, understanding how social processes are interpreted by these young women helps in understanding the
range of perceptions, expectations, and experiences of young African-
American women. From a broader societal context, Hooks (1989) asserted
that scholarship can effect cultural change and have an impact on public
policy. Research on African-American adolescent women has the potential
for providing decision makers with knowledge to support the aspirations
and reduce the difficulties faced by growing numbers of youth from non-
European backgrounds (Schorr, 1988).

The conclusions of this study are not drawn from a representative
sample of African-American adolescent females, nor can the results be
generalized in a statistical sense to a larger population. Yet, their individual stories are powerful and can illuminate the lives of other young women
of color and provide valuable insights for policy makers, program devel-
opers, and those who work directly with youth.

The massive amounts of data generated by this type of research create
dilemmas for researchers and perhaps more so for new researchers who

often are flying by the seat of our pants. We read books and articles about how to do qualitative research, but we really are feeling our way along. Many contemporary qualitative researchers may be in this situation. That I am not alone is a consolation. I worry, though. I worry whether I was accurate in my interpretations. I tell myself that I had to have some understanding of the research participants in order to gain entree into their worlds. This increased the likelihood that I could accurately describe and interpret the perceptions of my informants. The qualitative methodology employed in this study gave entree into the unstructured thoughts and emotions of these young women. On the other hand, despite the relative lavishness of the quotes in this article, I am left feeling as if I know much more than I can ever tell.

REFERENCES

Butler, A. (1990). A content analysis of education and social science research related to young African-American females. *Dissertation Abstracts International, 52/011, 128A.* (University Microfilms No. 91-14911.)

Brown, Lyn Mikel & Carol Gilligan (1992). *Meeting at the crossroads: Women's psychology and girls' development.* Cambridge, MA: Harvard University Press.

Daly, K. (1992). The fit between qualitative research and characteristics of families. In J. Gilgun, K. Daly, & G. Handel (Eds.), *Qualitative methods in family research.* (pp. 3-11). Newbury Park, CA: Sage.

Dill, B. (1983). Race, class, and gender: Prospects for an all-inclusive sisterhood. *Feminist Studies, 9,* 131-150.

Ferree, M. (1990). Beyond separate spheres: Feminism and family research. *Journal of Marriage and the Family, 52,* 866-884.

Giddings, P. (1984). *When and where I enter: The impact of black women on race and sex in America.* New York: Bantam.

Gilgun, J. F. (1994). A case for case studies in social work research. *Social Work, 39,* 371-380.

Glaser, B. & Strauss, A. (1967). *The discovery of grounded theory: Strategies for qualitative research.* Chicago: Aldine.

Gorelick, S. (1991). Contradictions of feminist methodology. *Gender and Society, 5,* 459-477.

Harding, S. (1987). Introduction: Is there a feminist method? In S. Harding (Ed.), *Feminism and methodology* (pp. 1-14). Bloomington, IN: Indiana University Press.

Herring, C., & K. Wilson-Sadberry (1993). Preference or necessity? Changing work roles of black and white women, 1973-1990. *Journal of Marriage and the Family, 55,* 314-325.

Hewitt, J. (1988). Determinants of career choice: Women elementary teachers' perspective on the elementary principalship. *Dissertation Abstracts International, 51/02*, 360. (University Microfilms No. 90-16524.)

Higginbotham, E. (1981). Is marriage a priority? Class differences in marital options of educated black women. In P. Stein (Ed.), *Single life* (p. 262). New York: St. Martin's.

Higginbotham, E. (1992). African-American women's history and the metalanguage of race. *Signs: Journal of Women in Culture and Society, 17*, 251-274.

Hooks, B. (1981). *Ain't I a woman: Black women and feminism.* Boston: South End Press.

Hooks, B. (1984). *Feminist theory: From margin to center.* Boston: South End Press.

Hooks, B. (1989). *Talking back.* Boston: South End Press.

Hooks, B. (1990). *Yearning: Race, gender, and cultural politics.* Boston: South End Press.

Ladner, J. (1972). *Tomorrow's tomorrow: The black woman.* Garden City, NY: Doubleday.

Ladner, J. (1987). Introduction to *Tomorrow's tomorrow: The black woman.* In S. Harding (Ed.), *Feminism and methodology* (pp. 74-83). Bloomington: Indiana University Press.

Lorde, A. (1984). *Sister outsider.* New York: The Crossing Press Feminist Series.

Marshall, C. (1981). Organizational policy and women's socialization in administration. *Urban Education, 16*, 205-231.

McAdoo, H. (Ed.) (1988). *Black families* (2nd ed.) Newbury Park, CA: Sage.

McIntosh, P. (1989). White privilege: Unpacking the invisible knapsack. *Peace and Freedom*, July/August, 10-12.

Mies, M. (1983). Towards a methodology for feminist research. In G. Bowles and B. Klein (Eds.), *Theories of women's studies* (pp. 117-139). London: Routledge & Kegan Paul.

Oakley, A. (1981). Interviewing women: A contradiction in terms. In H. Roberts (Ed.), *Doing feminist research.* London: Routledge & Kegan Paul.

Okin, S. *Justice, gender, and the family.* New York: Basic Books.

Olsen, C. (1993). The perceptions of African American adolescent females about their social location in the world in relation to gender, race, and class. *Dissertation Abstracts International, 54/02*, 443. (University Microfilms No. 93-16747.)

Reinharz, S. (1992). *Feminist methods in social research.* New York: Oxford University Press.

Schorr, L. (1988). *Within our reach: Breaking the cycle of disadvantage.* New York: Doubleday.

Scott, K. (1991). *The habit of surviving: Black women's strategies for life.* New Brunswick, NJ: Rutgers University Press.

Scott-Jones, D., & Clark, M. (1986). The school experiences of black girls: The interaction of gender, race, and socioeconomic status. *Phi Delta Kappan, 67*, 520-526.

Smith, B. (1983). Introduction. In B. Smith (Ed.), *Home girls: A black feminist anthology* (pp. xix-lvi). New York: Kitchen Table, Women of Color Press.

Smith, P. (1994). Talking back: Life stories of nine African-American school administrators. Paper presented at the meeting of the Women in Educational Administration Conference, Lincoln, NE.

South, S. J. (1993). Racial and ethnic differences in the desire to marry. *Journal of Marriage and the Family, 55*, 351-370.

Zinn, M., & Eitzen, D. (1987). *Diversity in American families.* New York: Harper & Row.

Mama Still Sparkles:
An Elder Role Model in Long-Term Care

Helen Q. Kivnick
Heidi L. Jernstedt

SUMMARY. This case study is part of a larger, ongoing project that considers exemplars to explore successful aging among individuals who require some form of long-term care. The project departs from narrow, decontextualized operationalizations of successful aging to begin to develop holistic conceptualizations that involve the daily, multifaceted lives of elders in their families. The project also departs from the dominant misery perspective that emphasizes deficits, illness, and decline in old age. Instead, it contributes to developing a resource perspective that seeks to maximize human adaptation, assets, and skills in later life. This project seeks to understand the dynamics and spirit of successful aging, as this process is illustrated by individual elders who are, in spite of severe disability and the need for ongoing services, identified by their colleagues as role models, as exemplars of successful aging. *[Article copies available for a fee from The Haworth Document Delivery Service: 1-800-342-9678. E-mail address: getinfo@haworth.com]*

KEYWORDS. Elder role models, Life cycle theory, Qualitative research, Gerontology, Long-term care

---

Helen Q. Kivnick is Associate Professor, and Heidi L. Jernstedt is a master's degree student, School of Social Work, University of Minnesota, Twin Cities, 386 McNeal Hall, St. Paul, MN 55108.

[Haworth co-indexing entry note]: "Mama Still Sparkles: An Elder Role Model in Long-Term Care." Kivnick, Helen Q., and Heidi L. Jernstedt. Co-published simultaneously in *Marriage & Family Review* (The Haworth Press, Inc.) Vol. 24, No. 1/2, 1996, pp. 123-164; and: *The Methods and Methodologies of Qualitative Family Research* (ed: Marvin B. Sussman, and Jane F. Gilgun) The Haworth Press, Inc., 1996, pp. 123-164. Single or multiple copies of this article are available for a fee from The Haworth Document Delivery Service [1-800-342-9678, 9:00 a.m. - 5:00 p.m. (EST). E-mail address: getinfo@haworth.com].

123

Empirical research has explored successful aging in terms of such variables as stamina (Colerick, 1985), life-satisfaction (Fisher, 1988), self-concept (McClelland, 1982), functional independence (Roos & Havens, 1991), and longevity (Vaillant, 1991), identified largely from a misery perspective of old age (Tornstam, 1992) that emphasizes deficits, illness, and decline (Albert, 1987). Sherman (1993) calls for a resource perspective on aging, for an approach that emphasizes assets and positive adaptation. Nonetheless, empirical research conducted from this perspective operationalizes "resources" in terms of such variables as physical health (House et al., 1992; Revicki & Mitchell, 1990), socio-economic status (House et al., 1992; Wykle & Musil, 1993) and social support (Dean, Kolodny, & Wood, 1990; Revicki & Mitchell, 1990). Whether the underlying perspective emphasizes misery or resources, decline or adaptation, each of the above operationalizations represents only a single, decontextualized element of successful aging. Measuring these variables one at a time does little, either to relate them to one another or to use them to construct an appropriately rich, complex, comprehensive understanding of the overarching process of successful aging.

Successful aging is not congruent to a freedom from dependence, as implied by Roos and Havens (1991), or to life satisfaction, as suggested by Caspi and Elder (1986). It is more. We know that it includes the vitality, the grit, the underlying purpose (Nadelson, 1990) and commitment to values that constitute the infinite resource of the human spirit. Throughout life, this spirit sparkles in the people and relationships that inspire us to keep trying. It is what permits a pair of professional, middle-aged women to care for their 85-year-old mother-in-law—suddenly blind and reluctantly transplanted from the rural South to the urban North—and, somehow, to have them all draw strength from the process. It is what lets the 92-year-old granddaughter of a slave remain active in her church and maintain a long-held clerical position despite nearly crippling arthritis. As individual elders, as family members and professional caregivers, and as a whole society, we must understand the dynamics and spirit of successful aging, nurture them, and learn to use them to fullest advantage.

THEORETICAL BACKGROUND

The project is grounded in the theoretical framework of Erik Erikson (1950) as reinterpreted and revised by Erikson, Erikson, and Kivnick (1986). In its original—and still most widely disseminated—interpretation, this theory describes psychosocial development as a lifelong, epigenetic process. From Infancy through Old Age, the individual is discussed as moving through eight life stages, engaging successive thematic conflicts. Each stage is directed toward resolving one particular conflict; each stage's resolution becomes the foundation for subsequent development (Hubley & Hubley, 1976). Several major problems limit the usefulness of this original interpretation in understanding successful aging.

Dynamic Balance of Opposites

In its original interpretation, development is conceptualized in terms of a battle between the syntonic and dystonic tendencies of a theme (e.g., Integrity *vs.* Despair). Healthy thematic resolution is traditionally described as a victory of the syntonic tendency over the dystonic, i.e., a destruction of the dystonic by the syntonic. Thus, healthy resolution of Old Age's conflict between Integrity and Despair would essentially require the elimination of Despair by a well-developed sense of Integrity. As Erikson et al. discovered in their study of vitality and involvement in later life (1986), this interpretation is so greatly oversimplified as to be outright wrong. Later life is a period characterized by inevitable physiological deterioration. Even among the healthy aged, the strength and endurance peaks of earlier adulthood sink. Sensory acuity diminishes. Social, political, and technological changes add elements of strangeness and unpredictability to the world our elders once learned to understand as familiar. Old friends face the prospect of losing one another to death or major geographic moves. Long-time partners confront widowhood and its attendant grief and loneliness. Individuals face the fear of helplessness and dependence. All of these events are expectable. All are reasonable causes for despair, and to suggest that psychosocial health in Old Age somehow requires their subordination to an acceptance of the more distant past is tantamount to prescribing widespread denial.

As clarified by the principle of Dynamic Balance of Opposites (Erikson et al., 1986; Kivnick, 1993), healthy resolution of the tension between Integrity and Despair does not imply the elimination of Despair. Rather, it requires the development of a robust sense of Integrity *together with* an also realistic sense of Despair. Indeed, around each psychosocial theme, at every stage in the life cycle, healthy development requires an essential capacity for the syntonic tendency, *in dynamic balance with* an also essential capacity for the opposing, dystonic tendency. Understanding successful aging must therefore involve an understanding of conventionally recognized healthy processes of reflection, acknowledgement, and coming to terms, as these processes are related to the discouragement and dissatisfaction conventionally seen as unacceptable.

Process in Time

A second major problem with the traditional presentation of Erikson's theory is the misunderstanding that each developmental stage represents a window of opportunity for resolving one particular psychosocial focal theme. Adequate or inadequate, so this common misunderstanding goes, thematic resolution is essentially frozen at the end of the relevant developmental period. We enter each new stage armed with the quality of our cumulative resolutions of earlier conflicts; our ability to resolve new conflicts depends wholly on this quality. Not only does this interpretation imply that inadequate resolution in early stages necessarily predetermines developmental difficulties throughout the rest of life. And not only does it imply that adequate resolution of an early-focal theme, e.g., Autonomy and Shame/Doubt, eliminates the need for subsequent concern with this theme. This interpretation also implies that the major goal of old age–a period now regarded as lasting from 20-40 years or more–is limited to coming to terms with the past. When Old Age was a stage reached by a few, hardy elders and enjoyed by these survivors for a few short years before death, this interpretation may have been accurate. However, we now live in an era in which average life expectancies are 78.2 years for women and 72.1 years for men (Wadhera & Strachan, 1993), in which women and men who reach 65 years of age are likely to live 19 and 15 more years, respectively (Aronson, 1994). It hardly makes sense to think about a period of 15-40 years–even though they may be the final 15-40 years–of a lifetime as focusing, monolithically, on the personal past.

The process variously referred to as anticipating and renewing, as previewing and reviewing, and as preworking and reworking (Erikson et al., 1986; Kivnick, 1993), addresses this problem. According to this process, all eight psychosocial themes are operational at every stage in the life cycle. While the focal psychosocial theme may dominate experience during a particular stage, the individual is, during this very same stage, simultaneously involved in reviewing thematic balances and renewing them in an age-appropriate way, for all those themes that are no longer focal. In addition, the individual is also involved in anticipating, in age-appropriate, rudimentary terms, all those psychosocial themes which will become focal at a future period in the life cycle (see Figure 1).

Although the original misunderstanding confines psychosocial development to the eight boxes that constitute the ascending diagonal line in Erikson's familiar chart, this process of anticipating and renewing makes clear that psychosocial process takes place in all 64 boxes of the chart. Each life stage or period is represented by one row of the chart; stage names appear along the left axis of Figure 1. The box that sits on the

FIGURE 1. Psychosocial Stages of Life*

Stage	1	2	3	4	5	6	7	8
Older Adulthood	57	58	59	60	61	62	63	64 Integrity & Despair. WISDOM
Middle Adulthood	49	50	51	52	53	54	55 Generativity & Self-Absorption. CARE	56
Young Adulthood	41	42	43	44	45	46 Intimacy & Isolation. LOVE	47	48
Adolescence	33	34	35	36	37 Identity & Confusion. FIDELITY	38	39	40
School Age	25	26	27	28 Industry & Inferiority. COMPETENCE	29	30	31	32
Play Age	17	18	19 Initiative & Guilt. PURPOSE	20	21	22	23	24
Toddlerhood	9	10 Autonomy & Shame/Doubt. WILL	11	12	13	14	15	16
Infancy	1 Basic Trust & Basic Mistrust. HOPE	2	3	4	5	6	7	8

*Adapted from Vital Involvement in Old Age; used with permission from W.W. Norton & Co.

127

familiar ascending diagonal represents the focal psychosocial theme. In any row, the boxes to the left of the diagonal represent those themes that are no longer focal, and are, during the period in question, being renewed, reviewed, and rebalanced. Similarly, the boxes to the right of the diagonal represent those themes that have yet to become focal, as they are currently being anticipated, previewed, and preworked in age-appropriate, anticipatory form.

Thus, Old Age's focus on balancing Integrity with Despair is inextricable from this period's simultaneous involvement in rebalancing those themes that have passed their time of ascendancy. They must now be renewed in terms of the issues and circumstances of later life. We must therefore understand successful aging not only in terms of balancing a sense of Integrity with an opposing sense of Despair. We must understand successful aging *also* in terms of renewing age-appropriate balances around the other seven psychosocial themes: Trust and Mistrust; Autonomy and Shame/Doubt; Initiative and Guilt; Industry and Inferiority; Identity and Confusion; Intimacy and Isolation; Generativity and Self-Absorption.

A related problem concerns a misunderstanding of Erikson's theory as entirely developmental, i.e., as focusing entirely on an individual's progress through one stage and then another, over the entire life course. Although the theory *does* clearly address these issues, in its revised form it *also* addresses issues of the thematic psychosocial dynamics that take place within each and every stage of the life cycle. The theory considers both psychosocial development over time, and also the dynamics of psychosocial functioning at any one point in time. Thus, this theory may, indeed, be expected to contribute to our understanding of the overall life course of an individual whom we, today, identify as an elder role model. Equally important, the theory may be expected to enhance our understanding of the ways this elder experiences his/her contemporary life in terms of all eight psychosocial themes. That is, this theory provides a useful conceptual framework for understanding the current psychological and social dynamics of an elder role model in long-term care.

Vital Involvement

While Eriksonian themes are most often understood as referring to underlying predispositions, attitudes, and feelings, Erikson et al. articulated the principle of Vital Involvement to illustrate that this theory can serve to provide a scaffolding for understanding the broadest spectrum of human behavior (1986). A theme and its associated psychosocial work may, indeed, be reflected in internal affect and unconscious process. But each theme is also inextricable from the behaviors through which the individual expresses involvement with the people, materials, living things, ideas, relationships, institutions, and more, that constitute the "social" world that gives "psychosocial" development such an important part of its meaning.

In summary, revised Erikson theory holds that healthy resolution of each psychosocial theme rests on a dynamic balance of the thematic syntonic *and* dystonic tendencies. The theory also holds that regardless of when in the life cycle any psychosocial theme is focal, all eight themes are operational, in one way or another, at each stage of the life cycle. Thus, Old Age's struggle to balance Integrity with Despair is inseparable from the process of reviewing, reworking, and renewing *the seven earlier psychosocial themes*. Finally, the theory holds that all behaviors, attitudes, and feelings may be understood as reflecting thematic psychosocial process. Thus, the revised Erikson theoretical framework usefully encompasses the whole of human functioning. It can meaningfully accommodate all information, concerning any life period, about a particular respondent, and it can suggest a thematic understanding of the unique pattern of strengths and weaknesses that constitute the respondent's psychological and social adjustment in old age.

The Elder Role Models in Long-Term Care project makes two major theoretical contributions to the field of successful aging. First, the project conceptualizes successful aging in the context of the entire life cycle. The researchers have been concerned not only with the lives of our respondents today, in later life, but also with their earlier lives. That is, the project has considered the earlier-life experiences, lessons, and relationships that have prepared respondents to live as the elder role models they are today. Second, the project conceptualizes successful aging in terms of thematic psychosocial process. Such conceptualization permits the comparison of exemplars to one another on specific dimensions, and the contribution of understanding derived from each exemplar to an overall body of knowledge.

In addition, this project makes a theoretical contribution to our fundamental understanding of thematic psychosocial process. Qualitative research is often described as effective at creating rather than testing theory (Kirk & Miller, 1986). Indeed, a major strength of qualitative strategies is the extent to which findings, both theoretical and substantive, are grounded in the data (Patton, 1990). Researchers must not misinterpret this essential strength as a requirement that all theory-focused qualitative research generate new theory. Qualitative work is also extremely effective at building, refining, and elaborating theory that has already been created. Rather than starting from scratch, such theory-building research analyzes

data in terms of already existing concepts and categories in an attempt to
clarify their boundaries, their substructures, and their patterns of inter-rela-
tionship, and to identify additional concepts and categories. Constant comparison in data analysis constitutes an ongoing test of the validity of
theoretical development. Theoretical development, in turn, provides an
ever more useful tool for analyzing and understanding the data. Engaging
this iterative process permits this project to contribute to our understanding of successful aging, as discussed above. It also permits this project to
make a major contribution to the ongoing development of Eriksonian
theory.

METHOD

This project sought to understand successful aging among the recipients
of long-term care through comprehensive examination of a small number
of exemplars, i.e., of information-rich cases. Respondents are identified
using a purposeful sampling technique through which potential referral
sources are asked to identify elder long-term care recipients about whom
they would make one of the following observations: (1) "When I get to be
that age, I hope I'm very much like her/him"; or (2) "My mother/father is
having trouble being 80. I wish she/he could somehow learn what this
individual knows, and I know she/he would do much, much better"; or
(3) "Even though this individual is extremely frail and requires a great
deal of care and service simply to survive from day to day, somehow when
I leave her/him, I always feel uplifted or inspired." Referral sources are
individuals involved in the long-term care enterprise, either professionally
or personally. Each source is asked to explain why he/she views this
particular elder in this way. Wherever possible, a second referral source is
asked to confirm the first source's informal assessment of the elder.

From among identified elder role models in long-term care, respondents are selected to represent variation in age, gender, race, class, disability, living circumstances, life style, and specific life strengths. Underlying
this maximum variation sample is the logic that common patterns emerging from great variation are particularly valuable in capturing the central,
shared aspects, the core, of the phenomenon of interest (Patton, 1990). In
addition, this variation permits exploration of the breadth and range of
what it is, to be an elder role model in long-term care.

Data Gathering

This study uses a qualitative, interview-based research design, as is
particularly appropriate for work that delves in depth into complexities

and processes, and work that emphasizes the subjects' frames of reference (Marshall & Rossman, 1989). Interviews do not focus on "being inspiring" or on "being an elder role model," or even on being old or impaired. Rather, they focus on the respondent's entire life and reflections thereon, from his/her current vantage point. The interview process and attention to retrospective life story build on Butler's seminal work on life review (1963; 1980), on Birren and Deutchman's recent work on guided autobiography (1991), and on Coles' work on stories (1980). For each respondent, the interview process takes 3-5 sessions, lasting an average of two hours apiece. Each session is semi-structured in nature, as described below.

A detailed interview guide identifies a large number of issues each respondent is expected to address, concerning life experiences, events, circumstances, values, attitudes, and reflections from older adulthood, middle adulthood, early adulthood, adolescence, school age, play age, and before. The interview guide provides a variety of differently worded questions designed to tap each issue. For any given respondent, the process is seen as finished at saturation, i.e., when all issues in the interview guide have been addressed, and when material being raised largely repeats material already discussed.

The interviews are not–nor are they intended to be–identical across respondents. Rather, they rely on the interviewer's clinical skills and sensitivities to elicit comparable information across respondents. That is, rather than asking all respondents identical questions, the interviewer makes sure that all respondents discuss comparable issues. The tone of the interviews is neither formal nor scholarly. William Carlos Williams told the young Robert Coles, " 'Their story, yours, mine–it's what we all carry with us on this trip we take, and we owe it to each other to respect our stories and learn from them' " (Coles, p. 30). In eliciting information, the interviewer conveys precisely this respect for elders' stories; individuals respond very much in kind.

Often, respondents will move seamlessly from one topic to another, addressing several identified issues without the interviewer having to ask more than a single, introductory question. When respondents do not broach identified issues spontaneously, the interviewer must ask questions to elicit information. Addressing a particular issue by asking several differently worded versions of the same question allows the interviewer to explore each respondent's multiple perspectives. It also frequently gives the interviewer access to material that is not specifically identified in the guide but that is, clearly, of importance to the respondent. For example, a respondent may respond to a particular question with a long and heartfelt discussion of an issue quite different from the one the interviewer had hoped to tap. The interviewer follows the respondent's train of thought to its logical destination, noting connections between this unexpected material and the other issues discussed in the interview, Then the interviewer uses a different wording of the original question, in an attempt to return the respondent to the issue she had initially tried to tap. As patterns suggest themselves, the interviewer rewords the respondent's remarks in order to "check out" her understanding or interpretation of the ideas being expressed.

Occasionally a respondent will, in the process of trying to answer a question, begin to explore an issue that proves particularly–and often unexpectedly–painful. Although the interviewer is an experienced, licensed psychotherapist, and although this interview process bears some structural similarity to psychotherapy, the authors must emphasize that the interviewer maintains clear boundaries between these research, life-history interviews, on one hand, and psychotherapy sessions, on the other (Schein, 1987). In psychotherapy, the client is identified as having some kind of problem for which he/she seeks help from a paid professional. It is the responsibility of the professional to guide the "conversation" of therapy in such a way as to help the client meet his/her treatment needs, even if particular topics prove to be extremely painful and the client attempts to avoid them.

In this life-history research, by contrast, many of these circumstances are reversed. The elders are not therapy clients, identified on the basis of their problems. Rather they are research respondents, identified on the basis of their strengths. The Investigator seeks out the elders. At her request, they agree to be interviewed in order to help meet her scientific goals. The researcher conducts an institutionally approved process of informed consent/protection of human subjects, informing each elder, at the outset and in writing, of the procedures, goals, possible dangers, and anticipated benefits of involvement. The researcher thus incurs an ethical responsibility to use her professional skills to protect respondents from dangers both foreseen and unexpected, and to maximize respondents' benefits from participating in the study. Rather than encouraging respondents to continue to explore painful issues, the interviewer provides every opportunity for respondents to bring such issues to meaningful closure and to move on.

Data Analysis

The data gathered through the interview process described above are characterized by the thick description that permits researchers to understand the world as seen by respondents. Data analysis comprises two major components, conducted roughly alternately for each respondent.

Component 1. All interviews are tape-recorded and then transcribed in their entirety. The research team conducts a thematic analysis of each protocol, using Erikson's psychosocial themes as sensitizing concepts, as discussed above. The team is experimenting with various software applications (e.g., FileMaker Pro; HyperRESEARCH) to mechanize and adapt the coding and charting procedure developed by Erikson et al. (1986). This procedure allows for the ultimate "translation" of nearly all of the interview material for each respondent into a 64-cell life-cycle chart, displaying each life event, behavior, feeling, etc., in terms of the life stage in which it occurred, and in terms of the psychosocial theme(s) it most powerfully expresses (see Figure 1). Analysis for each respondent yields a unique individual pattern of thematic psychosocial strengths and weaknesses as expressed over the entire life cycle, and in old age, in particular.

Data comprise up to 200 pages of transcript for each respondent. More than 75% of the material in each transcript is coded. In many qualitative studies, a relatively small proportion of each open-ended interview is ultimately coded as conceptually relevant to the focus of the research. For example, in Kivnick's (1993, 1987) study of the meaning of grandparenthood, although elder respondents were interviewed about older-, middle- and younger adulthood, and childhood, the researcher coded only those passages in each interview in which the respondent directly addressed the experience of grandparenthood. Observations like "My maternal grandmother was the light of my childhood," or "When I think of that little girl [granddaughter], I just have to stop what I'm doing and smile," were coded for subsequent analysis. Other observations that may be equally central to respondents' lives (e.g., "My mother taught me my earliest lessons about discrimination and tolerance, and she taught by example, not so much by preaching") were not analyzed because they did not directly concern the focus of that study. Since this study's theoretical foundation comprises psychosocial themes concerning the *entirety* of life's experience, essentially all of the material discussed by each respondent is conceptually relevant; it would be difficult to identify any behaviors, events, experiences, attitudes, or the like as conceptually irrelevant. Two general types of material are excluded from coding: (1) Verbatim (or nearly verbatim) repetitions of ideas that are not separated by an intervening thought; and (2) Lengthy descriptions of individuals, places, or objects. In addition, paragraphs of relevant description are occasionally paraphrased in condensed form and coded as such.

Each transcript is coded, independently, by the investigator and by a research assistant who has completed at least two years' training in this theoretical approach. Each coder identifies as a "data bit" every text passage that, either in terms of face value or in terms of our ever-deepening understanding of the respondent, describes a life experience, attitude, value, attribute, behavior, practice, event, circumstance, relationship, or any other meaningful life aspect. A bit may be as short as "Married at age 19," or as long as "Makes a point of teaching her daughters the traditional way of making her favorite Mexican dishes so that the dishes will not disappear with her death," or, in the case of long direct quotes, even longer. A bit may constitute a direct *quote,* a *summary* or observation based directly on the transcript, or a theoretical *interpretation* made by the coder. Each bit is clearly identified as one of these three types. To avoid forcing the data to "fit" the theory, appropriate bits are assigned multiple codes in this component of analysis, thereby insuring that each category includes the broadest range of applicable material. In fact, data are forcing expansion of the boundaries of each thematic category. Appropriate multiple coding of data also increases the likelihood of identifying meaningful links between categories, ultimately facilitating the development of a tightly woven theory rather than a weaker structure of isolated theoretical pillars.

Each data bit is coded according to two parameters: *(1) Expressing one or more of the eight psychosocial themes,* such as the statement "I worked hard in school. Everyone always knew me as a good student. I graduated from high school with honors" expresses the theme Industry and Inferiority. Depending on context and respondent, this statement may also express such additional themes as Identity and Confusion, and Intimacy and Isolation; and *(2) Relevant to one life stage or more.* Working hard in school is probably relevant to the life stages of School Age and Adolescence. Graduating from high school with honors is, unless a particular respondent is "off time," relevant to Adolescence. Data bits which are categorized within multiple themes are memoed, in order to clarify links between categories, as mentioned above.

Both coders meet to review the coding for each transcript, of each respondent. Coding uses the qualitative process of constant comparison (Corbin & Strauss, 1990), whereby each new item in a category (i.e., each new data bit in a theme) is compared to all the items that are already in the category. Bits that accumulate within each theme begin to support the development of abstract concepts and categories within the theme. Bits that differ greatly from other data in the theme or that do not fit into developing thematic subcategories are re-examined for possible recoding, or for reconceptualization of subcategories. Each discrepancy between the two coders (e.g., differently identified data bits; differently coded bits) is discussed thoroughly, until the two coders agree on a conceptualization.

For each elder role model in long-term care, this component of the analysis provides an overall, thematic psychosocial profile. Themes begin to surface as those in which this respondent has concentrated most of his/her energy, and in terms of which this person has experienced his/her world over the years. (Does this woman experience life primarily in terms of caring and being cared for? Does she meet new challenges by figuring out how to provide care, and secure necessary caring? Or does she rely more on ingenuity, meeting each new challenge by devising a uniquely appropriate strategy?) In addition, an understanding begins to emerge about the unique nature of the individual's strengths and weaknesses around each theme. (For example, one elder's strength around Intimacy and Isolation may rest on participation in a mutually rewarding, 60-year-long marriage. Another's strength in this same theme may be grounded in a satisfying network of old and new friendships with people of differing ages, interests, family circumstances, etc.) Finally, facing an elder's unique pattern of strengths, weaknesses, and life circumstances today in old age permits the reviewing of earlier life experiences for clues as to how he/she has been able to live a disabled old age in such an inspiring or remarkable way. (For example, what are the roots of the industriousness that drives a 92-year-old arthritic with a degenerative back condition to continue to work at a clerical job from which colleagues nearly thirty years her junior are choosing to retire?)

Component 2. The second component of data analysis constitutes an orientational approach (Patton, 1990) to inductive analysis (Charmaz, 1990; Corbin & Strauss, 1990) of each psychosocial theme. Starting with the analyzed data from the first respondent, and then comparing and revising based on the data for each new respondent, the research team has conducted an inductive analysis of the data bits that are categorized in each psychosocial theme. For example, the respondent discussed in this paper repeated, in her interviews, that she was never dependent on her husband because she had learned in childhood to be independent. This observation was thematically coded as Autonomy and Shame/Doubt and as Intimacy and Isolation. Within the "Autonomy and Shame/Doubt" theme, this observation has become part of a category currently referred to as Self-Reliance/Independence. Within the "Intimacy and Isolation" theme, this observation has become part of a category emerging as Spouse: Abstract attitudes/beliefs. Categories are subdivided, as warranted by the data that accumulate within conceptual labels. When appropriate, categories are also grouped into larger, more general categories, based on the content of their data. This analytic component has resulted in a network of concepts that constitutes the underlying theoretical structure of each psychosocial theme.

Data

This case study presents a thematic portrait of a particular elder role model. That is, the authors present the life story of Ana Martinez, an inspiring older Latino woman who, despite current disease, disability, and injury, continues to express the unique combination of caring, competence, and creativity that have long encouraged the devotion of her thirteen children, 59 grandchildren, and 41 great-grandchildren. And her story is presented in terms of eight psychosocial themes which give the story new shape and suggest new understanding, both of this woman's individual life and also of a particular style of successful aging in long-term care.

Case studies like this one allow the "ordinary great" (Nadelson, 1990) to serve as role models for their elder contemporaries, for the not-yet-old, and for practitioners and researchers in the fields of aging and family studies. In addition, the collection of case studies that constitute the overall project contribute substantially to our understanding of the underlying structure of a psychosocial, developmental theory that holds enormous promise for the practice and the study of aging and family life.

I first met Ana Martinez at a senior day health program in Minneapolis, where I had been scheduled to conduct a focus group with a group of participants, about values and preferences in later life.[1] Ana stood out in this group of her peers. A small woman confined to a wheelchair, she nonetheless seemed to be a source of encouragement and support for others in this group. Her hair is very black and curly. Her bright smile flashed so frequently that the smile lines never fully faded from her cheeks. Ana's hands are arthritic, and the last two fingers on each hand are frozen in a semi-extended position. Nonetheless, her nails are long and painted an eyecatching red. On that first day she wore a colorful, striped velour top and a heavy silver necklace. I could not see whether she wore slacks or a skirt, because her legs were covered with a carefully tucked blanket.

The group members knew one another well. Throughout the discussion, individuals confirmed each other's stories and reminded one another of forgotten details. But Ana's contributions were somewhat different from the others'. "You may say you stopped cooking after coming back from the nursing home," she told one woman, "but I remember that the very first day you were up boiling chicken and cutting vegetables." "It's not true that you've given up on crafts," she corrected another. "Just yesterday you were making ruffles for a basket." It was not so much that Ana was proving her friends wrong. Neither was it that she was besting them. Rather, she seemed to be reminding them that things were better than they felt at the moment, that they were stronger and abler than momentary despair would sometimes let them show. Finally one of the other women addressed Ana directly. "You know, you are the only reason I don't give up altogether. I am always in pain. And when I try to walk, every step hurts. But then I look at you, and I know you are in more pain than I am. And you can't even move out of your chair. And I know you can only use two fingers. But you always find something to smile about. And you are always making some new little thing and giving it away to make someone happy. So how could I quit?"

A few weeks later I phoned an administrator at this day health program, asking if she knew anyone she would call an elder role model in long-term care. I read off my three criteria. She interrupted before I finished the third. "We have one client who comes to mind immediately," she said. "I might be able to think of a few others, but this first woman is exactly what you're talking about. Upbeat. Energetic. Never feels sorry for herself. Always cheering other people up." It was Ana Martinez that had come to her mind.

Ana lives in a brightly painted, mustard yellow house in a working-class section of Minneapolis. On a block dominated by grey-green shingles and dirty white clapboard, her house shines like a beacon. She expresses pleasure with the way the color has brightened up the whole neighborhood.

Ringing the doorbell and knocking brought no-one to let me in. Peering through the window, I saw Ana in her wheelchair, working at a table. I knocked on the glass. She pointed at the door. Again I rang, knocked, and waited, and again no-one came. I went back to the window and knocked again. Again she pointed. We hollered back and forth for a while about the door being locked. After some time, a woman opened the door and gestured me inside. Ana introduced her as "my live-in."

Ana lives on the first floor of the house, which is crowded with belongings that must at one time have furnished several rooms. Shelves and cabinets display brightly painted ceramic vases, pots, and animals–interspersed with school photos of children of all ages–all the way up to the ceiling. Surfaces are piled with papers and children's books, with crocheted doilies, and with decorative baskets and pillows. Although an ornately carved television cabinet dominates one wall of the living room, a portable television blared in what must have once been a dining room.

Now Ana sleeps in that room, and a small bed is wedged between cabinets and clothes racks.

We set ourselves up in the living room. I cleared sitting space on a couch and crawled around to plug in the tape recorder while Ana wheeled her chair up to the coffee table that stood between us. She has attached a wooden slat to the arm of her wheelchair, which she uses as a flat surface for signing papers. As she signed the consent form, she explained that she does some paper work every day–bills, authorizations, coupons, and "all that stuff" and needs to be sure she can write whenever she needs to.

OVERVIEW

Older Adulthood

Ana's physical condition is worse than meets the eye. At 74, she has been in a wheelchair with arthritis for nearly 25 years. It was her knees that first put her in the chair. After four or five years she agreed to hip replacement surgery. "The doctors were after me . . . , and they told me that they could make me walk in three months. I kept on putting it off and putting it off. Finally, I decided, well, I better do something, because I still wanted to do the things that I was used to doing." Ana was dropped during a bed-to-chair transfer shortly after surgery, and the hip was severely injured. Infection set in and spread, and she ultimately lost a good deal of one side of her pelvis. The nurses never acknowledged having dropped her. There were no witnesses, and the hospital has never acknowledged responsibility for her condition.

Six months after the initial surgery, Ana returned home from the hospital minus one hip joint, permanently confined to a wheelchair. One leg " . . . is not connected. Just with my muscles and my nerves . . . I can never lift it." Since then, she has been far less mobile, and far more dependent, physically, than she had been before. "Even though I was in a wheelchair before, I still could do my personal care. I still could get in the tub and take a bath or get in the shower and take care of myself. Now I can't even do that . . . I was in my chair, but I could stand up and I could transfer." Now she must be washed and dressed. She must be lifted from chair to toilet, and back; for toileting emergencies she has learned to use a cleverly cut bleach bottle. She relies on a Hoyer lift to get her in and out of bed. She describes being in constant pain and engaging in an unending struggle to balance the relief of pain medication with the associated drugged helplessness that makes her feel "just like a zombie." She has recently developed a thyroid condition that requires daily medication.

Nonetheless, Ana fills each day with the activities that are most important to her. She has always felt most like herself when she is in the kitchen, cooking. Although her live-in aide prepares many of her daily meals, Ana has arranged her kitchen so that, with help, she can do a good deal of cooking from her wheelchair. She describes ongoing delight in preparing food to welcome her children and grandchildren when they come to visit. Since her family is large and she never quite knows who will drop in when, she makes sure she always has homemade Mexican treats on hand. Many older cooks train themselves to scale down the recipes from which they have always fed housefuls of hungry people; Ana has never made this accommodation. Although her children were launched decades ago, they and their families visit frequently and Ana still " . . . like[s] to cook *a lot* so that I have enough."

She has enjoyed handcrafts since childhood. Painting, ceramics, needlepoint, crocheting, embroidering, basketry and more have all, at one time or another, captured her fancy. At home Ana works primarily with needle and thread. She takes advantage of out-of-home daytime programs to engage in crafts that involve paints, clay, and other potentially messy materials. As she has for decades, she stays on top of her own legal and financial matters. Continuing to clip coupons for the sake of thrift remains a matter of stated pride.

Life History

Ana Martinez was born in 1918, in Dallas, Texas, into a family whose other children were already teen-agers and pre-teens. Her mother had come to this country from Spain as a child, and her father had come from Mexico as a young adult. When Ana was three, her parents were killed when a train crashed into the car in which they were riding. Ana and her next oldest sister were moved to New Mexico, where they lived with their aunts until they returned to Dallas four years later. From ages 8-12 Ana lived with her sister Maria's family. They all worked as migrants in Minnesota and South Dakota in the summer, and they helped run the sisters' Mexican restaurant in Texas when the Upper Midwest froze over each winter. Ana washed dishes. From the age of eight, she proudly recalls, she worked hard and pulled her own weight in this family enterprise. She also recalls having paid attention and used every experience as an opportunity to learn. She learned how to cook from watching her sisters, while she was washing dishes. She learned about picking sugar beets from watching the older migrants. She learned to sew, knit, crochet, and embroider while relaxing in the park with her sisters. She learned to sing and to play the guitar and the piano from listening to the radio. She learned Mexican dancing as part of family tradition. She learned child care from helping with her nieces and nephews.

When Ana was 12, the sisters sold the restaurant and moved permanently to the Twin Cities. She was 13 when she attended school for the first time. All along, she had been learning from her sisters to read, write, and do arithmetic in Spanish. She did well academically and was double-promoted three times. During adolescence she also sang and danced in a small Latino band, with a group of friends. The band did some touring and was well-received, and Ana dreamed of becoming a singer or a dancer.

She had to quit school after 11th grade, to get a full-time job. For several years she worked as a seamstress, using a heavy-duty power machine. Then she became a file clerk at the court house. Then she dusted crystal in a furniture store, worked in a packing house and in a foundry, sewed sacks for a flour company, served as a Floor Lady in an appliance store, ground hamburger and dressed chickens in a meat market, fixed drills on an assembly line, and, after the War, worked on an assembly line that manufactured toys.

Ana married at seventeen, a man she had met at church, and with whom she says she fell in love at first sight. Despite her dreams of performing, Ana quit the band when she got married. At the same time she abandoned hopes of returning to school.

Career dreams or aspirations notwithstanding, Ana had always assumed that she would stay home as a married woman and raise her children, and she says she had always counted on being a mother and wife, as her major roles in adult life. But financial circumstances required her to continue to work until the birth of her first child. Even as a mother, she started working again after only a few years, when the family needed money. For most of her childrearing years, she worked two jobs and then came home to cook and clean for the family.

Although she describes herself as never having been without a job, Ana describes her children as the focus of her life. She had always known she would be a mother, and she put more of herself into raising her children than into anything else. She smiles as she says, "My life was my kids' lives. They meant everything to me. . . . I enjoyed everything right from the beginning. I cuddled the little ones and went out with the older ones." She made sure their clothes were always clean and pressed. She gave them their haircuts. She took them to church each Sunday, and for ice cream or on picnics or fishing afterward. She loved caring for them, and she recalls how she loved teaching them things, and passing on life's important lessons.

Ten or 12 years into the marriage, Ana's husband began the drinking that would destroy their relationship. They divorced after roughly twenty years together. Ana had become close to an elderly couple, the Garcias, and after her divorce, she says, they took her in. They owned a restaurant, and she began to work for them in the evenings, after her day job. When Ana was just under forty, the Garcias retired, and she took over their restaurant. Here, she worked 18-hour days. But the place was hers. She talks of how it allowed her to carry on her family's "sister thing," to do the cooking that she loved, and to provide for her family while, at the same time, providing for the neighbors who were her customers. And it promised steady employment and income forever.

"A restaurant can't tell you how old you can be to do that," Ana says softly, and she would gladly have worked there until she died. However, chronic arthritis interfered. She worked through several years of increasing disability, until, at 50, she was told by her doctors that she could not work on her feet any more. Soon after she was confined to a wheelchair she sold the restaurant.

Ana and her children rely on one another. The children visit her frequently, and they take responsibility for her chores. They take her on day-long family outings and extended family vacations. Although Ana says that she can always call on them when she needs help, she is proud to add that they usually call and come and do whatever they can before she can even realize that she needs anything. For both children and grandchildren, she is a valued source of advice and comfort. She is proud to remain the family's emotional pillar.

At Christmastime, Ana's extended family rents a hall for their annual party. Despite her confinement and disabilities, she still tries to take responsibility for preparing the main dish. Giving hot tamales–by the dozen–is a holiday tradition in her family. Every year, Ana says, she makes tamales with a different one of her daughters. They work around the clock, making tens of dozens of tamales, so that they can give every family member a respectable portion.

These days, Ana goes to a day center several times a week. There she can be showered and have her hair washed. There, too, she can do the ceramics and, sometimes, the painting that are too messy to do at home. Perhaps most important, she says, the Center gives her an opportunity to see other people and to help cheer them up. Before her accident, she used to visit nursing homes and read to patients, or talk to them and fix their hair. And she used to volunteer assistance on a local cardiac unit. Now, she tells me, she ministers to her peers at the day center. She makes a point of saying something nice to someone she can tell is unhappy. She gives away little hand-painted ceramics and crocheted baskets. Indeed, the encouragement I saw her providing during that initial focus group is as characteristic as anything else, of the way Ana Martinez is living this period of her life.

PSYCHOSOCIAL PROFILE

Trust and Mistrust: Hope

Conceptual Summary.[2] From its earliest ascendancy at the beginning of the life cycle, the theme of Trust and Mistrust concerns the individual's reliance on a predictable, responsive environment, in balance with discriminating caution and skepticism about the realistic unpredictabilities and malignancies of that same environment. Individual heritage, demographics, and basic life circumstances constitute a stable foundation—that is shaken and must be re-established with each major circumstantial change. Rules and customs provide additional security. Routines, cultural practices, and religious behaviors and strictures all contribute to the sense of knowable reliability that informs daily conduct and that colors individual responses to the actions of others.

Religious participation and beliefs about God or a Supreme Being also express the individual's efforts to balance trust with suspicion, optimism with pessimism, calm expectancy with anxiety and fearfulness. Similarly, belief in spirits, superstitions, and the supernatural become part of the personal understanding of the world's predictability. Related to this spirituality are universal concerns (traditionally more powerful with increasing age) about the meaning of life and old age, and about the personal future and its connection with death.

Over the course of the life cycle, the process of establishing a personal view of self in relation to the vastness of time and space leads to the development of mature faith. This faith incorporates enduring, pervasive images from childhood. In turn, it supports those fundamental beliefs that are taught to the next generation, and that come, by the end of life, to constitute each individual's personal philosophy of life, and belief in the meaning of life.

Elder analyses: Current. Ana Martinez displays hope and optimism that seem startling in the face of the blows life has struck against these particular strengths. Her parents were killed when she was three. Her childhood was peppered with major moves and discontinuities. Money was never plentiful. Most recently, she was betrayed by the medical professionals to whose assurances she had subordinated her own realistic mistrust. The result of this decision is that she has been, for nearly twenty years, and will be for the rest of her life, far more disabled and in far more pain, with far less prospect of improvement than had been the case when nature was taking its own course. Understandably, she trusts neither physicians nor their recommendations and prescriptions. She trusts no-one but her son to transfer her, because she is afraid of being dropped.

For all this, Ana is, today, a woman of religious faith and good spirits. After the accident, she used to find herself thinking, "In a few days I'm going to get out of this wheelchair and start walking." Now she often repeats one of her aunt's sayings, "It's gloomy today, but it will be nicer tomorrow." And she finds ongoing security in knowing that all her thirteen children are nearby, in the Twin Cities, and that if she needs someone she ". . . can call and they will come right away." She has devised strategies for restoring a sense of security in the face of anxiety. She practices positive self-reflection, consciously responding to agitation by thinking of ". . . when I had better times . . . Good things [that] have really happened before. Good things that you did. Good deeds. You kind of say, 'Well, gee, I think it was pretty good,' and you kind of get out of it." When she is alone and hears noises, she turns her thoughts to the Lord and she is comforted. She relies on prayers to give her help in living, and she sees her relationship with the Lord as a major personal strength.

Elder Analysis: Historical. Despite its slings and arrows. Ana's life has involved a good deal of the structure, predictability, and responsiveness that are essential to basic trust. When her parents died, she and a sister went to live with aunts who cared for them well, who loved them, and whose homes ran according to the strict rules of religious practice and of secular propriety. Ana carries with her the memory of taking the train to New Mexico after her parents' death, of leaving her uncle in Texas and seeing ". . . those big wheels. They were so big to me, and all the smoke coming out, and I was scared." But life with her aunts was secure. And when she returned to Texas to live with her sister Maria, her life was much the same. Her experiences of fear are, most often, accompanied by reassurance and stability. She learned early that ". . . you just have to do with what you have, and there was no use thinking, 'I'm going to get this,' or, 'I'm going to get that,' when I knew I wasn't going to." She also learned that her life would be quite difficult, and it has been so. But it has been predictably so, and because of the predictability she has been able to develop the skills to adapt.

Ana grew up speaking Spanish as well as English, learning traditional Mexican songs, dances, and recipes, and obeying such social traditions as ". . . the younger ones couldn't go over the older. You had to mind her [the older sister]." Although she did not live in a household she would describe as middle class, Ana cannot think of her childhood as poor because "my sisters had restaurants," and "there was a lot of love in our family." For her, a family restaurant came to represent trust and security. The work was hard and unending. But the rewards were survival and a feeling of security. And the enterprise was infused with love.

Once she became a mother, the structure of Ana's life remained relatively stable. She had grown up looking forward to Sunday as the day for church and family, and she enjoyed creating that same predictability for her own children. She always worked. She knew she needed to have at least one job. And she knew she was a good enough worker that, "If I was laid off one place, I would go and the next day I had a [new] job." She cooked and cleaned and cared for her children. She had friends. She had activities. She had God. She had love. She still does.

Ana grew up with a familistic ideology characteristic of the working class in which she lived (Hareven, 1977; Laslett, 1972). Family members were expected to live, work, struggle, and–it is to be hoped–survive together.[3] Acting on this ideology, for Ana's sisters in her childhood, or for herself in adulthood, was far more a matter of course than of personal decision. And it is precisely this element of internalizing and then fulfilling expectation that has allowed Ana to draw the strength of basic trust from a set of extremely difficult life experiences.

Autonomy and Shame/Doubt: Will

Conceptual Summary. The tension between autonomy and shame/doubt is focal during the toddler's struggle to differentiate "self" from "not self," to control the physical body that is "self," and to exert the indirect control of will on that which is "not self." Toddlerhood's issues of walking and toilet training give way to childhood's concern with strength and coordination. Toddlerhood's separation and *rapprochement* become adolescence's independence and stubbornness, and adulthood's self-reliance, hesitation, and acceptance of help. Throughout life, the theme of Autonomy and Shame/Doubt concerns the body. It concerns capacities and limits. It concerns injuries, illnesses, and health. It concerns ability and helplessness, power and victimization. And it concerns boundaries–physical and emotional–and their capacity to contain the essential goodness or badness of what is within. Associated with every element of this theme is the notion of control, of determination. Who controls me? What and whom do I control? With whose suggestions and instructions will I comply? Whom and what will I oppose? With whom will I cooperate? How much assistance can I accept, and from whom, without somehow denying my fundamental control over my self and my destiny–without denying my essential self?

The process of development from infancy through adulthood is, in some ways, a chronicle of the increasing autonomy that accompanies heightened physical maturity and prowess. As development proceeds through older adulthood, physical prowess inevitably diminishes, and a new balance is required between independence and self-control, on one hand, and interdependence and cooperation, on the other. Although many cultures emphasize the importance of cooperation and responsible group membership through adulthood, our American mainstream places its highest value on self-reliance and independence. In such a culture, old age's deteriorations not only challenge physical independence and control. Far more serious, they may also threaten an essential sense of self.

Elder Analysis: Current. Since before she was 50, Ana's arthritis has seriously challenged her abilities to work for a living, to maintain her own home, and to carry on the capable, self-reliant life she had been establishing from childhood. "Ever since I was eight," she declares, "I was able to do housecleaning, wash dishes, and take care of children. . . . I learned how to be independent very young. My sister never had to do my laundry. I did it myself. We had to scrub. . . ." The arthritis required her to give up her career. The pain interfered with even minute activities, many times a day. But these challenges pale beside the injury she suffered after her hip replacement surgery, and her consequent lifelong disability, dependence, and often desperate feelings of helplessness. This is the theme in which Ana experiences more weaknesses than any other. Numerous times each day she is reminded of all the things she cannot do for herself. She cannot reach light switches. She cannot always feed herself. She needs help bathing and dressing. She needs help going in and out of the house, getting in and out of a car, going up and down the stairs.

Ana says she does not like having to depend on others for things she has always done for herself. She does not like to burden her children and grandchildren. Even less does she like having to depend on aides who come and go so often that they are rarely more than strangers, and with whom she finds herself engaging in annoying tests of will.[4] But she knows that accepting certain kinds of assistance is the *sine qua non* for maintaining the essential self-reliance and control which are still possible. And so she does. From minute to minute and from day to day, she doesn't call someone for help unless she has to. She does her own nails. She chooses her own clothes and jewelry each day. She has her hair dyed and she wears makeup, to present the physical appearance she chooses. She keeps her own financial records and does her own paperwork. She cuts coupons. She continues to do handicrafts. She signs her own name. She keeps children's books and toys where she and the great-grandchildren can use them without having to involve anyone else. She keeps canned goods and spices in the kitchen, in places where she can reach many of them without assistance. Even now, she says, "I can cook by myself if I have to."

Elder Analysis. Historical. Ana tells me that she learned early to cope with life, to take things as they come, and to depend on herself. There was much in her life about which she had no choice. She did not choose to become an orphan at three, or to become a seasonal migrant worker at eight. She would have liked to finish school, or stay home with her children, but she felt she had no choice. She would certainly have liked to remain strong and healthy, but about this, too, she had no choice. She learned early that she could rely on herself to meet the challenges she wished she didn't have to confront in the first place. And she learned that she could survive in good spirits, whatever the circumstances called for. These capacities continue to serve her well.

Initiative and Guilt: Purpose

Conceptual Summary. After Toddlerhood's focus on exercising capacity simply in order to demonstrate control, the Play-age child attends to using capacities for the purpose of accomplishing goals. The activity of walking ceases to be primarily an expression of body control and coordination, and it becomes a means of moving from here to there most efficiently, or a basis for learning to run, to climb, to dance. Throughout life, the sense of initiative involves curiosity, creativity, and ingenuity. But these expansive tendencies must be balanced by the anticipatory guilt that becomes the capacity for self-restraint. Over the life cycle, the individual learns to act on some good ideas and not on others, to express some products of an active, whimsical imagination, and to refrain from expressing others.

This is the lifelong theme most closely associated with playfulness, recreation, and enjoyment. It supports humor and exuberance. It is associated with the arts, with the aesthetic, with a sense of beauty. Initiative sustains the enterprise that prompts elder and child, alike, to abandon the inertia of rest in favor of purposeful exploration and activity. When inadequately balanced with self-restraint, initiative can impel ill-considered—and often later-regretted—courses of action. In the opposite direction, imbalance can result in a failure to follow through, and can lead to entanglement in an immobilizing web of painful anticipations, recriminations, and hesitations.

Elder Analysis: Current. I saw Ana's twinkling eyes as an instant indication of inner activity. Although disability confines her body and subdues her expressiveness, her perceptive comments reveal a lively attentiveness to her social environment. Belying a soft, slow, speaking style and an imposed leadenness to her physical movement, her flashing smile suggests to me that in earlier years she bustled with the busyness of employment, child rearing, housework, recreation, and aesthetic hobbies. Disabilities notwithstanding, Ana still does needlepoint, crocheting, embroidery, and other small handicrafts that permit her to create lovely objects. On display these trinkets offer pleasure and delight. When used as gifts and tokens, they allow Ana to continue to participate in the relationships of support and kindness that have always grounded her life.

Elder Analysis: Historical. Her lifelong enjoyment of cooking, sewing, singing, and dancing all developed in the context of a working class childhood within Latino tradition. She describes cooking and sewing as essential survival skills; they became opportunities for self-expression and creativity, as well. She learned singing and dancing as part of the essential body of knowledge that each community makes sure to transmit to each new generation. Here, too, these activities became a basis for personal imagination, dreams, and expression.

Although life has required Ana to spend more time in work than in play, she has been able to create enjoyment within the everyday activities that might otherwise have weighed as heavy burdens. In addition, she has fond memories of recreation. She took her children horseback riding, bicycling, and skating. They went fishing and on picnics together. While her marriage was still solid, she and her husband went dancing together each weekend.

Ana has not spent her time sitting and waiting. As a child, she always had work to do. And when she wasn't working, "I was a little nosy girl. I was right there watching." She says she was a mischievous child. "As soon as they got me dressed up, I used to run to the pump . . . and get all wet." She recalls using her older sister's makeup while she was out. As a mother, she had a free-flowing stream of ideas and projects around the children. Now, from her wheelchair she says, "It just seems like I naturally want to do something. I keep myself busy." At the day center, she participates in exercise and crafts sessions. In between, she makes a point of getting outside and enjoying the porch. At home she bakes regularly, so that she can offer dessert to unexpected visitors. She admits that she does get tired and depressed, sometimes. Initiative is clearly at work when she ". . . snap[s herself] out of it. I say, 'Go do something. Go talk to somebody.' When I get real depressed I call somebody on the phone."

Ingenuity has always characterized the way Ana fulfills life's responsibilities. In order to keep thirteen children dressed nicely for school, ". . . I learned how to be a seamstress, and I cut things up from old hand-me-downs." She made up stories that entertained her own children and their friends for hours. Today, she has devised her arm-chair system for producing a signature. She has arranged her kitchen so that she can reach and open essential spices without an assistant. Most often, she prays to God in prayers she makes up herself.

Ana's lifelong ingenuity is not accompanied by the resolute purposefulness that is often seen as the main strength of this theme. There are things she wishes she had done, that she simply didn't do. She would have liked to stay in school, but she never seriously tried to work out a plan for continuing her education. She very much wanted to be a performer, but she quit her band entirely when she married and had children. She says, "I never thought, here, I'm going to get a job. Things just happened to me." Rather than in planning and carrying out particular courses of action, Ana has expressed her considerable initiative in reacting creatively to the actions life has imposed upon her.[5,6]

Industry and Inferiority: Competence

Conceptual Summary. This psychosocial theme challenges the individual to balance a tendency toward hard work and accomplishment with opposing feelings of inadequacy and ineptitude. During school age, the child struggles to learn facts and to master formally taught skills, catalyzed by a dystonic–but less than overwhelming–sense of current inability. Underlying the pull toward mastery and the push away from inadequacy is an ever-growing competence, characterized both by demonstrable skills and knowledge, and also by an invisible, experienced sense of fundamental ability.

Perhaps even more important than specific competencies are the internal capacity to work hard and the accompanying confidence of being able, with enough disciplined effort, to achieve almost anything. Adulthood's most widely recognized expressions of industriousness concern working at a job, and competing for success. Less clearly acknowledged are the related behaviors of solving problems, of taking charge, of continuing to learn, and simply, of working hard.

Elder Analysis: Current. Ana is concerned with doing things well, and she attends to details. She gave up painting, she explained, when she could no longer manipulate the tubs and the different kinds of brushes well enough to create on canvas the images she worked out so painstakingly in her head. When she cooks with her daughters, she tries to make sure that they learn subtleties of each recipe–both in terms of ingredients and also in terms of the grinding and pinching and rolling and boiling that are integral to each dish. Without these details, she tells me, the recipes she learned from her sisters might just as well be lost, and the family might just as well eat from cans.

Ana's own industriousness and conscientiousness leave her particularly intolerant of and outraged at the hospital staff who caused her accident. She is proud to say that she, herself, has never put out halfhearted effort, and that she has always taken responsibility for mistakes. That she should be incapacitated is a personal tragedy. That she should be so because of the carelessness and irresponsibility of other workers is a tragedy for the next generation as a whole.

Elder Analysis: Historical. As much as any other, the theme of Industry and Inferiority has dominated Ana Martinez's life. She was raised in a culture that values the efforts of children, and in economic circumstances that required her contributions from the very beginning. She learned the skills of housework and child care while still in her own childhood, and she was a fully contributing member of Maria's household and of her sisters' Mexican restaurant from the time she was eight. From childhood through the disastrous hip replacement, Ana was almost never without at least one paid job. And when she wasn't working for money, she was working at tasks that contributed to her family's well being.

Ana chronicles some of her work settings. Sugar beet fields. Restaurant kitchen. Filing department. Crystal showroom. Sweatshop. Toolmaking assembly line. Toy making assembly line. Appliance store and showroom. Butcher shop. Corn factory. Family restaurant. Her own restaurant. When she describes her jobs, she speaks proudly of the hard work required. Rather than bemoaning the physical labor or the unending need to keep working, she takes pride in her industrious achievements. She is proud to have learned skills quickly, first by watching and then by doing. She learned to sew, crochet, knit, and quilt by watching her sisters. She learned to do housework in the same way. From tortillas to matzo balls she has picked up recipes, without written instructions or calibrated utensils, simply by watching. She learned songs on the piano just by listening. She learned dances by looking on. Before she was fluent in English, she could read and do mathematics in school by translating from the Spanish. In each case, Ana came to develop considerable mastery. She knows what her skills are, she is confident about her potential in these areas, and she describes great satisfaction in her performance.

Formal schooling is perhaps the one arena for traditional industry in which Ana is personally disappointed. Although she didn't attend school until the age of 13, her sisters had taught her to read, write, and do arithmetic in Spanish, and she made rapid progress in English. She was double-promoted repeatedly, and she was sorry to have to quit after eleventh grade, to take a full-time job. She married shortly thereafter. As with many bright women in similar circumstances, Ana subordinated academic achievement and aspirations to the industriousness of the workplace. And then, for a time, she subordinated the workplace to the industriousness of housekeeping and childrearing. In keeping with each generation's age-old commitment to enabling the next generation to do better, Ana made sure that her children all completed high school. She helped the two youngest secure scholarships to a private Academy when her neighborhood changed; she had always been good at working hard to solve problems, and the problem of her children's education was too important to be an exception.

Identity and Confusion: Fidelity

Conceptual Summary. The adolescent consolidates a sense of self in terms of the beliefs, values, abilities, relationships, activities, and dreams that, from the multitude of experiences life has offered, resonate as "truly me." As with every other psychosocial theme, identity can be robust only in the presence of a measure of confusion. Confident self-knowledge is meaningful only in terms of an ongoing awareness and consideration of what one is not, coupled with the recognition that for all its enduring sameness, identity undergoes change with the lifelong process of renewing.

In later life the individual is challenged to make sense of the self that has lived through many decades of past, that lives in a moment experienced as present, and that will continue to live into a future that looms ever more finite. "What is it that lets me feel most like myself?" is a question that becomes increasingly meaningful and, for the fortunate, increasingly easy to answer. Family, ethnicity, and status continue to influence the sense of self from outside, along with personality traits, preferences and dislikes, appearance, and physical attributes from within. Inevitably, the elder must struggle with the role of limitations and disabilities in essential identity. Inevitably, too, the elder must incorporate into a sense of self the changes in roles, relationships, and respect that accompany every journey along life's path. Where young adults may identify themselves in terms of what they hope to accomplish, elders place increasing emphasis on what they have learned, what they want to pass on, and how they want to be remembered.

Elder Analysis: Current. Even after 25 years' distance, Ana essentially identifies herself as a restauranteur. Recently she has somewhat modified this identity into something that might accurately be worded "one who cares for others by cooking." She treasures her family's annual Christmas feast, and she is proud to cook the main course each year. She would not be herself if she could not offer home-cooked food to the children whose visits are always a surprise but never wholly unexpected. A proud Latina, Ana is eager for her daughters to learn the Mexican recipes that exist nowhere but in her head, both as a way of transmitting a legacy, and also as a way of being well-remembered.

Also central to Ana's sense of self is her role as a mother. From early childhood, she says, "My thoughts were all that I was going to be a mother someday." All she had of her own mother was a visual image. "She was short and very beautiful, like a doll. She had light hair, green eyes, and her hair was combed in a bun." Ana describes having been loved by her aunts and her sisters, and she used the way they brought her up as a model for her own motherhood. Family was everything.

Ana speaks, today, of her long-ago dreams of a performing career, but these dreams were incompatible with those of marrying and raising children. At the time, in her niche, there was no question about which path was the right one for her to follow. "I got married and started having children, and I thought that was my role. That's all I knew, being a mother." Now, too, with the added perspective of nearly 60 years, she remains sure about this element of her identity. "My children meant everything to me. My children were my world . . . My life was my kids' lives . . . Like every mother's, [my dream] was to do the best for them and let them have it all." Although she is wistful about having given up on her dreams of performing, she says she does not regret the dreams she chose to fulfill, instead. And though she would have liked to pursue her education, she knew that "College wasn't for me."

Ana made these early choices based on a solid sense of who she was, and what her bedrock commitments were. Nearly 60 years later those commitments remain much the same. Ana Martinez is wise enough to know both that she could not choose two incompatible alternatives at the same time, and that the choice she made was the right one for her.

Unlike many elders, Ana maintains her lifelong attention to the appearance that has always been part of her sense of self. Her expression is proud when she tells me that she makes a point of keeping herself presentable. Ana describes herself as a kind of lapsed Catholic. She tells me, ". . . a good Catholic goes to church and participates and stuff, and I don't do that." Nonetheless, she sees herself as a very good Christian, adhering to the rules and commandments that are the essence of religion for her. She thanks the Lord regularly, for His many blessings. She believes in being truthful, in keeping her promises. She values her word. When she gives it, she means it.

Elder Analysis: Historical. Perhaps because she could never quite take it for granted, perhaps more because of the familistic ideology noted earlier, Ana has always strongly identified herself in terms of family and family relationships. Daughter. Niece. Sister. Mother. Everything that has mattered most in her life is somehow part of these. Her sense of herself as a competent worker developed as part of a childhood in homes where love and work were inseparable, and where the call for both was never-ending. Her skills at multiple arts and handicrafts developed in the same way.

Ana learned to cook while working in her sisters' restaurant. When asked what activity allows her to feel most like herself, Ana does not hesitate before answering, "Cooking." She says she has always thought of herself as a cook and a restauranteur, and for her these roles are closely intertwined with her sisters and with family continuity.

Like all disabled elders, Ana struggles to come to terms with an imposed invalid status. Like other elder role models in long-term care, she does not identify with the role of invalid. It is not that she denies her obvious disabilities. Neither is it that she complains about them. Rather, she lives with her disabilities without *becoming* them. Ana's family has no history of arthritis. With characteristic industriousness, she did as much family research as possible when this disease first affected her. And she discovered only that no-one in her family had had arthritis. Restaurants are part of her family identity. Arthritis is not.[7]

Ana has been incapacitated for more than 25 years. She has been in a wheelchair far longer than she owned her restaurant. She has been disabled for the most recent one third of her life. Still, the self that she experiences is a mother. A cook. A sister. A worker. An honest person. A good Christian. Independent. Honest. Cheerful. Essential to her identity in old age are all these qualities which have matured throughout life. Ana has learned her life's lessons well. Her life has been difficult in many ways, but *she* is not her life's difficulties. *She* is the person who has triumphed in spite of—or perhaps because of—them.

Intimacy and Isolation: Love

Conceptual Summary. By participating in relationships of closeness and in experiences of being alone, the individual fashions a capacity to engage with others whom he/she can love and be loved by, with true mutuality. Early associations with siblings and, later, with friends and other age-mates introduce elements of reciprocity and equivalency into the intimacy first experienced in relation to a primary caretaker. Throughout life the individual participates in many different kinds of close, loving relationships, all of which, together, contribute to an overall capacity for love.

In renewing earlier-life balances between intimacy and isolation, elders find themselves both revisiting earlier issues and also confronting the new demands that accompany new circumstances. Coming to terms with long-term marriage and sexuality may consume the energy of older widows, divorcees, and married people, alike. Elders also find themselves revisiting marriages, courtships, and love relationships of long ago, regardless of their duration. Old friends and long-term love of all sorts assume increasing importance as these irreplaceable people pass away. Being along takes on new meaning in the face of losses that are both increasingly frequent and increasingly expectable. Elders must bear the painful reality that "You can't make a new friend old." In response, they find themselves forging new intimacies across generational lines, within and across family boundaries, and based on qualities and criteria that acquire new meaning as former criteria become irrelevant.

Elder Analysis: Current. Ana's current face-to-face peer relations exist largely within the Day Center where, as she describes it, "I've got acquaintances but not friends." Although she does not experience closeness in these relationships, they do offer a measure of social contact. She learned early in life to ". . . get along with anybody," and to make friends easily, and these peer relations permit her to continue to exercise this facility. Ana feels good about people's generally warm reactions to her. She feels good, too, that people still come to her with their problems. She looks pleased when she tells me that colleagues at the Day Center miss her when she is away, and that the paid staff love her. Although none of those relationships is truly intimate, together they allow her to exercise the caring, the encouragement, and the optimism that she describes in her closest friendships.

Old age not only robs elders of intimacy they treasure. It also imposes relationships that may be entirely unwanted. Like all elders in long-term care, Ana finds herself involved with people in ways over which she has no control. She certainly has not chosen to have to rely on someone else to assist with her personal care. Neither does she like the fact that she has little control over who her personal care and live-in workers turn out to be, or over how long they work with her before moving on to other jobs. These relationships, like many others in later life, enforce contact, both casual and intimate, between people who might never have chosen to relate to one another, at all.

Elder Analysis: Historical. Ana does not speak of her former husband nearly as often or as passionately as she speaks of her children and sisters. She had had many boyfriends, whom she met through church picnics and parties. Alejandro, her future husband, was "a very good looking man." When she met him, "It was love at first sight." They were married when

Ana was 17, and their first child was born shortly thereafter. Early in the relationship, she says, she and her husband " . . . used to be together all the time." They visited with friends, they went dancing, and they were quite happy together. Alejandro did not like Anu's working outside the home, and this necessity became an early thorn in the side of the marriage. While Ana structured her own life around the children, she experienced Alejandro as increasingly uninvolved. When she took the children on family outings, he chose to visit with friends; when she arranged for family activities, he had to work. Ana both cared for her children and enjoyed being with them. She nurtured them and had fun with them. Alejandro became increasingly disengaged from all these relationships. Ultimately, though, it is his drinking that Ana holds responsible for killing their marriage. He became accusing and suspicious of her, until, at age 35, she divorced him and formally accepted the responsibility for raising their thirteen children on her own.

Because of her own experience in marriage, Ana says, she worked hard to teach her sons that they should be good to their wives. She points to their happy marriages as a sign that she has made good use of a lesson painfully learned. Ana is proud to say that she never denied Alejandro access to the children. Over the years, they have remained friends. Occasionally she invites him over for dinner. These days, she says, he phones three or four times a week just to talk.

Over her life, Ana has had close friends whom she describes as ". . . better than sisters because I raised their kids and they raised mine. . . . You do anything for them and they do anything for you. We were close just like sisters." In these relationships, affection and devotion seem to have been a product of shared life experiences and mutual activities. These friendships are very much in keeping both with historical descriptions of women's personal relationships (Sapiro, 1990), and with contemporary descriptions of closeness and interdependence among working-class women (Komarovsky, 1967). Related also to traditional Chicano sex-role segregation (Dill, 1995) and to the widespread belief among Latinas that most men are undependable and untrustworthy (Espín, 1995), Ana describes far more mutuality with these women than she discusses with her husband.

In later life, these kinds of sharing become more difficult. One of Ana's close friends has recently passed away. Another has moved away to be near her son. A third can't get around easily, as Ana can't. Since they can't do things together any more, their relationship is increasingly limited to the telephone. Ana does not really like the telephone. She is willing to make calls to transmit information. She enjoys brief exchanges of greetings. And she values being able to call friends and relatives as a way of snapping herself out of loneliness or depression. But she cannot use the phone as a medium for conducting relationships that were, in the first place, based more on doing than on talking. She finds herself dreaming about old friends who have passed away, and she takes pleasure in recalling pleasant times shared with people she can no longer see.

Throughout life, Ana says, she has been closer to her sisters than to anyone else. After the death of their parents, the aunts taught Ana and her sisters ". . . to stay together, love each other, and look after each other." They learned these lessons well. Serving as siblings and parents, peers and mentors, friends and teachers, her sisters provided the diverse kinds of love and care that children most often experience in many different relationships. Perhaps these unusual circumstances are responsible for the fact that for Ana, being close to and taking care of have always been inextricably intertwined. Her sister Maria is the person to whom she was closest. As a child she went to the park with Maria, embroidered with her, and baked with her. They washed clothes together. They listened to the radio and worked in the fields together. They sat together in silence. Like many working-class children, Ana did not have friends with whom she played dolls and other childhood games. Instead, it was Maria and her other sisters with whom she spent time (most often working) and whose company she craved. Ana wanted Maria's approval on everything she did, and she was reluctant to leave home for activities that did not include Maria. Looking back, Ana thinks that perhaps she and Maria were too close. She sighs. "It seemed like I lost a part of me when she died."

Generativity and Self-Absorption: Care

Conceptual Summary. "The experiences of caring, nurturing, and maintaining . . . make of the stages of life a life cycle, re-creating the beginnings of the cycle in each newborn. These same experiences make of the sequence of life cycles a generational cycle" (Erikson et al., 1986, p. 73), binding each generation to the one before, that created it, and the ones after, for which it is responsible. Throughout life, the generative providing of selfless, loving care must be balanced with the capacity to take necessary care of the self. In order to provide consistent nurturance for those for whom one is responsible, the individual must see to it that s/he, too, receives essential care.

The infant and toddler anticipate generativity as they receive the loving care that is, or is not, provided by their primary caretakers. In addition, first unconsciously and later with more awareness, children begin to learn from and to emulate their caretakers. These adults are, after all, the most pervasive models children have for this crucial set of behaviors. Caring for younger children and for pets and plants, playing at parenting, comforting peers in distress, and coming to terms with selfishness—all these are ways in which children continue to anticipate the generativity and self absorption that become focal with childrearing, and in middle adulthood It is not only procreativity that expresses essential care, and not only nurturance of children. Creativity and productivity, too, may affirm this central life strength.

In later life, elders continue to seek a balance between caring for others and securing necessary care for themselves. And they may develop a newly imperative concern for society at large, for humankind, for all the world's children. Elders continue to provide the next generations with all possible supports while, at the same time, counting on receiving essential services in return. At this stage, however, indirect expressions of generativity assume increasing importance. Elders take particular pleasure in identifying with members of the next generations, in seeing family ties remain strong, and in celebrating the myths and traditions according to which the family continues to grow and thrive. In passing on concrete objects and in transmitting personal values and goals, the elder firmly takes his/her place in the generational cycle that is all most of us will ever know of immortality.

Elder Analysis: Current. The capacity to care for others is the strength I first saw in Ana Martinez, in the focus group where I met her. Rather than listening to her peers in respectful silence, she made comments she explicitly intended to lift their spirits. She does not simply use the Day Center as a place to receive essential services. Rather, she says clearly that she regards it as an opportunity to soothe other people's problems and to find little ways to brighten their day. Before her accident, she used to read to patients in nursing homes, and to volunteer on a cardiac unit. When she gets depressed now, she worries that "I'm not doing any good for anybody."

Ana's family is both primary recipient and provider of her generativity. She continues to cook for her children and grandchildren, and to provide advice on their problems. Despite the confinement of the two rooms where she spends most of her time, she keeps piles of children's books ready to entertain grandchildren and great-grandchildren, when they come to visit. She relies heavily on the devotion of her family.

Ana says that she sees herself reflected in her children, in the way they all work hard and take care of their families. Hard work and loving care have dominated her life. She is pleased to have succeeded in passing on these values. Although she is distressed that not all her children have accepted her devotion to religion, she is proud that they all have children and take care of them well. She is also proud that they are all working. Most of her children went to college or completed vocational training, and her eyes shine as she enumerates their jobs. Hairdresser. Shop owner. Butcher. Bricklayer. Mechanic. Tailor. Teacher. Nurse. Ana, herself, moved from one relatively unskilled job to another. She takes great pride in the fact that her children have real professions. "I have given each one [of my children] a part of me," she says. "They make me proud knowing that I did well bringing them up."

Ana takes both pleasure and pride in her intergenerational family. The happiest experience of her year was when the whole family—13 children, 59 grandchildren, 41 great-grandchildren—came together for the annual Christmas party. She says she takes great satisfaction in the family's strength. Only two of her children have been divorced, she proclaims, and since her former son-in-law is the father of her grandchildren, she still considers him part of the family. She has "pretty close" relationships with most of her grandchildren.

Elder Analysis: Historical. Despite being orphaned at age three, Ana was well cared for by her aunts and sisters. Rather than dwelling on her orphan status, she summarizes her childhood with the observation, "There was a lot of love in our family." Loving care and nurturance were inseparable from hard work; all three pervaded her childhood. The oldest sisters took care of the younger ones, and, as they grew, the younger ones took care of new nieces and nephews. The sisters were unwilling to see Ana placed in an orphanage, and she tells me that they made whatever sacrifices were necessary to raise her themselves. Indeed, she remembers that at ten or twelve her sisters involved her in sewing clothes to send to the orphanage. Caring for and working hard were just the way her world was. It didn't cross her mind until much later that life could be any different.

Her childhood prepared her well for a life of raising children; her aunts and sisters were excellent role models. In addition, she believes that "God gave me the talent of knowing how to take care of my children and guide them." Although she knew she could not give them the tangible things they wanted, she provided the intangible guidance, support, and presence that are the essence of true nurturance. She made sure their school clothes were clean and well-fitting. She involved them in sports to keep them out of trouble. She accepted their friends. She structured their life with church, school, and family activities. She taught them the values she thought were important. And when her neighborhood became intolerably dangerous, she found a way to move out and place her youngest children in good schools.

For one who has spent so much of her life caring for people, Ana draws a clear, sharp line between those who do and do not receive her care. Although she expresses concern about children who are neglected and maltreated today, she shrugs helplessly and says only, "My children were never abused." She has never voted, and she does not see how doing so might be related to concern for others.

Integrity and Despair: Wisdom

Conceptual Summary. In its final stage the life cycle turns back to its beginnings, as the individual weaves a lifetime of strengths and weaknesses, joys and sorrows, gains and losses, dreams and disappointments into a unique fabric of experience. This is the integration that must guide the elder through the life time that remains—whether it be marked in months or in decades. This, too, is the integration that must see each elder through the death that brings to an end all we know for sure about life.

The process of integration involves far more than simple life review and uniform acceptance of the past. It requires a real, and often painful, coming to terms with choices made and not made, actions taken and not taken, hopes fulfilled and not fulfilled. This kind of honest stock-taking, taken with the perspective of time, is essential to clarifying the lessons learned from a lifetime of experience. It is these lessons that give rise to the wisdom that makes it all worthwhile.

Elder Analysis: Current. There is much about life that people often wish were different now or had been different earlier. Ana wishes she had had her parents. She wishes the kids of her childhood had not teased her for having no father. She wishes that she could have had a singing career. She wishes her sisters were still alive. She wishes she were not confined, helpless, to a wheelchair, and that she could get out and drive, go shopping, and do all the other things that used to occupy her time. But Ana knows clearly what she can effect and what she cannot. And she has no illusions about how rosy her life was before her accident. "I don't regret what I went through," she says. "My life never has been easy. Even when I was walking." She moves on quickly. "[But] there is people that are worse than I am. I get depressed sometimes, but I snap out of it myself . . . I say 'Go do something. Go talk to somebody.'" Taking her own advice, she goes to make a phone call, or crochet a doily, or think of a way to cheer up someone at the Day Center, or make a list of ingredients she'll need someone to buy so she can make the molé she'd like to have ready for her next visitors.

Ana pairs her wishful thinking about how things might have been different with acceptance of the way things were, and with pride and satisfaction at what she made of them. "We didn't have very much," she says about her childhood, "but we didn't have all these [bad things] that are going on now. I think I was fortunate because I've learned life skills. I've learned a lot by experiences." Ana used her learned skills and acquired knowledge to raise thirteen children whose successes confirm to her, every day, that she did well at the mothering that was more important than anything. She expresses pride in the gracious way she handled her relationship with her ex-husband Alejandro, pride that she has never mistreated anybody, and pride that in spite of her difficulties, people have always regarded her as a source of comfort and inspiration.

She is sorry that her marriage fell apart as it did, but she is able to forgive Alejandro for the things he did wrong. "He's the father of my kids," she says now, "and I don't hate him for the things that were done." To be sure, we know nothing of his story of the marriage, or of her story as she would have told it then. What we do know is that she is not racked, today, with the resentment that embitters so many other women in her marital position. We know that she treasures her relationship with each of her children. We know that she even takes some pleasure in her current relationship with Alejandro. Surely she has made an acceptable peace with this part of her past, and she is living out this part of her present in the best way her wisdom will permit.

Elder Analysis: Historical. With the untimely death of her parents, Ana confronted profound personal loss far earlier than children usually do. She was raised by adults who loved her. She grew up with secure family ties, and she created a new family based on love and devotion. Still she says, wistfully, "I always wish that I could have had my parents." As is true for many elders, Ana has now lost many of the people she has loved most. Her sisters have all passed on. Some of her friends have passed; others have been lost to disease or geography. Sometimes she dreams about these lost companions. Other times she thinks of them and grows lonely.

In some ways, Ana was prepared both for aging and for death from a very young age. Her aunt always told her, "You're going to get older, so age gracefully." So she tries to do so. She has long believed that learning from experience is part of aging gracefully, and she is able to look at many of her adversities as a source of learning. From very early, her aunt and uncle told her, "One day we won't be here any more. We'll be gone." Although her parents' deaths were entirely unexpected, she was readier for subsequent losses. I wonder how clearly she sees that practicing funeral songs with her daughter is, in part, an attempt to pass on her own early preparation for death, for which she remains so grateful.

Although Ana draws clear boundaries around the limits of her care, she does have thoughts about the future of the world. She believes that today's children are rushing life too much; she thinks it is important for them to look ahead to what will be in years to come. Unlike many elders who, like her, see serious problems with contemporary society, Ana does not romanticize the past. "I wouldn't want them to go back to my times of working in the fields," she says firmly. Today may be bad in some ways. But yesterday was bad in other ways, and there is no virtue to trading one bad situation for another.

As Ana looks back on her life, her observations reflect the very personal strategy that this one woman developed for living through the unique set of circumstances in which she found herself. "I learned very early that you just have to do with what you have, and there was no use thinking, 'I'm going to get this,' or 'I'm going to get that,' when I knew I wasn't going to do it." She learned, too, to use work as a distraction from unrealistic dreams. Some people would view these lessons as a prescription for giving in. To them, dreams constitute the aspirations or ambitions that give life its meaning and direction. To them, the value of dreams is the way they catalyze behavior.

It is not that Ana has lived without dreams, or that she has failed to achieve her goals. And it is not that she has accepted adversity without fighting back. Rather, it is that she has defined the limits of her struggles. Just as she imposes boundaries on the extent of her care, so she has closely defined the boundaries of her ambitions.

What Ana has not done is use her early dreams as a basis for trying to create a life far beyond her own experience. Ana has not been a visionary; she has lived as a pragmatist. She has defined clear goals and, whatever the obstacles, she has worked as hard as necessary to achieve them. She has derived great satisfaction from her successes. She has not failed at anything she has truly worked for. Ana has taken advantage of her considerable strengths of Competence and Care. Rather than using her imagination to expand her horizons, she has used it, instead, to cope with adversity and to enjoy the fruits of her efforts. As she comes to terms with her life thus far, her aunt's saying keeps coming to mind. "It's gloomy today, but it will be nicer tomorrow."

PSYCHOSOCIAL SUMMARY

When Ana puts into words what she has learned about life, many of her lessons echo the wisdom and philosophy of other elder role models. "The most important thing I learned was to accept others." "People should keep on having a positive attitude." "Life must go on." "I get depressed sometimes, but I snap out of it myself." "I'm probably here because of my children." "All I want is my health. After that I can cope with anything that comes along." These are the lessons Ana has learned from life, and according to which she has learned to live. They are the principles that guide her life today, the hallmarks of her successful aging. In some ways they are the common sense that is often acknowledged as being all too uncommon. They are what she has distilled from her experience as worth hanging onto, herself, and, further, as worth putting into words to pass on to others.

Seen through a psychosocial lens, these lessons crystallize Ana's particular emphases in each psychosocial theme. She certainly does not think of herself or her own life in the language of Eriksonian psychosocial theory, but this language allows us to understand her wisdom and the example she sets in terms that are broader than any one life can be. In the preceding psychosocial profile we have seen that Ana Martinez demonstrates special strength in the themes of Generativity and Self-absorption, and Industry and Inferiority, and that for her, these two themes are closely related. When all else may be questionable, Ana does not doubt that she is here for her children, and that she will be–as she has always been–good for them. Ana also does not doubt her ability to work her way out of a problem. Given her health, she says, she will work diligently and persistently and effectively enough to cope with anything that life may present. Ana also demonstrates particular strength in the theme of Trust and Mistrust. Associated with her religious faith and underlying her indomitable stamina is the relentless optimism that allows her to advise others to maintain a positive attitude, and to remind herself that tomorrow will be brighter.

These are the major thematic strengths with which Ana has met life's challenges; they remain the basis of her style of successful aging today. Ana demonstrates strength in all themes, balancing expectable thematic weaknesses and conflicts. For her, however, as for each individual, a unique profile of strengths characterizes the way she lives her life. Because Ana Martinez is an elder role model, an extraordinary ordinary elder, we can look to her psychosocial profile as one possible model for less successful contemporaries. We can also regard this kind of profile as a clarification of the strengths that each elder has at his/her disposal, to help compensate for more readily assessed weaknesses. Finally, we can use this profile to begin to develop a theoretical understanding of successful aging as a whole.

NOTES

1. The interviews for this case study were conducted by the Investigator, as a young woman eager to learn from the experience of an older one. To convey pur sonal involvement in the interview process, we have chosen to write about elements of this process in the first person, singular. Throughout this paper, the pronoun "I" refers to the Investigator, Helen Q. Kivnick.

2. Through the Psychosocial Profile section of this paper, each Conceptual summary is written to discuss all the categories and subcategories that have emerged, thus far, within each theme.

3. The sensitizing concepts around which this particular research team has structured its understanding of these data are those of psychosocial life-cycle theory. Accordingly, these are the concepts we use in discussing Ana's life, and, reciprocally, these are the concepts we seek to enrich with what we learn from her. Theories of gender, class, ethnicity, and their historical interaction are certainly relevant to Ana's life story and she, like every human being, is characterized by each of these parameters. However, since this manuscript tells the story of Ana Martinez's lifelong psychosocial strengths, we pay far less explicit attention to the theoretical paradigms whose concepts would lead us to focus on different stories in Ana's life. We make no claim that our story is the only valid or "true" story to be told about this elder role model. We maintain only that it is a story that makes sense and fits the data (Peshkin, 1988). We believe that it illuminates the data, as well.

4. Ana never referred to the woman who currently provides round-the-clock assistance as anything other than her live-in. She explained, over the course of the interviews, that this woman is relatively new in her life, being the second in a series of replacements for "... the girl who lived with me for many years." Ana had been extremely fond of her long-time assistant–who left to take a better-paying job.

5. For a working-class woman who has learned to expect life to be both difficult and unpredictable, creatively rolling-with-the-punches was probably a far more adaptive–and certainly more common–expression of initiative than struggling to actualize dreams would have been.

6. Individuals conventionally presented as role models are most often those who stand out as different from, and somehow better than, those around them. We are far more accustomed to thinking of an exemplar as the one person in his/her group who broke free from traditional limitations, than we are to considering someone who lives well, with integrity, within an existing niche. We researchers do not wish to diminish the importance of conventional role models, but these outstanding individuals do not necessarily demonstrate behaviors that can serve as meaningful examples to large numbers of their peers. In this study, we are considering "extraordinary ordinary" people as role models. That is, we are looking at elders whose expressions of psychosocial strength are, in quantity and consistency, greater than those of their peers but are, in quality, very much like those with which peers can identify.

7. This quality–transcending difficulties without denying them, in one direction, and without being consumed or defined by them, in the other–may prove to be a hallmark of the people we are studying as elder role models.

REFERENCES

Albert, G. (1987). Mental health past age fifty: A growing specialty in psychotherapy. *Journal of Contemporary Psychotherapy, 17*(1), 34-37.

Aronson, S. M. (1994). Days of our years. *Rhode Island Medicine, 77*(5), 131-2.

Birren, J. E., & Deutchman, D. E. (1991). *Guiding autobiography groups for older adults: Exploring the fabric of life.* Baltimore, MD: The Johns Hopkins University Press.

Butler, R. (1963). The life review: An interpretation of reminiscence in the aged. *Psychiatry, 26,* 65-76.

Butler, R. N. (1980). The life review: An unrecognized bonanza. *International Journal of Aging and Human Development, 12*(1), 35-38.

Caspi, A., & Elder, G. H. (1986). Life satisfaction in old age: Linking social psychology and history. *Journal of Psychology and Aging. 1*(1), 18-26.

Charmaz, K. (1990). "Discovering" chronic illness: Using grounded theory. *Social Science and Medicine, 30*(11), 1161-1172.

Colerick, E. J. (1985). Stamina in later life. *Social Science Medicine, 21*(9), 997-1006.

Coles, R. (1980). *The call of stories: Teaching and the moral imagination.* Boston: Houghton Mifflin.

Corbin, J. & Strauss, A. (1990). Grounded theory research: Procedures, canons, and evaluative criteria. *Qualitative Sociology, 13*(1), 3-21.

Dean, A., Kolodny, B., & Wood, P. (1990). Effects of social support from various sources on depression in elderly persons. *Journal of Health and Social Behavior, 31,* 148-61.

Dill, B. T. (1995). Our mothers' grief: Racial ethnic women and the maintenance of families. In M. L. Andersen & P. H. Collins (Eds.). *Race, class, and gender: An anthology* (2nd ed.) (pp. 237-259). Boston: Wadsworth.

Erikson, E. H. (1950). *Childhood and society.* New York: W.W. Norton.

Erikson, E. H., Erikson, J. M., & Kivnick, H. Q. (1986). *Vital involvement in old age.* New York: W.W. Norton.

Espín, O. M. (1995). Cultural and historical influences on sexuality in Hispanic/ Latin women: Implications for psychotherapy. In M. L. Andersen & P. H. Collins (Eds.). *Race, class, and gender: An anthology* (2nd ed.)(pp. 423-428). Boston: Wadsworth.

Fisher, J. C. (1988). Impact of anomia and life satisfaction on older adult learners. *Educational Gerontology, 14*(2), 137-146.

Hareven, T. K. (1977). Family time and historical time. *Daedalus, 106,* 57-70.

House, J. et al. (1992). Social stratification, age, and health. In K.W. Schaie, D. Blazer, & J. House (Eds.), *Aging, Health Behaviors, and Health Outcomes* (pp. 1-32). Hillsdale, NJ: Earlbaum.

Hubley, J. & Hubley, F. (1976). *Everybody rides the carousel* [Film]. The Hubley Studio. Distributed by Pacific Arts Video Records, Carmel, CA.

Kirk, J. & Miller, M. L. (1986). *Reliability and validity in qualitative research.* Newbury Park, CA: Sage.

Kivnick, H. Q. (1987). Grandfather John Heller: Generativity through the life cycle. In S. Reinharz & G. Rowles (Eds.). *Qualitative gerontology* (pp. 64-81). New York: Springer.

Kivnick, H. Q. (1993). Everyday mental health: A guide to assessing life strengths. *Generations, 17* (1), 13-20.

Komarovsky, M. (1967). *Blue collar marriage.* New York: Vintage.

Laslett, P. (1972). Introduction: The history of the family. In P. Laslett & R. Wall (Eds.), *Household and family in past time.* Cambridge: Cambridge University Press, 1-89.

McClelland, K. A. (1982). Self-conception and life satisfaction: Integrating aged subculture and activity theory. *Journal of Gerontology, 37*(6), 723-732.

Marshall, C., & Rossman, G. B. (1989). *Designing qualitative research.* Newbury Park, CA: Sage.

Nadelson, T. (1990). On purpose, successful aging, and the myth of innocence. *Journal of Geriatric Psychiatry, 63*(3), 3-12.

Patton, M. Q. (1990). *Qualitative Evaluation and Research Methods* (Second Edition). Newbury Park, CA: Sage.

Peshkin, A. (1988). Virtuous subjectivity: In the participant-observer's I's. In D. N. Berg & K. K. Smith (Eds.). *The self in social inquiry: Researching methods* (pp. 276-281). Newbury Park, CA: Sage.

Revicki, D., & Mitchell, J. (1990). Strain, social support, and mental health in rural elderly individuals. *Journal of Gerontology, 45*(6), 267-74.

Roos, N. P., & Havens, B. (1991). Predictors of successful aging: A twelve-year study of Manitoba elderly. *American Journal of Public Health, 81*(1), 63-68.

Sapiro, V. (1990). *Women in American society* (2nd ed). Mountain View, CA: Mayfield.

Schein, E. H. (1987). *The clinical perspective in fieldwork.* Newbury Park, CA: Sage.

Sherman, E. (1993). Mental health and successful adaptation in later life. *Generations, 17* (1), 43-46.

Tornstam, L. (1992). The quo vadis of gerontology: On the scientific paradigm of gerontology. *The Gerontologist, 32*(3), 318-326.

Vailliant, G. E. (1991). The association of ancestral longevity with successsful aging. *Journal of Gerontology, 46*(6), 292-298.

Wadhera, S. & Strachan, J. (1993). Selected mortality statistics. *Health Reports, 5*(2), 233-36.

Wykle, M. L. & Musil, C. M. (1993). Mental health of older persons: Social and cultural factors. *Generations, 17* (1), 7-12.

Discovering Women's Work:
A Study of Post-Retirement Aged Women

Lynn M. Meadows

SUMMARY. While the range and nature of Canadian women's work has varied at times and places due to a variety of factors, that work has usually contributed to the family economy. The discussion here focuses on women who were married during the period from just prior to the First World War until the end of the Second World War. Data were gathered from a sample of 22 ever-married women using unstructured face-to-face interviews. Immersion and crystallization were used to analyse the data. Similarities were found in women's experiences during early transitions in marriage, including the marriage bar and making ends meet. Fairly quickly, however, the effect of socioeconomic status became more salient. Four categories of women's experiences were identified, including volunteer work, paid work for "extras," necessary but hidden paid work, and family provisioning by single women. It is apparent from this study that women's work included not only paid and unpaid work, but Goffmanian labor that contributed to their families' class and status. *[Article copies available for a fee from The Haworth Document Delivery Service: 1-800-342-9678. E-mail address: getinfo@haworth.com]*

Lynn M. Meadows is Assistant Professor, Alberta Primary Care Research Unit, Department of Family Medicine, University of Alberta and The University of Calgary, Unit 52, PlC, 3500-26 Avenue, N.E., Calgary, Alberta, Canada T1Y 6J4.

This research is based on the author's (1991) PhD dissertation entitled "Women's Contributions to Family Resources," funded in part by the Social Sciences and Humanities Research Council Canada (Grant # 756-91-0391).

An earlier version of this paper was presented at the Annual Meeting of the National Council on Family Relations, Orlando, FL, November 1992.

[Haworth co-indexing entry note]: "Discovering Women's Work: A Study of Post-Retirement Aged Women." Meadows, Lynn M. Co-published simultaneously in *Marriage & Family Review* (The Haworth Press, Inc.) Vol. 24, No. 1/2, 1996, pp. 165-191; and: *The Methods and Methodologies of Qualitative Family Research* (ed: Marvin B. Sussman, and Jane F. Gilgun) The Haworth Press, Inc., 1996, pp. 165-191. Single or multiple copies of this article are available for a fee from The Haworth Document Delivery Service [1-800-342-9678, 9:00 a.m. - 5:00 p.m. (EST). E-mail address: getinfo@haworth.com].

KEYWORDS. Women's work, Family economy, Qualitative research, Feminist research, Post-retirement

Research on women, their families, and work involves the exploration of intersections among gender, family, economic opportunities and structures. Until recently, enquiry into family economic organization and related issues attracted little intellectual curiosity—especially the conceptualization of women as important social actors in the intersection of these realms. Resources that come to families from a variety of sources may or may not be shared in egalitarian ways, and perceptions of contributions of work that is paid are often much more positive than that which is not. Indeed, when reflecting upon what is known of families in the first half of this century, many of the common cultural images are framed and interpreted within the context of the breadwinner ideology (Bernard, 1981), and its relationship with the cult of true womanhood (Welter, 1966).

While the range and nature of women's work has varied at times and places due to technology, geographic location or period in history, in North America that work has usually contributed to the family economy. The work of past researchers has documented the experiences of families, their members, work and the economy in England and France (Tilly & Scott, 1987/1988); the interplay of industrialization, ethnicity, race, cultural and class differences and family work patterns in the United States (for example, Hareven & Modell, 1980; Hareven, 1982;); and women, work and family in the Canadian context (Crease, 1988; Parr, 1990; Prentice et al., 1988; Silverman, 1984; Strong-Boag & Fellman, 1986). These historical perspectives, and studies in Canada such as Luxton's (1980) work on three generations of women have begun to cumulate a body of research that documents the varied and complex factors that affect family economies, particularly the roles placed on various members.

The discussion here focuses on a topic on which empirical insight is still to be gained: women who were married during the period from just prior to the First World War until the end of the Second World War. This paper is based upon the qualitative component of my study of four generations of women and their work. I gathered data for the three younger generations (reported elsewhere) using a self-report questionnaire. In exploring the experiences of these women, I acknowledge the theoretical contribution of the concept of social reproduction.

Important work has already been done on senior or retired women, examining the importance of ethnicity (Hareven & Modell, 1980), urbanization (Modell & Hareven, 1973); women in the settlement days of western Canada (Silverman, 1984), differences between the work of married and never-married women (Keating & Jeffrey, 1983) and the ideological and structural influences of the concept of the private sphere of women and the public sphere of men (Lopata, 1993). My intent here is to examine these women's experiences within the context of the influence of the extant ideological and structural constraints, but to add a filter of the influence of class consciousness as individual women formed families with members working together to emulate the ideal-typical breadwinner family.

Women who married and formed families in the time period between the First World War and the end of the Second World War did so at a time of apparent laissez-faire family provisioning. As Bernard (1981) has pointed out, for a significant period in history male breadwinning implicitly involved not just putting food on the table and a roof over one's family, but also provided proof of the very success of one's manhood. The cult of true womanhood (Welter, 1966) ordained that women's post-marital activities were to be centred around caring for their families, ideally becoming domestic engineers–experts in the care and comfort of their families. Pre-marital education, even that beyond the mandatory, and paid labour were targeted towards preparing women for their true vocation–wife and mother. This paper presents a substantive record of the work of a group of post-retirement aged women, and details of the methodological approach used to collect that information.

THEORETICAL AND METHODOLOGICAL CONTEXT

This study employs a methodology grounded in a feminist political economy, and guided by a critical feminist epistemology, to explore the work and family experiences of a group of post-retirement aged women. Feminist theory proposes that at the macro-level, existing but unquestioned gendered differences are constructed both ideologically and structurally. At the macro-level, women's experiences are affected by the emphasis on definitions of work that are directed toward the accumulation of profit. This ideological reinforcement at the micro-level is usually accomplished in intimate networks of face-to-face associations. In turn, women's and men's experiences of differential valuation of work and the gendered division of labour within marriage are embedded in and permeated by the macro-structure (Lengermann & Niebrugge-Brantley, 1988). When the concept of social reproduction is invoked, it is possible to see that it includes both necessary labour (in the Marxian sense), the work of maintaining existing life and reproducing the next generations, *as well as* the organization of social reproduction (Brenner & Laslett, 1991). Thus scholars and others concerned with conceptualizations surrounding work can come to a broader definition of what constitutes work, and gain a better understanding of women's work as it contributes to their family resources and provisioning.

In this paper I conceptualize feminist political economy as adopting elements from both Canadian political economy and feminist approaches to family theory. Marchak (1985) describes Canadian political economy as the study of power relations. These relations are anchored in a system of property rights. These property rights go beyond the traditional Marxist view that attaches rights and obligations to one's relationship to the means of production. Within the Canadian political economy perspective these relations also encompass sources of inequality, subordination, and resistance. Feminist theoretical insight recognizes and explores the process and working of an internal stratification of family life, as well as in the world of work. Through this organization, men have greater power and control than women (Cheal, 1989). They also receive more benefits than women as a result of their perceived greater resources.

The key conceptual contribution of a feminist political economy to a study of women's work is the integration and interdependence of the family and the macro economy, as they intersect and affect the economy of the family in its gendered organization and reality. A feminist political economy approach offers to a study of women's work a connection to the macroeconomic structure in which family lives are situated, and the opportunity to take advantage of past historical research (Maroney & Luxton, 1987).

A feminist approach to expanding our knowledge of women *begins* with the goal of discovering from women in a variety of vantage points how they come to understand their world. One focus of this paper is, therefore, an examination of the role of class consciousness in families' (and more particularly women's) strategies for accumulating adequate resources (both monetary and non-monetary) for survival. In working toward identifying similarities and differences in these approaches, a critical feminist epistemology argues that researchers must search for patterns of experience in women's lives, to begin to reveal categories of generalization that will allow us to test and build a cumulative body of work. While there is no reductionist "TRUTH," neither can there be endless multiplicities of experience. Thus understandings and emergent patterns can be critically evaluated based upon evidence that contradicts or supports their existence (Hawkesworth, 1989).

The use of a feminist political economy to investigate women's contributions to their family resources takes as given the formation of individuals' identity and understanding of their lives and work as affected by the context of their gender and economic location. A central issue in a feminist sociology is understanding how researchers can 'know' social reality, given our individual perceptions (as private citizens or scholars), which are partial and interest-based. "Thus a feminist sociology seeks to understand how people come to their views of social reality, how they justify those views, condone their own behaviour according to those views, or reconcile themselves to their social situation according to those views" (Lengermann & Niebrugge-Brantley, 1988, p. 312). The challenge here is to take information from many sources, search for patterns of experience, and provide insight from women's experiences, in their early similarities, and as their class and status develop or change, and present these without discrediting their expertise.

Using the insight from feminist political economy, the concept of social reproduction, and realizing that while there are many individual realities, knowledge is only advanced by seeing how many experiences are similar or different, in the following pages I describe the methodology and insight provided by this study. I argue that contrary to extant ideological prescriptions and normative structural constraints, women played a vital, necessary and active role in family provisioning.

METHOD

The study from which this paper was written was not designed following a single methodology, rather it was influenced by the guidance of concepts stemming from a feminist political economy. The central methodological goal was to find a way to have post-retirement aged women share with me descriptions of their post-marital work, of whatever kind. Thus I wanted to capture the meanings of that work for women themselves, apprehend a view of that *Lebenswelt*, and then look at those data from the perspective of a feminist political economy. Given those needs, I decided to undertake face-to-face interviews with post-retirement aged women.

A key issue in the sampling was to generate information richness (Patton, 1990). Concerns with targeting a vulnerable population (those in care facilities or institutions, of post-retirement age) combined with a suspicion that these women might not identify themselves as having anything to contribute to a study of women's work, led to my decision to spread the word of the study to acquaintances and to contact directors or managers of several residences and care facilities for those of post-retirement age (greater than 65 years old).

When initiating contact with residences or care facilities, after an introduction by phone of the goal of the study, I made arrangements to meet with the person in charge of each location. Contacts were asked to identify ever-married women, with the only stipulation being that, in care institutions, the person be lucid. Ethically it was necessary and desirable to first have institutional approval, then have women approached by my contact person already known to the potential participant. Contact persons presented the women with a study information sheet and asked, if they were interested, for permission for me to contact them individually about the study. I then contacted potential interviewees by phone for an appointment. In the case of those in a care facility, the director, matron or other contact person arranged the appointment time. Those women living independently who agreed to participate in the study were contacted by phone for an appointment. The purposeful sampling technique, combining both snowball and convenience sampling, reflects the insight of Lincoln and Guba (1985), Marshall and Rossman (1989), McCracken (1988) and Patton (1990) that 12-20 persons are commonly needed when looking for disconfirming evidence or to achieve maximum variation. One unanticipated consequence of this strategy was that the resultant sample is not ethnically or racially diverse.

Participants ranged in age from 65 to 102. All face-to-face interviews took place at the women's place of residence. Four women lived independently, three were in an extended care institution, four were in an exclusive seniors' residence (individual apartments with common dining room and recreational and entertainment facilities), and the remainder were in middle-range residences with greater or lesser health care personnel or facilities available.

Of the twenty-five women who agreed to participate in the study, two interviews could not be completed (due to problems of recall or some confusion with chronology of events), therefore the experiences of these 2 women are not included in the study results. Two women requested that the interview not be recorded. Instead of transcript text, notes made on the interview guideline at the time of the interview, with field notes recorded after the interview are the source of recorded data included here. Field notes were made for all interviews.

I always started the interviews with an explanation of the project, reassurance that paid work was not the central focus of the study and the assurance that any information shared would be gratefully accepted. Time was then spent, usually, in general small-talk as rapport was established. Discussion or talk often began with reference to pictures of family or places, moving toward a focus on the woman's particular experience from educational completion toward marriage and family. While the direction provided was usually, "tell me about your life from leaving school through your marriage," I asked questions directly if childbearing, employment activities or other key issues did not emerge from the conversation. Given the sensitive subject matter of this study, gentle probes were used to explore the range of post-marital activities undertaken, such as, " 'did you ever take in sewing?'; 'did your activities change when your children went to school?'; 'when your husband was ill/unemployed/absent how did your activities change?' "

Besides basic demographic data and an employment history, women were encouraged to provide information regarding spousal discussions of family provisioning, attitudes toward women's work (both paid and unpaid), changes to financial circumstances during their marriage, and other comments or reflections on their work since marriage. I also gathered information on spouses' occupations, presence and numbers of children, and other topics volunteered by respondents. Allowing and encouraging women to "talk" (DeVault, 1986), rather than using a structured interview, provided for incorporation of the perspective of these seniors in the research design itself.

One important point of exploration was whether their family financial circumstances changed dramatically at any time during their marriage. That question was intended to explore the influence of husbands' changing ability to provide financially for the family, and explore in that relatively safe context the possibility that married women worked for pay—an event certainly stigmatized at that time in Canadian history in all but the most extreme circumstances.

Interviews ranged from ten minutes to two hours. The ten-minute interview was one that was not recorded. Unfortunately so much information was communicated so rapidly that its richness could not be captured, thus that participant is not part of the experiences reported here for twenty-two women. While obviously more detail was presented in longer interviews, the time for debriefing or moving back to more general conversational topics varied as well. Every effort was made to be attuned to the emotions arising from contemplation of events that were often fifty, sixty or seventy years in the past. In addition, it was important to acknowledge the differing comfort levels women have in sharing details of their lives with a virtual stranger. Thus the variation in length of interviews, and what some might call their brevity, was not unintentional.

Data Analysis

As the study proceeded, I transcribed tapes for content. Interviews not audio-recorded were transcribed from notes. After each interview I recorded field notes. At times these notes recorded information shared by participants after the tape had been turned off; in other cases the information noted the setting of the interview, the demeanour of the woman, or other relevant contextual information. Field notes were added to the files for each participant by appending the material to the transcript of the interview.

Initially I used a process of immersion and crystallization (Crabtree, 1994) in working with the data. This analytic style is often found in the interpretivist approach to qualitative data analysis, whereby the interest is in interpretations of meanings made by social actors and researchers (Miles & Huberman, 1994). When used by phenomenologists, this approach looks for a practical understanding of meanings and actions–the *Lebenswelt* of the social actors (Miles & Huberman). In this study, it was the technique most familiar and comfortable for me. Essentially, immersion and crystallization involves a process of submerging oneself in the data of interest, through reading and re-reading the available materials in an effort to become intimate with the data. The crystallization phase occurs as relationships between individual pieces of information are revealed or become apparent. To those unfamiliar with this method, this analytic technique may seem ad hoc or difficult to validate. However, as the patterns in the data emerge and are identified, the technique can become very similar to thematic analysis, and may incorporate matrices.

From the initial immersion and crystallization stage, I moved to a comparison of individual women's experiences with those of other women. One goal was to discover patterns or ideal typical work experiences among the women in the study. Miles and Huberman (1994) report that cross-case analysis enhances generalizability and deepens understanding and explanations. As part of the cross-case analysis used in this study, I created a content-analytic summary table. At a later stage, I developed a case-ordered descriptive meta-matrix (Miles & Huberman). This matrix displayed the four groups of women identified in the analysis according to some of their basic and family characteristics. It is presented in Table 1.

While some terminology used by Miles and Huberman (1994) is utilised here for clarity in explaining the process of data analysis, it is important to note that this is a post hoc description. At the time the analysis was done, the process would have been described by me as 'getting intimate with the data, and working with it until themes, categories and patterns emerged.'

In the following pages, the data are presented to first illustrate similarities among this group of women during the lifecycle transition from single to married status. Differences among women's experiences are then pre-

TABLE 1. Characteristics of Women's Families

CHARACTERIZATION	EDUCATION	PRE-MARITAL EMPLOYMENT	HUSBAND'S OCCUPATION	NO. OF CHILDREN	FINANCIAL DISCUSSION	POST-MARITAL EMPLOYMENT
Vital Volunteers N = 4	University	Teacher (2) Optometry Clerk	Professional (Accountant; MD)	1 - 2	Absolutely not!	Volunteer work
Good Homemakers N = 6	Normal School	Teacher (2) Clerk (3) Nurse	Job or career (Sales, Administration)	0 - 9	No	Paid work for extras
The Sustainers N = 6	High/Normal School	Teacher (3) Music Teacher Store Clerk (2)	Working class (Sales, manual labour)	1 - 3	Yes	Invisible work
Single Survivors N = 6	One: Grade 11 Others: University	Commerce Nurse (2) Sales (3)	Job to professional (Farmer to MD)	0 - 5	Female Provider	Paid work

sented to reflect the greater salience of class and status as families became established or circumstances changed radically. I argue here that for women who remained married, class consciousness and status indicators, in large part visible through accounts of Goffmanian labor (Collins, 1991; Goffman, 1959) would ultimately affect later stages of the lives of women and their families. For women who became sole providers for their families their emergent class consciousness became directed at facilitating a secure future for first their children, and then themselves. Quotes in the text are identified by a first name only, not the real name of the participant, to preserve anonymity.

FAMILY LIVES AND WOMEN'S WORK

Women in this sample were born between the years 1889 and 1917. They were married during the years 1916 to 1946. These women are well educated, with their formal education completed at marriage ranging from Grade 11 to two university degrees. Although there was some correspondence between women's educational achievement and their spouses' occupations, it is important to note that the limited areas of employment for women at that period in history, e.g., teaching, nursing, clerical or sales work, is represented across the range of their husbands' occupations. These occupations ranged from casual labourer (e.g., rail worker, manual labourer, truck driver), to farmer, to salesmen and professionals (e.g., accountant, physician, lawyer). While presence and numbers of children are not a focal point in this discussion, it is interesting to note that there is no clear distributional difference according to husband's occupation, or apparent family socio-economic-status. Details of the study findings are initially presented using the life stages of developing and organizing married lives.

Leaving 'Work,' Joining Families

As at other stages of women's lives, family formation required some learning, changing and adapting on the part of the couple. In spite of the marriage bar (Lewis, 1986) that prohibited employment after marriage for most women in Western Canada at that time, many of these women were responsible for their own economic survival before marriage. It was taken for granted that they would not 'work' after marriage, no matter what the new family's financial circumstances. The change from employee to wife was strikingly consistent:

> I taught until I was married. Then you couldn't work anymore. It was a rule. In [her city] in [her province]. I don't know about the other provinces. (Katherine)

This was the case in other locations, and a situation not without its problems for newlyweds trying to manage on their own:

> So we worked things out that I would teach till the end of June and then we got married. In 1933. When you got married you couldn't work if they [the local school board] knew it. I had one [friend] ask how she could get out of her predicament (i.e., remain in paid employment after marriage). (Noreen)

These rules were not just in the professions, but were the practice in most women's occupations. Office workers as well were affected:

> And when I married in 1916 I was automatically out of work [as a department store clerk] because they didn't employ married women in those days. That was in the First World War. (Jane)

The formal marriage bar in the workplace, a result of fear for men's jobs, and the ideological prescriptions of the 'proper' place of women, combined to formally and informally ensure that a married woman's place was in the home.

While macro-structural factors appear to have left little choice in the matter, at the more micro level some husbands, too, were explicit in their expectations. We see a variety of reports of how decisions were made by the couple or the husband that for the wife, paid work ended. One woman, in response to a question asking if she remained employed after marriage, said:

> No, because there wasn't any war and in those days men had quite a bit to say about that and he didn't approve of me working. (Mary)

This was not an isolated experience:

> After the war—we were engaged before my husband went overseas— and then when he came home we got married. And there was NO QUESTION that I worked after he came back, you know, no question. [Did you discuss your working after marriage?] Well, we hadn't discussed it, and I didn't want to work and he was working and then you have a baby. (Barbara)

Even when women were employed in an area in which expertise was in short supply, marriage and the roles that came with it took precedence over employment.

> And when we got married I was earning $250 a week, and he was earning $240 per week. Then [a national firm] said to me, "Miss, we are just waiting for you to just move in here and start working on Monday morning." And my fiance said over my dead body and that was it [laughter]. And that was it you see. And most of my friends were the same. (Barbara)

The one exception to this pattern was a woman with a very non-traditional approach to married life:

> I know I had difficulty adapting to women's role at that time. I thought it was very narrow. And of course all the magazines in the '50s that really, if you took the magazines seriously you'd be hopping around madly doing things in the home. But I wasn't very talented in these things. (Maggie)

Of most salience to women at this time of transition was a role change, from single woman to wife and often soon, mother. At the early stages of family formation, these experiences were shared by women who were teachers, sales clerks, nurses, and other professionals. Although some women married budding professionals, whether physicians or accountants, and others married labourers, farmers and salesmen, the establishment of a new family and the comforts of home were a struggle for most. Women moved from city to country, from one city to another, and still others from family homes to places of their own. There was also the expectation that women would automatically know, and be prepared to undertake, the activities ideologically associated with becoming a wife, and shortly thereafter a mother.

Family Beginnings

Although there was little question that paid employment would cease at marriage, sometimes initial expectations and plans had to be changed as economic and other realities of marriage emerged. In becoming part of a couple and new family, often both women and men had to adapt to changing roles and circumstances. One young teacher married an electrical engineer, who was initially employed in a large city after their wedding. But the 1930s were difficult times:

Things flattened out you know, and the farm next to his father's was being sold, and he bought it so that was where I lived. (Doreen)

Women were expected to be ready for all aspects of marriage, and to be flexible in adapting to the circumstances in which they found themselves:

That was understood that you had to be ready to set up your own home before you got married. It was my life and I had nobody to talk to. I did most of the sewing for my children (4 girls and 5 boys) until they were in their teens–and then I thought they should have tailored clothes. In my days we knew what it was to scrub on a scrub board to do our own washing! (Jane)

The work was challenging, with women drawing on their own innovation and strength to do what had to be done. Although women were not unaware of the related duties in becoming a wife, then as now the change in roles was not always easy:

He was a farmer and also a handyman. Well, I didn't live on the farm but I had to learn to cook meals, cook good meals, and of course there was no time until my little girl came along and my mother lived with me too, she had arthritis, and so I had a baby and a new husband [laughter] and my mother. I didn't want to look for other work. (Joyce)

This type of learning quickly to care was the experience of other women in the sample. New roles, much larger than merely that of wife, were thrust quickly upon women at marriage. Although questions about how the family managed financially were not directly asked, many statements help us to understand the ways in which women learned to cope, with or without acknowledgement that it was necessary.

Making Ends Meet

Especially as these new families were formed, women's labour was often substituted for the modern conveniences that money couldn't, at that stage, purchase. Family finances were seldom a topic of discussion for married couples. Instead, women innovated in the function of resources, both their own and those to which they had access, for many and varied uses. Although evidenced more at later stages of marriage, we see here evidence of women drawing on their past training to innovate in a manner suited to their position vis-à-vis the ideal typical breadwinner family:

> Although my husband was a chartered accountant, it took time to get established. So when I went shopping I had to take the children with me, and they got bored. So I would take them to the pet store, and they would watch the pets while I went shopping.
>
> And sometimes they would just stay at home. And of course we really couldn't afford that much so I would get the pattern catalogues, you know the small ones, and we would use them as cut-outs for the children. (Thelma)

Some women didn't care to elaborate on their post-marital financial circumstances, but acknowledged that living on one income had its challenges:

> Well, when we decided to get married, we got married. I knew that I wouldn't be able to work, mmmm [pause] we managed. (Katherine)

And from another:

> When you got married you couldn't work if they knew it. . . . There were a lot of times when you could really have used that money, really needed it and but [sic] we just bought things as we could. (Leslie)

These quotations illustrate the variety and commonality of women's experiences as they formed families and began to establish routines and responsibilities for various aspects of family life. Women clearly saw a dichotomy between real work, that which is paid, and the activities that they undertook as wives and mothers. However, it is also evident that in undertaking the myriad tasks that arose through challenging circumstances with which they were presented, these newlywed women contributed significantly to their family resources, substituting their managerial skills, if not their labour, in lieu of family income. We also see an awareness that while their marriage contract came with certain expectations for their roles as wives, there was room for innovation and use of existing skills, some discretionary possibilities in how these roles were played out, and expectations that emanated from women's gendered class and status positions.

Aside from one group who were to become single providers, women's conversation regarding their post-marital work was minimally focused on childcare. The question of 'getting by' was relevant for most during the early years of their marriage, as even future and new professionals were getting established. During the early years of marriage, patterns that continued throughout the marriage began to emerge. I will now report on distinctions between the kinds of work women did as the effect of socio-economic status became more salient.

Gendered Responses to Class Differences

The almost universal experience of women who married in the interwar and early WWII years was that employment ceased at marriage. Although this occurred in the face of reluctance for some women, others were quickly absorbed by the demands of husbands, households, childbearing and childrearing, and care of extended family. Many families struggled economically as husband's careers were established, homes were purchased or improved, and children were added to the family. The strategies that women employed as they managed and contributed to their family resources varied according to husband's occupation and income, as patterns for the future began to be established, but also according to women's individual reactions to the intersection of gender and class.

It is important to note that it was not the husband's occupation alone that created the family's status vis-à-vis the breadwinner ideal. The public appearance of the family's status was also an influential factor in women's work (cf. Meadows, 1991). The nature of that work did, nonetheless, vary according to the family's socioeconomic status.

After initial analysis of the data, I identified four post-hoc categories of women's work. The categories were based on the question, "What was a core influence in the different types of work these women performed?" The categories were also influenced by Collins' (1988, 1991) discussion of women's Goffmanian labour. This labour includes that which is done backstage (behind the scenes) to present a public (or frontstage) image of a particular type of family. The first group is composed of families who became upper middle-class, the second group are generally middle class, the third group are working class, and the fourth group reflects the experience of women who became the sole supporters of their families.

The categories presented here were developed by me in analysis of the data for my dissertation. At that time I struggled to name the categories without labelling women according to their husbands' socio-economic status. The Vital Volunteers are characterized by their ability to apply their skills to the important challenges of volunteer work, with an attitude of gusto (Meadows, 1991). The Good Homemakers embraced the ideal typical role of the efficient domestic engineer, while seeing to it that their husbands were publically and privately acknowledged as the family breadwinner. The Sustainers earned money to keep bodies together, and maintained a proper public image for their families, keeping souls together as well. The Single Survivors provided financially for themselves and their families, often not just surviving but flourishing. They took a proactive approach to the everyday lived realities of being a wife, mother and woman. Illustrations from women's experiences in this class and gendered milieu are presented below. They depict the full continuum of possibilities, from compliance to resistance.

Vital Volunteers: Women in Upper Middle-Class Families

The received view of traditional families is that the wives of relatively well-to-do men spend their hours in conspicuous consumption and other leisured pursuits. A more realistic depiction of their lives adds entertainment of husbands' clients and an array of volunteer labour to their pursuits. Women in this study whose families' socio-economic status appeared upper-middle class in retrospect are identified here as the Vital Volunteers. Although they may not initially have enjoyed comfortable economic circumstances, their husbands' careers were on the road to success, with the apparent 'volunteer' extraction of wife work including that of a career helpmate and front-stage (Goffman, 1959) appearance of a leisured life.

The precise nature of those activities and services appropriate for the wives of budding or established professionals varied, although the central goal was a common one. The Vital Volunteers produced status for their families through the giving of gifts (i.e., services) that were not reciprocated on the material level, awarding status to the giver (Collins, 1988). One woman described her activities this way:

> And over where my husband worked he said they were desperate for people to volunteer, and *that would be a good thing for me to do.* And of course it didn't pay and all and besides I was the wife of the head of the place and of course everything was rosy. So I started off with one of the volunteer organizations, delivering goods and yakking to the men and I found I loved it. (Emphasis added.) (Barbara)

This woman chose volunteer work as a way to get away from a "flippin' hovel" much different from the home she was used to, but also because, for her husband's career (and thus implicitly the wife's role), it was the proper thing to do. As she used her talents in this apparently necessary way, she also found work that was acceptable for one in her position, and that she loved. Another wife of a professional man stated:

During the War years I didn't really didn't need to work. My husband was head of a chartered accountant firm, so I did lots of entertaining. I needed to help my husband with his career. (Thelma)

The rhetoric surrounding these volunteer and entertainment activities suggests that women (at least in retrospect) saw the connection between their volunteer efforts and their husbands' careers. Although clearly these endeavours were part of the support network for the family provider, wives' work was not understood as a direct contribution to their family resources, or the success of their husbands' careers. Yet women provide the sense that there was enjoyment in these tasks as well, albeit within the prescriptions of the breadwinner ideology, and the resultant gender-specific normative practices:

Quite a few of them [friends] were university graduates and their husbands said they could do aaalllll the volunteer work you like and you can do Junior League or anything else but you can't take pay. We just accepted it. We just accepted it. . . . And we [herself and her husband] had a strong feeling that it really wasn't fair for me to take a job that some young girl that wasn't married might need. (Barbara)

And although there were many hours and much skill involved in co-ordinating fund-raising, entertaining veterans and entertaining guests, these activities were perceived externally as 'to fill the time,' and part of women's leisure. Seldom did women attribute skill to the volunteer work which they undertook, similar in fact to work which took place in the market place:

I volunteered for the symphony and the ballet. I usually ended up being treasurer. There was lots of responsibility, especially when we had these big sales. (Katherine)

And yet this same woman stated:

My sister was very clever. I don't think I was. . . .

The apparently leisured lives of the wives of upper middle-class professionals were filled with both homemaking (discounted to the point of non-discussion in the interviews), and challenging schedules of social and volunteer events. Even when financial concerns were not central, women required resilience in dealing with the circumstances of their lives:

> [A]fter my husband died I lived in that big home by myself, and I
> had trouble with gardeners and other help. Being a woman alone,
> you know. . . . (Thelma)

Women dealt with the intricacies of balancing volunteer work, entertaining for husbands, or raising children and running a home. The nature and
range of activities undertaken by the Vital Volunteers, although apparently
contributing to societal, rather than family good, were nevertheless part of
the family resources. Although these family women *appeared* to attain the
ideological goal of leisured pursuit of consumption and entertainment,
their own words refute that image:

> See all these young people who might go into it [volunteer work],
> whose husbands might be in the positions and so on, they have
> suddenly decided they want to get out and into the business world.
> But that's why it is [the current volunteer shortage], because they
> don't have to work but they want to get out and do things, you can't
> do both because it takes a lot of time if you have a house to run.
> (Katherine)

For these women the public visibility of their contributions to their family
resources rendered them redefined as leisure rather than as connected to
family resources. Many of these activities were a vital link in the ability of
husbands to be the good providers that they were. What this group of
women help make clear is their adaptation of pre-marital skills and training to the circumstances in which they found themselves, contributing to
their families in a necessary way, but also finding ways to self-fulfilment
in a context of ideological and micro and macro-structural constraints.

Good Homemakers: Women in Middle-Class Families

The calling of the Good Homemaker was to be a good wife and mother:
to provide care and a comfortable home for her husband and children,
through activities that publically affirmed her husband's success in providing, and her own as a domestic engineer. Good Homemakers left the paid
labour force at marriage, but sometime during their married lives many of
them undertook employment or activities that resulted in financial gain.
Their paid labour was, however, only perceived as for 'extras,' for fun or
to help out a friend. From the perspective of these women, their husbands
were the providers, and good ones at that. These husbands ran farms or
worked in offices, bringing in money or goods to meet basic family needs.
As wives, women's role was to see that their home ran smoothly, through

exercise of their skills in domestic engineering. This was often accomplished through innovative adaptation of formal workplace experience to married life where women were expected to instinctively know how to translate extant ideological and structural prescriptions into praxis.

In the country, women with city upbringings had to learn to do the appropriate chores for a farm wife. The hours were often long, and the labour strenuous, and sometimes recreation was all in the interpretation:

> We had 125 chickens and we sold the eggs because . . . they gave an extra good cross for laying or eating. And we used to take them [up to the nearby town] every week. It was kind of fun because you didn't get away much. My sister-in-law and I would go—it was nice to get away for an afternoon. (Mae)

Although clearly in retrospect this woman was contributing to family finances, at the time, and through her own contemporary illustration, she had an afternoon off from household and farm duties when travelling into town. Good Homemakers often spoke of their paid work in terms of voluntary forays into the wider world, something new to do, out of the ordinary routine, but never alluding to increased income that complemented or was necessary in addition to that of their husbands, the good providers. Indeed their need to exert autonomy in spite of circumstances comes subtly through in their accounts. As one woman described it:

> My husband was very very wonderful, very kind and helpful. [I took the job] just because, you know, I've always been active. [He] at first didn't like it, but then he drove me down and picked me up each day. (Jane)

Although in this family the husband had a good income, as long as the wife's paid employment was viewed as helping out someone who needed her, the employment was acceptable, especially because the request came from a fellow parishioner. And the woman had a chance to use her talents in an arena (college matron) that provided positive feedback. Given the prevailing ideology, any work for pay undertaken by wives of men supposedly earning a family wage needed to be framed in a context far from provisioning. For another woman who sold sterling silver over the phone:

> Well, and he was away in the War, and I liked to be doing something. So I sold people their silver, and that way I earned our own flatware set! (Alice)

Other women in this group did sewing for friends, neighbours and strangers, nursed entire communities for a thank you, and shared their skills with young wives of their acquaintance. One woman was astonished at the thought that her rural neighbours would actually pay or provide farm produce for her services (Bertha). In contrast to the Vital Volunteers, Good Homemakers did sometimes work for pay. However, when asked, Good Homemakers never worked because they needed pay–and seldom saw what they were doing as work. After all:

> I didn't go out in the fields and work! (Mae)

In this group, women's activities, even when generating remuneration, were seen to be in pursuit of fun, or to pay for extras like vacations and store-bought clothing. The Good Homemakers fulfilled the role for which they had prepared–secure with their good providers. The attitudes they evinced were positive, with their willingness to do whatever needed to be done apparent. Our third group, the wives of working-class men, had a more difficult job–that of living in a world attuned to the middle-class ideal of the breadwinner family, while circumstances made making ends meet an everyday struggle for them.

The Sustainers: Wives in Working-Class Families

In contrast to the first two groups of women, this group, called the Sustainers, was a necessary resource to their families' financial survival, a reality more often than not recognized and possibly even discussed by the couple. Their contributions to family resources involved more than the physical labour with which they tended their homes and their children. It also involved their undertaking of tasks in lieu of the benefits of the industrialization of housework, public creation of the illusion of domestic attainment of the breadwinner ideal, financial negotiations and management, the taking in of boarders, or work from other families that was invisibly completed behind the walls of the household. The Sustainers were women whose paid work, although often invisible, facilitated, whether consciously or unconsciously, public presentation of their husbands as good providers, thus garnering the familial status of breadwinner family. While often in difficult circumstances, these women often succeeded despite the structural and ideological constraints that surrounded them. Rather than a sense of having been somehow let down by their 'good provider,' there is evidence of the added work that these women did in protecting the pretence of male family wage, and their public role in maintaining this image. Said one woman of their finances on the day she was married:

> [In 1942] I had $40.00 in the bank, and he had $10.00 in his pocket. (Anne)

While they were both aware of their shaky fiscal situation, times were hard for many couples, and this did not deter them from entering into marriage optimistically. Children came quickly for this couple, but they did have their own home within a few years. However, small children couldn't be left home alone. The solution to the need for added income was very close to home:

> We had boarders from the time the young girls were three or four. We heard about the nursing aid program at a local college, all girls, and the government allowed them $45.00 for board and room. We (sic) gave them all their meals, all the beds, the towels and that, but otherwise they did their own rinsing out. We figured that at least we'd have food. (Anne)

Through the intensification of women's household labour, food was put on the table for the family. Just a bit more washing up, a few more meals and beds to make. Just housework. Sometimes hard work was joined by faith that families would get by:

> I wondered how we would get by. I didn't know what to do. And then I turned to my Faith, and decided to let Someone Else show me how to handle these problems. They weren't really in my hands, or my control. And things worked out. (Clara)

In this case, things worked out through taking in boarders, an idea suggested by a helpful neighbour. In a time when men were supposed to be the providers, one had to pretend not to know the neighbours knew the boarders were a key source of income. At other times women reported earning money through taking the census, sewing clothes for others, and negotiating with the corner grocer for credit. One woman reported working in a munitions factory doing inspections of seventeen-pound shells. She lived entirely on her own salary, banking that of her husband while he was overseas at war. This woman was sorry when the war ended, and her job with it.

As the Sustainers talked, the demands of childcare, husbands, boarders, putting food (literally) on the table, and getting by are obvious. None of these women mentioned that what came home in their husbands' pay packet wasn't enough to sustain the family. Rather, over and over again I heard women ask how *they* were going to get by. Whether eating just potatoes and turnips because that was what the grocer was willing to provide on credit, hoping a Higher Being would lend a helping hand, or using income from boarders to feed the family, the Sustainers were actively involved in keeping their families going. Retrospectively it is clear that their lives never even approximated the breadwinner family. However, the influence of that mythical ideal seems so ingrained that one of these women mentioned being the most consistent source of income for her family for a number of years only after talking about her husband as provider for over an hour! Clearly for these women their work involved all aspects of social reproduction: support of male workers, nurturance of their families, paid labor, and an attempt to conform publically to the prescriptive ideological context of their period in history, yet involving great innovation on their part to be part of a resource-gathering team.

These three groups of women all contributed directly to their family resources and economies, as their efforts operated in combination with either their husbands' earnings or position to facilitate adequate and complete social reproduction. The final group of women in this study found themselves at some point in their marriage in quite different circumstances: they became their family's sole source of resources, and were explicitly the good providers for their families. For the Single Survivors, restraints of a particular social class became moot at the loss of their husband. What became most germane was the care and education of their children, and ensuring a present and future for them all.

Single Survivors: Women on Their Own

Several of the women in this study were married for a relatively short period of time before their husbands ceased to be part of their lives— whether through death, separation or divorce. It is assumed that these women entered into their marriages with roughly similar expectations to others in the study: they too were surrounded by structural factors such as the breadwinner ideology and censure of married women's paid work. Within their marriages they found themselves in a variety of socio-economic circumstances. However, upon the demise or absence of their husbands, Single Survivors became the sole support for their families.

For three women in this study the Second World War exacerbated the unconventional behaviour of their husbands. Within a few years after the War their marriages ended (either formally or informally). Left alone with children and little if any financial support, these women consciously planned and undertook strategies that would provide for their families, including themselves, their children and at times their present but incapacitated husbands. In speaking of their lives as family providers they unanimously were determined that in addition to the basics of food and shelter, their children would receive a good education, to prepare them for later life. Summing up her efforts, one woman said:

> I've had sort of a struggle but I think I had it good compared to what some people had. I didn't have children that were trouble, and one thing and another, and I was very lucky to have the health to be able to work so long. I knew I had to, so I just made up my mind to make the best of it and I did. So many of them, like I was bound I wasn't going to go on welfare. So many of them were on relief of some kind. They didn't try. I made up my mind "no!" (Norma)

Left alone with her children, this woman sought and found resources to keep her family off social assistance. In the lean years before her employment, her family helped out. Later, when she was working full time, her concern was that her children stay in school.

Another woman, left alone with two young children and a farm, returned to her earlier career as teacher to provide for her family:

> I taught English and a bit of math. I would have liked all math, but in those days the women didn't get math. I taught there for ten years. Well, I retired from there. It had plus sides, and I had the children. Well, it was high school and the children and the house and everything, that's a full time job. (Victoria)

Women on their own with their children had to provide not only for the present, but also for the future. In spite of facing societal disapproval for married women (even without husbands) taking up jobs, the Single Survivors displayed resilience and courage as they embraced the role of provider. They not only did what was necessary, they made the best of it:

> [When my children were still at home] I did all sort of handicrafts and things like that along with my little [hairdressing] business and I got by somehow. When they both [children] left home I went out and took my grade 12 and went back to the local college and got my degree. I taught school at a vocational school until I retired. It really surprised me because when I went back to study I had been out of school for 31 years. It was very challenging, but I liked it though, and I enjoyed teaching. And that is about the story of my life. (Beth)

The matter-of-fact conclusions and mundane nature attributed to these activities by the Single Survivors echo those of the women in the three previous groups. Like the others, when they had to, they coped with all the exigencies of providing for the resources for their families. While circumstances were not always similar to the existing vision of the ideal family, women made the best of what they had to deal with, and to a woman, they 'got by.' The Sustainers demonstrated evidence of an important and increasingly visible class of women, those who defied or overcame gender and class constraints and actively sought a good life for their children, and when possible, themselves. In spite of prescriptive gendered roles, they showed an independence of spirit and willingness to do what was necessary to nurture the needs of themselves and their families, rather than the public expectations for women and their economic roles.

DISCUSSION

In the foregoing pages, we have seen through description and in women's own words how their work was part of the intricate web of resources that provided for the survival and public presentation of their families as whole and well. At the macro level, the breadwinner or good provider ideology set the context for and supported the structural marriage bar prohibiting the explicit paid employment of married women. At the micro level both the structural and ideological influences were reinforced in face-to-face interaction: a husband's assertion that his wife would work "over his dead body"; friends asking how to pass as still single to keep their teaching jobs; and married women not wanting to take a job from a single woman. Clearly in the norms and mores of the time, as well as in the formal rules of the paid workplace, women were wives, and men were workers.

Even in spite of this social and cultural context, we see diversity and innovation in women's contributions to their family resources. Sometimes women found they liked the options open to them; in other cases women railed against "hopping around the house doing things madly," or restrictions on paid employment. While the interplay of structure and ideology were much in evidence and influential, we see that for many women, those were merely two more factors to be juggled in their lives as mothers, wives and women.

A feminist political economy embraces enquiry into the connection and interdependence of work and family. The expanded definition of work, including all activities, both physical and mental, that are aimed at transforming materials into a more useful form, renders a larger scope of women's activities open to enquiry and explanation. Thus we see that women used formal education or employment as they planned or executed strategies for their families' survival, including adaptation to ideological and structural constraints. From the perspective of a feminist political economy, paid and domestic labour are two sides of the same coin, both leading to the reproduction of classes and capital accumulation. Thus, in concert these women and their husbands (when present) worked together in various forms to foster capital accumulation. When men's paid labour did not bring cash into the home, or came in an insufficient amount, women's paid labour was substituted. When men's career included the facets of volunteer work or business entertaining to complete its obligations, domestic and volunteer labour were contributed by women. And when women chose to work for pay, their wages were apparently only "for extras," as they worked for "something to do." When class constraints became superfluous to family needs, women acted in the best interests of their families, at times tailoring their strategies to their own needs as individuals within those families.

In these strategies great strength and wisdom can be identified. Surrounded by the ideology of the mythical breadwinner family, given gendered differences in the division of labour, and the economic realities of both their personal lives and the inter-war macro economy, these women cast clear eyes on their social reality. When shopping had to be done, the pet store served as a babysitter. A day marketing eggs was a day of leisure. Volunteer work and running a house take a lot of time–BUT something that would be "a good thing to do" could also be an activity that one loved.

In bringing these accounts of many individual women's lives together, it has been possible to discover patterns of similarity and differences in their lives. While generalizations must be confined to women of which this group is representative, it is clear that during the time period described their gender and economy intersected then, as now, with family. Furthermore, just as other social institutions impact families, families and their members have a reciprocal relationship. The women in this study were not victims of the time and place in which they lived. Rather they were often facilitators of change and innovators in dealing with realities in spite of social myths and ideologies.

In undertaking this study, it has been necessary not only to invoke past training, but also to be willing to push at the parameters of my own *Weltanschauang* (world view) to be willing and able to better understand and share the experiences of other women. The challenge of melding eclectic pieces of theoretical approaches and methodologies into a form that is understood by a wider audience hopefully provides both insight for other researchers, and knowledge of its use to a wider audience as we come to know both our past and our present. As we come to better understand women's work, we gain in our knowledge of the intersection of family, gender and economy.

REFERENCES

Bernard, J. (1981). The good provider role: Its rise and fall. *American Psychologist, 36,* 1, 1-12.

Brenner, J. & Laslett, B. (1991). Gender, social reproduction, and women's self-organization: Considering the U.S. Welfare State. *Gender and Society, 5,* 3. 311-333.

Cheal, D. (1989). Theoretical frameworks. In G. N. Ramu (Ed.), *Marriage and the Family in Canada Today* (pp. 19-34). Ontario: Prentice Hall.

Collins, R. (1988). Women and men in the class structure. *Journal of Family Issues, 9,* 1, 27-50.

Collins, R. (1991). Women and men in the class structure. R. L. Blumberg (Ed.), *Gender, Family, and Economy,* Newbury Park, CA: Sage.

Crabtree, B. F. (1994). Overview of approaches to qualitative research in the clinical setting. *10th Annual ASPN Convocation of Practices,* Colorado Springs, CO, February.

Crease, G. (1988). The politics of dependence: Women, work, and unemployment in the Vancouver labour movement before World War II. *Canadian Journal of Sociology,* 121-142.

DeVault, M. (1986). *Talking and listening from women's standpoint: Feminist strategies for analysing interview data.* Paper presented at The Society for Study of Symbolic Interaction.

Goffman, E. (1959). *Presentation of Self in Everyday Life.* Garden City, NY: Anchor.

Hareven, T. K. & Modell, J. (1980). Ethnic families. In S. Thernstrom (Ed.), *Harvard Encyclopedia of American Ethnic Groups.* New York: The Guilford Press.

Hareven, T. K. (1982). American families in transition: Historical perspectives on change. In Froma Walsh (Ed.), *Normal Family Processes* (pp. 446-466). New York: The Guilford Press.

Hawkesworth, Mary E. (1989). Knowers, knowing and known: Feminist theory and claims of truth. *SIGNS, 14,* 3, 533-557. Chicago: The University of Chicago.

Keating, N. & Jeffrey, B. (1983). Work careers of ever married and never married retired women. *The Gerontologist, 23,* 4, 416-421.

Lengermann, P. M. & Niebrugge-Brantley, J. (1988). Feminist sociological theory: The near future prospects. In George Ritzer (Ed.), *Frontiers of Social Theory: The New Synthesis* (pp. 282-325). New York: Columbia University Press.

Lewis, J. (editor) (1986). *Labour & Love: Women's Experience of Home and Family 1850-1940.* Oxford: Basil Blackwell Ltd.

Lincoln, Y. S. & Guba, E. G. (1985). *Naturalistic Enquiry.* Beverly Hills, CA: Sage.

Lopata, H. A. (1993). The interweave of public and private: Women's challenge to American society. *Journal of Marriage and the Family, 55,* 176-190.

Luxton, M. (1980). *More Than a Labour of Love.* Toronto: The Women's Press.

Marchak, P. (1985). Canadian political economy. *Canadian Review of Sociology and Anthropology, 22,* 673-709.

Maroney, H. J. & Luxton, M. (1987). *Feminism and Political Economy: Women's Work, Women's Struggles.* Toronto: Metheun.

Marshall, C. & Rossman, G. B. (1989). *Designing Qualitative Research.* Newbury Park, CA: Sage.

McCracken, G. (1988). *The Long Interview.* Beverly Hills, CA: Sage.

Meadows, L. M. (1991). *Women's contributions to family resources.* Unpublished dissertation (Sociology). The University of Calgary, Calgary, Canada.

Miles, M. B. & Huberman, A. M. (1994). *Qualitative Data Analysis (2nd ed.).* Thousand Oaks, CA: Sage.

Modell, J. & Hareven, T. K. (1973). *Family Socialization and Interaction Processes.* Chicago: University of Chicago Press.

Parr, J. (1990). *The Gender of Breadwinners: Women, Men, and Change in Two Industrial Towns 1880-1950.* Toronto: The University of Toronto Press.

Patton, M. Q. (1990). *Qualitative Evaluation and Research Methods* (2nd ed.). Newbury Park: Sage.

Prentice, A., Bourne, P., Cuthbert Brandt, G., Light, B., Michinson, W. & Black, N. (1988). *Canadian Women: A History.* Toronto: Harcourt Brace Jovanovich.

Silverman, E. L. (1984). *The Last Best West: Women on the Alberta Frontier 1880-1930.* Montreal: Eden.

Strong-Boag, V. & Fellman, A. C. (Eds.) (1986). *Rethinking Canada: The Promise of Women's History.* Toronto: Copp Clark Pitman.

Tilly, L. A. & Scott, J. W. (1978/1988). *Women, Work and Family.* New York: Holt, Reinhardt and Winston.

Welter, B. (1966). The cult of true womanhood: 1820-1860. *American Quarterly, 18,* 151-74.

Using Pattern Matching
and Modified Analytic Induction
in Examining Justice Principles
in Child Support Guidelines

Kathryn D. Rettig
Vicky Chiu-Wan Tam
Beth Maddock Magistad

SUMMARY. This paper reports on the design of a study using procedures of modified analytic induction to investigate how courtroom procedures followed or did not follow child support guidelines. Using concepts from principles of procedural fairness and distributive justice, the research team coded transcripts of public hearings on child support guidelines. This paper reports on work in progress and does not report results or conclusions. The coded examples of justice

Kathryn D. Rettig is Professor, Department of Family Social Science, College of Human Ecology, University of Minnesota, Twin Cities, 1985 Buford Avenue, St. Paul, MN 55108. Vicky Chiu-Wan Tam is a PhD candidate, Department of Family Social Science, University of Minnesota, Twin Cities. Beth Maddock Magistad is a PhD student, Department of Family Social Science, University of Minnesota, Twin Cities.

The study was funded by The Minnesota Agricultural Experiment Station, Project 52-054, "Justice Principles in Divorce Decision Procedures and Resource Allocations," Kathryn D. Rettig, Principal Investigator; and The McKnight, Bush, Bigelow, St. Paul, and Emma B. Howe Foundations. Interpretations of the results are the responsibilities of the authors and do not represent views of funding agencies.

[Haworth co-indexing entry note]: "Using Pattern Matching and Modified Analytic Induction in Examining Justice Principles in Child Support Guidelines." Rettig, Kathryn D., Vicky Chiu-Wan Tam, and Beth Maddock Magistad. Co-published simultaneously in *Marriage & Family Review* (The Haworth Press, Inc.) Vol. 24, No. 1/2, 1996, pp. 193-222; and: *The Methods and Methodologies of Qualitative Family Research* (ed: Marvin B. Sussman, and Jane F. Gilgun) The Haworth Press, Inc., 1996, pp. 193-222. Single or multiple copies of this article are available for a fee from The Haworth Document Delivery Service [1-800-342-9678, 9:00 a.m. - 5:00 p.m. (EST). E-mail address: getinfo@haworth.com].

principles demonstrate how procedures of modified analytic induction lead to the refinement of conceptual definitions when tested against lived experiences. *[Article copies available for a fee from The Haworth Document Delivery Service: 1-800-342-9678. E-mail address: getinfo@ haworth.com]*

KEYWORDS. Child support, Distributive justice, Induction, Congruence, Qualitative research, Hermeneutics

People who speak at public hearings about political issues are often the ones who have intense interests in a particular policy, strong feelings about alternative proposals, or who expect increased resources to result from the outcome of the policy debate. People who have the motivational energy to speak at public hearings about needed changes in child support guidelines probably have had direct or indirect experiences concerning the injustices resulting from applications of the guidelines to particular cases. Therefore, a public hearing about child support guidelines could be expected to provide personal stories about injustice experiences. An injustice experience presupposes that another person or institution has violated the victim's justified entitlement either by action or by omission. As Montada (1994) wrote, "Perceived injustice involves views about moral or legal norms, associated entitlement, and judgments about responsibility for harm and loss" (p. 6).

Deutsch (1983) concluded that there was little research concerning actual experiences of those who suffer injustice. Most existing studies using justice theories were conducted with experimental and survey designs and not in natural settings (Cohen, 1987; Mikula, 1984). Little is known about the emotions that follow the perception of injustice (Greenberg, 1984), the cognitive processes that are elicited (Mikula, 1986), or the different justice principles that adults are able to understand, define, and implement in a variety of situations. Most studies have focused on one or two dominant justice principles and few have examined intimate relations where there are multiple competing principles that require compromises (Tornblom, 1992). In addition, there are limited numbers of studies that have applied justice theories to family issues such as supporting children following divorce (Rettig & Dahl, 1991, 1993; Rettig, Magistad & Tam, 1994). In view of our limited understanding of perceived injustices, it seemed important to conduct an in-depth exploration of an actual situation in order to determine if the theories that developed through the methods of positivistic science could be found in everyday life.

The natural setting of the research originated from a federal mandate that states conduct periodic evaluations of numeric child support guide-lines. One state conducted four public hearings in 1990 to gather informa-tion about how the guidelines affected parents and children. These hear-ings were tape recorded and transcribed for later analyses. The investigators acquired these recordings because their ongoing divorce research project included a policy evaluation of child support guidelines. The transcripts provided an opportunity to analyze an additional data source for the pur-pose of looking for answers to the same research questions as the quantita-tive analyses of the ongoing project. The focus of inquiry for the present study was: What are the perceived injustices of the child support guide-lines and the child support system? The informants for the study were people who spoke at the hearings. We assumed they spoke because they had experienced or known about the injustices of child support guidelines, had read or heard about the hearings in advance, and were available to speak at the particular time and place.

The purposes of the research project were both substantive and method-ological. The substantive purposes were to examine perceptions of injus-tice in the child support guidelines using procedural and distributive jus-tice principles as theoretical standards for the interpretation of speakers' perspectives and to investigate whether the patterns represented in justice theories would emerge in a natural setting. The long-term objectives of the project were to contribute to a general understanding of perceived injus-tices associated with supporting children following divorce, to facilitate theory development by refining and adding to the theoretical definitions of procedural and distributive justice constructs, to supply rationale for pro-posed policy changes in the state child support guidelines, and to assist professionals in articulating justice principles during conflictual decision processes of divorcing parties. The process of restoring justice is only possible when people can clearly explain the violations that have occurred and the patterns of the violations can be summarized with a coherent organization of ideas. The underlying assumption of the research was that justice theories might provide a more systematic way of summarizing the injustice experiences with child support guidelines.

The methodological purposes of the present paper are to demonstrate the qualitative research processes of design, coding, and analysis data gathered in naturalistic setting. A deeper understanding of these research processes may be helpful to readers who are interested in applying existing theories to an actual life situation. This paper includes an explicit descrip-tion of the theoretical principles and an interpretive group process for coding by pattern matching. The ideas of speakers were matched to prior theoretical definitions of justice principles. There is also a description of one of the first steps of analytic induction where theoretical definitions were revised for greater precision. The research reported in this paper is work in process and therefore does not include results or conclusions. Coded examples of the justice principles are provided in order to demonstrate processes of refining theoretical definitions.

THEORETICAL BACKGROUND

Justice theories assume that "justice" has multiple meanings and that individuals use these internal meanings as guidelines to evaluate the fairness of decision procedures and the justice of resource distributions. It is expected that individuals in the same decision situation may use different internal meanings of justice and that these multiple perspectives contribute to the difficulties in communication and understanding that lead to conflicts. These internal guidelines have been called justice "principles," "values," and "decision rules" (Deutsch, 1985). Procedural justice theories are concerned with the fairness of decision procedures through which resource distributions are made (Tyler, 1987). Distributive justice involves moral decisions about comparative allotments of material goods, or social conditions, roles, opportunities, duties, or responsibilities (Cohen, 1987).

Procedural Fairness Principles

The fairness of formal decision procedures of divorce can be evaluated on the basis of several principles outlined in procedural justice theories (Austin & Tobiason, 1984; Leventhal, 1980; Lind & Tyler, 1988) including accuracy, bias suppression, consistency, correctability, ethicality, and representativeness.

Accuracy. The principle of accuracy requires that decision procedures be based on accurate information. This requires accountability of persons who produce information and records.

Bias suppression. The principle of bias suppression is upheld when the self-interests, doctrinaire views, and prior beliefs of the decision maker are suppressed during the allocation process. The decision procedure should consider all points of view, each of which must receive adequate and equal consideration.

Consistency. The principle of consistency requires that decision procedures be consistent across persons and situations over time.

Correctability. The principle of correctability requires that there be opportunities for modification or reversal of decisions. There must be grievance and appeals procedures.

Ethicality. The principle of ethicality states that decision procedures for resource allocations should be based on prevailing moral and ethical standards. Deception, bribery, and invasion of privacy should be avoided.

Representativeness. The principle of representativeness requires consideration of the concerns, values, and outlook of all recipients and subgroups in the population. The decision maker should be representative of the consensual attitudes and values of society during decision procedures.

Distributive Justice Principles

Distributive justice theories have identified principles people use to evaluate resource distributions. The three major distributive justice principles (or decision rules) are contributions, needs, and equality (Cohen, 1987; Deutsch, 1985; Schwinger, 1980). The other central principles are legality, justified self-interest, adhering to commitments, ownership, and status (Leventhal, 1980).

Contributions. The contributions principle requires that resources be distributed in relation to the amount and kind of contributions that were originally made. Equity is achieved when there is equality of outcomes per unit input. A prerequisite of using the contributions rule is the requirement that contributions of participants can be reliably measured.

Needs. The needs principle requires that more resources must be allocated to persons with greater needs. Requirements for applying the needs rule are that needs can be reliably measured and there is accurate information on the character and intensity of individual needs as well as consensus on the comparability and hierarchy of needs across persons.

Equality. The equality principle states that everyone must receive the same outcome, regardless of needs and/or contributions.

Legality. The legality principle is observed when resources are distributed according to existing laws.

Justified self-interest. The justified self-interest principle states that in some circumstances it is appropriate for an individual to take as much for himself as possible.

Adhering to commitments. The adhering to commitments principle requires that resources be distributed to those who have been promised these resources in the past.

Ownership. The ownership principle dictates that the owner has the right to decide when and how his/her resources will be allocated.

Status. The status principle states that more resources can rightfully be allocated to persons of higher social rank compared to persons of lower rank.

There is perceptual overlap between the procedural and distributive justice perspectives since most people have difficulty separating in their minds the decision procedures from the decision outcomes (Thibaut & Walker, 1975). One assumption of justice theories is that the fairer the decision procedure, the more psychologically acceptable the outcomes are likely to be (Folger & Greenberg, 1985). Procedural and distributive justice theories have seldom been examined together in actual life situations and the nature of their importance in the thinking of adults is unknown (Tornblom, 1992). The present study examined both procedural and distributive principles of justice with adult informants who were not asked directly about their perceptions of justice-injustice and who were unaware that the transcripts would be examined from the perspectives of justice theories.

THE RESEARCH DESIGN

The steps of designing naturalistic inquiry outlined by Lincoln and Guba (1985) serve as the organizational outline for presenting the design features of the present study: (a) focus of inquiry, (b) fit of focus to paradigm, (c) fit of the inquiry focus and paradigm to the theories selected to guide the study, and (d) nature of the data. These steps unfolded in a different sequence and are challenging to describe in the present example. The design of the study began after the data were received rather than according to a proactive plan. The data for the study are presented as the first step of the research design process since data collection had been completed prior to the initiation of the study. The research approach was similar to both naturalistic inquiry and ethnomethodology approaches but did not exactly match either of these. The study also crossed positivistic, interpretive, and critical science paradigms (Hultgren & Coomer, 1989) without fitting exactly into any one of these. The nature of the data fit record, document, narrative, and discourse analysis without fitting any one of these labels exactly. However, the fit of the theories to the natural setting of the research and the inquiry focus and scientific paradigm were appropriate.

The Nature of The Data

The research procedures can be outlined by describing the data; the processes of sampling hearings, sites, and informants; the processes of theoretical sampling from the text, coding by pattern matching speakers' meanings to prior theoretical constructs; and revising theoretical definitions in light of interpretations derived from the analysis of data. The data, sampling of hearings and informants, and description of informants are design issues for the present study, while the processes of theoretical sampling from the text, coding by pattern matching, and analyzing using procedures of modified analytic induction will be described as methods.

Public hearings as records or documented discourse. The data were written transcripts from taped recordings of four public hearings held in one state to gather information about the effects of child support guidelines on parents and children. The hearings were initiated by the State Department of Human Services Office of Child Support Enforcement and Policy Studies Incorporated in order to comply with the federal mandate for regular evaluations of numeric child support guidelines. Two hearings were held in cities and two in small towns in order to obtain opinions from residents in all geographic regions. The format of hearings involved the Director of Child Support Enforcement and the President of Policy Studies Incorporated as the official listeners who also asked some clarifying questions and occasionally provided factual information to speakers.

The data did not fit Lincoln and Guba's (1985) definition of records that attest to some formal transaction such as marriage certificates or driving licenses and yet the hearings were recorded for official and not personal reasons. The hearings were not historical or prepared for personal reasons as are letters and diaries that are defined as documents (Hodder, 1994), but documents are closer to speech than records and require more contextualized interpretations as these hearings required. In addition, these documents represented important meanings about the material culture and how the past was reconstructed and constituted in the present (Denzin & Lincoln, 1994).

The data were not exactly like the naturally occurring talk that is described in discourse analyses (Holstein & Gubrium, 1994) because the hearings were intentionally planned and tape recorded and the talk was not conversational or interactional. Instead, there were speakers talking to people who were formally defined as listeners. The text of the transcripts was a record because it was recorded for official reasons, was a document because the existence predated the research and the information was personal, and was discourse with some direct interaction with the leaders and some indirect interaction that was told in narrative form about previous interactions among family members. Yet the narratives were not stories with a beginning, middle, and end that are more typical for narrative analysis (Manning & Cullum-Swan, 1994).

Sampling hearings, sites, and speakers. The sampling processes of the present study were more theoretical (Glaser & Strauss, 1967) and purposive than representative (Guba & Lincoln, 1981; Patton, 1980) without fitting exactly into any one of these methods. The sampling strategy of analytic induction is to maximize the chances of obtaining negative evidence for the pre-existing theoretical premises (Gilgun, 1995; Manning, 1982).

The overall purpose of the present study was to learn about the many ways in which adults perceived the child support guidelines as failing to uphold the principles of justice. The effectiveness of the theoretical sampling processes could be compromised by several of the following conditions. First, the research situation may have isolated the extreme and deviant cases that might either be troublesome or enlightening. Second, the sites of the hearings, particularly those in cities, may have elicited the politically important or sensitive cases. Third, the informants at the hearings were self-selected because of convenience. It could be argued people who could not read announcements of hearings, did not have transportation to get there, or could not leave work or children were less likely to be represented. Fourth, the text of what informants actually said may have been selective in terms of typical cases. Alternatively, the text may represent critical cases or maximum variability of injustice perceptions. It is likely that people with the strongest opinions were present. On the other hand, remarks that highlighted important perceptions of injustice may be more helpful for theory development, identifying value priorities, and supplying rationale for policy changes.

Description of the informants. The informants for the study were 77 speakers of which 36 were men (46.8%) and 41 were women (53.2%). Forty-three speakers were present at the two city hearings (55.8%) and 33 spoke in the small-town hearings (42.9%). The perspective of child support obligor was presented by 40 speakers (51.9%) and the perspective of child support obligee by 33 speakers (42.9%). Four speakers were judged impartial (5.2%) concerning the perspective of obligor or obligee. These speakers presented reasonable balances in geographical locations, genders, and obligor/obligee perspectives.

The Focus of Inquiry

The first step of proactive naturalistic design is typically to determine a focus for the inquiry. The focus is important in order to establish the boundaries for the study and to determine the criteria for inclusion and exclusion of information (Lincoln & Guba, 1985). The focus of inquiry includes the type of inquiry and research setting, the content domain, the focusing research questions, and the research approach that is taken to answer the questions. The type of inquiry for the present study was policy evaluation of child support guidelines and particularly "policy-in-experience" because it involved policy as it is understood by a particular group (Lincoln & Guba, 1985, p. 227).

The research setting was naturalistic since the investigators had no influence on the antecedent conditions or the behaviors of speakers at the hearings. The content domain was interpersonal justice-injustice. The focusing question was: What are the perceptions of injustice in the child support guidelines and the child support system? The focusing question fit one of the standards for good interpretive research since it addressed how we are to interpret *meaning* in a particular text within the cultural and historical situation of the text (Brown, 1989). The observations were also time and context dependent as is typical of naturalistic inquiry (Lincoln & Guba, 1985).

The research approach differed from naturalistic inquiry, however, in terms of design, data, and coding processes. Naturalistic design is often called "emergent" since it evolves over time from the growing wisdom that results from the interactions of researchers and informants as the data collection progresses (Lincoln & Guba, 1985). The research design for the present study was not emergent, but rather unfolded after the data became available. The focusing question was retrospectively imposed on the existing data in much the same way that secondary analyses are imposed upon quantitative data. The data were not case studies or narratives as would be more typical of naturalistic inquiry. In addition, the coding method of imposing existing theories on the text of the hearings is not as typical of naturalistic inquiry (Lincoln & Guba, 1985).

The research approach had some characteristics representing central ideas from ethnomethodological approaches. The purpose of ethnomethodology is to reveal how "taken-for-granted or seen-but-unnoticed rules lie at the basis of everyday communications and interactions among social actors" (Van Manen, 1990, p. 178). The content domain in the present study was justice rules/principles that are known and assumed in interactions, but not articulated by social actors. In addition, the rules were organizationally embedded in the legal divorce institutional processes as is typical of ethnomethodological approaches (Holstein & Gubrium, 1994; Van Manen, 1990). However, the ideas presented at hearings were not exactly the naturally occurring discourse and interaction that is typically examined in ethnomethodological approaches due to the formality and the official nature of the hearings. In addition, the analyses did not center on the collaborative and constantly emerging structure of conversation (Holstein & Gubrium, 1994).

The Fit of Inquiry Focus to Paradigm

The present inquiry approach fit some dimensions of positivistic, hermeneutic, and critical science paradigms (Brown, 1989) without falling exactly into any one of these. The positivistic mode of inquiry was represented in the use of prior theory that was imposed upon the text, the attempt to verify theoretical patterns in actual situations (Carr & Kemmis, 1986), and the search for universal patterns of value priorities in the justice principles. The research also took post-positivist critiques into consideration by using a consensus criteria of truth (Thomas & Wilcox, 1987) in the data coding processes. Two coders had to discuss and agree upon the intended meaning of the speakers, the meaning of the definitions of the normative justice principles, and whether or not the meanings of the speakers matched the theoretical definitions of normative constructs. This was a more relativistic view of knowledge; therefore, the coding processes represented the interpretive science or hermeneutic mode of inquiry.

The critical science paradigm was represented in value-oriented research questions that reflected the emancipatory interest of knowledge and an interest in social change. The implicit question underlying the perceptions of injustice was: What needs to be changed about the child support guidelines and the child support system? The normative theories of justice provided guidance on what changes "should" occur according to the interpreted perspectives of speakers at the public hearings. Normative theories involve value constructs and modes of theorizing that legitimate different ethical, ideological, or policy positions with respect to what ought to be (Morrow & Brown, 1994). The ultimate use of the research to provide rationale for policy changes in child support guidelines also suggested the critical science mode of inquiry.

The Fit of Inquiry Focus and Paradigm to Justice Theories

Divorce in a family can involve conflicts of high intensity, particularly in regard to decisions about parental rights and responsibilities toward children. Intense feelings are indicators of perceived injustice (Mikula, 1986). Legal divorce calls for formal decision procedures and requires a redistribution of incomes and assets. Money is more likely than other resources to be distributed by deliberate decisions and money is precisely measurable. For these reasons, distributions of money are likely to require explicit justifications and thus provide an ideal setting for studying injustice perceptions (Soltan, 1987).

Divorce involves different views about how money should be distributed, about whose needs should take priority, and about the relative amounts of money, time, and human resources parents should contribute for support of children. The person obligated to pay child support (obligor) and the person who receives the money on behalf of children (obligee) have differing perspectives on how child support guidelines affect child support awards, how awards affect comparative financial contributions of parents to meet the financial needs of children, and how parents' levels of living are affected by their differing contributions. The procedures for making these decisions are often criticized because *accurate* information about incomes of parents was not used or *consistency* of treatment was not maintained across parents within a divorce case or across cases.

Decisions about distributions of parental incomes to financially supporting children after divorce involves the practical problems of: How much money should each parent *contribute* to meet the *needs* of children? Should the contributions be *equal?* If not equal, then what is equitable? How can equivalent levels of living be achieved? The decisions about child support obligations are "negative allocations" (Tornblom, 1992) that involve outcomes that are money costs as opposed to positive outcomes of money profits. These resource allocations can be evaluated on the basis of distributive justice principles. Therefore, the substantive theories chosen for the study fit the inquiry focus, paradigm, and the research situation.

The application of interpersonal justice theories to supporting children after divorce was an appropriate fit because it involved an actual life situation involving the consequences of both divorce decision procedures (procedural fairness theories) and resource distribution outcomes (distributive justice theories). The perceptions of injustice could be described by people who decided to speak at the hearings and could be examined without investigator manipulation of the situation. The fit of theory to research setting was one way that the study maintained ecological validity. Ecological validity requires that behaviors be studied in the setting in which they naturally occur and with minimal observer interference (Gibbs, 1979). In addition, ecological validity requires that the environment experienced by the subject will actually have the properties the investigator assumed were there (Bronfenbrenner, 1979).

METHOD

The methods of the study included sampling theoretically from the text, coding by matching patterns of speakers' meanings to prior theoretical constructs, and revising theoretical definitions. The theoretical sampling processes are described first.

Theoretical Sampling from the Text

The text was sampled theoretically by selecting quotations that were perceptions of injustice. There were several reasons for the exclusion of speakers, pages, paragraphs, or sentences from coding processes. These omissions were necessary, but may have introduced error in the study. The pragmatic aspects of the hearings, including introductions, microphone adjustments, and clarifying questions were not coded. Testimonies that did not talk about child support or justice issues were excluded from coding. For example, one student reported on a research project about outcomes for women and children following divorce. This speaker did not elaborate beyond the facts of the research in order to give opinions about injustices. A second speaker had a child in a residential treatment facility and the situation was expensive for her limited resources but was beyond the jurisdiction of child support guidelines.

Pages, paragraphs, or sentences were excluded from coding when the speakers told long introductory stories to set the stage for telling the justice concerns. In those cases, only the justice concerns were coded. Paragraphs or sentences were excluded when speakers talked about divorce in general, health insurance for the ex-spouse, retirement benefits, taxation, joint custody, and loss of AFDC due to remarriage. However, if speakers connected the topic (such as spousal maintenance) to child support, then the quotes were coded. The text was also excluded from coding when there were recording problems. For example, the tape would run out and there would be a short delay that, in some cases, prevented understanding of the speaker's train of thought. Sometimes there were sentences that simply could not be interpreted by anyone on the research team. Occasionally there was indication of a justice violation but insufficient information to code the idea. If neither coder thought that she could reasonably interpret the speaker's meaning, it was necessary to exclude the quote since the intent was to maintain the speaker's perspective.

Coding by Matching Patterns in Data to Prior Theoretical Constructs

The efforts to comprehend injustices from the perspective of the speakers and from the theoretical understanding of the researchers were important for maintaining interpretive validity (Maxwell, 1992). Standards for interpretive research require that the meaning expressed by the author of the text is respected in the interpretation (Brown, 1989). In addition, good interpretive research "reflects that interpretation has been made by interrelating the parts and the whole of the text" (Brown, 1989, p. 280) during the processes of data reduction (or coding). The data reduction processes required simultaneous interpretations of the meanings conveyed by speakers, the meanings of the justice principles applied to the speakers' intended meanings, and the precision of the match between the speakers' meanings and the theoretical definitions of the justice principles. These were intricate processes because multiple interpretations of meanings are always possible, particularly with value constructs. Pattern matching and procedures related to modified analytic induction were simultaneous, but for the sake of clarity in description, the coding methods are described first.

Interpretive group. The two coding methods used in the research included an interpretive group and an interpretive understanding process of hermeneutic circling. The "interpretive group" was recommended by Arnold and Fischer (1994) and Thompson, Locander, and Pollio (1989), and also is practice for researchers influenced by the Chicago School of Sociology, such as Benner (1994) and Strauss (1987). The group approach assumes people who share [pre]understanding are more likely to make similar interpretations of the same text. According to Arnold and Fischer (1994), "A group effort at interpretation may be useful since a group may collectively see patterns not recognized by any single researcher" (p. 58). The interpretive group in the present study consisted of two coders and a third person who listened, questioned, and gave occasional opinions. The discussions of the three people in the interpretive group provided the 'human as instrument' element that is important in the methods of naturalistic inquiry (Lincoln & Guba, 1985).

The people in the interpretive group are important in meeting one standard for trustworthy interpretive research. As Brown noted, "The research shows the researcher's familiarity with the topics which are the subject matter of the text and with cultural traditions and the historical-social context which shaped the meaning of the text" (p. 282). The interpretive group for the present study included people who were familiar with economic consequences of divorce, child support guidelines, distributive and procedural justice principles, and were familiar with the cultural traditions of divorce over a period of time. The group members were three people with age diversity representing the third, fourth, and sixth decades of life. They were also familiar with the culture of both place and ideas, an additional standard for trustworthy interpretive research (Brown, 1989). One person was a native of the state, the second a native of a neighboring state, and the third a native of another culture. Two people were from divorced families, both of whom had experienced remarried families, either directly or indirectly. The youngest person had received child support as a child and the oldest had received child support on behalf of children. The oldest person had a decade of experience with divorce research and was part of a community of professionals interested in the effects of child support guidelines on family economic well-being. The third person had lived in the United States for five years, and had an excellent command of the English language. The role of the person from another culture in the interpretation processes was critically important for both the meaning-making processes and for maintaining theoretical validity. Theoretical validity goes beyond accurately describing and interpreting the speakers' perspectives to a higher level of abstraction that provides theoretical explanation and understanding of the text. Theoretical validity refers to an account's validity as a theory of some phenomena (Maxwell, 1992).

Hermeneutic circling. The interpretive group tried to reach an understanding that was free of contradictions through the processes of hermeneutic circling. According to Arnold and Fischer (1994), "Hermeneutic understanding is an action-oriented, practical-moral knowledge brought to, and derived from, a specific situation or problem" (p. 59). The understanding process involves the ideal of a hermeneutic circle or interactive spiral of understanding that is a back and forth specific-general-specific movement of interpretation. The intent is to understand the specific elements of the text in the context of the whole text. In other words, the meaning of the whole text is determined from the specific elements of the text, while, at the same time, an individual element is understood by referring to the whole of which it is a part (Bernstein, 1983).

The first step in the interpretive processes required developing shared meaning among the coders concerning meanings of the speakers, meanings of the theoretical concepts, and the accuracy or precision with which the two meanings matched. Each person read the transcript from one city and attempted to code the speakers' ideas based on individual understandings of the justice principles. The codes were penciled in the margins. The second step was to go through the transcript as a group to discuss and agree upon whether or not the text was appropriately coded for a justice issue, what the speaker meant by the expressed ideas, and what justice principle was an appropriate match to the speakers' intentions. The initial group process required several weeks of group time beyond individual coding time for decision, discussion, verification, negotiation, and modification by compromise that were required to achieve shared meaning.

The codes that were agreed-upon by group process were cut out and pasted on a separate piece of paper so they could be visually examined for consistency within each justice principle. For example, the text that demonstrated 'equality' issues could again be examined to determine if each quotation appropriately fit the theoretical definition with precision. Quotes were removed when they were inconsistent with theoretical definitions. The process often required going back to the context of the quote to determine the overall meanings, to decide where ideas appropriately started and stopped, and to decide if more than one principle was demonstrated. A list was developed at this stage to keep track of quotes that were important justice issues that did not seem to fit the existing principles such as child support enforcement issues. A second list included quotes that seemed to represent the theoretical principles but did not match the existing theoretical definitions with precision such as issues of accountability of obligors in paying child support. The failure of obligors to pay support is not exactly a justice violation of "correctability," or "ethicality," or any of the other principles.

Coding the first hearing site required approximately three months. Once there was agreement on the codes for the transcript from the first city site, then the second city site was coded first by the two individual coders and then verified and/or modified by discussion, negotiation, and compromise. The quotations were grouped by theoretical principles and examined by group process for consistency with the quotes from the first hearing. It was then necessary to recode some of the text in the first transcript to incorporate the newly acquired meanings of the coders. Quotes that were inconsistent with the others within a given justice principle were removed by agreement of the interpretive group. The same processes of individual coding and group verification or modification were followed for the remaining two transcripts. The coding processes of decision, discussion, verification, negotiation, and modification by compromise were ways of establishing validity by the informal logic of argumentation that is important for trustworthy interpretive research (Brown, 1989). However, the disadvantage of the approach was the time intensiveness. The entire coding processes required twelve months of research time with one coder working more than quarter time, a second one alternating between quarter and half time, and the third one spending several hours weekly on the research project. The coding processes proved that it was impossible to match the meanings of speakers to the theoretical definitions without questioning the meanings of the theoretical constructs and questioning the limits of the meanings. The analytic induction process began during this questioning.

Modified Analytic Induction

The present study used modified analytic induction (Cressey, 1950; Gilgun, 1992, 1995; Manning, 1982; Miller, 1982; Robinson, 1951; Znaniecki, 1934[1]) as a research procedure. The advantages of analytic induction are in its capacity to generate conceptual formulations, induce theoretical revisions by examining negative evidence, integrate theoretical and judgment sampling processes into the social sciences, and create process theories. The negative features of the procedure are its time intensiveness and the limitations in predicting social behaviors (Manning, 1982).

Induction is the process of developing general conclusions from observations of a number of discrete facts. According to Manning (1982), "Analytic induction is a non-experimental qualitative sociological method that employs an exhaustive examination of cases in order to prove universal, causal generalizations" (p. 280). Analytic induction seeks to develop universal statements containing the essential features[2] of a phenomenon, or those things that are always found to be associated with the existence of a social occurrence (Manning, 1982). The essential features are those things that are always present when the phenomenon is present and, when they are absent, the phenomenon itself is absent. The definitional aspect of science is critical in analytic induction, and in the procedure, redefinition and reconceptualization are often required to narrow the range of applicability or the scope of the theory (Manning, 1982). The phenomenon must be precisely defined to eliminate the extraneous or unexplained cases. Exceptions or negative cases assume major significance in research procedures since explanations aim for completeness and universality.

Analytic induction is unlike other qualitative approaches since it begins with a pre-existing theoretical viewpoint or premise that guides the investigator's approach to the cases that are examined (Gilgun, 1995; Miller, 1982). Cressey (1950) outlined procedures of analytic induction that Robinson (1951) summarized:

> The procedure begins with an explanatory hypothesis and a provisional definition of something to be explained. The hypothesis is then compared with the facts and modifications are made in two ways: (a) The hypothesis itself is modified so that the new facts will fall under it and/or (b) The phenomenon to be explained is re-defined to exclude the cases which defy explanation by the hypothesis. (p. 813)

The first modification requires theoretical revisions. The second modification requires identifying the limits within which the hypothesis or definition is applicable. These modifications come about when the investigator finds negative instances (Miller, 1982). The present paper focuses primarily on the second modification concerning the definitional issues and finding the limits of the existing theoretical definitions.

As discussed, analytic induction is considered a method of causal analysis or as a method of proof (Miller, 1982; Robinson, 1951), but my analysis does not focus on cause. Furthermore, we realize that we will not develop definitions and generalizations that are universal, but, rather, we are developing working hypotheses and concepts that illuminate other similar situations (Gilgun, 1994, 1995). Because of these departures from classic analytic induction, the procedures fall under the category of *modified* analytic induction (Bogdan & Biklen, 1992; Gilgun, 1995).

The following paragraphs describe only the procedures used for isolating cases in which the justice principles were evident and excludes from discussion the next two steps of analytic induction that would first study only the cases that met the theoretical criteria in order to draw from them the universal generalizations and second to compare these cases with examples that fell outside of the definitions (negative cases) in order to revise the theoretical premises.

The research required identifying examples in the text that had the essential features of the principles of procedural and distributive justice, according to the theoretical definitions. The definition of each justice principle was then re-defined and examples were excluded that did not fit the more precise definitions. The analytical induction research procedures required deciding about (a) meanings of theoretical definitions, (b) whether the example fit in the category of procedural fairness or distributive justice principles, (c) which of the procedural or which of the distributive justice principles were most appropriate when there was conceptual overlap within theories, and (d) which examples were justice issues that were not fitting within the existing theoretical constructs.

Examples of Modified Analytic Induction

The first step of analytic induction resulted in revised theoretical definitions of procedural and distributive justice principles that are provided in Table 1. A summary of the revised procedural fairness definitions indicated 122 quotes that fit the definitions and 147 that were procedural fairness issues that were not a precise match with the definitions and will require further analyses. The quotes that fit revised procedural definitions, in order of frequency, were representativeness, correctability, accuracy, consistency, ethicality, and bias suppression. A summary of the revised distributive justice definitions indicated 169 quotes that fit the definitions and 194 that were excluded. The quotes that fit revised distributive definitions, in order of frequency, were: needs, equality, contributions, ownership, justified self-interest, legality, adhering to commitments, and status.

The following paragraphs give selected examples for procedural and distributive justice principles. The revised definition is followed by a

TABLE 1. The Original and Revised Definitions of Procedural Fairness and Distributive Justice Principles

Procedural	Original Definitions	Revised Definitions
Accuracy	Decisions must be based on accurate information. The rule requires accountability of persons producing information and accurate records.	Decisions must be based on correct information.
Bias Suppression	Personal self-interest in the allocation process should be prevented. The decision should not be made on doctrinaire grounds such that the decision maker considers only prior beliefs. All points of view must receive adequate and equal consideration.	Personal self-interest of the decision maker in the allocation process should be prevented. The decision should not be made on doctrinaire grounds such that the decision maker considers only prior beliefs.
Consistency	Decision procedures should be consistent across persons and situations over time.	Decision procedures should be consistent across persons within cases and across cases as well as within persons across time.
Correctability	Opportunities must exist to enable decisions to be modified or reversed such as in grievance and appeals procedures.	Opportunities must exist to enable decisions to be modified or reversed such as in grievance and appeals procedures. Modifications/appeals must be accessible with minimal barriers and constraints.
Ethicality	Resource allocations must be based on prevailing moral and ethical standards and avoid deception, bribery and invasion of privacy.	Resource allocations should not be based on intended deception, bribery or invasion of privacy.
Representativeness	The resource allocation process must represent the concerns of all recipients and the decision maker should be representative of the consensual attitudes and values of society.	The resource allocation process should represent the concerns of all recipients.

Equality	Resource allocations must guarantee that everyone receives the same outcome, regardless of needs or contributions.	Resource allocations should guarantee that everyone receives the same or similar outcomes, regardless of needs or contributions. Two types of equality directly stated (same) or implied (similar). In equality—implied the speaker focuses on the discrepancy of outcome in resource allocation implying that the equality rule has been violated (especially discrepancy in levels of living).
Needs	More resources must be allocated to persons with greater needs. A requirement for applying the needs rule is accurate information on the character and intensity of needs as well as consensus on comparability and hierarchy of needs.	Resource allocation should take needs into consideration. Two ways of expressing needs: In terms of "there is a need" or in terms of "not enough resources" (implicit).
Contributions	Resources must be distributed in relation to the amount and kind of contributions that were originally made. *Equity* is achieved when there is equality of outcomes per unit input. A prerequisite of using the contributions rule is the requirement that contributions of participants can be reliably measured.	Resources should be distributed in relation to the amount of contributions that were originally made. *Equity* is achieved when there is equality of outcomes per unit input. A prerequisite of using the contributions rules is the requirement that contributions of participants can be reliably measured.
Justified Self-Interest	The belief that in certain circumstances it is just for an individual to take as much for him/herself as possible.	The belief that an individual should receive a particular outcome simply because he/she wants it or deserves it.
Adhering to Commitments	Resources should be distributed to those who have been promised these resources in the past.	Resources should be distributed to those who have been promised these resources in the past.
Legality	The distribution of resources should be based on existing laws and/or policies.	The distribution of resources should be based on existing laws and/or policies.
Ownership	The owner of a resource has the right to decide when and how his/her property will be allocated.	The owner of a resource has the right to decide when and how much of and to whom his/her property will be allocated.

quote having the essential characteristics of the definition and a quote that was excluded along with some explanations of reasons for decisions that were made.

Procedural fairness principles. The first principle of procedural fairness is *accuracy* which requires that decisions be based on correct information. An example of a quote that was included is the following:

> I don't know what the judge based his decision on because it was nothing but a bunch of allegations and there was no real fact finding that I could tell. . . . And I just think when we're dealing with a temporary order, where there's been no real fact finding or real opportunity to defend yourself. . . . (M, 18)

Quotes that were excluded from the definition had characteristics that fit the meaning of "exactness" rather than "correct" information: "The rules on calculating net monthly income under the existing guidelines do not really address how we're supposed to calculate for the self-employed people" (R, 10).

The principle of *bias suppression* required that personal self-interest of the decision maker in the allocation process should be prevented. The decision should not be made on doctrinaire grounds such that the decision maker considers only prior beliefs. An example that fit within the revised definition was:

> We're in a small county, small court system, we can appeal those cases, but we only have one or two, maybe three, judges in our district, and you start appealing on your judges and you're basically going to start to tick them off, and they're not going to be real favorable with you, so that's a problem in itself. (F, 28)

Quotes that were excluded from the definition of bias suppression had characteristics of disrespectful treatment or threats: "I was told to shut up by the judge" (D, 4).

The principle of *consistency* was defined as decision procedures should be consistent across persons within cases and across cases as well as within persons across time. An included example of consistency was:

> It's interesting that the budget that I had to revise and re-do at least 10 times before my divorce has $500 less expenses with a family of four than my ex-husband claims as his expenses of one person, yet he does not have to explain or justify his expenses and I have to go line by line by line on mine to say, 'Yes, these are the expenses I have and this is why I need the child support.' (R, 5)

The quotes that were outside of the revised definition had the essential characteristics of the opposite of consistency: "I think each case needs to be looked at as a separate case by the judicial system" (F, 8).

The definition of *ethicality* stated that resource allocations should not be based on intended deception, bribery or invasion of privacy:

> For years he worked for himself, and he claimed zero income to the government so he wouldn't have to pay child support. He told me that he did this, and he said to me, 'Oh, K . . . , I'm going to go legit this year and I'm going to pay workman's comp and everything.' (D, 27)

The examples of ethicality that were excluded from the definition dealt with misuse of child support funds because the examples did not apply to the divorce decision procedures:

> My ex-wife two years ago spent six weeks in Europe. How can she afford that? I know. She's using my child support to do it. She spent five weeks out west a year ago. I haven't had a vacation in 10 years. (F, 11)

Distributive justice principles. The most problematic of the distributive justice principles for the application to child support guidelines was the principle of *contributions* which stated that resources should be distributed in relation to the amount of contributions that were originally made:

> The parent who financially contributes more than 50% of the children's needs should be the one claiming the children as tax exemptions on their IRS 1040 tax forms. (M, 13)

In other words, the financial reward (output) of a tax exemption should go to the person who contributed the most money in child support (input). The above example is stated from the perspective of the child support obligor and is easier to classify since the resource input involves money and the output or reward is the same resource. The coding decisions were more difficult when there were several resources involved in one statement and when the resource that was contributed was a different resource than the reward output. The following quote from the perspective of a child support obligee demonstrates that complexity:

> Fifteen years of earning no salary as a full-time wife, mother, and homemaker yielded me no portion of our marital income, labelled alimony, severance pay, or retirement benefits. I receive no dollar

amount for being on the job 24 hours a day for fifteen and a half years. (M, 4)

The coding was easier when the resources were more directly labeled such as one speaker who talked about the input of time and goods resources and the failure to receive financial resource benefits:

I spend approximately 30% of the time with my daughter. I get no credit for the food, clothing, household that I have to provide in order to keep her. (M, 39)

The quotes that were excluded from the revised definition of contributions talked only about input of resources: "Her income has usually been double, two and a half times his, yet she was never, ever ordered to pay any support" (M, 17).

The rule of *legality* requires that the distribution of resources should be based on existing laws and/or policies. An example that fit the definition stated:

According to the guidelines I should be paying roughly 20% of my net income. I'm paying between 45 and 60, and it just seems a little bit too far apart for me. (D, 21)

The quotes that were excluded from the definition were often more procedural in nature than the distribution of resources that is intended by the distributive justice principles:

Some judges are very good, and they take that responsibility seriously, and they apply those guidelines how they're supposed to be. A lot of judges don't. (F, 27)

In other words, in the procedures of decision making the guidelines are sometimes not followed. The exclusion of this quote required making a decision about whether the emphasis in the statement best fit the procedural or distributive justice principles. The decisions can be difficult when speakers are talking about resource distributions that are inequitable across cases as well as some of the decision procedures that lead to these inequities over time as was the following excluded quote:

Courts are misrepresenting, misinterpreting the guidelines of the maximum level of support for non-custodial parents, rather than the minimal level, as intended by the legislature. Deviations downward from the guidelines are much more common than upward deviations. (M, 34)

The *justified self-interest* principle is a belief that an individual should receive a particular outcome simply because he/she wants or deserves it:

> I'm not looking to go out and buy new cars or anything like that, but it would be nice to be able to go to McDonald's once in a while. (F, 10)

Prior theoretical constructs only included justified self-interest, but the coding processes demonstrated there could be justified interests for others, primarily children. An obligor stated: "And I have to say that I believe in child support. I think the kids deserve to be supported" (M, 30). This perspective was shared by an obligee who said: "Children of divorce are entitled to a lifestyle other than the basic food, shelter, and clothing" (M, 34). Quotes that were excluded from the revised definition were more process than outcome oriented as indicated by a grandparent:

> Our government should not do this to little kids, either, because it isn't just our grandchildren. We've heard of cases throughout the country, and it isn't fair to these little kids. (F, 5)

In other words, children are also entitled to receive certain resource outcomes as a result of the resource distributions of their divorcing parents.

Validity and Reliability Issues

The methods of pattern matching and analytic induction had both advantages and disadvantages in efforts toward maintaining validity and reliability. Lincoln and Guba (1985) clarified that for naturalistic inquiry the equivalent terms for internal and external validity are credibility and transferability while the equivalent terms for reliability and objectivity are dependability and confirmability. Credibility is enhanced through the activities of prolonged engagement, persistent observation, triangulation of investigators, peer debriefing, and negative case analysis (Lincoln & Guba, 1985) that were all used to some extent in the present study. The ultimate test of credibility is whether the analysis can represent the multiple constructions of reality presented by speakers at the hearings.

The principles of procedural and distributive justice offered meaningful ways to describe injustice experiences of informants. It could be argued, however, that these constructs were too limited to adequately describe the actual experiences of informants and that the constructs added a selective attention bias to the analyses methods of the investigators that would not have been present without the prior theory that was imposed upon the data. On the other hand, the theoretical constructs provided consistency of attention across cases for the investigators and also the advantage of transferability. It would have been possible to transfer these concepts to analyze child support hearings in other states. The ultimate test of transferability is whether the database makes transferability judgments possible for potential appliers (Lincoln & Guba, 1985) and this transferability seems possible.

The dependability of the analysis can be insured by using stepwise replication procedures and inquiry audits (Lincoln & Guba, 1985), both of which were used in the present study. The interpretive group processes of two coders working independently and then having to reach agreement by verification, discussion, negotiation, and compromise in a three-person group provided the "daily communication" processes for stepwise replication. The agreed-upon codes were then subjected to reviews by the group for their appropriateness, accuracy, and consistency after the completion of coding for each hearing site. These checking processes were a form of inquiry audit that reviewed the processes, standards, and product for its dependability.

The confirmability of an analysis is insured by the completion of a confirmability audit (Lincoln & Guba, 1985) that was also used in the present study with an audit trail of written records and notes in all stages of the coding. The decision and verification processes of the interpretive group also provided a formal agreement that the findings were grounded in the data, the inferences were logical, the negative cases had been carefully considered, and the results were as free from investigator bias as possible. Most of all, the formal agreement of the interpretive group could verify that the study was a continuously disciplined inquiry representing careful efforts.

DISCUSSION

The present study represents work in progress since analytic induction is incomplete in regard to developing universal generalizations. The work that has been completed indicates that it was possible to examine perceptions of injustices using procedural and distributive justices principles for interpretation of speakers' perspectives. It was also possible to verify that the theoretical patterns of justice can emerge in a natural setting. Many examples of injustice experiences were found in the text which demonstrated that justice principles are operating in the experiences of divorced persons. Coding by pattern matching using an interpretive group was an effective method of data reduction which yielded credible and dependable results. The interpretive group used a hermeneutic circling process of decision, discussion, verification, negotiation, and modification by compromise. Interpretations of value principles were difficult and the group process was a way of arriving at agreements about meaning that may be helpful to other qualitative researchers who struggle with interpreting value constructs.

The first methodological purpose of the paper was to demonstrate an interpretive process of coding by pattern matching to theoretical constructs. The coding process demonstrated that the theoretical definitions were present but were insufficient for describing the actual experiences of supporting children after divorce. The second methodological purpose of the paper was to demonstrate analysis by analytic induction to refine theoretical definitions. Only one modification of analytic induction was demonstrated, that of excluding cases that fell beyond the limits of the theoretical definitions. This limitation was originally unintended but practically necessary because of the time-intensive nature of analytic induction. The time requirements of the method were underestimated when initiating the research project. The interpretive group for this study certainly agreed with Manning (1982) that analytic induction demands "patience, time, and tenacity as well as a tolerance for ambiguity" (p. 290). Researchers who intend to use analytic induction should be prepared for its time intensiveness and the resulting mental exhaustion that may occur.

The coding and analysis methods outlined in the present paper could also be important for other researchers who apply existing theories to a natural situation. For example, Foa and Foa's resource theory (Foa & Foa, 1974; Foa et al., 1993) is a theory that specifies the resources that are exchanged between persons (love, status, services, information, goods, and money). Some of the theoretical concepts are normative and there are clear definitions for concepts, a structured network of relationships among these concepts, and many propositions. These exchange relations and propositions could be observed in naturally occurring family interactions as has been initiated by Vicki Loyer-Carlson (personal communication, 1994). The processes of coding and analyses of data will provide many of the same challenges that were faced in the current study. How does one separate (and code) the verbal transactions that are "love" from the verbal transactions that represent "status"? The second step of data reduction will require refining the definitions of love and status so the "limits" of each definition are clear and the verbal transactions can be classified as either "love" or "status."

The retrospective designing process that was demonstrated in the present study could be used any time a researcher has existing records, documents, diaries, case studies or stories and cannot return to the informants for additional information, clarification, or validation of interpretations. The focusing research questions must be created in such a way that the data can provide sufficient answers to the question and so that ecological validity can be maintained. In other words, the experiences of the subject must match what the investigator assumes is there and the context of the subjects must appropriately match the focus of inquiry. "Secondary data analysis" like this has many of the same disadvantages as it does when applied to quantitative data. It is not always possible to find the information that is ideally needed.

The research approach in the present study could also be applied to other kinds of data such as transcripts of therapy sessions, case studies, or narratives. Manning and Cullum-Swan (1994) explained that narrative analysis takes a number of analytic forms that vary in levels of formality. Formality is the "degree to which the internal coherence of the text is defined in advance with reference to codes, syntax, grammar, or forms" (Manning & Cullum-Swan, 1994, p. 464). The present study was a more formal approach and also what Manning and Cullum-Swan called a "top down" process. The top down process is one in which the investigators begin with a set of rules and principles and try to "exhaust the meaning of the text using the rules and principles" (p. 464). The research process that was presented in this paper tried to sample all of the personal stories about experiences with child support guidelines for the unjust consequences that resulted for the informants through the applications of these guidelines to particular cases. The justice principles were the rules that were used to interpret the coherence and meaning of the text. The top down approach that begins with theory differs from the grounded theory approach which is used to inductively discover theoretical principles from examining patterns in the data from the "bottom up." The research approach demonstrated in the paper can be used when the research begins with existing theory and the intent is to test the theory for its practical usefulness in everyday life.

The detailed description of pattern matching and analytic induction processes that are outlined in this paper may be of the most value to people who are trying to learn qualitative methods. It is easy to find in the literature examples of research results and conclusions that have been determined through various data analytic techniques. It is much more difficult to find more detailed explanations about how to do analyses with examples of the method. Students in research methods classes often request specific examples that will assist them in understanding general principles and ideas.

The researchers involved in the current project are hopeful that the advantages of analytic induction will outweigh the disadvantages. This would happen if the analyses result in theoretical revisions that show reasonable interpretations of injustice experiences concerning supporting children after divorce. A second advantage would result if these interpretations are important for changing the child support guidelines in ways that will be more equitable for greater numbers of people. If the study can provide rationale for proposed policy changes in child support guidelines and can assist professionals in more effectively articulating justice principles during divorce decision making procedures, then the research may meet the long-term objectives.

NOTES

1. " . . . enumerative induction abstracts by generalizing, whereas analytic induction generalizes by abstracting. The former looks in many cases for characters that are similar and abstracts them conceptually because of their generality, presuming that they must be essential to each particular case; the latter abstracts from the given concrete characters that are essential to it and generalizes them, presuming that in so far as essential, they must be similar in many cases" (Znaniecki, 1934, p. 251).

2. "Thus, when a particular concrete case is being analyzed as typical or eidetic, we assume that those traits which are essential to it, which determine what it is, are common to and distinctive of all the cases of a class" (Znaniecki, 1934, p. 252).

REFERENCES

Arnold, S. J., & Fischer, E. (1994). Hermeneutics and consumer research. *Journal of Consumer Research, 21,* 55-70.

Austin, W., & Tobiason, J. M. (1984). Legal justice and the psychology of conflict resolution. In R. Folger (ed.). *The sense of injustice: Social psychological perspectives* (pp. 227-297). New York: Plenum.

Benner, P. (1994). *Interpretive phenomenology.* Thousand Oaks, CA: Sage.

Bernstein, R. J. (1983). *Beyond objectivism and relativism: Science, hermeneutics, and praxis.* Philadelphia: The University of Pennsylvania Press.

Bogdan, R., Biklen, S. K. (1992). *Qualitative research for education* (2nd ed.). Boston: Allyn and Bacon.

Bronfenbrenner, U. (1979). *The ecology of human development.* Cambridge, MA: Harvard University Press.

Brown, M. M. (1989). What is good research? In F. M. Hultgren & D. L. Coomer (eds.). *Alternative modes of inquiry in home economics research Yearbook 9*, (pp. 257-297). Teacher Education Section of the American Home Economics Association, Peoria, IL: Glencoe.

Carr, W., & Kemmis, S. (1986). *Becoming critical: Education, knowledge, and action.* Philadelphia, PA: Falmer.

Cohen, R. L. (1987). Distributive justice theory and research. *Social Justice Research, 1*, 19-40.

Cressey, D. R. (1950). Criminal violation of financial trust. *American Sociological Review, 15*, 738-743.

Denzin, N. K. & Lincoln, Y. S. (1994). *Handbook of qualitative research.* Thousand Oaks, CA: Sage.

Deutsch, M. (1983). Current social psychological perspectives on justice. *European Journal of Social Psychology, 13*, 305-309.

Deutsch, M. (1985). *Distributive justice.* New Haven, CT: Yale University Press.

Foa, U. G., & Foa, E. B. (1974). *Societal structures of the mind.* Springfield, IL: Charles Thomas.

Foa, U. G., Converse Jr., J., Tornblom, K. Y. & Foa, E. B. (1993). *Resource theory: Explorations and applications.* San Diego, CA: Academic Press.

Folger, R. & Greenberg, G. (1985). Procedural justice: An interpretive analysis of personnel systems. In K. M. Rowland & G. R. Ferris (eds.). *Research in personnel and human resources management: A research annual, vol. 3* (pp. 141-183). Greenwich, CT: JAI.

Gibbs, J. C. (1979). The meaning of ecologically oriented inquiry in contemporary psychology. *American Psychologist, 34*, 127-140.

Gilgun, J. F. (1992). Definitions, methods, and methodologies in qualitative family research. In J. F. Gilgun, K. Daly & G. Handel (eds.). *Qualitative Methods in Family Research* (pp. 22-40). Beverly Hills, CA: Sage.

Gilgun, J. F. (1994). A case for case studies in social work research. *Social Work, 39*, 371-380.

Gilgun, J. F. (1995). We shared something special: The moral discourse of incest perpetrators. *Journal of Marriage and the Family, 57*, 265-281.

Glaser, B. G., & Strauss, A. L. (1967). *The discovery of grounded theory.* Chicago: Aldine.

Greenberg, J. (1984). On the apocryphal nature of inequity distress. In R. Folger (ed.). *The sense of injustice: Social psychological perspectives* (pp. 167-186). New York: Plenum.

Guba, E. G., & Lincoln, Y. S. (1981). *Effective evaluation.* San Francisco: Jossey-Bass.

Hodder, I. (1994). The interpretation of documents and material culture. In N. K. Denzin & Y. S. Lincoln (eds.). *Handbook of qualitative research* (pp. 393-402). Thousand Oaks, CA: Sage.

Holstein, J. A. & Gubrium, J. F. (1994). Phenomenology, ethnomethodology, and interpretive practice. In N. K. Denzin & Y. S. Lincoln (eds.). *Handbook of qualitative research* (pp. 262-272). Thousand Oaks, CA: Sage.

Hultgren, F. H. & Coomer, D. L. (1989). *Alternative modes of inquiry in home economics research Yearbook 9*, Teacher Education Section of the American Home Economics Association, Peoria, IL: Glencoe.

Leventhal, G. S. (1980). What should be done about equity theory? In K. J. Gergen, M. S. Greenberg, & R. H. Willis (eds.). *Social exchange: Advances in theory and research* (pp. 27-55). New York: Plenum.

Lincoln, Y. S. & Guba, E. G. (1985). *Naturalistic inquiry.* Beverly Hills, CA: Sage.

Lind, E. A. & Tyler, T. R. (1988). *The social psychology of procedural justice.* New York: Plenum Press.

Manning, P. K. (1982). Analytic induction. In R. B. Smith & P. K. Manning (eds.). *Qualitative methods:* Vol. II of *Handbook of social science methods* (pp. 273-302). Cambridge, MA: Ballinger.

Manning, P. K., & Cullum-Swan, B. (1994). Narrative, content, and semiotic analysis. In N. K. Denzin & Y. S. Lincoln (eds.). *The Handbook of qualitative research* (pp. 463-477). Thousand Oaks, CA: Sage.

Maxwell, J.A. (1992). Understanding validity in qualitative research. *Harvard Educational Review, 62,* 279-299.

Mikula, G. (1984). Justice and fairness in interpersonal relations: Thoughts and suggestions. In L. Berkowitz (ed.). *Advances in experimental social psychology* (Vol. 2, pp. 267-297). New York: Academic Press.

Mikula, G. (1986). The experience of injustice: Toward a better understanding of its phenomenology. In H. W. Bierhoff, R. L. Cohen, J. Greenberg (eds.) *Justice in social relations* (pp. 103-123). New York: Plenum. New York: Academic Press.

Miller, S. I. (1982). Quality and quantity: Another view of analytic induction. *Quality and quantity, 16,* 281-295.

Montada, L. (1994). Injustice in harm and loss. *Social Justice Research, 7,* 5-28.

Morrow, R. A., & Brown, D. D. (1994). *Critical theory and methodology.* Thousand Oaks, CA: Sage.

Patton, J. Q. (1980). *Qualitative evaluation methods.* Beverly Hills, CA: Sage.

Rettig, K. D. & Dahl, C. M. (1991). The unlikely possibility of justice in divorce settlements. *Proceedings, Theory construction and research methodology workshop.* National Council On Family Relations, Denver, CO.

Rettig, K. D. & Dahl (1993). Impact of procedural factors on perceived justice in divorce settlements. *Social Justice Research, 6,* 301-324.

Rettig, K. D., Magistad, B. M. & Tam, V. C. (1994). An application of interpersonal justice theories: Perceived injustices of child support guidelines. *Proceedings, Theory construction and research methodology workshop* (pp. 89-102). Minneapolis, MN: National Council on Family Relations.

Robinson, W. S. (1951). The logical structure of analytic induction. *American Sociological Review, 16,* 812-818.

Schwinger, T. (1980). Just allocation of goods: Decisions among three principles. In G. Mikula (ed.). *Justice and social interaction* (pp. 95-125). New York: Springer-Verlag.

Soltan, K. E. (1987). *The causal theory of justice.* Berkeley, CA: University of California Press.

Strauss, A. (1987). *Qualitative analysis for social scientists.* New York: Cambridge University Press.

Thibault, J. & Walker, L. (1975). *Procedural justice: A psychological analysis,* Hillsdale, NJ: Earlbaum.

Thomas, D. L. & Wilcox, G. E. (1987). The rise of family theory: An historical and critical analysis. In M. B. Sussman & S. K. Steinmetz (eds.). *Handbook of marriage and the family* (pp. 81-102). New York: Plenum.

Thompson, C. J., Locander, W. B. & Pollio, H. R. (1989). Putting consumer experience back into consumer research: The philosophy and method of existential phenomenology. *Journal of Consumer Research, 16,* 133-146.

Tornblom, K. (1992). The social psychology of distributive justice. In K. R. Scherer (ed.). *Justice: Interdisciplinary perspectives* (pp. 177-236). Cambridge, MA: Cambridge University Press.

Tyler, T. (1987). Procedural justice research. *Social Justice Research, 1,* 41-66.

Van Manen, M. (1990). *Researching lived experience: Human science for an action sensitive pedagogy.* New York: State University of New York Press.

Znaniecki, R. (1934). *The method of sociology.* New York: Farrar and Rinehart.

PART II:
LEARNING TO BE QUALITATIVE

Learning to Be Interpretive:
Hermeneutics and Personal Texts

Joyce A. Walker

SUMMARY. This paper presents my reflections as a graduate student writing a qualitative dissertation. The lessons learned in the process of hermeneutic interpretive research changed the way I investigate nearly everything. The power of positivism was deeply embedded in my beliefs about what real research looks like, my thinking about why and how research is done, and my language about how research is expressed and communicated to others. Because hermeneutic study seeks to make meaning of words and narrative and to gain understanding, it is a powerful tool to study intact texts. This article poses questions that may be helpful to novice and veteran researchers undertaking interpretive research. *[Article copies available for a fee from The Haworth Document Delivery Service: 1-800-342-9678. E-mail address: getinfo@haworth.com]*

Joyce A. Walker is Professor and Extension Educator, 4-H Youth Development Center, 340 Coffey Hall, University of Minnesota, Twin Cities, St. Paul, MN 55108.
This article is developed from the author's (1993) dissertation.

[Haworth co-indexing entry note]: "Learning to Be Interpretive: Hermeneutics and Personal Texts." Walker, Joyce A. Co-published simultaneously in *Marriage & Family Review* (The Haworth Press, Inc.) Vol. 24, No. 3/4, 1996, pp. 223-239; and: *The Methods and Methodologies of Qualitative Family Research* (ed: Marvin B. Sussman, and Jane F. Gilgun) The Haworth Press, Inc., 1996, pp. 223-239. Single or multiple copies of this article are available for a fee from The Haworth Document Delivery Service [1-800-342-9678, 9:00 a.m. - 5:00 p.m. (EST). E-mail address: getinfo@haworth.com].

KEYWORDS. Hermeneutics, Qualitative research, Dissertation, Post-positivism, Methodology, Letters

Doctoral students in my college feed their committee at the dissertation defense. For weeks before the event, I debated. Would it be pound cake or fresh fruit? Bagels or cucumber sandwiches? In January of 1993, I was happier concocting menus for faculty than responses to imagined grueling and antagonistic questions about my research. At my most desperate, I could hear the voices: "You call this a literature review?" "What did Hagenpooper et al. say about this? You didn't read Hagenpooper!" "Validity–I'm asking a simple question about validity!" "How can you be the researcher and one of the researched at the same time?" "Do I understand that you modified your findings based on the opinions of the *participants*?"

The dreaded scenarios that played in my head through many sleepless nights never materialized. On the contrary, my oral exam was a model of collegial discussion, questioning, and lively debate. In this article I reflect on the sources of my struggles and the factors in my success. The purpose of this article is to document the challenges of doing qualitative research at a time when it was not clear how a dissertation committee would respond to a hermeneutic interpretive approach. It is a story of worrying about the committee, making decisions and working alone, and creating the process as I went along. By sharing my experience with novice and veteran researchers, I hope to stimulate discussion about the similarities and differences with their own endeavors to frame sound interpretive research.

Hermeneutic studies of intact text can provide a systematic approach to make meaning out of recorded family histories, correspondence, diaries, journals, even extensive notations in family albums. The methodology provides a model for studying families and relationships using the words and voices of men, women, and children as the text for research. Because each collection of people is unique, meaning-making comes from the shared meanings and interpretations of many studies understood within the context of family theory and a body of contemporary research. My own plunge into a full blown hermeneutic study of intact text under the critical eye of a dissertation committee changed forever the way I understand and value research work. For this I am very grateful.

HERMENEUTICS: THE EXPLORATION OF INTACT TEXT

I brought three important things to my doctoral work: nearly a half century of life experience, 10 years of university work and teaching, and a box stuffed with letters from women. From the beginning, I was determined to focus my dissertation on these letters and the women who wrote them because I was convinced that the narratives contained significant insights into the self-described private lives of educated women experiencing marriage, motherhood, personal growth, and role conflicts in the second half of the 20th century. This belief was fueled by the women themselves. They had come to understand the rarity of their sustained and intimate correspondence. Eve (not her real name) wrote in 1984, "I liked *The Big Chill* but couldn't help thinking what a much better story we could tell. I wish somebody would take on the project." Despite my resolution to do so, I was not at all sure what the "much better story" was, and I had no clear idea how to move "the project" ahead in a productive way.

As I slogged through my required credit hours of statistics and an elective in quantitative methodology, I fretted over how to frame a hypothesis for my work. While this seems ill-conceived and even amusing now, I was determined to find a method to do my work, and the method I knew—the only one seriously discussed at all—was the standard procedure for empirical research. Finally, in an overview course in interpretive and critical theory research, I came to the essential understanding that ways of knowing and methods of research are not fundamentally all the same.

My research, entitled *Women's Voices, Women's Lives: Understandings About Personal Success From a 25 Year Correspondence* (Walker, 1993), is an interpretive work in the hermeneutic tradition. It is interpretive in that it seeks to understand the lived experiences and everyday meanings of the lives, thoughts, and ideas of the women who shared them. The knowing about the women is grounded in the narrative text of their letters. This is in contrast to a search for objective knowledge that offers scientific explanation, prediction, or generalization about the women based on their writings (Nielsen, 1990; Van Manen, 1990). This study focused on a particular group of women who attended a mid-sized midwestern public university between 1959 and 1963. The intention was to organize, interpret, and articulate the thoughts and ideas they shared over time in letters. Such interpretive study is premised on a stance that "social reality can only be understood by understanding the subjective meanings of individuals" (Carr & Kemmis, p. 86). As researcher, I can point out similarities to a larger body of social science theory and research, but connections between the experience of these 18 women and other women must be observed and claimed by the women. It cannot be assumed.

Interpretation of Meanings

The work is hermeneutic in its methodology and tradition in that it seeks to make meaning of human motives, ideas, and actions by critical

examination of texts–the narratives represented in the words in the letters–
and to interpret these understandings in a humane manner (Nielsen, 1990).
Hermeneutics, the theory and practice of interpretation, is a method of
knowing in the human sciences that acknowledges the possibility for
misunderstanding and the necessity of considered work to translate or
understand the text within the context or tradition of its origin (Van
Manen, 1990). Like the ancient abbey cleric trying to make meaning of
ideas in ancient scrolls, the hermeneutic scholar is challenged to come to a
deep understanding of what is described by trying to know the meaning
attached to it by the participants themselves (Nielsen, 1990).

My own challenge was to interpret the text at hand, 279 hand-written
and computer-generated letters exchanged annually over a quarter century.
My participants or informants–the letter writers–were 18 high achieving
women who, educated and prepared for work, found themselves 5 years
after college graduation consumed by the challenges of marriage and
family for which they were essentially unprepared. Every year since 1968,
each of the 18 fashioned a letter to share thoughts about herself, her life,
and her ideas. The letters were sent to a rotating editor who assembled and
copied them and distributed a packet to each one. My commitment to
make meaning out of the provocative stories that women from my college
days had been sharing each winter since 1968 held special significance
because I am one of these letter-writing women.

Prior to my dissertation research, I viewed qualitative research methods
as supplementary procedures to gain information to complement the statistical tests and to give life–perhaps a human face or story–to the findings. I
had worked with texts from interviews and focus groups that were carefully
designed to explore narrow questions related to the hypothesis. In other
words, I worked with texts generated by the researcher for the express
purpose of elucidating some aspect of a defined study. I had never simply
plunged into a vast pile of existing, fascinating, and apparently disorganized
letters inspired not by a researcher but by the women themselves. While the
letters energized and excited me, I had obstacles to overcome. How would I
remain a neutral researcher with my own letters in the data set? How would
I assure validity of my findings? Would I approach the cohort as individuals
or as a group? How would I measure the women's concepts of success and
achievement? Most important, what was the question?

POSITIVISM AND ME

I was discouraged to find that my own worst enemy was me! My
greatest surprise was the discovery that positivist thinking, empirical

methodology, and experimental research terminology were deeply embedded in my thinking. I am a product of my times and my education. I did not realize that I was, deep inside, an unquestioning repository of positivist rules, beliefs, and assumptions about research. I was burdened with a mindset of measures, significance, and procedures, with a language of data, comparisons, and cohorts. I couldn't shed the notion that if I only found and followed a neat, prescribed, scientific, linear process, the answer would be revealed as if on a huge computer printout. My deeply held beliefs about the purpose of research, the language of research, and the processes of research had never been examined. Now I was stumbling over them every day. Fundamentally, the successes and struggles I experienced around my dissertation research became an adventure once I confronted my own demon, the closet positivist.

Getting Unstuck

For months I was stuck. Even as I concluded that my study would most appropriately be a qualitative one, I could see no clear order or direction. A major breakthrough occurred when I realized that my difficulties in conceptualizing my research were epistemological not methodological. Qualitative research–interpretive work–is not simply a different way of doing research: it is an essentially different way of thinking about what you are doing. Gadamer (1981) gives firm expression to the view that interpretive study is fundamentally premised on an epistemology–or way of knowing what we know–different from that of the logical positivists. The challenge of interpretive work is to understand the meaning of the text rather than to measure, generalize, or predict outcomes from the data as is the case in the classic large random sample study of quantitative research.

Because contemporary hermeneutic scholars are absorbed in the methods and implications of interpreting meaningful human action, they spend considerable effort seeking to understand the context and the metaphors of human interactions that the participants themselves attach to those interactions (Nielsen, 1990). Hermeneutic scholars attach meaning and intentionality to the words of participants like the letter writers, and they work hard to make sense of the language, the lived experience, and the intimate understandings of their subjects. As the philosopher Gadamer (1981) said,

> Understanding is an adventure and, like any other adventure, is dangerous. Just because it is not satisfied with simply wanting to register what is there or said there but goes back to our guiding interests and questions, one has to concede that the hermeneutic experience has a far less degree of certainty than that attained by the methods of the

natural sciences. But when one realizes that understanding is an adventure, this implies that it affords unique opportunities as well. It is capable of contributing in a special way to the broadening of our human experiences, our self-knowledge, and our horizon, for everything understanding mediates is mediated along with ourselves. (pp. 109-110)

Interpretive epistemology challenges the fundamental tenants of positivist research: there is no need for a distanced, neutral, objective researcher. Particularly when focusing on a hermeneutic study of intact text, the interpretive research frame encourages making use of those who know best even if these informants are literally and figuratively close to the text. This was a powerful concept because it invited me into active engagement in the process of critical reflection and meaning-making along with the sixteen other letter writers. (One woman died in 1990; I am the eighteenth.) The recognition that those intimately involved understand in a special way legitimized my desire to bring each one of the women actively into the process, to seek their advice, and to use their knowing to keep me honest.

A second breakthrough came for me when I read Hans Georg Gadamer's (1981) book *Reason in the Age of Science* at the suggestion of my son, a graduate philosophy major. According to Gadamer, "One of the more fertile insights of modern hermeneutics is that every statement has to be seen as a response to a question and that the only way to understand a statement is to get hold of the question to which the statement is an answer" (p. 10). Interpretive work commonly begins with the answers and concludes with discovery of the question. The letters–the texts–exist intact. The answer is in hand. The challenge is to discover within the text the question to which the text is the answer. In a Carnak-like reversal reminiscent of Johnny Carson's late night television routine, the researcher sorts through the answers before the question is even framed. I found I had two important preliminary or framing questions to answer before I could identify the research question for the study: (1) What is the question to which these letters are a response? and (2) What do I want to learn from these letters? By focusing my attention on these two questions, I came to understand what the letters were about, what tied them together in a longitudinal chain of conversation. For the 18 women, the letters are an attempt to find the answer to the question, "What does it mean to be a successful woman now, in the second half of the twentieth century?"

The Text and the Women Lead the Way

One of the primary contributions of hermeneutic scholars has been their work with alternate research models that emphasize participant observation, oral histories, case studies, and narrative interviews. These models are participant or text-centered rather than researcher-centered because the substantive issues and even the questions are initiated by the participants or the text, not primarily from the researcher (Nielsen, 1990). My own study is clearly woman-driven. I did not initiate the contact: the women did. I did not set out to gather data: the women provided the narrative text in their letters. The study is constructed and organized around key questions, and these questions are not solely my creation. I did not frame the questions as in an interview or oral history. If questions are posed in the letters, the women ask them. They routinely ask–and answer–marvelous questions.

> What do I fear? Not growing old, for I don't feel old. I do fear disappointing others. What do I dream of? Having good health and just being me, not the me I think others want me to be. (Nel, 1987)

> Did we have it too good? Security is a hard thing to give up and harder yet to live without. Most parents try so hard to protect their kids and shelter them from pain and disappointment (especially girls). I wonder if that was the intended good result? (Jill, 1987)

> Why aren't we, many of us, highly paid, highly visible executives and vice presidents? Because we were programmed differently and have been living with the conflict all our adult lives between wanting to achieve individually and wanting to nurture and support others? (Leah, 1987)

> I am confused a lot about things I would think an adult should be sure. The concept of responsibility is often the conundrum for me–to whom? to self? to mate? to children? to other commitments? (Kate, 1982)

The women who ground this study are unique in their time, their place, and their personal history. Hermeneutic study honors this uniqueness and values it. The study is not intended to generate understandings that can be generalized to other women of other times, cultural backgrounds, social class or economic conditions, race, or nationality unless these other women hear the themes and claim an association. In presentations of my early work to groups of girls and women, I discovered large numbers who come up afterwards to reinforce their common questioning about the concept of success. One university student confided that the letters really helped her understand her mother's feelings of growth and independence when she divorced the girl's father. At this point I began to trust what I was learning—to listen to the voices of the women and understand what they were saying. When I finally faced this issue, I knew what I had to do and did it. I submerged myself in the voices and I listened, determined to let the text lead me for a while.

METHODOLOGICAL PROBLEMS AND STRATEGIES

My troubles were not over. Although the issues of epistemology and framing the question were out on the table, the process of interpretive research continued to frustrate and confuse me. I have tried to isolate these process issues and decision points so that others can recognize them and give them attention. In reality, they are not so distinct and they are interrelated, and they tend to link back to the fundamental methods and expectations associated with empirical research. I present these issues as questions because that is how they first came to my attention. My research strategies and lessons learned are not the only answers, so I hope that readers will take up the discussion and add their experiences and ideas to mine.

Text Management

How can I manage all this text? I had 25 years worth of letters, 18 different correspondents, and over 400 single space pages of text. The decision to use a computer-assisted text management system was ideal. I chose The Ethnograph (Seidel, 1988) because I was familiar with the software, but there are other packages on the market that assist in the coding, sorting, and retrieving of text. The development of a careful system for coding words and ideas must be designed, but once coded and entered into the computer using The Ethnograph, themes or categories can be retrieved and the relevant passages of text (previously marked) will print out in their entirety.

Boundaries

Where are the boundaries? There are none. It takes courage and encouragement to set them. (One of my advisors reminded me regularly that there was no expectation that my dissertation contain everything I knew.) The boundaries are difficult to set for several reasons. At the beginning, the dissertation is a work in progress; hence the parameters are not clear. The expectation (by self or others) that to complete a dissertation is to become one of the experts on the topic makes it difficult to stop reading, searching, and tracking down one more lead. Furthermore, since the quest for understanding nearly always requires work across disciplines, it is difficult to be certain that all the authorities on a given topic have been cited. The breadth of study can be exciting and problematic for graduate students determined to really become experts on a slice of their field. Yet human experience does not fall neatly into the disciplines of academia. I found that I had to read widely in psychology, the history of letters, philosophy, women's development, career development, and English literature in order to place some of my understandings in a research and theory context.

On the other hand, I made an assertive, and I believe well-grounded, decision early in my work to eliminate descriptive text passages that dealt solely with details of the activities and accomplishments of children. After several readings of the full text of the letters, organized both by woman and by year written, I came to understand that talk of children fell into two categories: (a) descriptive passages reporting on school activities, births, vacations, etc., and (b) personal passages that addressed the relationships, challenges, and feelings between the women and their children. I decided that in my line by line coding for The Ethnograph I would not code the former, the summary or descriptive passages that read like a stereotypical Christmas letter; however, I coded passages where women reflected on their children in ways that informed personal and family relationships. The decision to focus on the women and not the children created a boundary that allowed me to set aside portions of text, not because they were irrelevant, but because they are the subject for another study.

Correspondents as Collaborators

How can I really get my informants engaged in the research? The key is to invite them and reach out in ways that make it easy for them to get involved. Because the tradition of distance between the researcher and the researched is so strong, there are few guidelines for how and how much to involve the participants. I sent individual letters asking for their support in concept for a study based on the letters, and I solicited a short, honest reaction on a self-addressed and stamped post card. I sent each a dissertation abstract and a specific proposal to involve them along with the human subjects release form. I gave each a 3-5 letter code name to protect their identity. I visited personally with seven of them during business trips the year before I began serious analysis. I initiated each probe, and I set clear limits on the time they would commit in response to questions or calls. I sent each one a preliminary draft of the themes and followed up with a

15-30 minute phone call to discuss their ideas. Everyone participated including the family of the one woman who died after a chronic and debilitating illness in 1990.

It is essential to approach the work with the absolute certainty that participants and key informants have the answers to the important questions. They must become true partners in the research project. My telephone discussions with the women who did not contribute letters for long periods of time were very enlightening. Three of them shared at length their sense of disappointment and estrangement at the focus on marriage and motherhood in the early letters:

> I expected more of us: the academic/leadership women of one of the finest public universities. And when I saw you all evolving unprotestingly into your mother's roles, I was disappointed and angry. (Liz, 1992)

I worked to combine my interpretations with theirs and to understand their lived experience from their perspective.

I took the position that the women told the truth as they understood it in the letters they wrote. Overwhelmingly they confirmed this view. While most made it clear they never consciously censored their contributions, three talked about how they intentionally omitted things to protect themselves or others. The question is one of the degree of truth-telling. Rene's candid confession of the limits of her personal sharing reveal the complexities of truth-telling and underscore her remembered despair as well as the silence she maintained to protect her family:

> The one thing I've said, and I've said it to [husband] and a couple other people, is basically I could have given you through the years—everybody through the years—a whole bunch more, but I didn't dare. And it isn't like I didn't want to tell you, it's that this newsletter became something that everybody in my family read. My boys read it, my husband couldn't wait for it to come. And basically I was afraid at times to just unburden my soul and say some of the things I was thinking. As good as this [manuscript] is, it probably could have been better. I don't know if other families had the same situation occur or not. There were many times I wanted to say how despairing I was . . . but I didn't dare. (Rene, 1992)

The engagement of participants in confirming and validating the interpretations of the text makes a great deal of sense, but it flies in the face of positivist traditions in educational research that keep the participants at a healthy distance so as not to contaminate the results or compromise the findings. Nonetheless, the participant confirmation process is powerful for the participants and for the researcher. Carr and Kemmis (1986) wrote:

> To be valid, an interpretive account must first of all be coherent; it must comprehend and coordinate insights and evidence within a consistent framework. For many interpretive researchers, this is enough. . . . But a more stringent test may also be applied, either concretely or in principle: to be valid, the account must also be able to pass the test of participant confirmation. Researchers willing to take this more stringent test argue that an interpretive account must be recognized as a possibly true account of what is going on by those whose activities it describes. (p. 91)

The letter writers came to know the worth of their writings and to see the contribution their sharing made possible. I came to know that my single opinion about the meaning of the letters paled beside the congregate opinion of the sixteen. When the women said emphatically "Yes!" to the shared learnings and implications, the study gained a power to influence that I, as a single researcher, could not possibly achieve.

Getting Close to the Text

Why does this feel so messy and circular? Because it is. The tidy and prescriptive path of scientific inquiry began to look mighty appealing to me when I felt mired in questions and certain that the big ideas had once more escaped me. Interpretive work is not linear. Its beauty and frustration is the movement back and forth from text to coding, to a new idea, and back to text again. Sometimes I felt I wandered around in the dark for days, but when the light finally went on, it was exhilarating and the forward movement came in great bounds.

Sometimes the women were the ones who turned on the light switch. At a time when I was unable to frame a discussion of the marriages and divorces described in the letters, I visited with Rene between flights at her local airport. Her talk about the Great American Dream, the stereotypical goal of finding the perfect place and relationship to enjoy forever after, suddenly opened my eyes to the many statements and off-hand comments in the letters that were premised on the idea that there was some unspecified but vaguely alluded to place to end up or goal to attain.

The Language of Research

What language do I use? I had to adapt a new one. My research vocabulary was full of scientific, analytic language: data, cohort, measure, statistical significance, random samples, reliability, validity, hypothesis testing, and findings. Participants were "little n's" as in n = 18. Even the other women in the study noticed this language and commented on it. Ruth wrote on a draft, "Why call us a cohort? Very militaristic term! There must be something better–a group, maybe?"

There is a growing language that captures the new ways of knowing and making meaning. Much of it is in philosophy, feminist research theory, and anthropology. It took time and conscious effort to speak and to think humanely about texts, interpretations, understandings, lived experience, and meanings, but what a lovely, simple concept to finally refer to my friends, my correspondents, the participants with me in this study as the women.

Literature Review

Is my literature review as untidy as it seems? Yes, and that's to be expected. In order to incorporate work across disciplinary boundaries, my literature review had breadth, but not depth in every area. Readings, literature reviews, and acknowledged experts are often unfamiliar. I finally made this caveat at the beginning of my literature review chapter (Walker, 1993) entitled, "The Literature That Informs the Study":

> In such a contextual study, it was initially difficult to know exactly how to best make use of the literature review since it is usually used to establish the context for prediction or generalization. In this interpretive study, the literature serves a different purpose which is to alert the researcher to the possibility of issues. Consequently, this chapter is not a literature review in the traditional sense of a systematic survey of research and theory on a focused topic. This is a perusal through the books, authors, and ideas that this researcher found to be most informative in elucidating and understanding the themes and messages in the set of letters which compose the text for the study. (p. 78)

Finding an End Point

Why does this work feel incomplete, even at the end? It feels incomplete because understanding human motivation and behavior is on-going. I raised as many questions as I answered. I identified six themes fundamental to success for the women, themes they endorsed with only a few caveats. I was also left wondering. Do I sense a renewed interest in the spiritual life? What is the implication of living a life with different measures of success in the public and the private life? What do other women need to know to feel successful and competent in undertaking the important challenges of adult life? Is it reasonable to focus success on the rearing and teaching of children in a society that routinely trivializes these roles? Such is the nature of hermeneutic work. We expect to find a definitive answer and be done, but it seldom works so neatly.

Shared Status of Expert

After all this reading and work, why don't I feel like an expert? The concept of researcher as impartial expert is turned upside down when the researcher is a member of the group under study. Of course, if I had not been closely positioned as an insider, it is unlikely that the text would ever be studied or the findings confirmed by the other women. Expert status must be shared between the researcher and the participants as all are authors and equal experts on the meaning of the text. This poses particular difficulties in a doctoral dissertation if the graduate student feels compelled, by their own expectations or those of their committee, to establish singular expert status.

THE LESSONS OF HERMENEUTIC STUDY

The challenge is first and foremost to search deeply in the text so that the answer is understood and the question can be known. Interpretive research based on intact text centers on making meaning of the text so as to arrive at an understanding of the question to which the text is implicitly the answer.

It is critical to articulate the basic epistemological and theoretical assumptions fundamental to the study. I put them down on paper and kept them in front of me. I clarified and sharpened them. In addition to the study-specific assumptions associated with my own work, four epistemological assumptions are important to this interpretive way of knowing. First, there is no objective, independent reality governing explanations and understandings of human behavior. Knowledge is socially constructed and time dependent. Second, understanding of human behavior is subjective and dependent on the perspective of the participants. Third, people act with meaning, and language is the vehicle for interpreting and understanding the meaning people give to their actions. Fourth, there is no such thing as a totally disinterested or objective researcher.

Researchers need guidelines by which to judge their own work. I developed the set of principles noted here, based on Brown (1989) and Madison (1988), to guide me in determining the value of my interpretive work. I chose to rely on five criteria that are explicitly related to the methodology (designed as appropriate), that are definitive and without overlap, and that are understandable to a community of reviewers.

The interpretation must be *wide*. When the researcher considers the whole text respectfully, the study becomes unified and coherent. It must be comprehensive, dealing with the totality of the text without significant omission or serendipitous probing. It must be thorough, responding to all questions posed by and for the text. In my own work, line by line coding for The Ethnograph computer text management system helped to assure that the whole text was considered as did the systematic readings of the letters by woman and by year.

The interpretation must be *deep*. The researcher must push to the heart of the issues, exploring the central problems in a penetrating manner. It cannot merely deal with the obvious or surface ideas. Implicit in this criterion is the notion that the text selected for study must be substantive and in no way trivial. I had the advantage of knowing this text from its inception. I saw it grow from 18 letters to nearly 300 in 25 years. My interest in the subject and my connection to the writers strengthened my deep understanding.

The interpretation must be *contextual*. The text cannot be considered in isolation but in light of relevant cultural traditions and values as well as related historical events and ideas. Likewise, the interpretation must be reflective of and congruent with the larger body of the author's work and expression. My position as peer, friend, and contemporary of the women gave me an intimate perspective on the context of the letters. My life paralleled theirs from early collegiate experiences to marriage, mother-hood, and divorce.

The interpretation must be *connected*. The researcher must relate ideas of the past to each other and to the present and future. The interpretation must stimulate new ideas, offer potential for new connections, and link the theoretical and the practical. The work must demonstrate knowledge of the literature in the field. The literature review combined with my work in the area of youth and families, my experience as a woman, and my relation-ship to the women promoted connection.

Finally, the interpretation must be *authentic*. The researcher must be true to the language and intent of the author. The text and author must be taken seriously and treated with confidence that they represent ideas of value as they are communicated. The study draws heavily on the precise words of the women: their voices speak for themselves. Their participation as informants and as reviewers of the draft and final version helped assure their authentic representation.

Allow time for qualitative research. Above all, time. Investigator energy is spent less in the tasks of making arrangements and collecting data; however, extensive time is required for the thinking, synthesis, backing up, circling around, and re-thinking necessary to understand complex human behaviors. The process of coming to an understanding–of meaning making–is hard to rush, and time pressures can blind a researcher to simple, powerful evidence just waiting to be noticed. I had long puzzled over the meaning of the eclectic reading material referenced and shared by the women over the years. Then, on my vacation (to get away from the dissertation and the letters), I picked up Virginia Woolf's (1929) *A Room of One's Own* and Nicola Beauman's (1983) *A Very Great Profession: The Woman's Novel 1914-39*. And there it was–my missing theme: the essential space and private place the women claimed in the act of reading. It was only when I allowed my mind to open up and let in new air that I saw former disparate ideas come together with new understanding.

The absence of clear measures for the interpretation can cause doubts. After months of immersion in the letters, I lost track of what I really did know. Moreover, I began to lose sight of what was important. I began to think my understandings represented old information that everyone else already knew. This dismissive thinking, upon reflection, usually wasn't true. However, there is no data run and no "$p > .05$" to reference and rely upon. Interpretive work requires a keen sense of intuition; a willingness to follow a scent or pursue a faint trail; a system of tracking, moving forward, and circling back again to find answers. One must trust one's self and one's judgment. It also involves knowing what to trust, whether to pursue an "outlier" idea or set it aside. It means coming to a conclusion without reading absolutely everything ever written on any possibly related subject. It means knowing when to stop.

The rewards of working with intact text are significant. The language of intact text is usually very intentional. One advantage I found to studying letters was the careful construction and deliberate choice of words. Consider these examples:

> I grew up assuming a man would take care of me and my children, and my career work, if any, would be a supplement, an adjunct, a bonus or an insurance policy. I did not grow up believing that I would be responsible for taking care of myself. (Leah, 1992)

> My personal life is intact but akin to a finely cluttered satchel. (Clare, 1981)

> The most salient observation about our 17 year-old marriage is that, in spite of ongoing efforts, trying to nurture our own relationship is difficult. . . . We have recently discovered that when we imagined ourselves parents it was either with infants or grandchildren. We somehow neglected to envision these middle years. Probably just as well—we might have remained childless. (Nan, 1981)

The women confirmed that they took time and paid attention to the words they used in these letters. The text is intentionally conceived and written or recorded in precise and considered language. I think this is particularly true when the text is generated voluntarily. The researcher has the luxury of spending time in interpretation rather than in planning and collecting data. Also, because the text itself has a beginning, a middle, and an end, limits are put on the study.

It is ideal to have a team of people working on a qualitative study. A team creates an on-going forum to check out ideas and get reactions to insights. It was very lonely to work on an interpretive study for a dissertation. The women participants saved the day because they provided a group for consultation and confirmation. They shared stories with me that gave me energy and made me feel that the work was important (a fact that is easy to lose sight of). One of the women read the draft manuscript aloud to her 82-year-old mother who has severe vision impairment. Her mother wrote to me:

> This will probably be your first fan letter! Ruth and I just finished reading your interesting and entertaining draft of the [women's] letters. It has been a sort of special time—Ruth reading aloud while I listened. She would read a little, then stop so we could discuss someone's ideas or thoughts. It gave us thoughts to ponder and brought back memories. My comment as we went along was, 'This would make a great novel.'

Such interest and encouragement are invigorating. The study is not fiction, but the 82-year-old reader recognized provocative elements common to the life experience of many women as she attended to the thoughtful voices and carefully crafted words shared in the letters.

What is not in the text may be as important as what is included. What is absent can be as important as what is present. Never leave a study of intact text without asking, "What is missing? Why is it not here?" Always listen to informants with an ear to what is avoided and unspoken. In response to my observation that love affairs, mentors, intimate dealings with spouses, and contemporary friendships were topics never discussed in the letters, several women wrote to tell me that anger was also missing. As one explained, letters are not a good forum for dealing with anger–you put it out and it just lays there until the next year's letter.

Not long ago, thumbing through the 1994 summer issue of the *International Journal of Qualitative Studies in Education*, I came across a bibliographical note for a University of Warwick seminar paper (Macguire & Ball, 1994) entitled, "Why Didn't You Use a Survey So You Could Generalise Your Findings?" Again the specter of challenge to qualitative methodology rose before my eyes. But my experience and my reflections have given me a sound and practical grounding in the methods essential to making meaning and coming to understanding of narrative text. I appreciate the powerful affirmation of my women collaborators and the relief of setting aside the positivist perspectives that once ruled by thinking about research. My confidence and experience now give me great satisfaction, a fine thing considering that three years ago I was debating bagels or cucumber sandwiches!

REFERENCES

Beauman, N. (1983). *A very great profession: The woman's novel 1914-1939.* London: Virago Press.

Brown, M. M. (1989). What are the qualities of good research? In F. H. Hultgren & D. L. Coomer (Eds.). *Alternative modes of inquiry.* Washington, DC: American Home Economics Association, Teacher Education Section.

Carr, W., & Kemmis, S. (1986). *Becoming critical: Education, knowledge and action research.* London: Falmer.

Gadamer, H. G. (1981). *Reason in the age of science* (F. G. Lawrence, Trans.). Cambridge: MIT Press.

Madison, G. B. (1988). *The hermeneutics of postmodernity: Figures and themes.* Bloomington: Indiana University Press.

Maguire, M. and Ball, S. J. (1994). Researching politics and the politics of research: Recent qualitative studies in the UK. In J.A. Hatch & R. Wisniewski (Eds.). *International Journal of Qualitative Studies in Education, Vol 7,* 269-285.

Nielsen, J. M. (Ed.) (1990). *Feminist research methods: Exemplary readings in the social sciences.* Boulder: Westview.

Seidel, J. (1988). *The ethnograph 3.0: A user's guide.* Littleton, CO: Qualis Research Associates.

Van Manen, M. (1990). *Researching lived experience: Human science for an action sensitive pedagogy.* London, Ontario: Althouse.

Walker, J. (1993). Women's voices, women's lives: Understandings from women's twenty-four year correspondence. St. Paul: University of Minnesota (unpublished).

Woolf, V. (1929). *A room of one's own.* London: Harcourt, Brace.

Learning to Teach Qualitative Research: Reflections of a Quantitative Researcher

Cynthia Franklin

SUMMARY. This paper is a case study of my experiences as a quantitative researcher who taught myself to teach qualitative research at the Ph.D. level. I share my processes of learning qualitative epistemologies, research designs, data collection methods, and reporting styles. I included conceptual schemas, bibliographies, and other resources for teaching qualitative research in the hope that my work will be helpful to others who want to learn to teach qualitative research methods. *[Article copies available for a fee from The Haworth Document Delivery Service: 1-800-342-9678. E-mail address: getinfo@haworth.com]*

KEYWORDS. Teaching qualitative research, Paradigm debates, Reflexivity, Qualitative family therapy research, Post-positivism, Constructivism

Qualitative research methodologies are gaining acceptance within practice-based disciplines such as family studies, marriage and family therapy, social work, counseling psychology and education (Gilgun, 1992a, 1992c; Hartman, 1990; Heineman-Pieper, 1989; Howe, 1988; Lancy, 1993; Moon, Dillon, & Sprenkle, 1990; Piele, 1988; Pieper, 1985; Polkinghorne, 1984; Viney, 1989; Witkin, 1989, 1991). Recent transformations in the

---

Cynthia Franklin is Associate Professor, School of Social Work, University of Texas at Austin, 1925 San Jacinto, Austin, TX 78712-1703.

[Haworth co-indexing entry note]: "Learning to Teach Qualitative Research: Reflections of a Quantitative Researcher." Franklin, Cynthia. Co-published simultaneously in *Marriage & Family Review* (The Haworth Press, Inc.) Vol. 24, No. 3/4, 1996, pp. 241-274; and: *The Methods and Methodologies of Qualitative Family Research* (ed: Marvin B. Sussman, and Jane F. Gilgun) The Haworth Press, Inc., 1996, pp. 241-274. Single or multiple copies of this article are available for a fee from The Haworth Document Delivery Service [1-800-342-9678, 9:00 a.m. - 5:00 p.m. (EST). E-mail address: getinfo@haworth.com].

philosophy of science, including increasing awareness of the limitations of empiricist/positivist research methodologies for the human sciences, have increased enthusiasm for qualitative approaches to research (Gergen, 1985; Gregersen & Sailer, 1993, Hoffman, 1992; Polkinghorne, 1984). Several professional journals within marriage and family therapy, such as the *Journal of Marriage and the Family, Family Relations, Journal of Marital and Family Therapy* and *Family Process*, are soliciting manuscripts on qualitative research studies (Joanning, 1993). This volume will bring into print several examples of qualitative family research.

Academic researchers are grappling with how to teach qualitative research methodologies and some disciplines are publishing guides to help academics develop strategies for teaching (Hoshmand, 1989). Major professional associations such as the National Council on Family Relations, American Association for Marriage and Family Therapy, the Council on Social Work Education, and the American Educational Research Association are developing workshops and training sessions on qualitative methodologies to help educate researchers and practitioners.

Most academics and practitioners, however, have been trained in empiricist/quantitative methodologies and have little or no training in the interpretive/qualitative approaches to research. Learning to teach qualitative methodologies, therefore, requires a major re-focusing of a researcher's orientation to science and methods. It is difficult to make such a transition in a workshop or short training session. Epistemologies and methodologies of qualitative research are diverse and differ significantly from those of empiricist/quantitative approaches. At first glance, differences in research designs and methods make it difficult for those trained as quantitative researchers to appreciate and comprehend the complexity and richness of qualitative methods. Such differences present challenges to interested quantitative researchers who want to understand qualitative methods well enough to become effective teachers of qualitative research.

This paper will provide insights and resources for family researchers who want to learn to teach qualitative research methods. Trained in empricist/quantitative research methodologies, I will share my experiences in learning the methodologies and learning how to teach them at the Ph.D. level. I will provide a narrative of my learning processes and will share my teaching outline, conceptual schemas, bibliographies, and examples of studies from qualitative family research. My learning experiences parallel and are similar to the qualitative research process and demonstrate how qualitative methods are useful for investigating new areas. Although the paper discusses my experience as a quantitative researcher who learned to teach qualitative methodologies, the teaching methods and resources also may prove useful for those trained as qualitative researchers.

ACADEMIC CONTEXTS FOR LEARNING QUALITATIVE RESEARCH

Debates between academic researchers concerning the appropriateness of qualitative research are on-going in the practice disciplines that do research on families (c.f. Atherton, 1993; Atkinson, Heath, & Chenail, 1991; Berlin, 1990; Cavell & Snyder, 1991; Heineman, 1981; Moon et al., 1991; Schuerman, 1982). Unfortunately, in some cases, these debates have alienated qualitative researchers, resulting in continued disinterest and perhaps less opportunity for understanding what qualitative methods may offer. Quantitative researchers who are interested in learning qualitative approaches often do not have colleagues who supply them with resources and dialogue that would help them learn.

For example, at the time I was learning to teach qualitative research, Tyson (1992) published an article about the heuristic paradigm in the journal *Social Work*, the official journal of the National Association of Social Workers. This article presented a critical analysis of quantitative/empiricist research and presented a qualitative approach. One response to this article was a letter signed by 23 social work researchers from Canada and the U.S. that not only lambasted the premises of the piece but the journal's editorial board for publishing it (see Grinnell et al., 1994). Such a response might intimidate even the most intrepid of researchers. Though I was asked to be a signer of this letter, I refused, feeling awkward in the process, as if I were being asked to take sides in an ideological war. This incident touched me personally, but my experience probably is replicated many times in other disciplines, as the writings of others attest (e.g., Cavell & Snyder, 1991; Held & Pols, 1985; Held, 1990; and Liddle, 1991). This strife inhibits quantitative researchers from learning qualitative methods and thus from effectively teaching these methods to their students.

Changes in the philosophy of science and the interests of students and practitioners, however, are putting pressure on faculties throughout the country to offer courses in qualitative methods. Professors who teach research recognize changes in academic climate and are responding to the increased interest in qualitative methods. Well-known research texts that previously have not included methods on qualitative research have added substantive content on qualitative methods (i.e., Grinnell, 1993). Some authors of research textbooks have been challenged to find appropriate content necessary on qualitative research methods (Allen Rubin, personal communication, February 11, 1993). When academics want to learn how to teach and do qualitative research, therefore, they have been hampered not only by ideological debates but the relative lack of contemporary qualitative research within their own disciplines.

A QUALITATIVE RESEARCH PROCESS
TO LEARN QUALITATIVE RESEARCH

My dean asked if I would consider teaching qualitative research at the Ph.D. level. I was surprised since all my research experience was quantitative. I had taken no courses and hadn't even studied the approach. Consequently, I wasn't sure if I was the right person to teach this course. I also doubted the judgment of those who believed I was the best prospect. After careful reflection, a few bouts of ambivalence, and some coercion from those who really wanted me to teach the course, I agreed.

Upon reflection, the following seven steps helped me to learn how to teach qualitative research. These steps may be helpful to others trained as quantitative researchers. First, I developed relationships with qualitative researchers who agreed to support my learning. These researchers served as supervisors or mentors. Fortunately, I was able to identify qualitative researchers in my own department. Second, I did a literature search on qualitative research methods in areas near to my substantive areas (e.g., families) and read that literature. I found it necessary to narrow my search, however, because of the vastness of the literature within the family field. As pointed out by Grotevant (1991), family studies has expanded into many disciplines. The literature is large across different disciplines and specialties. For this reason, I limited most of my literature searches to clinical areas, my area of expertise.

Third, I talked to qualitative researchers about how they collected and analyzed data. They shared samples of their fieldnotes, memos, journals, and publications. In addition, they provided me with their syllabi and other teaching materials. I studied these materials assiduously. Fourth, I met regularly with qualitative researchers, once or twice a month, to discuss ideas and ask for supervision and feedback about my learning. During these meetings, we also talked about teaching processes and techniques, as well as the challenging practical and conceptual issues of doing qualitative research. Typical of the questions I asked were, How can you judge the credibility of key informants in the field? What are the connections between postmodernism and qualitative approaches?

Fifth, I taught the qualitative research class and received feedback from my students, as well as from experienced qualitative researchers. Sixth, I collected syllabi from other faculty in other universities who taught qualitative research. Finally, I arranged to work with a qualitative researcher on an ethnographic study of the relationships between low income, Latino families, and schools. As a part of that study I had my first experience in analyzing qualitative data and organizing data into a report. I then wrote a proposal that was funded to conduct a qualitative study of teen pregnancy prevention. My learning continues as I conduct this research.

I saw that my learning followed a process similar to qualitative research in that I started out on a journey of inquiry equipped with my own context, frame of reference, and sets of questions. When I began, I was unaware that I was following processes common to qualitative approaches. Intuitively, I followed this process, which probably is related to my training and experience in clinical social work and family therapy. Social work, in particular, trained me to proceed without a lot of prior knowledge, but gave me confidence that I would learn as I go. I also kept talking to qualitative researchers and used methods that were similar to those that were familiar to me as a social work practitioner (i.e., interviewing, observation, and written documents). Gilgun (1992c) made a similar point about the connections between direct practice with individuals and families and the processes of qualitative research. Family systems and social work theory taught me to seek understanding in context at many systems levels. I also already knew that there are multiple interpretations to be considered.

Consistent with my bent toward incorporating multiple perspectives, I simultaneously read literature from many domains and sought to locate every faculty member (key informants) who had conducted qualitative research. My sample of faculty consisted of a grand total of two people, and they did not know others. A sample of two people might not have much credibility to quantitative researchers, but these researchers guided me through my initial learning. Insiders, no matter how few in number, can be helpful. One of my informants was a social work faculty member trained by Lou Zurcher, a social psychologist and qualitative methodologist. Her research area was adoption. My second informant was an anthropologist who had on-going experience as an ethnographer. Her ethnographic research was on families and poverty. I was fortunate to find such excellent mentors with specialties in the family area, and I developed relationships with them. They seemed to enjoy their roles as "peer debriefers" as I tested my emerging ideas about qualitative methodology.

My faculty informants had funded research projects and served as living examples of the diversity of approaches within the qualitative research tradition (Jacob, 1989). The social work researcher relied more on objectivist approaches to qualitative research. She was quite structured, integrating quantitative and qualitative approaches in her research. In contrast, the anthropologist was a subjectivist. Her data management was almost entirely intuitive, relying on emerging themes from her field journals. She never used computers or quantitative methods. I found myself most comfortable with the more objectivist, structured researcher, but more intrigued with the subjectivist anthropologist. She served as an ideal or a prototype qualitative researcher for me. After all, she differed so much from my quantitative background. For this reason, I intentionally spent more time with her and worked on an ethnographic field study with her.

Intensive reading and discussions with the qualitative researchers continued until I reached a point of "saturation." Finally, what I was reading and discussing became familiar and repetitive. This point did not come until after about two years, when I had taught the class all the way through once. By then, I began testing my knowledge against other qualitative researchers through attendance at conferences and the gathering of syllabi from other faculty in other universities. I repeated the same process in the following year, learning all the time. My processes paralleled qualitative research processes.

Qualitative Research and Families

Another important part of my learning was connecting the qualitative methods to my understanding of families. Sprey (1988) is a helpful reference for understanding the importance of qualitative research for developing family theories. Sociology and social work also have long histories of using qualitative field methods to study families in natural settings. Up until the 1940s, for example, qualitative research methods were the dominant research paradigm in sociology. Family sociology is replete with examples of using qualitative methods to study family processes and other difficult-to-observe phenomena, such as homelessness, and criminality (Feagin, Orum, & Sjoberg, 1991).

The anthropological influences of Bateson's systemic approach also seem very consistent with qualitative methods. Some view Bateson as the father of family therapy. His recursive epistemology (Bateson, 1971; 1979) is similar to qualitative research perspectives inherent in ethnographic field methods. I made other connections between the qualitative research methods and the practice methods of family therapy. For example, the hypothesizing and circular questioning used in the systemic approach (second order cybernetics) characteristic of the Milan style of family therapy and their observational, team and research methods seem somewhat consistent with qualitative inquiry (Golann, 1987). Further, the "not knowing" conversational interviewing approaches of the Collaborative Language Systems practice approach (Anderson & Goolishian, 1988; Goolishian & Anderson, 1990) are similar to the ethnographic interviewing methods found in qualitative research. These connections are further exemplified by two papers that I subsequently wrote on the connections between qualitative research and clinical practice methods (Franklin, in press; Franklin & Jordan, in press).

STRATEGIES FOR TEACHING QUALITATIVE RESEARCH

As I designed my class, I developed an outline of the information I needed in order to teach qualitative methods. Appendix 1 is composed of references in five areas. Many of the references are related to family practice and other clinical areas encompassing child and family studies, which is consistent with my own substantive area. In particular, the references in Appendix 1 highlight several research designs and data collection methods that I studied and subsequently taught in my class. My goal was to be able to describe processes of qualitative research in the same manner that I had been taught to describe the steps of quantitative research.

Appendix 2 maps the steps I present to students for understanding and carrying out a qualitative research design. Below, I discuss epistemological issues and some of the specific teaching methods used in teaching qualitative research. When possible, I illustrate these methods with examples from the family literature.

Epistemologies

When I began learning about qualitative research, I devoted considerable attention to reading about the epistemological debates: constructivist/constructionist versus the positivist/objectivist orientation to research. In particular, I wanted to build my understanding of the underlying assumptions and beliefs of qualitative perspectives. I had a vague familiarity with some of this literature (i.e., Heineman-Pieper, 1982; Schuerman, 1982; Geismar, 1982; Pieper, 1985; Witkin & Gottschalk, 1988; Thyer, 1989; Atkinson, Heath & Chenail, 1991; Cavell & Snyder, 1991; Liddle, 1991; Moon et al., 1991; Harrison, Hudson & Thyer, 1992; Witkin, 1992). In reading the epistemological debates within my own discipline, social work, I concluded that each side did not seem to understand the other and that the debates were hopelessly circular. Or perhaps as Tyson (1994) recently pointed out, one side is defending a particular style of research (statistics and other quantitative tools) and the other is speaking about adopting a meta-theory for a human science. I quickly expanded my reading to epistemological discussions in some other disciplines: psychology, education, sociology, and anthropology (cf. Manicas & Secord, 1982; Geertz, 1983; Borgen, 1984; Brunner, 1986; Guba, 1990; Mahoney & Lyddon, 1988; Polkinghorne, 1984, 1991; Mahoney, 1988; Gholson, Shadish, Neimeyer, & Houts, 1989; Strong, 1991; Neimeyer, 1993). I wanted to see if there were some common threads across social science disciplines.

From my reading of the epistemological debates, common themes emerged across disciplines. I identified four core themes for a new meta-theory for science: (1) The acceptance of human values as a part of science, (2) the inevitability of multiple meanings, and the testing and assemblance of multiple evidences for those different meanings, with multiple methods, (3) realization that non-lineality and complexity are the norm, and (4) the acceptance of the improbability of ever knowing an objective reality. This view of science–new to me and many others–is rooted in the post-positivist and constructivist approaches to the philosophy of science.

Post-positivism. Post-positivism refers to a scientific paradigm that pursues knowledge from a view that the real world exists but that it is impossible for humans beings to see this world given their limited sensory and cognitive abilities (Guba, 1990). Post-positivist researchers use qualitative methodologies but believe in the possibility of objectivity. They use methods such as critical multiplism, or triangulation to gain multiple descriptions of an event. Post-positivists also accept critiques such as gender and ethnic biases inherent in traditional, "value free" oriented logical positivist science.

Constructivism. Constructivists and constructionists represent a range of views concerning cognitive, linguistic, and social construction of reality. To most constructivists or constructionists, importance is not given to the existence of an ontologically "real world," but rather they give importance to how human beings construe the world through meanings, language, and social interactions. This does not mean, however, that constructivists believe that nothing except mind or perception exists, which is the same as solipsism. In fact, there is a range of views associated with constructivism, beliefs concerning a knowable, ontologically "real world" (Franklin, in press). See Guba (1990), Mahoney (1991), Schwandt (1994), and Steier (1991) for a review of constructivist perspectives in theory and research. These authors offer multi-disciplinary review on constructivism, including some differing definitions, and viewpoints concerning methods.

Constructivist schools of thought appear to agree that inquiry is contextually bound. According to this view, theories are value-laden, as are "scientific facts." Contextualist ideas, however, are not exclusively qualitative in origin. Contextualism is consistent with newer quantitative theories such as those found in behavioral analysis and non-linear dynamics or complexity theory. In complexity theory, for example, all understanding and prediction are contextual and are subject to rapid and seemingly unexplainable variation and change. These changes produce complex but understandable patterns. Gregersen and Sailer (1993) argue that non-linear dynamics make qualitative research essential for the social sciences, and I might add the family sciences.

Qualitative researchers have a high regard for the complexities of interactions, and I found this orientation to be consistent with my training in family practice which made me question the simplicity of a lineal view. I was also aware of the significance of radical constructivism in family systems theories, as well as the increasing attention given to other constructivist and constructionist meta-theories (Alexander & Neimeyer, 1989; Hoffman, 1990; McNamee & Gergen, 1992; Segal, 1986; von Glasserfield, 1988). Neimeyer (1993) has a particularly enlightening review of constructivist family theories and constructivist approaches to research.

Gaining a Meta-Perspective About Epistemological Debates

Though I wanted to understand different sides of the epistemological debates so I could communicate these views to students, I want to acknowledge that I had always considered myself to be more in favor of the objectivist approach to science (Franklin, 1994). I found that one of the first encounters on my way to learning qualitative research was re-visiting these issues. Fortunately, I was not sold on the infallibility of quantitative methods and was willing to think about other viewpoints. Willingness to consider other viewpoints is essential to appreciating qualitative research. In examining my own views, I began to ask myself what I really liked about quantitative research. My answer was that I liked the objectivist devotion to defining methods that had theoretical and practical value and that were based in evidence. As I learned more about the qualitative research process, however, I discovered there were other methods for assembling evidence that had theoretical and practical value.

A viewpoint important to qualitative research is the possibility that human cognitive and emotional functioning make it impossible for us to make value-free observations. In other words, my observations are partly constructions of my own biology and/or social experiences, and my observations therefore cannot be completely separate from my own personal experiences. In my experience teaching qualitative methods, constructivist ideas sometimes were barriers. For me, the concept of "not knowing" became a challenge to personal beliefs about veracity and truth. Meanings appear to get lost in the translation between what can be observed and "the truth." For example, I found that many people became "upset" with the idea that a singular reality or truth does not exist. For such individuals, this belief may represent a "core ordering process" that resists challenge (Mahoney, 1991). These individuals, however, appear to be willing to acknowledge that people see events in different ways and have diverse values. I have found that explaining the constructivist epistemology from a cultural perspective or cognitive-perceptual perspective is helpful in moving beyond these epistemological blocks that hamper learning. It is also helpful to explain that not all qualitative researchers subscribe to a constructivist orientation and that you can use qualitative methods within diverse scientific paradigms (Guba, 1990).

I looked for meta-perspectives to help me understand the circular nature of the epistemological debates and found fruitful reading in Smith (1989) and Diesing (1991) who interpret the debates within the broader context of the search and struggle to find appropriate methods for a human science. Historically, there has always been a tension between quantitative and qualitative epistemologies, and there is a group of researchers who undoubtedly want to relegate qualitative research to the back seat of the bus. This does not mean, however, that qualitative methods are automatically given an inferior position in family research or the other social sciences. But rather, I found several viewpoints concerning the place of qualitative methods in family research. Appendix 3 describes five categories I developed in order to organize the multiple ways that qualitative research may be viewed. These categories range from non-acceptance to uncritical advocacy. Pragmatic acceptance, defined as openness to the potential usefulness of all research methods, is more or less a middle ground.

When teaching qualitative methods, I encourage my students to use these categories to help them in their perspectives on qualitative research. I also lead them through an exercise at identifying the positions of other individuals on our faculty and those they encountered in readings. I identify myself as a pragmatist and teach a pragmatist orientation. I try to give them a good representation of the constructivist view because I don't think that they will get this perspective elsewhere in our program.

I use the family therapy literature to illustrate multiple perspectives. For example, the family researchers Cavell and Snyder (1991) take the position of non-acceptance or critical acceptance of the qualitative research.

They state that qualitative research designs are subject to numerous threats to internal and external validity that greatly limit the conclusions that we can draw from them. They conclude that there is a need to use evidence from controlled experimental procedures and the criteria of validity and reliability to document informal observations. In their view, qualitative research may be useful for theory development but it has limited usefulness in evaluating theories or in or providing estimates of causation, such as in the effectiveness of treatment methods. Moon et al. (1991), on the other hand, take a different view. These authors believe that the quantitative and qualitative research methods are complementary. Both add a valuable approach to research analysis and synthesis. Finally, Atkinson et al. (1991) suggest a more exclusive acceptance view. They insist that qualitative research methods are most useful for family researchers and that researchers must abandon the notions of objectivity and the establishment of the validity and reliability of data. Trustworthiness of data should be determined by the community of research consumers who are the stakeholders.

RESEARCH DESIGNS

From my quantitative background I learned that a research design is a set of rules for how to collect data. By collecting data in a certain manner, we are assured of the internal and external validity of our findings. I soon discovered that qualitative researchers were equally interested in how data were collected, giving attention to the credibility of the sources of data and the consistency in which the data were collected. Often compared to validity and reliability of methods, these procedures for collecting data have a rigor equal to that of quantitative designs (Gilgun, 1994). At the same time, however, qualitative research designs differ in their flexibility and use of the reflexive and circular processes of data gathering and analysis. Copeland and White (1991) described qualitative family researchers as using research designs that collect data from "small samples who are interviewed and observed, or more accurately, are visited in the natural environment (e.g., their own homes)." Qualitative family researchers collect data "consisting of open-ended remarks made in the context of interview conversations between participants and researchers. Participants may also be asked their views on how the topic is being studied, and the qualitative researcher may alter her method in response to input from participants." Family researchers using qualitative designs are "involved intensely with participants through-out a time period, watching change unfold before them . . . "(p. 11).

Illustrations

In class, I use various family studies to illustrate the use of different research designs. One study that I have found helpful in illustrating grounded theory, for example, is on parental management of conduct problem children (Spitzer, Webster-Stratton, & Hollinsworth, 1991). For ethnography, I use a study by Newfield, Kuel, Joaning, and Quinn (1990) on the family therapy of adolescent drug abuse. This study helps illustrate how ethnographies may be used in different settings and for shorter, as well as longer periods of time. Of course, there are many examples of classic ethnographies on families that may be used from the anthropology and sociology literatures. A couple we have discussed at length, in class, include *Hard Living on Clay Street: Portraits of Blue Collar Families* (Howell, 1973) and *Street Corner Society* (Whyte, 1981).

Case studies are also frequently used in family research. To illustrate the case study approach, I use collective case studies that highlight individualism in American family life (Bellah, Madsen Sullivan, Swidler and Tipton, 1985). I have also used Jarret (1992), a family case study about the underclass debate. In addition, there are many fine classic case studies on family life in the sociological literature. Handel (1991) reviewed many of these studies, as well as summarizing the importance of case studies in family research.

Appendix 4 presents a summary teaching outline that describes teaching methods and the types of assignments that I use to help students master the content and skills associated with conducting qualitative research studies. Besides describing content on research design, the outline is divided into three other sections that encompass data collection methods, data analysis, and writing-up the results. Students are already familiar with these headings through their training in quantitative research. Below I discuss specific techniques for teaching these methods, and provide illustrations from the family literature.

METHODS OF DATA COLLECTION

As a quantitative researcher, I knew that the integrity of any research design was only as good as its measurement system. The measures or data collection methods used are central to the research task. I sought to understand what methods qualitative researchers use to collect data. I discovered that they used a repertoire of methods as shown in Appendix 4. These methods include interviewing, participant observations, and various types of documents. All methods relied heavily on researchers as the main data gathering instruments. To assure the credibility of the data, qualitative researchers often work in teams and go through a process of testing their data and data sources repeatedly through member checks, triangulation, and verifying interpretations through peer debriefing and going back to the original sources for verification of interpretations.

Qualitative research methods are especially relevant to studying families because there are many aspects of family process and interactions that are hidden, or may be too personal or complicated to be easily ascertained with quantitative methods such as structured questionnaires or standardized measures. Family researchers are "outsiders" to family life but qualitative research methods provide approaches that afford glimpses of the inside through the process of intense and prolonged observations or interviews in field settings.

Gilgun, Daly and Handel (1992) is the best text that I found for both discussing and illustrating qualitative family research. This text covers a breadth of data collection methods, including interviewing, participant observations, document sources and the integration of quantitative and qualitative procedures. Other references of this type are found in Appendix 1. In the class students practice data collection. For example, they conduct and write up fieldnotes on participant observations, interviews, and a set of documents. I set up these exercises like informal field experiments that the students do as homework assignments. They further practice collecting data by designing their own small qualitative research study that they can carry out in a semester.

DATA ANALYSIS

Analysis of narrative data is especially complex for a quantitative researcher accustomed to statistical methods such as significance tests, statistical power analysis, and effect sizes to decide if the relationships between variables hold meaning worth considering. How does a qualitative researcher build evidence and draw conclusions from the complexities of interview transcripts, field notes, recorded observations, memos (notes about notes or speculative insights about observations), and documents? I have found from teaching qualitative research that data analysis is terrifying to students. They respond well to opportunities for practicing data analysis.

For this reason, in my class I now provide experiential exercises that are opportunities for students to analyze existing data sets. I provide case records from a local family and children's agency. Students analyze relevant and contrasting themes concerning the characteristics of families who were discharged with an unfavorable outcome versus those who were discharged with a favorable outcome. In the future, I plan to ask students to analyze focus groups from my qualitative study of teen pregnancy prevention.

While there are many approaches to analyzing qualitative data including statistical approaches, I found the grounded theory method to be the most helpful method for aiding my overall understanding concerning the essence of the qualitative approach (Glaser & Strauss, 1967; Strauss & Corbin, 1990). Gilgun (1992a) does an excellent job of explaining the method when she listed 21 steps of the grounded theory process. I found her approach to be especially understandable. I taught the essence of this process to my students and encouraged them to use this method in their own data analysis of their qualitative research projects.

As mentioned, however, there are many other methods for analyzing qualitative data. An important analytical method that has been used in family studies is domain analysis based on the work of the ethnographer, James Spradley's (1979) Developmental Research Sequence Model. Domain analysis helps researchers to conduct a type of narrative factor analysis on their data. Sells, Smith, Coe, Yoshioka and Robbins (1994), for example, used this method to analyze data from family therapy sessions.

Detailed discussion of qualitative data analysis methods are beyond the scope of this paper, but I will highlight one conceptual scheme that I found to be useful for understanding different types of approaches to data analysis. As I learned about qualitative research, I discovered that qualitative data analysis could be more or less structured (Miles & Huberman, 1994). Crabtree and Miller (1992), from family medical practice, offer a useful typology for understanding the continuum of data analysis approaches for qualitative research. The continuum ranges from an objective, positivist a priori approach to data analysis to subjective, constructivist interpretive approach to data analysis. Appendix 5 summarizes several styles of data analysis, from pre-established categories to immersion methods.

Qualitative researchers have many data management methods available to them, ranging from color coding schemes, folders, word processing programs, to computer data analysis programs developed especially for managing these types of data. Computer programs such as ETHNO-GRAPH, HYPERQUAL, ATLAS, and NUD*IST make the data analysis process easier to manage. Programs are available for both the DOS and Macintosh systems. Several programs also offer a demo for a nominal cost to review the program for suitability. See Miles and Weitzman (1994) for a recent review of computerized, qualitative data analysis programs. I bought two of the programs, HyperResearch and NUD*IST, to use in my class and in my own research. I also found two qualitative data analysis interest groups available through E-mail that keep me abreast of the new developments in NUD*IST and other data analysis programs. You may contact these groups at mailing-list@qsr.latrobe.edu.au and mailbase-admin@mailbase.ac.uk/Qual-software.

WRITING IT UP

The writing up of qualitative research generally involves setting out the themes constructed in the analysis and illustrating them with quotes intended to represent the lived experience of informants. Stories, metaphors, diagrams, dialogue, and paradigm cases often are part of the write-up. Links to previous research and theory demonstrate the wide applicability of qualitative findings. Many qualitative researchers have a social change philosophy. They do research to give voice to the oppressed. Other researchers are content to explore multiple family realities with no particular agenda for social change. There are many approaches to writing up qualitative research, ranging from quantitative technical approaches that are read like a standard research report, to the reflexive, subjectivist, almost journalistic accounts.

Reflexivity. In class, I pay special attention to reflexivity because I've found that this style of writing is difficult to teach students, while at the same time it often has special meaning to social work practitioners. According to Gilbert and Schmid (1994), reflexivity "comprises critical introspection and analysis of the self as researcher, and deliberate, critical dialogue within research communities about assumptions and practices" (p. 4). At first, as a quantitative researcher learning qualitative research, I sometimes had negative reactions to reflexive analysis, something rarely present in the typical quantitative research report. I experienced the information revealed in the research reports as too personal and the conclusions drawn as too emotionally intense. For example, I remember reading one research report where the researcher revealed that she had been a victim of child sexual abuse. I wasn't sure I would feel comfortable revealing such intensely personal information about myself in a research report. Of course, I did agree that the researcher's personal experience was important to her study since she was investigating intrafamily sexual abuse. Eventually, I begin to gain a better appreciation for reflexive writing styles. Interestingly, however, several of my students also reacted to these self-disclosures in a similar manner. They especially reacted to the intensely personal reflexive accounts recorded in edited books such as Riessman (1994), whose researchers exemplify reflexivity in their narratives.

Actually, reflexivity reminds me of the type of personal analysis a family psychotherapist goes through in analyzing her personal reactions and countertranferences toward family members. Reflexivity is important to qualitative research and has particular implications for validity in the data analysis. For this reason, I require students to follow this more reflexive writing style in the design and analysis of their qualitative research study. I require students to devote a section of their studies to a discussion of their histories, assumptions, and feelings about the research problem, and its analysis.

Being reflexive promotes self-awareness and helps students interpret data. One student, for example, who was conducting research on victims of family trauma, gained a depth of insight about the "secondary trauma" she had experienced in working with these clients for many years. While discussing her reflexivity, another student who had worked for several years in women's advocacy and family policy, reported that she became aware that her feminist belief system sometimes did not match with the interview data she collected from women rape victims. The topic was women victims' experiences with polygraph tests. She struggled to accept that the women were not offended by the polygraph. She wanted to force the data into her own personal conceptualizations about how women who have been raped are victimized when they have to take the polygraph. She reported that for the first time in her life she became aware that some of her ideas about the societal oppression of women may not apply to all women. This was unsettling because she had formed strong ideas through her work in family advocacy. See Gilgun (1994) and Catlett (1994) for further examples of how reflexivity may be used in qualitative family research.

DISCUSSION

I have chronicled my experience of learning to teach qualitative research and have recorded some of my significant learnings. My experiences in many ways followed the process of qualitative research. As a researcher trained in quantitative research, I was challenged and rewarded. I worked hard to learn. Contrary to the opinions of some, qualitative research is not easy. I estimate that I read and searched for literature approximately 20-25 hours a week for six months before I felt comfortable with my basic understanding. In the beginning, I was cursing my decision to teach this class. I was increasingly surprised, however, at how much I enjoyed the reading. I knew that quantitative researchers sometimes have difficulty understanding or appreciating qualitative research, but I was not having this experience.

I hope my story helps others to teach qualitative family research. For this reason, I provided many examples of how I used the family practice literature to teach the different designs and methods of qualitative research. I also provided a teaching outline and materials on how to organize a class. In addition, I have provided several references and research examples from the family literature that other instructors may find useful.

Why did I put in the effort and time learn to teach qualitative research? I know that I did not gain this interest in qualitative methodology from my formal research training. Through introspection, I have come to believe that the qualitative process was interesting to me because of my cultural heritage, which is American Indian, and my clinical training in family practice. In fact, in some curious way, qualitative processes remind me of my family values. It especially seems similar to the clinical process of family therapy. Perhaps, my life experiences may have made it seem easier than it actually is for a quantitative researcher to learn to teach qualitative methodologies.

I enjoy teaching this class. I have taught the class for three years in my school, and I recently taught it at the doctoral level in a psychology department. My experience with learning to teach qualitative research has been personally fulfilling, and I hope other quantitative researchers will learn this approach.

REFERENCES

Alexander, P. C. & Neimeyer, G. J. (1989). Constructivism and family therapy. *International Journal of Personal Construct Psychology, 2*, 111-121.

Anderson, H. & Goolishian, H. (1988). Human systems as linguistic systems: Preliminary and evolving ideas. *Family Process, 27*, 37-393.

Atherton, C. R. (1993). Empiricists versus social constructionists: A time for a cease fire. *Families in Society, 74*(10), 617-624.

Atkinson, B., Heath, A. & Chenail, R. (1991). Qualitative research and the legitimization of knowledge. *Journal of Marital and Family Therapy, 17*(2), 161-166.

Bateson, G. (1979). *Mind and Nature.* New York: Dutton.

Bateson, G. (1971). *Steps to an ecology of mind.* New York: Ballantine.

Bellah, R. N., Madsen, R., Sullivan, W. M., Swidler, A., & Tipton, S. M. (1985). *Habits of the Heart: Individualism, and commitment in American life.* Berkeley: University of California Press.

Berlin, S. B. (1990). Dichotomous and complex thinking. *Social Service Review, 64*(1), 46-59.

Borgen, F. H. (1984). Reaction: Are there necessary linkages between research practices and the philosophy of science? *Journal of Consulting Psychology, 31*(4), 457-460.

Catlett, B. J. (1994). Reflexivity in the learning process. *Qualitative Family Research, 8,* 1-3.

Cavell, T. A., & Snyder, D. (1991). Iconoclasm verses innovation: Building a science of family therapy. *Journal of Marital and Family Therapy, 17*(2), 167-172.

Crabtree, B. F. & Miller, W. L. (1992). *Doing qualitative research.* Newbury Park, CA: Sage.

DeChillo N., Matorin, S., & Hallahan, C. (1987). Children of psychiatric patients: Rarely seen or heard. *Health and Social Work, 12*(4), 296-302.

Denzin, N. K. & Lincoln, Y. S. (1994). *Handbook of qualitative research.* Newbury Park, CA: Sage.

Diesing P. (1991). Hermeneutics: The interpretation of texts. How does social science work? *Reflections on practice.* Pittsburgh, PA: University of Pittsburgh Press.

Feagin, J. R., Orum, A. M., Sjoberg, G. [Eds.](1991). *A Case for the case study.* Chapel Hill, N C: University of North Carolina Press.

Franklin, C. (in press). Expanding the vision of the social constructionist debates: Creating relevance for practitioners. *Families in Society.*

Franklin, C. & Jordan, C. (in press). Qualitative assessment: A methodological review. *Families in Society.*

Franklin, C. (1994). Must social workers continually yield current practice methods to the evolving empirically supported knowledge base? Yes! In W.W. Hudson & P. S. Nurius (Eds.), *Controversial issues in social work research* (pp. 271-282). Boston, MA: Allyn and Bacon.

Geertz, C. (1983). *Local knowledge: Further essays in interpretive anthropology.* New York: Basic Books.

Geismar, L. (1982). Debate with authors. *Social Service Review, 56,* 311-312.

Gergen, K. J. (1985). The social constructionist movement in modern psychology. *American Psychologist, 40*(3), 266-275.

Gholson, B., Shadish, W. R., Neimeyer, R. A., & Houts, A. C. (Ed.). (1989). *Psychology of science.* Cambridge, MA: Cambridge University Press.

Gilbert, K. R. & Schmid, K. (1994). Bringing our emotions out of the closet: Acknowledging the place of emotion in qualitative research. *Qualitative Family Research, 8,* 1-3.

Gilgun, J. F. (1994). Reflexivity emerges as central: What does it mean for understanding and knowledge? *Qualitative Family Research, 8,* 1-3.

Gilgun, J. F. (1992a). Definitions, methodologies, and methods in qualitative family research. In J. F. Gilgun, K. Daly & G. Handel (Eds.), *Qualitative methods in family research* (pp. 22-40). Newbury Park, CA: Sage.

Gilgun, J. F. (1992b). Hypothesis generation in social work research. *Journal of Social Service Research, 15,* 113-135.

Gilgun, J. F. (1992c). Observations in a clinical setting. In J. F. Gilgun, K. Daly &

G. Handel (Eds.). *Qualitative methods in family research* (pp. 236-259). Newbury Park, CA: Sage.

Gilgun, J. F. (1994). A case for case studies in social work research. *Social Work, 39*(4), 371-380.

Gilgun, J. F., Daly, K., & Handel, G. (Eds.). (1992). *Qualitative methods in family research.* Newbury Park, CA: Sage.

Glaser, B. G. (1978). *Theoretical sensitivity: Advances in the methodology of grounded theory.* Mill Valley, CA: Sociology Press.

Glaser, B. G. & Strauss, A. L. (1967). *The discovery of grounded theory: Strategies for qualitative research.* Chicago: Aldine.

Glaser, B. G. (1992). *Emergence verses forcing: Basics of grounded theory analysis.* Mill Valley, CA: Sociology Press.

Goolishian, H. & Anderson, H. (1990). Understanding the therapeutic system: From individuals and families to systems in language. In F. Kaslow (Ed.), *Voices in Family Psychology* (pp. 91-113). Newbury Park, CA: Sage.

Gregersen, H., & Sailer, L. (1993). Chaos theory and its implications for social science research. *Human Relations, 46*(7), 777-801.

Grinnell, R. M., Jr., Blythe, B., Corcoran, K., Fraser, M., Gibbs, L., Green, R. G., Montgomery, D. H., Holden, G., Hudson, W. W., Ivanhoff, A., Jenson, J., Jordan, C., LeCroy, C. W., Longres, J. F., McMurtry, S., Nichols-Casebolt, A., Nurius, P., Royse, D., Sheafor, B. W., Tripodi, T., Thyer, B. A., Weinbach, R. W., Zastrow, C. (1994). Social work researchers quest for respectability. *Social Work.*

Grinnell, R. M. (1993). *Social work research and evaluation* (4th ed.). Itasca, IL: Peacock.

Grotevant, H. D. (1991). Forward. In A. P. Copeland, and K. M. White, *Studying Families (*pp. vii-viii). Newbury Park, CA: Sage.

Guba, E. G. (1990). *The paradigm dialog.* Newbury Park, CA: Sage.

Handel, G. (1991). Case study in family research. In J. R. Feagin, A. M. Orum, G. Sjoberg (Eds)., *A Case for the Case Study* (pp. 244-269). Chapel Hill: University of North Carolina Press.

Harrison, D. F., Hudson, W. W., & Thyer, B. A. (1992). On a critical analysis of empirical clinical practice: A response to Witkin's revised views. *Social Work, 37*(5), 461-464.

Hartman, A. (1990). Editorial: Many ways of knowing. *Social Work, 35*(1), 3-4.

Heineman, M. B. (1981). The obsolete scientific imperative in social work research. *Social Service Review, 55*(3), 371-397.

Heineman-Pieper, M. (1982). Author's reply. *Social Service Review, 56,* 312.

Heineman-Pieper, M. (1989). The heuristic paradigm: A unifying and comprehensive approach to social work research. *Smith College Studies in Social Work, 60*(1), 8-34.

Held, B. S. (1990). What's in a name? Some confusions and concerns about constructivism. *Journal of Marital and Family Therapy, 16*(2), 179-186.

Held, B. S. & Pols. (1985). The confusion about epistemology and "epistemology"-and what to do about it. *Family Process, 24,* 509-517.

Hoffman, L. (1992). A reflexive stance for family therapy. In S. McNamee & K. J. Gergen, *Therapy as social construction* (pp. 7-24). Newbury Park, CA: Sage.

Hoffman, L. (1990). Constructing realities: The art of lenses. *Family Process, 29,* 1-12.

Hoshmand, L. L. S. T. (1989). Alternate research paradigms: A review and teaching proposal. *The Counseling Psychologist, 17*(1), 3-79.

Howe, K. R. (1988). Against the quantitative-qualitative incompatibility thesis or dogmas die hard. *Educational Researcher, 17*(8), 10-16.

Howell, J. T. (1973). *Hard Living on Clay Street: Portraits of Blue Collar Families.* Prospect Heights, IL: Waveless Press.

Jarrett, R. L. (1992). A family case study: An examination of the underclass debate. In J. F. Gilgun, K. Daly, G. Handel (Eds.), *Qualitative Methods in Family Research.* Newbury Park, CA: Sage.

Jacob, E. (1989). Qualitative research: A defense of traditions. *Review of Educational Research, 59*(2), 229-235.

Joanning, H. P. (1993, October). *Qualitative research* presentation at the annual meeting of the American Association for Marriage and Family Therapy, Anaheim, CA.

Lancy, D. F. (1993). *Qualitative research in education: An introduction to the major traditions.* New York: Longman.

Liddle, H. A., (1991). Empirical values and the culture of family therapy. *Journal of Marital and Family Therapy, 17*(4), 327-348.

Lofland, J. & Lofland, L. H. (1984). *Analyzing social settings: A guide to qualitative observation and analysis* (2nd edition). Belmont, CA: Wadsworth.

Neimeyer, R. A. (1993). An appraisal of constructivist psychotherapies. *Journal of Consulting and Clinical Psychology, 61,* 221-234.

Mahoney, M. J. (1991). *Human Change Processes.* New York: Basic Books.

Mahoney, M. J. (1988). Constructive meta-theory: Basic features and historical foundations. *International Journal of Personal Construct Psychology, 1*(1), 1-35.

Mahoney, M. J., & Lyddon, W. J. (1988). Recent developments in cognitive approaches to counseling and psychotherapy. *The Counseling Psychologist, 16*(2), 190-234.

Manicas, P. T., & Secord, P. F. (1982). Implications for psychology of the new philosophy of science. *American Psychologist, 38,* 390-413.

Miles, M. B. and Huberman, A. M. (1994). *Qualitative data analysis: An Expanded sourcebook, 2nd. edition.* Newbury Park, CA: Sage.

Miles, M. B. & Weitzman, E. A. (1994). Choosing computer programs for qualitative data analysis. In M. B. Miles and A. M. Huberman, *Qualitative data analysis: An expanded sourcebook, 2nd. edition.* Newbury Park, CA: Sage.

Mishler, E. G. (1986). The analysis of interview narratives. In T. R. Sarbin (Ed.), *Narrative psychology: The storied nature of human conduct* (pp. 233-255).

Moon, S. M., Dillon, D. R., Sprenkle, D. H. (1990). Family therapy and qualitative research. *Journal of Marital and Family Therapy, 16*(4), 357-373.

Moon, S. M., Dillon, & Sprenkle, D. H. (1991). On balance and synergy: Family therapy and qualitative research revisited. *Journal of Marital and Family Therapy, 17*(2), 173-178.

Neimeyer, G. J. (Ed.). (1993). *Constructivist assessment: A casebook.* Newbury Park, CA: Sage.

Neimeyer, R. A. (1993). An appraisal of the constructivist psychotherapies. *Journal of Consulting and Clinical Psychology, 61*(2), 221-234.

Newfield, N. A., Kuel, B. P., Joanning, H. P. & Quinn, W. H. (1990). A mini ethnography of the family therapy of adolescent drug abuse: The ambiguous experience. *Alcoholism Treatment Quarterly, 7*(2), 57-79.

Newfield, N. A., Joanning, H. P., Kuel, B. P., & Quinn, W. H. (1991). We can tell you about "psychos" and "shrinks": An ethnography of the family therapy of adolescent drug abuse. In T. C. Todd & M. D. Selekman (Eds.), *Family therapy approaches with adolescent substance abuse.* Boston: Allyn & Bacon.

Orum, A. M. Feagin, J. R., & Sjoberg, G. (1991). Introduction, The Nature of the Case Study. In J. R. Feagin, A. M. Orum, & G. Sjoberg. *A case for the case study* (pp. 1-26). Chapel Hill, NC: The University of North Carolina Press.

Peile, C. (1988). Research paradigms in social work: From stalemate to creative synthesis. *Social Service Review, 62*(1), 1-19.

Pieper, M. H. (1985). The future of social work research. *Social Work, 21*(4), 3-11.

Polkinghorne, D. E. (1984). Further extensions of methodological diversity for counseling psychology. *Journal of Counseling Psychology, 31*(4), 416-429.

Polkinghorne, D. E. (1991). Two conflicting calls for methodological reform. *The Counseling Psychologist, 19*(1), 103-114.

Riessman, C. K. (1994). *Qualitative studies in social work research.* Thousand Oaks, CA: Sage.

Schuerman, J. R. (1982). Debate with authors: The obsolete scientific imperative in social work research. *Social Service Review, 56*(1), 144-146.

Schwandt, T. A. (1994). Constructivist, interpretivist approaches to human inquiry. In N. K. Denzin & Y. S. Lincoln (Eds.), *Handbook of qualitative research* (pp. 118-137). Thousand Oaks, CA: Sage.

Segal, L. (1986). *The dream of reality: Heinz Von Foerster's constructivism.* New York: Norton.

Sells, S. P., Smith, T. E., Coe, M. J., Yoshioka, M. & Robbins, J. (1994). An ethnography of couple and therapist experiences in reflecting team practice. *Journal of Marital and Family Therapy, 20*, 3, 247-266.

Smith, J. K. (1989). The origins of the current discussion. *The nature of social and educational inquiry: Empiricism versus interpretation* (pp. 37-62). Norwood, NJ: Ablex.

Spradley, J. P. (1979). *The ethnographic Interview.* New York: Holt, Rinehart, and Winston.

Sprey, J. (1988). Current theorizing on the family: An appraisal. *Journal of Marriage and the Family, 50*, 875-890.

Spitzer, A., Webster-Stratton, & Hollinsworth, T. (1991). Coping with conduct-problem children: Parents gaining knowledge and control. *Journal of Clinical Child Psychology, 20* (4), 413-427.

Steier, F. (Ed.) (1991). *Research and reflexivity.* London: Sage.

Strauss, A. & Corbin, J. (1990). *Basics of qualitative research: Grounded theory procedures and techniques.* Newbury Park, CA: Sage.

Strong, S. R. (1991). Theory-driven science and naive empiricism in counseling psychology. *Journal of Counseling Psychology, 38*(2), 204-210.

Thyer, B.A. (1989). First principles of practice research. *British Journal of Social Work, 19*, 309-323.

Tyson, K. B. (1992). A new approach to relevant scientific research for practitioners: The heuristic paradigm. *Social Work, 37*(6), 541-555.

Tyson, K. (1994). *New foundations for scientific social and behavioral research: The heuristic paradigm.* Boston: Allyn and Bacon.

Viney, L. L. (1989). Which data collection methods are appropriate for constructivist psychology. *International Journal of Personal Construct Psychology, 1*, 191-203.

von Glaserfeld, E. (1988). The reluctance of change a way of thinking. [Special Issue, Constructivism and Family Therapy], *The Irish Journal of Psychology, 9*, 84-110.

Weitzman & Miles (1995). *Qualitative Data Analysis Programs.* Newbury Park, CA: Sage.

Whyte, W. F. (1981). *Street Corner Society: The social structure of an Italian slum (2nd edition).* Chicago: University of Chicago Press.

Witkin, S. L. (1989). Towards a scientific social work. *Journal of Social Service Research, 12*(3/4), 83-98.

Witkin, S. L. (1991). Empirical clinical practice: A critical analysis. *Social Work, 36*(2), 158-163.

Witkin, S. L. (1992). Empirical clinical practice or Witkin's revised views: Which is the issue? *Social Work, 37*(5), 465-468.

Witkin, S. L. & Gottschalk, S. (1988). Alternative criteria for theory evaluation. *Social Service Review, 37*, 465-468.

APPENDIX 1

Learning Qualitative Research: Areas and References

Epistemologies

Atherton, C. R. (1993). Empiricists versus social constructionists: A time for a cease fire. *Families in Society, 74*(10), 617-624.

Atkinson, B., Heath, A. & Chenail, R. (1991). Qualitative Research and the Legitimization of Knowledge, *Journal of Marital and Family Therapy, 17*(2), 161-166.

Berlin, S. B. (1990). Dichotomous and complex thinking. *Social Service Review, 64*(1), 46-59.

Cavell, T. A., & Snyder, D. (1991). Iconoclasm verses innovation: Building a science of family therapy. *Journal of Marital and Family Therapy, 17*(2), 167-172.

Daly, K. (1992). The fit between qualitative research and characteristics of families. In Gilgun, J. F., Daly, K. & Handel, G. (Eds.) *Qualitative Methods in Family Research.* Newbury Park, CA: Sage.

Guba, E. G. (Ed.) (1990). *The Paradigm Dialog.* Newbury Park, CA: Sage.

Handel, G. (1992). The qualitative tradition in family research. In Gilgun, J. F., Daly, K. & Handel, G. (Eds.) *Qualitative Methods in Family Research.* Newbury Park, CA: Sage.

Harrison, D. F., Hudson, W. W., & Thyer, B. A. (1992). On a critical analysis of empirical clinical practice: a response to Witkin's revised views. *Social Work, 37*(5), 461-464.

Heineman, M. B. (1981). The obsolete scientific imperative in social work research. *Social Service Review, 55*(3), 371-397.

Jacob, E. (1987). Qualitative research traditions: A review. *Review of Educational Research, 57*(1), 1-50.

Jacob, E. Clarifying qualitative research: A focus on traditions. *Educational Researcher, 17*(1), 16-24.

Jacob, E. (1989). Qualitative research: A defense of traditions. *Review of Educational Research, 59*(2), 229-235.

Lancy, D. F. (1993). *Qualitative Research in Education: An Introduction to the Major Traditions.* New York: Longman (Chapter 1).

Liddle, H. A., (1991). Empirical values and the culture of family therapy. *Journal of Marital and Family Therapy, 17*(4), 327-348.

Lyddon, W. J. & Alford, D. J. (1993). Constructivist assessment: A developmental-epistemic perspective. In G. J. Neimeyer (Ed.), *Constructivist assessment: A casebook* (pp. 31-57). Newbury Park, CA: Sage.

Moon, S. M., Dillon, D. R., Sprenkle, D. H. (1990). Family therapy and qualitative research. *Journal of Marital and Family Therapy, 16*(4), 357-373.

Moon, S. M., Dillon, & Sprenkle, D. H. (1991). On balance and synergy: Family therapy and qualitative research revisited. *Journal of Marital and Family Therapy, 17*(2), 173-178.

Neimeyer, G. J. & Nelmeyer, R.A. (1993). Defining the boundaries of constructivist assessment. In G. J. Neimeyer (Ed.), *Constructivist assessment: A casebook* (pp. 1-30). Newbury Park, CA: Sage.

Patton, M. J., & Jackson, A. P. (1991). Theory and meaning in counseling research: Comment on Strong (1991). *Journal of Counseling Psychology, 38*(2), 214-216.

Pieper, M. H. (1987). Comments on Scientific imperatives in social work research: Pluralism is not skepticism. *Social Service Review, 61*(2), 368-370.

Polkinghorne, D. E. (1984). Further extensions of methodological diversity for counseling psychology. *Journal of Counseling Psychology, 31*(4), 416-429.

Polkinghorne, D. E. (1991). Two conflicting calls for methodological reform. *The Counseling Psychologist, 19*(1), 103-114.

Schuerman, J. R. (1982). Debate with authors: The obsolete scientific imperative in social work research. *Social Service Review, 56*(1), 144-146. Also read Heineman, Author's reply.

Smith, J. K. (1989). The origins of the current discussion. *The nature of social and educational inquiry: Empiricism versus interpretation* (pp. 37-62). Norwood, NJ: Ablex.

Strong, S. R. (1991). Theory-driven science and naive empiricism in counseling psychology. *Journal of Counseling Psychology, 38*(2), 204-210.

Witkin, S. L. (1991). Empirical clinical practice: A critical analysis. *Social Work, 36*(2), 158-163.

Witkin, S. L. (1992). Empirical clinical practice or Witkin's revised views: Which is the issue? *Social Work, 37*(5), 465-468.

QUALITATIVE RESEARCH DESIGNS/METHODS OF INQUIRY

Grounded Theory

Gilgun, J. F. (1992). Definitions, methodologies, and methods in qualitative family research. In Gilgun, J. F., Daly, K. & Handel, G. (Eds.), *Qualitative Methods in Family Research.* Newbury Park, CA: Sage.

Glaser, B. G. & Strauss, A. L. (1967). The discovery of grounded theory: Strategies for qualitative research. Chicago: Aldine.

Neuman, L. (1994). Qualitative Research Design. *Social Research Methods: Qualitative and Quantitative Approaches.* Needham Heights, MA: Allyn & Bacon.

Riessman, C. K. (Ed.). (1994). *Qualitative studies in social work research.* Newbury Park, CA: Sage (Part 1, Grounded Theory and Health, Chapters 1, 2 & 3).

Spitzer, A. Webster-Stratton, & Hollinsworth, T. (1991). Coping with conduct-problem Children: Parents gaining knowledge and control. *Journal of Clinical Child Psychology, 20* (4), 413-427.

Ethnography

Berg, B. L. (1989). Chapter 3, Ethnographic Field Strategies. *Qualitative Research Methods for the Social Sciences.* Boston: Allyn & Bacon.

Fetterman, D. M. (1989). Chapter 1, The first step, An overview. Chapter 2, Walking in Rhythm: Anthropological Concepts. *Ethnography: Step by Step.* Newbury Park, CA: Sage.

Gilchrist, V. J. (1992). Key Informant Interviews. In B. F. Crabtree & W. L. Miller, *Doing Qualitative Research.* Newbury Park, CA: Sage.

Kenemore, T. K. (1987). Negotiating with clients: A study of clinical practice experience. *Social Service Review, 61*(1), 132-143.

Lancy, D. F. (1993). *Qualitative Research in Education: An Introduction to the Major Traditions.* New York: Longman (Chapters 2 & 3).

Newfield, N. A., Kuel, B. P., Joanning, H. P., & Quinn, W. H. (1990). A mini ethnography of the family therapy of adolescent drug abuse: The ambiguous experience. *Alcoholism Treatment Quarterly, 7*(2), 57-79.

Newfield, N. A., Joanning, H. P., Kuel, B. P., & Quinn, W. H. (1991). We can tell you about "psychos" and "shrinks": An ethnography of the family therapy of adolescent drug abuse. In T. C. Todd & M. D. Selekman (Eds.), *Family therapy approaches with adolescent substance abuse.* Boston: Allyn & Bacon.

Sells, S. P., Smith, T. E., Coe, M. J., Yoshioka, M. & Robbins, J. (1994). An Ethnography of couple and therapist experiences in reflecting team practice. *Journal of Marital and Family Therapy, 20*, 3, 247-266.

Case Studies

Gilgun, J. F. (1994). A case for case studies in social work research. *Social Work, 39*(4), 371-380.

Handel, G. (1991). Case study in family research. In J. R. Feagin, A. M. Orum, & G. Sjoberg, *A Case for the Case Study* (pp. 244-268). Chapel Hill, NC: The University of North Carolina Press.

Jarrett, R. L. (1992). A family case study: An examination of the underclass debate. In Gilgun, J. F., Daly, K. & Handel, G. (Eds.), *Qualitative Methods in Family Research.* Newbury Park, CA: Sage.

Lancy, D. F. (1993). *Qualitative Research in Education: An Introduction to the Major Traditions.* New York: Longman (Chapters 5 & 8).

Matocha, L. K. (1992). Case study interviews: Caring for persons with AIDS. In Gilgun, J. F., Daly, K. & Handel, G. (Eds.), *Qualitative Methods in Family Research.* Newbury Park, CA: Sage.

Merriam, S. (1988). Case study research in education. San Francisco: Jossey-Bass Publishers.

Orum, A. M., Feagin, J. R., & Sjoberg, G. (1991). Introduction, The Nature of the Case Study. In J. R. Feagin, A. M. Orum, & G. Sjoberg. *A case for the case study* (pp. 1-26). Chapel Hill, NC: The University of North Carolina Press.

Trepper, T. S. (1990). In celebration of the case study. *Journal of Family Psychotherapy, 1*(1), 5-13.

Heuristics and Hermeneutics

Heineman-Pieper, M. (1989). The Heuristic Paradigm: A Unifying and Comprehensive Approach to Social Work Research. *Smith College Studies in Social Work, 60*(1), 8-34.

Diesing P. (1991). Hermeneutics: The interpretation of Texts. How does social science work? *Reflections on practice.* Pittsburgh, PA: University of Pittsburgh Press.

Polkinghorne, D. (1983). Existential-Phenomenological and Hermeneutic Systems. *Methodology for the human sciences: Systems of inquiry.* Albany, NY: State University of New York Press.

Robinson, J. A. & Hawpe, L. (1986). Narrative Thinking as a Heuristic Process. In T. R. Sarbin, *Narrative Psychology: The Storied Nature of Conduct* (pp. 111-125). Westport Connecticut: Praeger.

Scott, D. (1989). Meaning construction in social work practice. *Social Services Review, 63*(1), 39-51.

Tyson K. B. (1992). A new approach to relevant scientific research for practitioners: The Heuristic paradigm. *Social Work, 37*(6), 541-555.

DATA COLLECTION METHODOLOGIES

Interviewing

Allen, K. R. & Walker, A. J. (1992). A feminist analysis of interviews with elderly mothers and their daughters. In Gilgun, J. F., Daly, K. & Handel, G. (Eds.), *Qualitative Methods in Family Research.* Newbury Park, CA: Sage.

Berg, B. L. (1989). A dramaturgical look at interviewing. *Qualitative research methods for the social sciences.* Needham Heights, MA: Allyn & Bacon.

Daly, K. (1992). Parenthood as problematic: Insider interviews with couples seeking to adopt. In Gilgun, J. F., Daly, K., & Handel, G. (Eds.) *Qualitative Methods in Family Research.* Newbury Park, CA: Sage.

Feixas, G., Procter, H. G., & Neimeyer, G. J. (1993). Convergent lines of assessment: Systemic and constructivist contributions. In G. J. Neimeyer (Ed.), *Constructivist assessment: A casebook* (pp.143-178). Newbury Park, CA : Sage.

Fravel, D. L. & Boss, P. G. (1992). An in-depth interview with the parents of missing children. In Gilgun, J. F., Daly, K. & Handel, G. (Eds.), *Qualitative Methods in Family Research.* Newbury Park, CA: Sage.

Murphy, S. O. (1992). Using multiple forms of family data: Identifying pattern and meaning in sibling-infant relationships. In Gilgun, J. F., Daly, K. & Handel, G. (Eds.), *Qualitative Methods in Family Research.* Newbury Park, CA: Sage.

Neimeyer, R. A. (1993). Constructivist approaches to the measurement of meaning. In G. J. Neimeyer (Ed.), *Constructivist assessment: A casebook* (pp. 58-103). Newbury Park, CA: Sage.

Rojiani, R. H. (1994). Disparities in the social construction of long-term care. In Riessman, C. K. (Ed.), *Qualitative studies in social work research.* Newbury Park, CA: Sage.

Siedman, I. E. (1991). *Interviewing as qualitative research.* New York: Teachers College Press-Columbia University.

Snyder, S. (1992). Interviewing college students about their constructions of love. In Gilgun, J. F., Daly, K. & Handel, G. (Eds.), *Qualitative Methods in Family Research.* Newbury Park, CA: Sage.

Yorke, M. (1989). The intolerable wrestle: Words, numbers and meanings. *International Journal of Personal Construct Psychology, 2,* 65-76.

Observations

Gilgun, J. F. (1992). Observations in a clinical setting: Team decision-making in family incest treatment. In Gilgun, J. F., Daly, K. & Handel, G. (Eds.), *Qualitative Methods in Family Research.* Newbury Park, CA: Sage.

Jorgensen, D. L. (1989). The methodology of participant observation. *Participant Observation: A methodology for human studies.* Newbury Park, CA: Sage.

Lightburn, A. (1992). Participant observation in special needs adoptive families: The mediation of chronic illness and handicap. In Gilgun, J. F.,

Daly, K. & Handel, G. (Eds.), *Qualitative Methods in Family Research.* Newbury Park, CA: Sage.
Solomon, C. (1994). Welfare workers' response to homeless welfare applicants. In Riessman, C. K. (Ed.), Qualitative studies in social work research. Newbury Park, CA: Sage.

Documents, Personal Accounts and Narratives

DeChillo N., Matorin, S., & Hallahan, C. (1987). Children of psychiatric patients: Rarely seen or heard. *Health and Social Work, 12*(4), 296-302.
Harbert, E. M., Vinick, B. H., & Ekerdt, D. J. (1992). Analyzing popular literature: Emergent themes on marriage and retirement. In Gilgun, J. F., Daly, K. & Handel, G. (Eds.), *Qualitative Methods in Family Research.* Newbury Park, CA: Sage.
Hoshmand, L. T. (1993). The personal narrative in the communal construction of self and life issues. In G. J. Neimeyer (Ed.), *Constructivist assessment: A casebook* (pp.179-205). Newbury Park, CA: Sage.
Hydèn, M. (1994). Woman battering as a marital act: Interviewing and analysis in context. In Riessman, C. K. (Ed.), *Qualitative studies in social work research.* Newbury Park, CA: Sage.
Lancy, D. F. (1993). *Qualitative Research in Education: An Introduction to the Major Traditions.* New York: Longman (Chapters 6 & 9).
Larossa R., & Wolf, J. H. (1985). On qualitative family research. *Journal of Marriage and the Family, 47*(3), 531-541.
Robinson, R. A. (1994). Private pain and public behaviors: Sexual abuse and delinquent girls. In Riessman, C. K. (Ed.), *Qualitative studies in social work research.* Newbury Park, CA: Sage.
Viney, L. L. (1993). Listening to what my clients and I say: Content analysis categories and scales. In G. J. Neimeyer (Ed.), *Constructivist assessment: A casebook* (pp. 104-142). Newbury Park, CA: Sage.

DATA ANALYSIS: ANALYTIC AND INTERPRETIVE PROCEDURES

Crabtree, B. F. & Miller, W. L. (1992). A template approach to text analysis: Developing and using codebooks. In B. F. Crabtree & W. L. Miller (Eds.), *Doing Qualitative Research* (pp. 93-109).
Gale, J. E. (1991). Methodology and procedures. *Conversation analysis of therapeutic discourse: A pursuit of a therapeutic agenda.* Norwood, NJ: Ablex.
Gilgun, J. F. (1992). Hypothesis generation in social work research. *Journal of Social Service Research, 15,* 113-135.

Glaser, B. G. (1978). *Theoretical sensitivity: Advances in the methodology of grounded theory.* Mill Valley, CA: Sociology Press.

Glaser, B. G. (1992). *Emergence verses forcing: Basics of grounded theory analysis.* Mill Valley, CA: Sociology Press.

Neimeyer, G. J. (Ed.) (1993). *Constructivist Assessment: A Casebook.* Newbury Park, CA: Sage.

Jorgensen, D. L. Analyzing and Theorizing. *Participant Observation: A methodology for human Studies.* Newbury Park, CA: Sage.

Fielding, N. G. & Lee, R. M. (1992). *Using Computers in Qualitative Research.* Newbury Park, CA: Sage.

Miles, M. B. & Huberman, A. M. (1984, 1994). *Qualitative Data Analysis: A sourcebook of new methods.* Newbury Park, CA: Sage.

Mishler, E. G. (1986). The analysis of interview narratives. In T. R. Sarbin (Ed.), *Narrative Psychology: The storied nature of human conduct* (pp. 233-255).

Smith, T. S., Sells, S. P. & Clevenger, T. (1994). Ethnographic content analysis of couple and therapist perceptions in a reflecting team setting. *Journal of Marital and Family Therapy, 20,* 3, 267-285.

Strauss, A. & Corbin, J. (1990). Part II: Coding Procedures and Chapter 5, Open Coding. *Basics of Qualitative Research: Grounded theory procedures and techniques.* Newbury Park, CA: Sage.

Strauss, A. & Corbin, J. (1990). Chapter 6, Techniques for enhancing theoretical sensitivity, Chapter 7, Axial Coding. *Basics of Qualitative Research: Grounded theory procedures and techniques.* Newbury Park, CA: Sage.

Tesch, R. (1990). *Qualitative Research: Analysis Types and Software tools.* New York: Falmer.

Yin, R. K. (1989). Analyzing case study evidence. *Case study research: Design and methods.* Newbury Park, CA: Sage.

WRITING UP YOUR STUDY

Berg, B. L. (1989). Writing research papers: Sorting the noodles from the soup. In B. L. Berg, *Qualitative Research Methods.* Boston: Allyn & Bacon.

Lofland, J. & Lofland, L. H. (1984). Writing reports. In J. Lofland & L.H. Lofland, *Analyzing social settings: A guide to qualitative observation and analysis.* Belmont, CA: Wadsworth.

Wolcott, H. F. (1990). *Writing up qualitative research.* Newbury Park, CA: Sage.

APPENDIX 2

MAJOR ATTRIBUTES OF QUALITATIVE RESEARCH DESIGNS

1. *Selecting Research Topics*: The researcher selects a topic based on personal interests, life experiences, guiding theory, desire to solve a problem, etc. . . .
2. *Research Designs*: Designs or methods of inquiry for collecting data are flexible and emergent. Hypothesis and research questions emerge and may change as the data is collected. Researcher starts out with a question and a guiding purpose or design but goes with the flow after they enter the field setting. Prolonged engagements in a field setting are preferred. A study may last months or even years.
3. *Subjects*: Selection of participants for the study is guided by the topic and the availability of viable subjects. Cases are usually relatively few in number.
4. *Sites or Settings*: Qualitative research takes place in natural or field settings. Researchers usually gain entry into and attach themselves to one or more field settings. Relatively few sites are usually chosen.
5. *Measurement Instruments*: The researcher is the principal instrument of data collection. Qualitative researchers use a self-reflexive stance and own their biases, beliefs and life experiences associated with the research study. Guiding theories are also acknowledged. Researchers strive to record subjective reality of participants. Researchers use a wide angle lens to record the context surrounding phenomena under study. Sequences of events and depth of information are also emphasized. Multiple methods are used in the interpretive process as an alternative to validity. Detailed and meticulous recording of data and how it was interpreted, and using multiple interpreters and confirmation checks are an alternative to reliability.
6. *Data Interpretation*: Qualitative researchers rely primarily on analytic and interpretive procedures in their data interpretations instead of statistics and mathematical procedures. An analytic schema or set of interpretive procedures such as grounded theory is used to analyze the data. Raw data is used to support interpretations.
7. *Reporting Results*: Reports use a narrative format that reads like a story with several episodes. The actual words and phrases of participants are interwoven throughout the story. Diagrams, pictures, and other graphic methods may be used to report results. Metaphors, case histories, and narrative dialogue are also frequently used.

APPENDIX 3

RANGE OF VIEWS CONCERNING QUALITATIVE METHODS

NON-ACCEPTANCE/RESISTANCE to accepting qualitative research as a viable way to carry out research. Arguments against qualitative research are based on realist/positivist ontologies, and desire to control and maintain the current research enterprise. Also, fears that acceptance of qualitative methods will lead to skepticism, subjectivism and relativism, and undermine the advancement of knowledge and technologies for the human sciences.

CRITICAL ACCEPTANCE of qualitative research but with the amendment that the methods withstand the same tests of validity and reliability used in the experimental sciences. Qualitative methods are to be evaluated in the same way as other methods of research within the empiricist research traditions, and are challenged to demonstrate that they can produce empirical outcomes and useful technologies.

CONTINGENT ACCEPTANCE FOR DISCOVERY AND EXPLORATORY UTILITY ONLY and should be incorporated along a continuum of research methodologies that ranges from the more exploratory to the more experimental research methods. A definable research hierarchy is implicit in this classification.

PRAGMATIC ACCEPTANCE of all research methodologies including qualitative methods. There are many ways of knowing and multiple methodologies may be used to generate useful knowledge. Each method should stand on its own abilities to generate helpful and pragmatic knowledge. Both qualitative and quantitative methods may be used in concert with one another. It is not appropriate or necessary, however, for there to be a research hierarchy, and qualitative methods do not have to evaluated according to the tenets of empiricist research. Usefulness of all research methods should be interpreted in the consensus of a community of scientists and practitioners who evaluate the usefulness of their findings.

EXCLUSIVE ACCEPTANCE of qualitative research methods and the overthrow of the empiricist research paradigm and enterprise. Qualitative research methods are seen as more useful than quantitative methods for the human sciences. Quantitative research is seen as mechanistic and unable to capture the fluidity and complexities of human experience. The reductionistic aspects of quantitative methods limit their usefulness, and the quantitative research enterprise is not believed to have produced great discoveries within the human sciences. Practice-based professions such as social work, and marriage and family therapy are encouraged to abandon these methods in favor of qualitative methodologies.

APPENDIX 4

TEACHING OUTLINE

Teaching Methods

Research Designs

Lecture and discussion concerning several designs: grounded theory, ethnography, case studies, heuristics, and hermeneutics.

Data Collection Methods

Lecture, discussions, and demonstrations, of interviewing, participant observations, and the use of documents and personal accounts in the field.

Data Analysis

Lecture, discussions, and demonstrations of conceptual data analysis approaches, such as grounded theory, domain analysis, and heuristics.

Assignments

Assigned readings illustrating each approach. A notebook of five studies of each design, collected and analyzed by the student. Student conceptualizing own design for mini qualitative research study that is carried out during class.

Readings and research tools that are used, such as interview schedules, field notes, journals, memos, and transcriptions. Practice exercises on methods. Collecting data for own qualitative study.

APPENDIX 5

DATA ANALYSIS METHODS FOR QUALITATIVE RESEARCH

Content Analysis and Quasi-Statistical Methods

Develop an a priori codebook or pre-established categories formulated from previous research or literature review.

Examine text using an a priori codebook to guide data management and analysis.

Identify data sources or units that apply to codebook.

Statistically determine connections between codes or data sources.

Verify and report results.

Quasi-statistical methods have their origins in manifest and latent content analysis which provides quantitative procedures for analyzing text data.

Template Analysis Methods

Develop an a priori template or one after scanning the data. Templates differ from codebooks in that they are flexible and may be changed in the process of collecting the data or data analysis.

Examine text using template for data management and data analysis.

Identify data sources or units that apply and match with the template.

Revise codes and categories in the template if needed to match with the data.

Reapply codes and categories from the new template to the text. Repeat above steps until you are satisfied that the template is able to code and sort the data satisfactorily.

Interpret and determine connections between the categories and date sources.

Verify interpretive results by checking them against the text.

Report results.

Template approaches to data analysis have their origins in qualitative positivism and ethnographic content analysis.

Editing Analysis Methods

Interpreter enters the text without a template or codebook. Interpreter tries to identify and separate preconceptions before reading the text. Underlying assumptions and pre-existing notions should be brought into awareness. Approach to the text is one of discovery looking for elements of an emergent hypothesis.

The interpreter enters the text searching for meaningful segments of text that relate to the study, and separates and organizes the segments into categories or codes.

Interpreter examines the categories and codes and makes connections between the patterns and themes that may exist within the text. Categories and codes may be revised after examination of the text. Other data may be collected to confirm or disconfirm an emergent hypothesis.

Categories and codes may be revised after further examination of the text and/or collection of new data. The new categories and codes may then be applied to the new test. Categories and codes may go through other revisions until the interpreter is satisfied that there is an appropriate match between the emergent categories and codes, and the text.

Interpretations and connections are made between the categories, and emergent themes are discovered. An hypothesis may emerge.

Report results.

The editing data analysis approach comes from several traditions including but not limited to phenomenology, symbolic interactions, hermeneutics, ecological psychology, grounded theory, and ethnography.

Immersion/Crystallization Analysis Method

Interpreter/reflector enters the text with the intent of empathetically immersing themselves until an intuitive insight/interpretation or crystallization of the text emerges.

Concerned reflection, intensive inner searching, and the yearning for insight are the modes of investigation and interpretation. Intuition is relied on to gain insights in the same way that a clinician might rely on clinical hunches to interpret case materials.

A cycle of empathic immersion with the text and crystallization are repeated until an interpretation happens.

Once an insight or interpretation emerges from immersion with the text, the results may be reported.

The immersion and crystallization analysis method comes from heuristic research which emphasizes self-reflection in the research experience.

Research and Practice:
A Reflexive and Recursive Relationship–
Three Narratives, Five Voices

Jerry Gale
Ronald Chenail
Wendy L. Watson
Lorraine M. Wright
Janice M. Bell

SUMMARY. In this multiply-authored account, five academicians discuss the connections between their work as clinicians and their clinical qualitative research. Each saw connections between practice and research, and each in her or his own domain of interest has found that practice informs research and research informs practice. This article also introduces three major types of qualitative clinical family research: conversational analysis, recursive frame analysis, and hermeneutic phenomenology. *[Article copies available for a fee from The Haworth Document Delivery Service: 1-800-342-9678. E-mail address: getinfo@ haworth.com]*

Jerry Gale is Associate Professor, Department of Child and Family Development, The University of Georgia, Athens, GA 30602. Ronald Chenail is Dean, School of Social and Systemic Studies, Nova Southeastern University, Fort Lauderdale, FL 33314. Wendy L. Watson is Associate Professor, Marriage and Family Therapy Graduate Programs, Brigham Young University, Provo, UT 84602. Lorraine M. Wright is Director, Family Nursing Unit, Department of Family Sciences, and Professor, Faculty of Nursing, University of Calgary, Alberta, Canada T1Y 6J4. Janice M. Bell is Research Coordinator, Family Nursing Unit, and Associate Professor, Faculty of Nursing, University of Calgary, Alberta, Canada T1Y 6J4.

[Haworth co-indexing entry note]: "Research and Practice: A Reflexive and Recursive Relationship–Three Narratives, Five Voices." Gale, Jerry et al. Co-published simultaneously in *Marriage & Family Review* (The Haworth Press, Inc.) Vol. 24, No. 3/4, 1996, pp. 275-295; and: *The Methods and Methodologies of Qualitative Family Research* (ed: Marvin B. Sussman, and Jane F. Gilgun) The Haworth Press, Inc., 1996, pp. 275-295. Single or multiple copies of this article are available for a fee from The Haworth Document Delivery Service [1-800-342-9678, 9:00 a.m. - 5:00 p.m. (EST). E-mail address: getinfo@haworth.com].

KEYWORDS. Qualitative research, Practice and research, Phenomenology, Self reports, Recursive frame analysis, Hermeneutics

To write this paper, the first author contacted the other four authors about a collaborative piece regarding their experiences connecting practice and research. Each author began his/her professional career as a practitioner. While each of the following stories stands on its own, together they weave a broader narrative. The first piece presents a practitioner's development from a family therapist to a therapist/researcher and his discovery that research and practice could recursively inform one another. The second piece describes how a family therapist/researcher uses Recursive Frame Analysis to track the process of change in conversations. Specific examples are given of how this knowledge allows him to be a reflective discourse analyst while simultaneously conducting therapy. The third story tells how two nurse practitioners and a family therapist employed hermeneutic inquiry to generate new discoveries and insights of their clinical practices and a passion for working as a clinical research team.

A PRACTITIONER'S ENTRY INTO RESEARCH
JERRY GALE

In 1986, following many discussions with my wife, we decided it would be valuable for me to receive a PhD. Having worked in a number of clinical settings (e.g., group homes, foster homes, juvenile courts, community based programs and private practice) for the previous ten years, we agreed that a doctorate would improve my clinical abilities as well as increase my earning potential. At that time, I had a master's in guidance and counseling (1979) which provided me with minimal background in research. Through workshops, seminars and supervision, I had a lot of clinical training in family therapy and Ericksonian hypnosis.

Upon entering the Department of Human Development and Family Studies at Texas Tech University, specializing in marital and family therapy, my identity-story was dominated by an emphasis towards clinical practice. Though a therapist and not a researcher, I was interested in investigating the communication aspects of the therapeutic process. My curiosity about communication processes developed primarily out of early childhood experiences with a speech impediment (Gale, 1991b) and my post-graduate training in Ericksonian psychotherapy, with its emphasis on language and relationships.

Studying Clinical Communication

While at Texas Tech, I enrolled in a number of courses that fueled my interests in studying clinical communication. One course was an introduction to ethnography (taught in my home department of human development and family studies). Additionally, courses taught by Brad Keeney, and lectures from visiting faculty (e.g., Heinz von Foerester, Stephen Tyler and Harry Goolishian) stimulated my interest in theoretical aspects of communication (second order cybernetics, linguistic systems and constructivism).

These classes and lectures nurtured a respect and appreciation for qualitative methods. I became very interested in studying methods and procedures for gathering and analyzing phenomenological experiences. This quest and interest in communication led me to take classes in the Department of Speech Communication. In my second year in the program I participated in a study interviewing families receiving care from pediatric cardiologists at the University Hospital (Chenail, Douthit, Gale, Stormberg, Morris, Park, Sridaromont, & Schmer, 1990). This project entailed interviewing families, and introduced me to data collection, data immersion, transcribing, category development via discourse analysis, collaborating with colleagues, the rigors and commitment of time of doing qualitative research and the excitement of writing and publication. In order to learn how to carry out this research, four of us took a directed readings class with G. H. Morris in the department of speech communication.

From this project, I developed an appreciation for the rich, thick landscape of the interviewees' descriptions. As a practitioner, I had valued and used clients' detailed stories. However, the interviewing component of the pediatric family study suggested that there was more to listening than I had previously suspected. The family interviews further highlighted for me how narratives are co-constructed through the participation of many (family and community members) and the power that these stories had to impact health.

Performative Aspects of Language

As I approached my dissertation, my research and theoretic paradigm was shifting toward the performative aspects of language (Austin, 1962; Potter & Wetherell, 1987), and tracking the therapeutic conversation. That is, how verbal and non-verbal interactive processes themselves are practical activities that create and maintain social realities. These ideas were impacting my clinical practice! I was more attentive and sensitive to the micro-communication practices of the clients and myself. It was useful to consider how the verbal and non-verbal interactive processes themselves are practical activities that create and maintain social realities. At this time, it made sense to me that qualitative methods were appropriate for addressing these issues. Further, the qualitative literature that I was reading (conversation and discourse analysis, ethnomethodology and marital and family therapy process research) informed and enhanced my clinical skills as well as my instructional skills. I was becoming a better listener and a better communicator as well as developing an understanding of how knowledge is actively constructed. My research pursuits were positively impacting my clinical skills! My prospectus proposed doing a conversation analysis of a marital therapy case.

Obtaining a videotape of a single session consultation conducted by Bill O'Hanlon (internationally acknowledged as a master clinician of solution focused therapy, see O'Hanlon & Weiner-Davis, 1989), I made an audio-tape and transcribed the session. I spent about 80 hours viewing the videotape and listening to the audio-tape. I developed nine themes through the iterative processes of transcribing, developing categories and conducting constant comparative analysis (Gale, 1991a; Gale & Newfield, 1992). While the analysis focused on the collaborative communication of the therapist and couple, the themes developed highlighted the rhetorical procedures used by the therapist.

Doing the Dissertation

Doing the dissertation, which captured my attention and passion, was also a tedious and frustrating process. Many times I experienced doubts about my abilities to complete the project. (I questioned if I was really a researcher, and I struggled to see the data from different perspectives.) It was only through many discussions and support from faculty, colleagues, other researchers, and my wife, that I persevered.

This study greatly affected my clinical and research practice, and it contributed to a deeper understanding of conversations as both social and constructive phenomena. The powerful relevance of micro-details of talk also became apparent. From a clinical perspective, this awareness increased my sensitivity to the non-verbal and verbal exchanges between myself and clients. Analyzing the rhetorical skills used by the therapist in my study pointed to a sophistication of communication practices that had heuristic value (Gale, 1991a; Gale & Newfield, 1992) and have since affected my teaching practices as well. This knowledge supported a respect for the politics of talk that occurs at the micro-level. This challenged my previous view of therapist neutrality, and contributed to the pursuit of collaborate relationships between myself and client/research participants.

Unexpected Shifts in Identity-Story

My activities in graduate school, somewhat to my surprise, led to a shift in my identity-story. New possibilities for action as well as conceptualization opened up. I discovered that conducting research and reading research articles informed my clinical practice, and that my clinical practice informed my research activities. I now reflect more than ever on my clinical work and in teaching and research spend a great deal of time creating a balance between theory, practice and research. Conducting research became a rich and interesting endeavor with practical implications.

In writing this narrative, and reflecting upon my experiences, I believe that it was important to have a community that supported and tested my development as a researcher, clinician and instructor. As when working with a team to develop one's clinical skills, having access to qualitative research courses (or colleagues to consult), and faculty and colleagues to guide, challenge and support one's research is consequential. Through this support, one can develop rigor, imagination and ethical practices in research, practice and instruction.

RESEARCHER/PRACTITIONER: CLOSER TO THE TALK *RONALD J. CHENAIL*

For the past seven years as a qualitative researcher and family therapist, I have studied the practice of therapy by closely examining the way therapists and their clients speak in clinical sessions. I have not been particularly interested in the psychological or social systems theories that underlie the practice of therapy. Instead, I am more curious about how therapists, clients, supervisors, and other participants in therapy conduct themselves in these therapeutic conversations.

Use of Words in Therapy

I like to study how people speak when they are being therapists or clients. I want to know how people use words in their attempts to express their emotions, ideas, situations, and problems. I am fascinated with the ways therapists use their words to open up new vistas in conversations and how these fresh avenues in the talk seem to help people feel better and allow them to try new ways of living in and relating to the world.

My curiosity with talk in therapy extends to my practice as a family therapist. I have come to believe that whatever theories of personality, family, or systems a therapist holds, the practice of therapy boils down to having a conversation: albeit a particular kind of a conversation, but a conversation nevertheless. To be a therapist, I have to know how to use words. I have to be able to listen to what others say in the therapy room. I have to be able to speak with clients, to use their language.

I have to be able to track what is happening in a particular therapeutic conversation. Conversations are tricky phenomena, especially with families in therapy contexts. It seems in a moment's notice that a calm, constructive flow of talk can erupt into a chaotic, destructive torrent of screams and yells. Like all face-to-face interactions in language, therapy conversations can turn on a word. For instance, a "things are getting better" line of talk in a session can quickly turn into a "I still can't understand why he did it" refrain simply by the use of one little word: "but."

Redundant, Stagnant Talk

At other times, the talk can become redundant and stagnant to the point that there appears to be no movement. In these moments, therapist and client cover and re-cover the same stretch of talk over and over again. The pattern of talk in the therapy sessions takes on the same stuck pattern the clients have been experiencing in their out-of-session conversations.

As the therapist I feel that I need to track the talk and to recognize this change, or lack of change, in the conversation. By doing so, I can better choose how I will participate in the conversation. Hopefully, these choices made will help to increase the possibilities that the conversations we have together as therapist and clients will become alternatives to the troublesome ones in which they have been participating and to help us all reach a more therapeutic way of interacting.

Recursive Frame Analysis

In this essay, I want to discuss how I have conducted a number of qualitative studies as a therapist and as a researcher to learn more about talk and talk about talk of therapy. To this end, I will describe a qualitative approach to the study of discourse I have helped to develop called Recursive Frame Analysis (RFA). First, I want briefly to discuss some basic assumptions and techniques of RFA. This should help acquaint those readers who have not been previously introduced to Recursive Frame Analysis. Second, I want to illustrate how taking a closer look at clinical discourse through an RFA lens has helped to inform the way I speak and listen in therapy sessions.

To learn more about how others and I use and understand language in therapy and other such conversations, I have helped to lead a qualitative research project dedicated to the construction of a practical and useful way to "get closer to the talk." The system which has evolved in our project is called Recursive Frame Analysis (RFA) (Chenail, 1991). Created by Bradford Keeney, RFA is a method for understanding and presenting conversations. It is a type of sequential analysis which helps researchers and therapists to note their perceptions of semantic shifts in a conversation.

I have used this method to research a variety of conversations. These studies include an examination of parents' conversations about their children's heart murmurs (Chenail, 1991), a description of family therapist-supervisor talk behind the one-way mirror in a therapy session (Chenail & Fortugno, in press), an analysis of divorce mediator-disputants discourse in child custody dispute resolution (Chenail, Itkin, Bonneau, & Andriacchi, 1993; Chenail, Zellick, & Bonneau, 1992), and an in-depth look at systemic family therapy discourse (Rambo, Heath, & Chenail, 1993). Through each of these studies I was able to learn something different and something new which can happen when two parties sit down to discuss how to solve a problem.

RFA Assumptions

The roots of Recursive Frame Analysis can be traced to the work of Gregory Bateson (1972) and Erving Goffman (1974). Bateson and Goffman understood frames as being our conceptual or cognitive views of particular situations. For instance, do we perceive a story we hear from a client to be a tale of problems or of solutions? Our choices of frames help us to hear certain aspects of the talk, while not helping us to hear other parts of the conversation.

Along with this conceptual understanding of frames, Recursive Frame Analysts also employ what Deborah Tannen and others (Tannen & Wallat, 1993; Putnam & Holmer, 1992) call "interactive frames." Interactive frames are linguistic patterns through which we create meaning in our conversations. We build our conversations word-by-word and understand the words we hear and use in conversation by how we contextualize them. To contextualize or to frame a word is to connect it with other words. Context is built by the ways individuals connect words with other words in conversations.

For example, each sentence I have used so far in this essay has been built by connecting words. For you, the reader, each word I use already comes with a "dictionary" meaning. Each word has its own meaning for you prior to my using it in a sentence. When you come across a word like "frame," you have to look around at the other words I have used along with "frame" in order to construct how I am using and not using "frame" in a particular sentence. "Frame" understood in context means that you construct the meaning of "frame" by understanding it along with the other words around it.

The notion of recursion comes into play with Recursive Frame Analysis in that our cognitive frames are in recursive relationship with the linguistic frames we speak and hear. Our understanding of a situation helps us to grasp "what is going on." At the same time, as we experience "what is going on" in a situation, our understandings of that event can be re-shaped or reframed.

For example, if a therapist understands therapy as a "teaching" situation, he or she organizes therapy into "lessons" and "evaluates" how well the client has "learned." If the client does something in therapy which the therapist has never experienced before, the therapist may then see therapy as a "learning" opportunity and begin to appreciate what can be learned from the client-as-teacher.

Also, in conversation, there is a recursive relationship between text and context. A particular piece of text contextualizes other text, and in turn, is also contextualized by the other surrounding bits of text. If someone talks about success in business in terms of "scoring big with a contract" or "slam-dunking the competition," we can hear that this person contextualizes business in a sports frame. At the same time, these juxtapositions can lead us to think of sports in business terms too. For instance, newly hired chief executive officers in businesses can sign contracts that pay them for scoring big, and basketball players can compete against each other for money in slam dunk competitions during all-star games.

RFA Practice

With RFA, researchers listen to or watch a recording of a conversation while reading and re-reading a transcript of the discourse in question. They (a) discuss their observations of the subject matter of the conversation being developed (i.e., an emphasis on content or what is being said) and (b) note shifts from one subject to another in the course of a conversation (i.e., an emphasis on process or how things are being said).

An RFA analysis proceeds as follows: After the recording has been perused numerous times, the team members note instances when speakers use words repetitively. Then the team begins to "chunk" these instances into informal groupings. In RFA, chunking is the process by which an observer or team of observers makes sense of a collection of data by gathering together those discourse examples which seem to the observer(s) to have some characteristics in common. In RFA lingo, we say that we chunk these frames into galleries.

For example, in a therapy conversation, one gallery that can usually be constructed is a Problem Gallery. A problem gallery is a chunking that would contain all those frames uttered by the client(s) that the therapist or researcher understands as "problems." Another gallery commonly chunked by therapists would be a Solution Gallery. Again, this gallery would be a chunking of all the frames understood as being solutions or possible remedies by the therapist or researcher. In both cases, the therapist's or researcher's chunking of the frames may or may not be the same as how the client understands the conversation. In addition, other therapists or researchers may also differ on how they chunk the talk.

From an RFA perspective, this type of disagreement is fine because the purpose of RFA is not to make the map of the interaction, but only to make your map of a conversation: One based upon your understanding of the talk. When I write up RFA research, I present the analysis as my conceptualization of discourse. I re-present the data alongside my analysis and I encourage readers to judge the readability of my RFA map: Can readers follow how I have delineated the galleries and frames? Do readers agree with my rendering of the case? Readers could make their own RFA maps from the transcripts.

Similarly, as a therapist, I use RFA to chart how I understand a therapeutic conversation to be unfolding as I participate in the session. Again, I understand that these chunkings of the talk are my own constructions. In therapy, these RFA's are not as detailed as those I construct as a researcher. The speed at which a conversation unfolds in real-time does not allow me to create an intricate map as a therapist.

Also, I judge my in-session RFA's as good only when they help me work with the clients. Therefore, I keep my patterns of galleries simple and readily discard them if they do not help me get closer to the client's talk. For instance, I can always tell if my mapping of the talk is "off" in a session because the clients will tell me that what I am saying does not make sense to them, or they will continue to repeat their story several times in the therapy. If either situation occurs, I do not argue with the clients and tell them that my map is the map and that they are wrong about their understanding of their own situation. Rather, I know I must discard my present RFA understanding, listen anew to the clients' stories, and create a new pattern of galleries and frames.

RFA-Informed Therapy: Three Examples

To help the readers understand how RFA research has informed my practice of therapy, I would like to discuss briefly three in-the-room-processes that I first noticed as an RFA researcher and then subsequently used as a therapist. These patterns of talk are torqued talk, opening up closings, and closing down closings. Most of the therapy I practice and supervise nowadays is organized by these three talk distinctions. As a result, I find that by concentrating on whether I think the talk seems to be "standing still" (torqued talk), or whether I gather that the talk is "moving from one gallery to another" (opening up closings), or whether the talk only appears to be moving from one gallery to another, I can better gauge how I want to participate in the conversation at a particular moment in time.

Torqued talk. Most clients come to therapy because they feel that they are stuck. They do not know what to do with a life situation, or, if they do know what to do, they are unable to accomplish their goal(s). By tracking the frames in therapy with RFA, I can usually notice how tight the talk can be for clients. They will repeat their stories, sometimes word for word, again and again in the sessions. The rigidity or tightness I experience in these conversations led me to describe this talk as being torqued. By torqued, I mean that the talk seems twisted tightly and that I am having trouble hearing any changes in the clients' wordings.

In a recent study (Rambo, Heath, & Chenail, 1993), I examined a full-length family therapy session. The family had come to therapy to discuss how a son, "Randy," could move into his father "Ted's" home to live. The son's mother and father had been divorced a number of years. During that time, the son had lived on and off with his mother and her new husband, his father, and an uncle.

During the session, I had chunked a number of frames into a gallery I called "Randy and Ted Getting Together Talk," a possible solution gallery. The talk in the conversation returned to that gallery nine times. Seven of those nine times, the "getting together talk" was followed by another gallery, "Ted's Problem with Randy Talk," a problem gallery. To me, the repeated solution gallery and problem gallery juxtaposition seemed to be a good representation of torqued talk.

Many therapy sessions can be seen as having a pattern of torqued talk similar to the one I experienced in studying the case with Randy and Ted. Until some new bit of talk can be introduced into the conversation, both the talk in the therapy room and the clients' situation outside of the room will remain stuck. One technique I have learned that can help in untorquing talk is the opening up closing.

Opening up closings. RFA can be used for conducting a sequential analysis of discourse. As in the case above, the Recursive Frame Analyst charts the flow of conversation and marks when conversations shift from one chunking to another. For instance, the analyst may mark when a conversation shifts from talk about the children's school problems to talk about the children's problems at home. The talk may then shift from talk about children's problems to talk about the husband's and wife's problems. In each instance, the researcher or therapist would mark or take note of when they would notice one of these shifts.

Along with charting changes in meaning, or semantic shifts in these conversations, a Recursive Frame Analyst may also take note of who is initiating these shifts and how the particular speaker is able to successfully move the talk from one gallery to another. The term I use to note this shifting phenomenon is called opening up closings (Schegloff & Sacks, 1973), a distinction I have borrowed from conversation analysis. With an opening up closing, the speaker uses certain words which open up a new line of conversation, while simultaneously closing down the current topic of talk. In RFA terms, one gallery is opened up as another is closed down.

In studying the discourse of divorce mediation, a group of colleagues and I (Chenail, Itkin, Bonneau, & Andriacchi, 1993, October; Chenail, Zellick, & Bonneau, 1992, October) became curious about how divorce mediators were able to help disputing parties come to resolutions regarding child care, custody, and support. In many of these cases, the ex-husband and ex-wife had not had much success in getting along with each other, much less working out complex agreements over their child or children.

When we examined the transcripts of more than 30 divorce mediation cases from an RFA perspective, we noted a number of times that the mediator was able to open productive resolution talk, while at the same time closing down unproductive fighting talk. As we looked closer at these gallery transition moments, we noticed that the talk took its turns when the mediator reminded the parties that they were both at the mediation sessions for the best interests of their child or children. That move on the part of the mediator helped to open up a new line of talk different from the preceding line of conversation in most of the cases we observed.

Closing down openings. My RFA research on conversations has also helped me to notice another interesting speech act, the closing down opening. This type of talk occurs when one speaker appears to offer an opening such as, "I really think that that might work . . . " and then follows it up with a closing down ending such as, " . . . but not with this situation." In other words, whereas an opening up closing opens up a new talk gallery while closing down a currently active gallery of talk, a closing down opening only appears to offer the possibility of a new gallery to the other in a conversation. Closer attention to the use of "Yes, but" in therapy has helped me understand how seemingly promising lines of therapeutic talk can be quickly shut down, and how I can possibly change the situation without becoming part of the torqued talk.

In the full session analysis (Rambo, Heath, & Chenail, 1993) which I mentioned above in the Torqued Talk section, I became fascinated with how the various members of the family used "Yes, but's" to create what seemed, on the first take, to be openings for solution talk, but on the second take, appeared to move the talk nowhere. For instance, Ted, the dad in the session, said " . . . and, he's (Ted's roommate Nathan) said right now he doesn't mind. He won't mind if Randy (Ted's son) comes in, but he told me point blank if we have any problem one of them is going to go" (Rambo, Heath, & Chenail, 1993, p. 175). Ted's talk about Nathan not minding sounds like an opening for a "Ted, Nathan and Randy Getting Along" Gallery. The promise of such an opening comes crashing down just a few words later as Ted says, " . . . if we have any problem one of them is going to go" (p. 175).

I like the irony of this type of speech act: The words appeared like an invitation to an opening, but in truth they were helping in keeping the talk so stuck. If the therapist made a move to open up some "Getting along" talk, the "one of them is going to go" closing of Ted's speech cuts off that gallery. If the therapist heard the "one of them is going to go" talk as an opening up of a "Ted, Nathan, and Randy Not Getting Along" Gallery, the previously opening up talk of the "right now he doesn't mind" now becomes a closing down line to that gallery.

Presented with such a dilemma in conversations, I have learned from my qualitative discourse analyses to treat closing down openings not as "either/or's," but as "both/ands." To do so, I have to build a new gallery in which both lines of a closing down opening talk (i.e., the "Yes" part and the "but" part) can become woven together. In the case mentioned above, I could use an opening up closing such as, "It sounds like both possibilities could happen: that Nathan and Randy might get along and then again, they might not be able to get along. Given that situation, Ted, how do you want to proceed?" In this way, I can ask Ted to open up a new gallery (i.e., a "What to do" line of talk) and listen to where that gallery takes us.

Conclusion. From the years of analyzing sessions from an RFA perspective as a researcher, I feel as if I am operating from within the talk in therapy. As I am engaged in the clinical hour as a therapist, I am also participating as a discourse analyst. I find this reflective stance helps me to stay closer to the process within the therapy room both as therapist and as researcher.

After seven years of using RFA as an aid to my listening, I have begun to develop "a sharper ear." Now, I find that I can trace what is being said, who is saying it, how the talk has changed, how the talk has stayed the same, and how I can participate in the conversation, all at the same time. It is almost akin to listening to a symphony: you can follow the melody, note the key in which it is being played, notice what part the violins are playing, all while humming along with the tune. In this way, RFA has given me a whole new appreciation for talk and how it works.

ONE CLINICAL RESEARCH TEAM'S EXPERIENCE WITH HERMENEUTIC INTERPRETATION
WENDY L. WATSON
LORRAINE M. WRIGHT
JANICE M. BELL

"There is something different about your clinical work." In the mid-80s that phrase became a theme of the comments on our national and international presentations. The commendation that our work was different from others caught our attention especially when voiced by other clinicians who were familiar with the work of those who had influenced our clinical practice: the Milan team's systemic elegance, Michael White and David Epston's narrative notions, and Maturana's biology of knowing.

Through 10 years of clinical practice we (Watson and Wright) had co-evolved a clinical approach that we have named Systemic Belief Therapy (SBT). One of the major premises of SBT is that the belief about the problem is the problem. For example, when a family is experiencing difficulties with cancer, depression or marital conflict, we believe it is their beliefs about the problem that become the problem. Our clinical effort was therefore focused on drawing forth and challenging the belief at the heart of the matter, i.e., the constraining belief that perpetuates and is perpetuated by the problem.

But how did we really do that? What *was* "different" about our clinical work? What was involved in the process of our therapeutic approach that brought about those seemingly "miraculous" changes with families? What happened in the therapeutic conversation between the clinician and the family so that the constraining belief was challenged and facilitative beliefs were supported or offered? What was the process of therapeutic change involved in our clinical approach, Systemic Belief Therapy?

Our previous research had focused on examining: (1) the relationship between chronic illness and family functioning (Watson, Bell & Wright, 1992; Wright & Bell, 1989); (2) the effectiveness of family systems nursing/family therapy interventions (Watson, Bell & Wright, 1992); (3) family outcomes; and (4) the education and supervision of family systems nursing/family therapy clinical practice (Wright & Bell, 1989).

Transitions to Clinical Research

The ideas gleaned from those research projects were useful. After a while, however, as a clinical research team, the three of us were asking questions we found compelling and that invited different research approaches. We wanted answers that were more than statistically significant. We wanted clinical significance! We wanted to engage in research that would push our understanding and articulation of our clinical practice to new and higher levels. We were dissatisfied with examining clinical work in a manner that had little relevance for clinicians. Examining effectiveness is a useful enterprise, but clinicians want to know they are making a difference. The usual effectiveness designs have little meaning in terms of changing, shaping, refining, and articulating the clinical work. We were attracted to process research that allows clinical research teams to ask different questions about the clinical work and allows a different kind of research to emerge. Qualitative methods are particularly well suited to looking at the therapeutic process.

Nursing and Qualitative Research

At that time, the three of us were working in the discipline of nursing. Nursing, like education, has been a discipline that historically has been attracted to qualitative research. In fact, many of the leaders in the qualitative movement have been and continue to be nurses, including Patricia Benner (1994), Katharyn May (1991, 1994), Janice Morse (1992), Patricia Munhall (1988), Margarete Sandelowski (1986, 1984), Phyllis Noerager Stern (1991), and Toni Tripp-Reimer (1985a, 1985b). Our dissatisfaction with quantitative approaches centered on the compression of human experience into a few variables as well as the ongoing clinical sense that there was something more to discover than quantitative measures and procedures could offer us. This dissatisfaction nurtured our desire to approach our next inquiry through a qualitative research approach.

Qualitative methods were appealing to us as clinical researchers. They seemed rich, humane, and congruent with our beliefs that clinician/researchers are part of the observing system. Qualitative methods also resonated with our beliefs about reality. For years in our clinical practice and teaching we had eschewed positivism, the foundation of quantitative research approaches. Our belief that realities are not embedded in certainty but rather are co-evolved through our interactions with others drew us toward qualitative approaches. Thus, our passion for qualitative research with families grew. We saw it as the preferred way for us to study families in general and family intervention and change in particular. We increased our appreciation of qualitative research approaches' appreciation of the lived experiences of families *and* of researchers.

Research on the Processes of Therapeutic Change

In 1992 we received funding to study the processes of therapeutic change. We were ready and keen to articulate our clinical practice. Janice Bell, a colleague who joined our team as research coordinator in 1986, was the principal investigator of the study. Our consultant was Catherine Chesla, a former student and colleague of Patricia Benner (1994), a respected hermeneutic nursing researcher. Under Chesla's tutelage, we developed our skills in hermeneutic interpretation.

Our clinical research team (Bell, Wright and Watson) reviewed all the families with whom two of us (Watson and Wright) had worked from 1988 to 1992 and chose five exemplary cases. What constituted "an exemplary case?" It was a case where the family showed: (1) dramatic cognitive, affective or behavioral change during the family therapy sessions which ranged from 2 to 5 sessions (both during session change and across session change was noted); and (2) improvement in the presenting problem 6 months following termination of the family therapy sessions.

We began our journey into "Hermeneutic Discovery Land" by viewing the previously videotaped clinical sessions of one exemplary case. This overview gave us an initial sense of the clinical work with the family. Next, each member of the research team separately selected segments of the interview she considered salient to the process of therapeutic change. This was done by studying each interview to see how the clinician responded to the family and how the family responded to the clinician. The question that guided each team member's selection was, "Would there have been as much change with this family had this particular interaction not have occurred?" Our research team then convened to discuss their choice of change segments to arrive at consensus among the team and to exchange rationale (sometimes passionately) for and against the selection of a particular change segment. Once team consensus was reached, the change segments were transcribed.

Hermeneutic Analysis

Our hermeneutic analysis proceeded in stages. The first stage was separate analyses of the transcribed change segments. The second stage was discussing our analyses. We videotaped our discussions, and, in the third stage, we analyzed the videotape for further insights into therapeutic change processes.

In our separate analyses, we each answered the following questions: (1) What is the broad and the immediate context of this change segment? (2) What is happening here from the clinician's perspective and from the family's perspective? (3) Is this move or intervention unique or is it similar to another? and (4) What else could we call it? Each of us wrote our responses to these questions.

We were continually trying to give new language and see with new eyes the kinds of movements that were occurring in the segments salient to the process of change, and the written word afforded us that opportunity. One of our team members (LW) described her experience with hermeneutic interpretation of the transcriptions this way:

> My initial reaction to the idea of the hermeneutic process was that observing videos and then transcribing and interpreting the transcriptions would be time-consuming and unnecessary. After 20 years of clinical experience, I felt quite able to target segments of change and comment on them without having to review text. However, this came to be one of the greatest and most humbling changes in my beliefs about "seeing" and interpreting clinical work. The reason being that what I "saw" on video and what I "saw" in the transcriptions were not the same. Therefore, my interpretations were also different. I entered into a totally different domain through the analysis of text. It was as if I was at times, looking at therapeutic change and my clinical work with an entirely different lens and therefore discovering some aspects of my clinical work for the first time. Themes, patterns, and powerful uses of language leapt off the page at me and there was the privilege of being able to ponder the words, reflect on a phrase and marvel at the change evident on a single page.

> One of the research families was a young 27 year old man experiencing MS, and his parents. During the second interview, a change segment was identified which our research team labelled as 'distinguishing the illness experience.' In the videotaped version of this change segment, I observed myself seeking to draw forth various distinctions about the illness, i.e., asking difference and relative influence questions. However, in my hermeneutic analysis of the text

of this change segment, I wrote, 'One belief of mine that is challenged from the text but that I do not remember having an impact on me during the interview, nor in the videotape review, is the notion that the son does not believe that he influences his illness but rather believes there are things that he 'does in spite of' his illness. This response lifts the illness experience out of the control paradigm, upon which the line of inquiry about relative influence is based, and moves the illness experience into some other paradigm . . . perhaps the 'in spite of illness' paradigm. I will not forget this notion. The latter was a totally new idea for me reading the text.' This was one of many examples of how the written word invited new reflections and new distinctions.

I have come to believe that the text speaks a different language and we involve ourselves with text much differently than with videotaped or live sessions. It has reminded me of the phenomena of going to a movie and then reading the book. There has always been the tendency to criticize the movie for not capturing what was in the book–but how can it (or vice versa)? This was the same experience with observing our videos of our clinical work and then reading the transcripts of the sessions. They are totally different domains of understanding and of course one cannot give what the other gives. But I believe both are essential for any clinical researcher to experience in order to truly capture the many subtle nuances and changes that occur within individual family members, within the clinician and between the clinician and family.

When each team member had analyzed the transcripts and written out their analyses, we sequestered ourselves for days at a time with only our individual analyses, lots of food, laughter and a great desire to learn to sustain us. We called ourselves the "Hermeneutic Hermits!" Our research assistant and the video-camera were poised and ready to record our comments, concerns, conversations and hopefully some cutting edge ideas. We engaged in intensive, synergistic processes, hoping that from these team hermeneutic interpretation sessions we would construct a proliferation of pearls of understanding about the therapeutic processes that had previously eluded us.

The convincing "data" that the research process was exciting and synergistic are the numerous videotapes of the three of us completing the hermeneutic analysis as a team following our individual analyses. This is an unusual collection of data and we are unaware of other research teams that have videotaped their process of conducting hermeneutic analysis. It would be useful for another researcher to analyze those videotapes for the process events of our particular team. However, the most significant examples of our synergism and co-evolution of ideas were the writing of interpretive memos.

Interpretive Memos

We wrote interpretative memos about "creating the context for change," "distinguishing change," and "beliefs." Through the offering of ideas and asking questions of each other regarding these macro-moves, we experienced the excitement and exhilaration that accompanies the co-evolving and co-generation of further clarifications, distinctions, and descriptions of important clinical moves. We found ourselves under the hermeneutic spell. We consistently and more passionately were committed to the incredible process of weaving in a multiplicity of ideas and building upon each other's ideas, savoring the experiences of synchrony as well as the serendipitous conceptual leaps. We were most amazed that the labor intensive process was predominantly energizing, not enervating; productive, not pathetic; and actually fun, not frustrating!

Just a footnote: In the spirit of giving moves and interactions new names, we initially called these team interpretation sessions, "Synergistic Hermeneutic Interpretation of the Team," but abandoned it when we realized the acronym "S.H.I.T" did not in any way capture how we felt about these tremendous think tank times.

The process of: (1) team overview of all sessions; (2) individual selection of change segments; (3) team consensus of change segments; (4) individual hermeneutic interpretation of transcriptions of change segments; and (5) team hermeneutic interpretation was then repeated with the other four exemplary cases.

What did this qualitative process unfold? We discovered and uncovered aspects of our clinical work that had been out of our awareness. We co-evolved a new language, a refined understanding and an increased ability to articulate our clinical practice. For example, for many years we had encouraged our students to "create a context for change." But now, we had micro-moves that were part of our way of creating the context for change: therapeutic micro-moves such as "the goodness of fit conversation," or "proclaiming the prematurity of progressing at this point."

Major moves such as "distinguishing the illness," "distinguishing change," "challenging beliefs" and "solidifying beliefs" accompanied by a multitude of micro-moves were among the other "outcomes" which defined our clinical practice. Some of the micro-moves involved within the major moves were: (1) clearing away the debris; (2) the goodness of fit conversation; (3) proclaiming the prematurity of progressing; (4) the gambler's rhythm; and (5) reciprocal balancing.

Additionally, other palpable products of our hermeneutic inquiry included: (1) the power of language (by family members and the clinician); (2) the power of family beliefs about illness; (3) the power of the beliefs of health care professionals in empowering or disempowering families; and (4) the power of witnessing/validating families.

Journeys into Commitments

The journey into "Hermeneutic Discovery Land" was also a journey into commitments. Through our qualitative research experience we have discovered a greater desire to acknowledge the learning that families give us and to give that learning back to other families and to give credit where credit is due by telling other families where we gained that knowledge that we are passing on. We have an ever increasing desire to conduct research for the purpose of helping families, not for pleasing funding agencies, or for our own merits and rewards within academic life. We desire to scrutinize our clinical practice, teaching, and research with the question, "Will this help us help families?"

And finally we are more passionate about working as a clinical research team even though separated by a thousand miles on a day to day basis. We have come to believe that, as in therapy, the most creative, thoughtful, and perhaps even ethical work is that which occurs within a *team* of researchers. The synergism, the co-evolution of ideas, the multiple minds add to the richness and credibility of both the process and the outcome of the work.

REFERENCES

Austin, J. L. (1962). *How to do things with words.* Oxford: Clarendon.

Bateson, G. (1972). *Steps to an ecology of mind.* New York: Ballantine.

Benner, P. (1994). *Interpretive phenomenology: Embodiment, caring and ethics in health and illness.* Thousand Oaks, CA: Sage.

Chenail, R. (1991). *Medical discourse and systemic frames of comprehension.* Norwood, NJ: Ablex.

Chenail, R. J., Douthit, P., Gale, J., Stormberg, J., Morris, G. H., Park, J., Sridaromont, S., Schmer, V. (1990). "It's probably nothing serious, but . . . " Parents' interpretation of referral to pediatric cardiologists. *Health Communication, 2,* 3, 165-188.

Chenail, R. J., & Fortugno, L. (in press). Resourceful figures in therapeutic conversations. In G. H. Morris & R. J. Chenail (Eds.), *The talk of the clinic: Explorations in the analysis of medical and therapeutic discourse.* Hillsdale, NJ: Lawrence Erlbaum.

Chenail, R. J., Itkin, P., Bonneau, M., & Andriacchi, C. (1993, October). Managing solutions in divorce mediation: A discourse analysis. Paper presented at the Twenty-first Annual Society of Professionals in Dispute Resolution International Conference, Toronto, Canada.

Chenail, R. J., Zellick, S. Z., & Bonneau, M. (1992, October). How to do mediation with words: I. Involvement strategies. Paper presented at the Twentieth Annual Society of Professionals in Dispute Resolution International Conference, Pittsburgh.

Gale, J. E. (1991a). *Conversation analysis of therapeutic discourse.* Hillsdale, NJ: Erlbaum.

Gale, J. (1991b). The use of self in qualitative research. *Qualitative Family Research Newsletter,* 5(1), 6-7.

Gale, J., & Newfield, N. (1992). A conversation analysis of a solution-focused marital therapy session. *Journal of Marital and Family Therapy, 18,* 2, 153-165.

Goffman, E. (1974). *Frame analysis: An essay on the organization of experience.* Cambridge, MA: Harvard University Press.

O'Hanlon, W. H., & Weiner-Davis, M. (1989). *In search of solutions: A new direction in psychotherapy.* New York: Norton.

May, K. A. (1991). Interview techniques: Concerns and challenges. In J. M. Morse (Ed.), *Qualitative nursing research* (rev.ed.) (pp. 188-201). Newbury Park, CA: Sage.

May, K. A. (1994). Abstract knowing: The case for magic in method. In J. M. Morse (Ed), *Critical issues in qualitative research methods* (pp. 10-21). Thousand Oaks, CA: Sage.

Morse, J. M. (Ed.). (1992). *Qualitative health research.* Newbury Park, CA: Sage.

Munhall, P. (1988). Ethical considerations in qualitative research. *Western Journal of Nursing Research, 10,* 2, 150-162.

Potter, J., & Wetherell, M. (1987). *Discourse and social psychology: Beyond attitudes and behavior.* London: Sage.

Putnam, L. L., & Holmer, M. (1992). Framing, reframing, and issue development. In L. L. Putnam & M. E. Roloff (Eds.), *Communication and negotiation* (pp. 128-155). Newbury Park, CA: Sage.

Rambo, A. H., Heath, A. W., & Chenail, R. J. (1993). *Practicing therapy: Exercises for growing therapists.* New York: Norton.

Sandelowski, M. (1986). The problem of rigor in qualitative research. *Advances in Nursing Science, 8,* 3, 27-37.

Sandelowski, M. (1994). The proof is in the pottery: Toward a poetic for qualitative inquiry. In J. M. Morse (Ed.), *Critical issues in qualitative research methods.* Thousand Oaks, CA: Sage.

Schegloff, E. A., Sacks, H. (1973). Opening up closings. *Semiotica,* 7, 289-327.

Stern, P. N. (1991). Are counting and coding a cappella appropriate in qualitative research? In J. M. Morse (Ed.), *Qualitative nursing research* (pp. 147-162). Newbury Park, CA: Sage.

Tannen, D., & Wallat, C. (1993). Interactive frames and knowledge schemas in interaction: Examples from a medical examination/interview. In D. Tannen (Ed.), *Framing in discourse* (pp. 57-76). New York: Oxford University Press.

Tripp-Reimer, T. (1985a). Reliability issues in cross-cultural research. *Western Journal of Nursing Research, 7,* 3, 391-392.

Tripp-Reimer, T. (1985b). The Health Heritage project. *Western Journal of Nursing Research, 8,* 207-224.

Watson, W. L., Bell, J. M., & Wright, L. M. (1992). Osteophytes and marital fights: A single case clinical research report of chronic pain. *Family Systems Medicine,* 10(4), 423-435.

Wright, L.M., & Bell, J. M. (1989). A survey of family nursing education in Canadian Universities. *Canadian Journal of Nursing Research,* 21, 59-74.

Wright, L. M., Bell, J. M., & Rock, B. L. (1989). Smoking behavior and spouses: A case report. *Family Systems Medicine,* 7(2), 158-171.

PART III:
ESSAYS ON METHODOLOGIES

An Ethnographic Approach to Understanding Service Use Among Ethnically Diverse Low Income Families

Avery E. Goldstein
Lynn Safarik
Wendy Reiboldt
Leonard Albright
Carol Kellett

Avery E. Goldstein is Assistant Professor, Child Development and Family Studies, Department of Family and Consumer Sciences; Lynn Safarik is Lecturer, Occupational Studies; Wendy Reiboldt is Assistant Professor, Consumer Affairs, Department of Family and Consumer Sciences; Leonard Albright is Professor and Coordinator, Graduate Program, Occupational Studies; Carol Kellett is Professor and Director, The Urban Families Initiative and Professor, Department of Family and Consumer Sciences; California State University at Long Beach, Long Beach, CA 90840-0501.

[Haworth co-indexing entry note]: "An Ethnographic Approach to Understanding Service Use Among Ethnically Diverse Low Income Families." Goldstein, Avery E. et al. Co-published simultaneously in *Marriage & Family Review* (The Haworth Press, Inc.) Vol. 24, No. 3/4, 1996, pp. 297-321; and: *The Methods and Methodologies of Qualitative Family Research* (ed: Marvin B. Sussman, and Jane F. Gilgun) The Haworth Press, Inc., 1996, pp. 297-321. Single or multiple copies of this article are available for a fee from The Haworth Document Delivery Service [1-800-342-9678, 9:00 a.m. - 5:00 p.m. (EST). E-mail address: getinfo@haworth.com].

SUMMARY. Poverty is linked to disparity in families' access to basic human services and an incapacity to fulfill basic needs. The study described in this paper uses a qualitative research design to address the ecology of service use in the family within the broader social and physical environment. While the focus of this paper relates to the methodology of the study, some substantive results are used for illustrative purposes. Through an in-depth study of families in the contexts of their neighborhoods, our task is to search for patterns and their meanings. This process may uncover the motives and beliefs underlying service use and access among the families in our study. *[Article copies available for a fee from The Haworth Document Delivery Service: 1-800-342-9678. E-mail address: getinfo@haworth.com]*

KEYWORDS. Low-income families, Family diversity, Cross-cultural interviewing, Family ecologies, Service use, Urban families

Poverty is linked to disparity in families' access to basic human services and an incapacity to fulfill basic needs (Garbarino, 1992). Inequality in individual earnings and family income is greater today than 20 years ago. Approximately 14.2% of Americans (35.7 million) were living in poverty in 1991 with the incidence of poverty highest among African American and Hispanic families (U.S. Department of Commerce, 1992). Immigration contributes to the complexity of providing support for families in urban areas. In Los Angeles County, for example, the Anglo "majority" is the *minority*, comprising only 40.8% of the population (Clifford & Roark, 1991). A multicultural population increases the complexity of developing effective solutions to social and economic problems.

Qualitative methods are particularly amenable to the study of diverse families as they focus on the "processes by which families create, sustain, and discuss family realities" (Daly, 1992, p. 4). In order to capture family realities and to understand the meanings of family resource use, we find qualitative methods to be invaluable. As we examine the resources families access to ease their daily lives, we expect that taken for granted family meanings may offer insight to resource use. Because the focus of this study is on diverse families, many of whom do not speak English, these methods are particularly appropriate.

The social welfare system tends to categorize problems of culturally diverse children and families into discrete boxes, failing to acknowledge interrelated causes and solutions that exist in many different parts of the social system. Melaville and Blank (1992) report that a lack of functional communication among public and private sector agencies that serve familics limits the ability to implement comprehensive solutions. Gardner (1993) has labeled the lack of coordination and collaboration among service agencies "failure by fragmentation." Present policies and programs for families living in poverty allocate large amounts of funding to intervention and remediation while they provide limited funding for prevention (Naisbitt, 1994; Schorr, 1988). Collaboration and prevention, however, require new policies and programs that underscore the significance of the physical, social, and economic environments that influence families and how they function. Families are diverse, and such a recognition places more demands on policy, programs, and implementers to accomodate to the values, culture, neighborhoods, and communities in which families live (National Resource Center for Family Support Programs, 1993).

In response to these concerns, the study described in this paper uses a naturalistic approach to address the ecology of family service. We believe that the methods we used are responsive to the unique characteristics of culturally diverse families and that these methods will help us understand the coping mechanisms families use in their daily lives. Implicit in our methods is a preventative approach that builds on a family strengths model. Since we are midway through data collection, some descriptions are presented in the past tense while others are presented in the future tense. The focus of this paper relates to the methodology of the study. Substantive results will be used only for illustrative purposes.

PURPOSE AND GOALS

Five major goals guided the effort to understand service-use among diverse urban families: (1) Identify *family and community dynamics* in three families within each of three selected urban neighborhoods; (2) determine neighborhood *resources* that affect families; (3) examine how families *access* services; (4) discover *innovative service delivery* models; and (5) *evaluate the research methodology.*

We will explicate the last goal since this paper focuses on our research methodology. To evaluate an emergent research methodology requires an on-going critical examination of the efficacy of the qualitative research procedures used in this study. The present endeavor to elucidate these methods is helpful in generating key formative evaluation questions. Are there certain procedures that yielded particularly rich data? Do the methods fit the diversity of families being studied (Gilgun, 1992)? Since the population is a particularly difficult one to study, were the issues of language (immigrant families are often not fluent in English), access (e.g., families living in poverty may not have phones—how can we reach them?)

and literacy (new immigrants may not be able to read or write their native language or English) effectively addressed by the research methods? Did we consider multiple perspectives during data collection/analysis? Systematic attention to methodological issues will enhance our research goals.

CONCEPTUAL FRAMEWORK

Two decades ago Urie Bronfenbrenner (1974) stated that "much of American developmental psychology is the science of the behavior of children in strange situations with strange adults" (p. 3). Currently, according to McKinney, Abrams, Terry and Lerner (1994), the majority of child development research continues to focus on middle-class European-American children in laboratory settings. The present study uses a conceptual framework that encompasses an ecological perspective (Bronfenbrenner, 1974, 1979).

The conceptual framework for the study helped us to identify the study's parameters. Though the general purpose of the study was to obtain an in-depth understanding of the daily lives of poor families, the specific purpose was to gain insight regarding their service use patterns. The conceptual framework helped us to organize the data. In addition, the framework helped the research team develop common perspectives on the specific goals, process and outcomes of the study to avoid what Miles and Huberman (1984) describe as "fruitless, empirical anarchy" (p. 33). When researchers share a common conceptual framework, multiple researchers collecting data in multiple sites are more likely to reach research goals.

Throughout data collection, the Bronfenbrenner framework will be used to organize and comprehend the multitude of complex influences on a person's choices about services. The conceptual framework enables the researchers to manage data within and across families and neighborhood sites in a systematic way. Using the framework, the researchers can seek out patterns at any one system level across families or neighborhoods or look for patterns within a family across system levels. Information about why a mother does or does not use the city health services may emerge at the microsystem level (her physician does not speak Spanish), at the mesosystem level (the hours conflict with her work and child-care arrangement), the exosystem level (a neighborhood association is offering services at the school site), or the macrosystem level (the clinic lost funding due to a weak economy).

METHODOLOGY

The rationale for using a naturalistic paradigm for this research is based on the belief that "there are multiple constructed realities that can be studied only holistically . . . and the inquirer and the 'object' of inquiry interact to influence one another" (Lincoln & Guba, 1985, p. 37). A set of assumptions and a conceptual framework regarding the phenomena being investigated guides the choice of methods. An ethnographic methodology, which is field-based, humanistic, and holistic (Dobbert, 1982) is a suitable approach for this study. Ethnography is the primary method of social anthropologists. Van Maanen (1979) explains the prime analytic task of the social anthropologist: "to uncover and explicate the ways in which people in particular settings come to understand, account for, take action and otherwise manage their day-to-day situation" (p. 540). Through an in-depth study of families in their neighborhoods, our task is to search for patterns and their meanings with the hope that this process will uncover the motives and beliefs underlying service use and access among the families in our study.

Although we state that the research is rooted in the tradition of social anthropology, the methods described in this manuscript draw extensively from the guidelines offered by Miles and Huberman (1994) who state that their orientation is "transcendental realism" (p. 4). Tesch (1990) offers a definition of transcendental realism as, "describing as precisely as possible the range and the local and historical contingencies of social regularities in social behavior" (p. 51). She explains how this relatively obscure approach to qualitative research allows researchers to use tools systematically in data collection and analysis. The researchers found the more structured, systematic procedures to be helpful in coordinating the efforts of multiple investigators in a multiple-site design.

Though we are interested in the philosophy of science related to our methodological choices, we also were frankly pragmatic: we concentrated on selecting methods that were most suitable for our purposes. We intended to examine service use and access from the "inside out." Data collection started in the home and gradually moved out into the neighborhood, then into the agencies. Our inquiry was family-driven; that is, we used their cues to direct the study. In order to understand service use choices, we believed we needed to learn as much as we could about the people who made the choices. This meant we would have to spend time with families, in their homes, and in their communities.

Design

The goals of the project will be accomplished through data collection within three neighborhoods over a two-year period. Activities include pre-fieldwork activities, data collection and analysis phases. Throughout the project, consultation with a Research Council, an advisory group consisting of experienced qualitative researchers, helped guide and verify methodology and procedures. Project researchers have a variety of backgrounds, including child development and family studies, occupational education, consumer affairs and teacher education. Because the team is multidisciplinary, the project benefits from an array of experiences, philosophies, and world views.

The first six months of the study involved pre-fieldwork activities, including rapport building, establishing credibility and accessing communities in the area. During pre-fieldwork activities neighborhood sites were selected, focus groups commenced, and key informants were identified. We also hired family interviewers and selected families for interviews. Data collection involves interviewing families and service providers in three phases over eighteen months. Currently, we are approximately half way through the project, and have completed the first wave of data collection. Since the design is emergent, methods will evolve throughout data collection.

In order to understand service use among families living in poverty we will gain a holistic view of these families through (a) understanding how, when, and where families in multiple sites access services using their own perspectives; (b) spending prolonged time within neighborhoods; (c) collecting data from multiple sources; (d) isolating themes using multiple data sources. Researchers will use the culture of settings to explain and understand service use among families living in poor urban neighborhoods.

Multiple Methods

This section addresses four major components of the method: pre-fieldwork, sampling, data collection, and data analysis. Various activities designed to build rapport and gain access to neighborhoods and families are discussed in "pre-fieldwork." In the next section, purposive sampling techniques as they were used for site and family selection are explicated as well as the use of focus groups and key informants. Three primary data collection methods, including interviews, participant observation, document analysis, as well as unique variations of these methods (e.g., photojournaling, and resource mapping) are explained in the data collection section. This section also includes a description of the procedure used to record the researchers' reflections. In the data analysis section coding, credibility, within- and cross-site analyses are elucidated. It is important to note that many of these procedures were interactive; for example, interview data helped focus specific participant observation activities, document analysis helped generate new interview questions, and participant observation at community events provided opportunities to collect documents.

Pre-Fieldwork

A critical aspect of field-work is the establishment of rapport and credibility with the community under study (Lincoln & Guba, 1985). With this in mind, for the first several months of the project, we undertook a series of pre-fieldwork activities including informal interviews, neighborhood meetings, walking tours, and tours by cars in the company of community informants. This helped us to gain access to the neighborhoods and families. We viewed rapport building as a "developmental process that continues through the entire investigation" (Stainback & Stainback, 1988, p. 33). We also expected to accumulate contextual data over the life of the project.

The research team held several *informal interviews with various community members*, including police officers, community activists, and city administrators and collected information about city-wide and neighborhood-specific contextual elements. We learned practical information, such as crime awareness and historical background, during these interview sessions as well. In addition to orienting the researchers to neighborhoods, these informal interviews provided important contacts with key individuals who later proved to be instrumental in accessing families.

Another strategy used to gain entry into the communities was *attendance at neighborhood grassroots organization meetings*. The researchers participated in neighborhood collaboratives, city-wide community events, and professional gatherings. This type of participant observation enabled the researchers to interact with residents and service providers, while gaining an understanding of the naturally occurring variables that were influencing them. We wrote fieldnotes, and collected minutes, agendas, and other literature, all of which are part of our data base.

We explored possible research sites during *neighborhood driving tours or "windshield surveys"* (Andranovich & Riposa, 1993) *and guided walking tours*. Tour guides included a city planner, a neighborhood organization leader, and a long-term resident and local activist. The driving tours, or "windshield surveys," were conducted prior to site selection in an effort to familiarize the researchers with the neighborhoods being considered for selection. We took notes during the driving tours to document impressions and observations about the neighborhood, e.g., graffiti, trash, condition of homes and the activities of people. The driving tours were also helpful in that they allowed the researchers to compare their impressions about the neighborhoods and to see similarities and differences across neighborhoods. Again, these observation activities served the dual purpose of facilitating site selection and building rapport with gatekeepers to the community. The differing perspectives of the tour guides, time of day, and seasonal factors were taken into account in interpreting observations made during the tours

The pre-fieldwork phase also included a cursory *review of the literature* to help focus the inquiry. The multidisciplinary research team members brought unique perspectives to the issues of poverty, family dynamics, cultural diversity, and social service delivery by sharing current published work in their respective fields. Researchers kept abreast of ongoing research and policy trends.

Purposive Sampling

Sampling procedures in qualitative research can hardly be separated from data collection. A purposive or theoretical approach to sampling is used to capture the "full array of multiple realities" which exist and to maximize the researchers' ability to "devise grounded theory that takes adequate account of local conditions, local mutual shapings, and local values . . . " (Lincoln & Guba, 1985; p. 40). We used three purposive sampling processes. First, key informant sampling identified especially knowledgeable individuals who increased our understanding of neighborhood conditions (Miles & Huberman,1994). Second, maximum variation sampling (Patton, 1980) was used to document unique variations in ethnicity, level of neighborhood organization, and level of neighborhood deterioration. The purpose of maximizing the variation in both site and family selection was to compare and contrast commonalities and differences as they emerged among sites to provide richer interpretations (Patton, 1980). Third, we used snowball sampling to develop networks for gaining access to families and other potentially productive data sources. Whereas these sampling strategies were primarily used for selecting the three sites (neighborhoods) and the three families in each neighborhood, we made on-going sampling decisions in the selection of events, documents, literature, times, locations, etc., to be included in the research. Detailed strategies for site selection, focus groups, key informants and family selection are described below.

Site selection. In an effort to select low income, ethnically diverse communities, we reviewed census data that provided information on income, ethnicity, receipt of public assistance, home ownership, and migration patterns. The neighborhoods selected were in the lowest income category in the city of Long Beach. In addition, to obtain maximum variability in ethnicity, we selected neighborhoods with "pockets" of minority groups. In Long Beach the neighborhoods chosen for this study were predominantly Hispanic. However, each of the neighborhoods varied with regard to the existence of other minority groups. Among the three sites, one of the neighborhoods had a relatively large number of African-Americans, while the other two neighborhoods had a relatively large proportion of Filipino-Americans and Cambodian-Americans.

Another criterion for neighborhood selection was the level of existing collaborative and intervention efforts within the neighborhoods. A program entitled Neighborhood Improvement Strategies (NIS) was in place in several neighborhoods in Long Beach. NIS is a city-sponsored community development program that identifies neighborhoods at risk based on public safety, physical conditions, and social conditions. NIS organized neighborhood groups to discuss ways to improve conditions within identified neighborhoods. In an effort to obtain maximum variability among our three sites, we used this NIS designation to see if we could observe differences in neighborhoods or families based on the level of NIS involvement. One neighborhood was an NIS level 1 area (most severe decay). The second neighborhood selected was an NIS level 2 (approaching severe decay), and the third neighborhood was not classified by the city as an NIS neighborhood.

Focus groups. The purpose of the focus group process was multi-faceted and involved a variety of participants. We conducted focus group meetings to obtain community feedback regarding interview procedures, build rapport in the neighborhoods, identify and meet key informants, familiarize neighborhood members with the project, and learn about community organizations. Focus groups provided the opportunity for participants to become more explicit about their own views as a result of group interaction, i.e., the "cueing phenomenon" (Morgan & Krueger, 1993, p. 17). In addition, the dynamics of focus groups enabled us to provide a less threatening atmosphere in which open and honest discussion ensued. Those involved in focus groups included community residents, school personnel, clinic workers, clergy, agency administrators, and community police. It was important to thoroughly explain the goals of the project and help the participants understand the nature of the research. We indicated that the project was important because we were learning about service-use directly from the families. We explained that the focus group provided an opportunity to gain their perspectives regarding family and community strengths and solutions. Participants were anxious to share their thoughts in an effort to improve conditions in their neighborhoods and community agencies, and saw participation in this study as a vehicle to do so.

Researchers asked focus group participants a range of questions, some to do with method, others to do with compensation for participation, and still others related to general substantive areas. For example, we asked about culturally appropriate ways to contact and interview families. We learned some important strategies, such as who should be the initial contact in Cambodian families (the oldest male). We found that the meaning of simple gestures such as making eye contact or shaking hands varied across the cultures of the families in our study.

We were also concerned about ways we could compensate the families for their participation. Therefore, we asked focus groups whether families should be offered food coupons, monetary stipends, or other compensation. Focus-group participants were queried about how the community would receive university members. Would families be distrustful of the researchers, or rather, pleased to be a part of the research?

We had other questions related to interview sites and qualities sought in those persons who would help us in conducting the interviews. Would they be comfortable meeting in their homes, or would they rather meet at a neutral place, such as a community center? What age group, gender, and knowledge of a specific dialect would be most helpful in indigenous research assistants? We also asked for guidance about how to gain access to families, a usual challenge in studies such as ours. Would service providers allow us to use their facilities as a place to meet and recruit families?

We gained a great deal from these focus groups. Most important, these meetings opened the doors to the neighborhoods. Focus groups provided leads to a variety of data sources.

Key informants. Key informants were critical in the collection of data. Burgess (1985) discusses the central role of key informants in ethnographic research as a "collaborative enterprise with a group of informants" and distinguishes the multiple roles of the key informant as a "guide, assistant, interpreter, and historian." (p. 79). The key informants for this study were obtained through multiple sources including focus groups, city government, neighborhood associations and service agencies. Serving as *guides*, key informants provided access to neighborhoods and families. They were gate keepers of the community in that we would have been unable to get access families without them. Key informants provided on-going *assistance* with family selection and data collection. They served as *interpreters* of the neighborhood environments and family culture. Finally, they provided a context, or *history*, within each neighborhood.

We developed a Neighborhood Access Tree where we recorded information on the names and titles of informants, and dates and locations of meetings. This Tree helped us to trace the chain of contacts within each neighborhood.

Neighborhood access and key informants varied significantly between neighborhoods. In some neighborhoods just one "well connected" individual provided a plethora of information while in other neighborhoods more extensive networks yielded access. For example, in one neighborhood a community police officer was able to gather focus group participants (community members, agency and school personnel) and provide family names and phone numbers to researchers to assist in family recruitment.

In contrast, in another neighborhood the key informant network was more extensive. In this neighborhood, a representative of a grassroots collaborative program called "Healthy Start" suggested that the researcher contact the community worker at a local elementary school in order to identify families for the study. The community worker sought approval to assist the researcher from the school principal. The school principal, who had learned about the research project at Healthy Start meetings, was cooperative. The community worker at the local school contacted a family, described the project, and arranged for the family to meet the researcher.

Overall, a variety of agency personnel and community workers served as key informants. A community police officer, school community workers, a representative of a Healthy Start collaborative and a grass-roots organizer were the primary key informants. They provided us with access to families and a history of neighborhoods. They continue to provide on-going assistance with data collection and insights into the contexts in which we are conducting the study.

Family selection. Utilizing information gained through focus groups and key informants, we selected three racially/culturally diverse families within each poor neighborhood to participate in the study. Inclusion criteria included being in a low-income group so that we could investigate interactions between service-use and poverty. Racial and ethnic diversity were other criteria. We wanted our sample to represent the demographic characteristics within each neighborhood. Participants chosen from one neighborhood included two Mexican-American families and one African-American family. In the second neighborhood, two Filipino-American families and one Mexican-American family participated in interviews. In the third neighborhood, two Cambodian-American families and one Mexican-American family were interviewed.

Data Collection

We had multiple sources of data: interviews with family members and service providers and analysis of documents such as photo-journals that families composed especially for this research, and resource maps that the interviewed constructed. Researchers also kept reflective journals. We also collected many documents circulating within neighborhoods, such as flyers and community newpapers.

Family interviewers. Persons who were members of the cultural groups of interest conducted the interviews with university researchers. These individuals were fluent in either Spanish, Tagalog, or Khmer. During orientation sessions, time was spent on the goals and methods of the study, but just as important was developing rapport within the research teams. Part of rapport building was mutual brainstorming on the most effective ways to conduct interviews. In this way, the indigenous interviews made a major contribution to the study's methods and, in the process, became part of the research team. The importance of a good "fit" between researcher and family interviewer cannot be stressed enough. This team works in tandem to build trust, collect first-order concepts and translate these into second-order concepts (Van Maanen, 1983). It is through their close-knit relationship that rich data are collected and useful insights are gained.

Family interviews. Since the perspectives of multiple family members were important (Handel, 1994), we invited all family members 10 and older to participate. We were partially successful: Within each family, between one and six members were interviewed. We also tried to involve as many men as possible, using such strategies as inviting them simply to observe interviews with other family members. We continue to work on how best to involve multiple family members and the men in families.

Most of the of interviews took place in the homes of the families, while others were in schools and community centers, depending upon the choices of the families. When families agreed, the interviews were tape recorded and transcribed. In some instances, data were collected without the use of recorders. In fact, when this happened, researchers found that these interviews were particularly informative. Simply "visiting" was a fruitful approach. The families may have felt more relaxed in these informal sessions.

The interviews were semi-structured and composed of questions that gave researchers latitude in wording, timing, and sequencing. As analysis ensued, new sets of questions continued to be developed. Interviews also included family- and site-specific questions to gain in-depth understanding of a particular family or neighborhood. Initial interviews were predominantly exploratory in nature, aimed at establishing rapport with the families and refining the data collection procedures. The research teams were trained to use recursive interviewing techniques (Stainback & Stainback, 1988) which "allow the researcher to treat people and situations as unique and to alter the research [questions] in light of information fed back during the research process itself" (p. 54). The following questions served as a guideline during the first round of interviews:

1. Describe your family. (Probes–how many, who lives in the household, extended relationships, ages, stability and changes within family structure, who works, who's in school.)
2. Describe your neighborhood. (Probes–how long have you lived in the neighborhood and home, boundaries, likes, dislikes, services, businesses, schools, parks, describe the people in your neighborhood, stability or significant changes/events in the neighborhood.)
3. How did you come to live here?
4. How do you get around your neighborhood and the city?
5. What do you do when a family member is sick?
6. How do you find out about jobs for you and/or your family members?
7. If you work outside the home, who cares for your children while you are at work? When you go to the store?
8. Do your children attend school? If so, where do your children go to school? Who do you talk to at the school? (e.g., other parents? teachers? principals?)
9. How do you get food for the family?
10. Where do you get clothing for the family?
11. Does your family celebrate any special holidays or events?
12. Who cares for your older family members?
13. Who do you go to when you need help? If they can't help, what do you do?

Service provider interviews. The research design emphasizes the importance of examining family service use patterns from the "inside out." When family interviews revealed the use of formal and informal resources (e.g., family/friend networks, health clinics, local grocery stores), researchers followed up with service agency interviews in order to gain a holistic view of service provision in the neighborhood.

Length of interviews varied but, on average, lasted one hour. The preliminary set of questions included:

1. What is the goal of your agency? Why was it started? What programs and services are offered by your agency?
2. What is the philosophy of the agency?
3. How are agency services delivered?
4. Are there similar services in the area?
5. How does your agency compare to and relate with other similar projects?

6. Who are the key agency personnel and what are their roles in service delivery to families? What is the relationship between management staff and service providers?
7. Describe interactions between the agency staff and neighborhood clients.
8. How do families take advantage of available services?
9. How successful has the agency been? What are the most significant achievements/failures?
10. What future directions are anticipated for your agency?

Photo-journals. One of the techniques used to get an insider view of service use in various neighborhoods was photo-journaling. In this procedure, we gave families disposable cameras and asked them to take pictures of people, places, and things that they believed either improved their quality of life or made their life worse. Any member of the family could take the photographs. After researchers developed the film, we asked family members to assemble the photos in albums that we gave them. During interview visits, we asked family members to describe each photo. In addition, the researchers will probe to find out how families relate these pictures to services and resources in their neighborhood. Using photographs as a research tool has a long history (Harper, 1989; Stasz, 1979) and is used here to provide researchers with unique insider images of families in context. The use of photo-journaling in this study is derived from researchers who attempt to investigate "native ways of seeing" (Worth & Adair, 1972). Photo-journals will provide a rich understanding of families' lives.

Resource maps. Family interviewers constructed resource maps, which are graphic depictions of resources (broadly defined) in the community. Using a large scale, detailed street map of the neighborhood in which they were interviewing, the family interviewers did multiple neighborhood walk-throughs and windshield surveys and recorded the resources, services, and activity they observed. Examples of resources and services are grocery stores, homeless shelters, clinics, restaurants, etc. Examples of activities included apparent drug deals, prostitution, and tagging. Each resource, service, and activity observed was coded into general categories (e.g., educational services, recreational services, etc.). These categories were assigned a short alpha-numeric and color code. Completed resource maps will later be shared with family members to elicit their comments and perceptions of neighborhood services. This data collection method was derived from Heath and McLaughlin's (1993) use of map drawing by teens asked to describe their neighborhoods.

Recording researcher reflections. An integral part of qualitative data collection is capturing the insights, impressions, and hunches of researchers as they occur before, during, and after contacts in the field. These reflective comments often provide the impetus for theory development. The researchers shared impressions about the families in two ways: through regular research staff meetings and through fieldnotes. The researchers were struck with the intensity of the family interview process; the act of entering someone's home and engaging in empathic conversation about the details of their lives was a powerful experience. Debriefing sessions between the researcher and the family interviewer became essential and automatic. These interchanges were either tape recorded or included in the field notes. In addition, the researchers kept detailed fieldnotes that included reflective comments that often noted the subjective sides of conducting the research and memos that were more theoretical in nature.

Document analysis. We collected several types of documents as we became familiar with the neighborhoods. Minutes and agendas of meetings, newspaper articles, and agency literature are examples. Criteria for including a document for analysis included relevance to an individual or neighborhood included in the sample. Research assistants were assigned the task of reviewing documents for these criteria and completing document summary forms. Forms were then reviewed for consistency. Document summary forms were modeled after those presented by Miles and Huberman (1994). These forms served to elucidate relevant themes (e.g., violence in a neighborhood) and helped the research team manage a large volume of pertinent written materials. Researchers reviewed document summary forms to provide a larger contextual framework for family interviews.

Data Analysis

Data analysis is ongoing, including a preliminary analysis phase and successive analysis cycles following each of three data collection waves (waves were not necessarily mutually exclusive). A constant comparative strategy (Glaser & Strauss, 1967; Stainback & Stainback, 1988) is used to build a pattern of relationships from data collected from the nine families and synthesized into theories about service use by poor, urban families in the three Long Beach neighborhoods. The process of constant comparison involves many iterations of reviewing the data for recurring themes, issues, and events; creating categories to accommodate these patterns; and seeking out new incidents of these categories in subsequent data collection waves. Through the continued comparison of specific incidents in the data, refinement of the categories, identification of their properties, and exploration of their relationships with one another, the data will be integrated into coherent theories about the families and neighborhoods being studied. Below is a discussion of the specific data analysis procedures including contact summary forms, coding, credibility and within- and cross-site analysis.

Contact summary forms. Preliminary data analysis was facilitated through the use of contact summary forms (Miles & Huberman, 1994) which researchers used to summarize interview data after each contact. These forms helped emphasize salient points, emerging themes, and methodological concerns and comments. Both the researcher and family interviewer completed the form after reviewing transcriptions of the interviews in an effort to share impressions, verify data, and gain perspectives of both interviewers and families.

This method of reducing family visit data had several purposes, including the development and refinement of a coding system and assisting the researchers with planning for subsequent data collection. The contact summary forms helped the researchers reorient themselves to the interview data when transcription caused time lags and enabled the five researchers to efficiently and effectively communicate their findings during team analysis.

Coding. Data were further reduced and analyzed through the process of assigning codes. The initial coding process began as an organizational tool and will become progressively interpretive as patterns and relationships in the data emerge, reflecting several levels of analysis. The provisional coding system used in the research adapted two accounting schemes as described in Miles and Huberman (1994). Both etic codes (those which come from the researchers' perspective) and emic codes (those which are related to the participants' view) were included (Dobbert, 1982). The process of coding was guided by the research questions and conceptual framework (pre-defined) and but also allowed for the inductive creation of codes that were context-sensitive (post-defined). The codes will be revised, subdivided, and refined throughout the many iterations of data collection and analysis. The HyperQual2 data analysis software (Padilla, 1993) will be used to manage the data for analysis. We selected HyperQual2 due to its suitability for conducting descriptive/interpretive research (Tesch, 1990) and ease of entry of various forms of field data, i.e., unstructured interviews, documents, observations, and researcher notes.

Miles and Huberman (1994) recommend conducting a code check to ensure that researchers share a common understanding of what codes mean. To accomplish this the researchers analyzed one interview from each of the neighborhoods, collaboratively developed and defined a preliminary coding scheme, and then independently applied the coding system to another interview transcript. This process was utilized at the preliminary data analysis sessions and coding procedures will evolve as the study progresses.

Since the study sought answers to questions about service use from the "inside out" as previously described in the paradigm section of this manuscript, analysis included the ongoing identification of formal and informal service providers in the data. These data were coded, retrieved, and communicated to other researchers assigned to follow up with focused interviews with the identified service providers. Later, an analysis of the participant and service provider perspectives will be conducted to gain a holistic understanding of the effectiveness of services.

Credibility. Qualitative data are inherently subjective, dynamic, and changeable over time. However, several procedures for ensuring credibility of the data were utilized and are presented throughout this manuscript. In summary, we have addressed credibility concerns by: (1) separating reflective, interpretive comments from primary data in the field notes; (2) using a team approach to conducting the research (the research team consisted of five researchers and three family interviewers) and building regular debriefing sessions into the analysis process; and (3) conducting member checks at regular intervals during the data collection and at the conclusion of the study.

Reactivity issues have been alluded to in other parts of this manuscript, (i.e., feelings experienced when entering a home for an interview) and are addressed in the Discussion section. The effects of researchers on families, and of families on researchers, are two potential areas of bias with which qualitative researchers struggle continuously. Examples of the researcher effects on participants included the tendency of families to present a favorable view of their family life in order to impress the researchers. In addition, informants may act to protect their self-interests or promote their own agenda. The researchers increased their awareness of these biases by debriefing with other researchers and family interviewers. In addition, triangulation (corroboration with other data sources) assisted in this process. Again, the researchers thoroughly and repeatedly addressed issues of reactivity during regular staff and analysis meetings.

Further, as Miles and Huberman (1994) suggest, the credibility of the data depends to a large extent on the capacity of the researchers and interviewers to maintain valid and reliable information gathering. Researchers possessed varying degrees of strengths in conceptualization skills, insight into the phenomena under study, and their interviewing skills. Through self-reflection and group processing, these skills were refined as the study progressed.

It was a great advantage to work within a research team. As Gilgun (1993) stated, "The single most useful way to do our work well is to work in teams . . . not only do we need previous research and theory and strong conceptual skills, but we also need at least one other person with whom to make sense of the data" (p. 179). Researchers continuously consulted with one another to understand data, develop coding concepts and themes as well as move toward theory generation.

Several types of triangulation (Stainback & Stainback, 1988) were used in an attempt to relate the various data collected through interviews, participant observation, and document analysis. First, data from a variety of participants (family member, service providers, and key informants) were analyzed to increase understanding about key research questions. Secondly, multiple methods, i.e., participant observation, interviews, and document analysis were utilized to ensure that findings were not an artifact of a single method. Finally, investigator triangulation was used by including at least two researchers during each analysis session, and through the teaming of researcher and family interviewer during data collection and debriefing sessions.

Within-site and cross-site analysis. The research design included three sites (neighborhoods) and three cases (families) within each site. A research pair of one university faculty (principal investigator) and one family interviewer collected data. Therefore, analysis was conducted at four levels: within-case, across-case, within-site and across-site. For clarity, the explanation of the multi-level analysis will replace "case" and "site" terminology with "family" and "neighborhood" respectively. Over time three waves of data analysis were planned. A wave is defined as a round of interviews that included all members of a family for all three families in the neighborhood. These waves, therefore, took varying amounts of time depending on availability of families and researchers and unforeseen circumstances such as sickness, childbirth, relocation, etc., that affected both families and researchers.

The process of developing theory can be facilitated by using matrices (Miles & Huberman, 1984). These visual displays of reduced data involve crossing two or more of the main dimensions of a study to see how they interact. The authors explain the benefits of using matrices:

> [D]isplaying your reduced data in a systematic way has immense consequences for your understanding. It requires you to think about your research questions and what portions of your data are needed to answer them; it requires you to make full analyses, ignoring no

relevant information; and it focuses and organizes your information coherently. (p. 239)

Throughout the data analysis process, we plan to use matrices to reduce and display data for the purpose of conducting within-site and across-site analysis.

DISCUSSION

As we have progressed through this study we have encountered some interesting dilemmas that deserve mention, including: maintaining the insider-outsider balance, family access, reciprocity and ethics, evaluating family interviewers, conducting interviews in languages other than English and finally, advantages of the collaborative nature of the research.

Maintaining the Insider/Outsider Balance

Maintaining the delicate insider/outsider balance was a challenge that the researchers faced throughout the research. At times the dual role of participant and observer became uncomfortable for the researchers; we felt compelled to contribute at community meetings. In some cases, researchers became key players in community grassroots efforts, and collaborators on grant proposals with city administrators. However, we were wary about spreading ourselves too thin when there were reams of interview transcriptions piling up to be analyzed. We resolved this conflict, especially during periods of intensive family interviewing, by separating responsibility for community work and research among the five researchers. As a result, one researcher became the primary contributor at community meetings so that the other investigators could concentrate on collecting data.

Family Accessibility

Family accessibility varied significantly between neighborhoods. When there was a previously established relationship between the researchers and community members through work in neighborhood collaborative groups, the process of accessing families was expedited. When there was no previously established relationship, researchers were required to make multiple contacts. With each contact, the researcher needed to re-explain the goals of the research project. In one of the three neighborhoods where there were no organized community groups, the school became an integral "organization" in which to identify and reach families. However, once inside the school structure, it was difficult to impose on the time of school personnel. School community workers were more than willing to provide names of families, and make the initial contact for the researchers. However, their supervisor was reluctant to take up their school hours for such a task. We resolved the dilemma by assuring both the supervisor and the school principal that the community workers would assist researchers only during their off hours, and would be compensated by the researcher project. This compensation also eased the discomfort felt by researchers for imposing on the busy schedule of valuable school employees.

Reciprocity and Ethics

Another challenge involved what Marshall and Rossman (1989) call "reciprocity and ethics" (p. 69), wherein when people give their time to help the interviewer, the researcher feels obligated to reciprocate. But, this reciprocity must fit within the constraints of personal and research ethics. In the aforementioned study, families devoted a great deal of time and energy to helping us understand service-use within neighborhoods. In turn, we feel indebted to them. As we conduct on-going interviews, family members have made specific requests to us for assistance (e.g., they have asked for help with immigration issues, legal issues, health issues, etc.). Since we are investigating service/resource-use we are hesitant to change the family eco-system by intervening. On the other hand, we cannot ethically refuse their requests. Our solution to this dilemma is to provide appropriate assistance while documenting all requests and responses as a part of data collection. Guidelines for assistance were developed to ensure that: (1) we were in compliance with state regulations for reporting child abuse, (2) we did not exceed our level of professional expertise, and (3) families were empowered to find their own solutions. We have, by necessity (and choice), become true participant observers.

One particularly dramatic example occurred when a mother revealed that her 11-year-old daughter had been troubled for some time by a school incident that occurred several years ago. Although the daughter was reluctant to speak, the mother described how her daughter was sexually assaulted by a group of young boys in the elementary school bathroom. The researcher cautiously ascertained the details of the incident. The mother expressed the long-lasting emotional effect of this violation on her daughter and expressed a need for psychological counseling. This revelation was accompanied by an intense emotional outburst from the daughter who was unable to stop crying despite comforting gestures by the mother, researcher, and family interviewer.

The researcher responded to this "cry for help" by asking the mother if she would like information about counseling services. Despite the daughter's protests, the mother was adamant about getting help. The researcher assured the mother that she would immediately obtain names and phone numbers of local counseling services. Fortunately, the research staff was familiar with a family services organization located at this child's elementary school. In making the referral, it was important to determine if the incident had been documented and reported in accordance with child abuse laws. When it was clear that the school had followed the appropriate referral procedures, the counselor contacted the mother. The researcher called the mother to confirm the referral. During the next several weeks, the researcher followed up, being careful to respect the daughter's right to confidentiality and to focus on issues germane to service access. Throughout this highly sensitive episode in the research, the researcher struggled to maintain her role as an empathic observer. She found discussions with the research team to be helpful.

Family Interviewers

An additional difficulty occurred in the interaction between family interviewers and family members. Our original conceptualization of interview procedures involved the researcher posing a question followed by the family interviewer translating the question into the native language of the family member and then translating the family member's response back into English. We quickly discovered that it is unrealistic to expect all interview discussion to be translated into English during normal discourse. Instead, there were periods of extended conversation between the family interviewer and the family member without opportunity for translation into English. The researchers felt uncomfortable with the periodic loss of "control" during family interviews but acknowledged that those extended periods of non-translated conversation were part of rapport building. Thus, researchers had to trust that the family interviewer would establish rapport and at the same time collect appropriate data without continuous direct guidance from the researcher.

We also struggled in our attempts to find effective family interviewers. We knew that pairing a researcher with a family interviewer who spoke the native language of the family would increase our access to family members. We even asked focus groups what characteristics of a family interviewer would be important (i.e., age, gender, education, dialect). While focus groups gave us useful feedback, throughout the course of the study, we learned more about choosing appropriate interviewers. It was important that the family interviewer understand the methodologies and communicate well with researchers. It was equally important that the interviewer be able to develop rapport with family members. One interviewer, while a good match for the family, did not fully understand the methodologies used, and therefore was unable to participate in the analysis of data. In another case an interviewer used vocabulary which was too sophisticated for the family. It became evident that a good match must be found among the family interviewer, researcher and family member. Thus, the research team met frequently to discuss "good" and "poor" matches while making appropriate staffing adjustments.

Authenticity of Transcription

Interviewing non-English-speaking families posed a special challenge. Using audio tapes during interviews provided an excellent opportunity to obtain word-for-word family perceptions as they occurred (as opposed to the use of field notes, etc.). Because interviews had a wealth of untranslated information (dialogue not translated into English during the interview) we found the need for a two-stage process in interview transcription. First family interviewers produced a word-for-word transcription of the interview. In the next stage, since researchers could only analyze data in English, all native language dialogue in the transcript was translated into English with a designation that it had originally been spoken in another language. In this way data were kept in their original form, avoiding the filter of the family interviewer which inadvertently changes the original form of family comments. Therefore, the authenticity of the data was maintained.

Collaboration

An arduous situation came from one of the study's greatest strengths—the collaborative nature of the study. The advantages of collaboration in research and service are well documented (McKinney et al., 1994; Gardner, 1993; Schuchardt, Marlowe, Parker & Smith, 1991). But, as we brought together researchers from a variety of disciplines, it became apparent that we did not necessarily share common paradigms or common terminologies. This led to misunderstandings and a lack of clarity in communication. It was imperative that we become conscientious communicators, replacing "mind reading" and assumed similarities with articulate, clear discourse. Some researchers on this project faced another challenge, the difficulty of transitioning from quantitative research to qualitative methods. We found that our training in quantitative approaches often times made it very difficult to enjoy the subjective nature of the research. In the positivist tradition, we are taught to disengage from the research and the "subjects." In this study we found it difficult to put our voices back into our work. In writing this paper we often struggled with this dilemma, taking extra effort to get closer to the research–to probe deeper and avoid falling back into creating "distance" in order to do good research.

The benefits of the collaborative nature of this research were plentiful. Discussions among the interdisciplinary research team about substantive and methodological issues as they arose yielded rich, and often diverse, interpretations. Therefore, creative solutions to the never-ending challenges of the research abounded. Unique strengths of individuals emerged throughout the project and the team learned how to use these to the greatest advantage. The importance of mutual support, often taking the form of "gripe sessions," cannot be underestimated. The trade-offs of collaboration were related to logistical problems such as the difficulty in coordinating multiple schedules given the inevitable competing priorities associated with academia. The highly ambiguous nature of the research intensified the frustration and conflict that naturally arises within research teams. Unknowingly, the team coped in accordance with Lincoln and Guba's (1985) advice, ". . . arranging for mechanisms such as systematic team meetings to discharge feelings or outside reviews that provide external anchor points for team members . . ." (p. 238).

Yet another one of the "mixed blessings" of having multiple sources of data collected by multiple researchers is, of course, that data seem to increase exponentially with each passing week. Managing the data is difficult enough; the task of analyzing this enormously rich data set is mind-boggling at times. As our project moves into a more intensive analysis phase, we rely heavily on expert advice and relevant data analysis literature for reassurance and direction.

Final Thoughts

The experience of doing qualitative research with families has been filled with both triumphs and anxieties. It seemed that at every turn we were faced with new challenges. As the study progressed, however, we became adept at finding creative solutions to these challenges. We looked forward to the time spent with the families. Our relationships with the family interviewers became more synergistic, and, as a result, data collection and analysis became more eloquent. The collaborative process of writing this manuscript has been especially helpful in solidifying the research design and sharpening our skills in data collection and analysis procedures. Having to organize, synthesize, and reflect on our methods at this interim stage in the research has forced us into thoughtful dialogue about every aspect of our work. In fact, it has provided further inspiration to move ahead.

REFERENCES

Andranovich, G. D. & Riposa, G. (1993). Doing urban research. *Applied Social Service Research Methods Series, 33*, Newbury Park, CA: Sage.

Bronfenbrenner, U. (1979). *The ecology of human development: Experiments by nature and design.* Cambridge, MA: Harvard University Press.

Bronfenbrenner, U. (1974). Developmental research, public policy, and the ecology of childhood. *Child Development, 45*, 1-5.

Burgess, R. G. (Ed.). (1985). *Strategies of educational research.* Philadelphia: Falmer.

Clifford, F. & Roark, A. C. (1991, May 6). Racial lines in county blur but could return. *The Los Angeles Times*, pp. A-1, A-20, A-23.

Daley, K. (1992). The fit between qualitative research and characteristics of families. In J. F. Gilgun, K. Daly and G. Handel (Eds.), *Qualitative methods in family research* (pp. 3-11). Newbury Park, CA: Sage.

Dobbert, M. L. (1982). *Ethnographic research: Theory and application for modern schools and societies.* New York: Praeger.

Garbarino, J. (1992). The meaning of poverty in the world of children. *American Behavioral Scientist, 35*, 220-237.

Gardner, S. L. (1993). The ethics of collaboration. *Georgia Academy Journal, 1(1)*, 2-4.

Gilgun, J. F. (1993). Publishing research reports based on qualitative methods. *Marriage and Family Review, 18*(1/2), 177-181.

Gilgun, J.F. (1992). Definitions, methodologies, and methods in qualitative family research. In J. F. Gilgun, K. Daly and G. Handel (Eds.), *Qualitative methods in family research* (pp. 22-39). Newbury Park, CA: Sage.

Glaser, B., & Strauss, A. (1967). *The discovery of grounded theory.* Chicago: Aldine.

Harper, D. (1989). Visual Sociology: Expanding Sociological Vision. In G. Blank, J. L. Mc Cartney, & E. Brent (Eds.), *New technology in sociology: Practical applications in research and work* (pp. 81-97). NJ: Transaction.

Heath, S. B. & Mc Laughlin, M. W. (Eds.). (1993). *Identity and inner-city youth: Beyond ethnicity and gender.* New York: Teachers College Press.

Lincoln, Y.S. & Guba, E. G. (1985). *Naturalistic inquiry.* Beverly Hills, CA: Sage.

Marshall, C. & Rossman, G. B. (1989). *Designing qualitative research.* Newbury Park, CA: Sage.

McKinney, M. H., Abrams, L. A., Terry, P. A., & Lerner, R. M. (1994). Child development research and the poor children of America: A call for a developmental contextual approach to research and outreach. *Home Economics Research Journal, 23*, 25-41.

Melaville, A. I. & Blank, M. J. (October, 1992). *What it takes: Structuring inter-agency partnerships to connect children and families with comprehensive services.* Washington, DC: Education and Human Services Consortium.

Miles, M. B. & Huberman, A. M. (1984). *Qualitative research methods.* Beverly Hills, CA: Sage.

Miles, M. B. & Huberman, A. M. (1994). *Qualitative data analysis: An expanded sourcebook* (2nd ed.). Beverly Hills, CA: Sage.

Morgan, D. L. & Krueger, R. A. (1993). When to use focus groups and why. In D. L. Morgan (Ed.), *Successful focus groups* (pp. 3-19). Newbury Park, CA: Sage.

Naisbitt, J. (1994). *Global paradox: The bigger the world economy, the more powerful its smallest players.* New York: Morrow.

National Resource Center for Family Support Programs. (1993). *Family support programs and comprehensive collaborative services.* Chicago: Family Resource Coalition.

Padilla, R. V. (1993). HyperQual2 Version 1.0 [Computer Software]. Chandler, AZ: Author.

Patton, M. Q. (1980). *Qualitative evaluation methods.* Beverly Hills, CA. Sage.

Piaget, J. & Inhelder, B. (1969). *The psychology of the child.* New York: Basic Books.

Schorr, L. B. (1988). *Within Our Reach: Breaking the Cycle of Disadvantage.* New York: Anchor Press/Doubleday.

Schuchardt, J., Marlowe, J., Parker, L., Smith, C. (1991). Low income families: Keys to successful outreach. *Advancing the Consumer Interest, 3*(2), 27-31.

Stainback, S. & Stainback, W. (1988). *Understanding and conducting qualitative research.* Dubuque, IA: Kendall/Hunt.

Stasz, D. (1979). The early history of visual sociology. In J. Wagner (Ed.), *Images of information: Still photography in the social sciences* (pp. 119-137) Newbury Park: Sage.

Tesch, R. (1990). *Qualitative research: Analysis types and software tools.* Philadelphia: Taylor and Francis.

U.S. Department of Commerce. Bureau of the Census. (August, 1992). *Poverty in the United States: 1991.* Current Population Reports, Series P-60, No. 181. Washington, DC: U.S. Government Printing Office.

Van Maanen, J. (1983). *Qualitative Methodology.* Beverly Hills, CA: Sage.

Van Maanen, J. (1979) The fact and fiction in organizational ethnography. *Administrative Science Quarterly, 24,* 536-611.

Worth, S. & Adair, J. (1972). *Through Navaho eyes: An exploration in film communication and anthropology.* Bloomington, IN: University Press.

The Composite Biography
as a Methodological Tool
for the Study of Childhood in History

Barbara A. Hanawalt

SUMMARY. This article presents a composite biography of an orphaned girl and her mother in Medieval London. Though the mother was sound in mind and body, she had no control over her daughter's inheritance and place of residence. In addition, her underage daughter was married without her consent. The composite biography can bring to life the otherwise dry renditions of families' experiences that are present in court records and other historical documents. *[Article copies available for a fee from The Haworth Document Delivery Service: 1-800-342-9678. E-mail address: getinfo@haworth.com]*

KEYWORDS. Family history, Historical documents, Composite biography

The study of childrearing and parenting, as well as community and governmental interfaces with families, increasingly seeks to add historical perspectives in order to see developmental patterns and variations. In this respect, historical studies of western families add perspectives similar to ethnography in that they permit alternative pictures of family relation-

Barbara Hanawalt is Professor, Department of History, University of Minnesota, Twin Cities, 614 Social Science Tower, Minneapolis, MN 55455.

[Haworth co-indexing entry note]: "The Composite Biography as a Methodological Tool for the Study of Childhood in History." Hanawalt, Barbara A. Co-published simultaneously in *Marriage & Family Review* (The Haworth Press, Inc.) Vol. 24, No. 3/4, 1996, pp. 323-334; and: *The Methods and Methodologies of Qualitative Family Research* (ed: Marvin B. Sussman, and Jane F. Gilgun) The Haworth Press, Inc., 1996, pp. 323-334. Single or multiple copies of this article are available for a fee from The Haworth Document Delivery Service [1-800-342-9678, 9:00 a.m. - 5:00 p.m. (EST). E-mail address: getinfo@haworth.com].

ships. The families and communities that appear in European history form the roots of our own structures. Historical examples, however, present problems of interpretation because readers see that both continuity and discontinuity, the familiar and the alien, are present when compared to contemporary families. A further problem for researchers is to make this sometimes scattered and esoteric evidence comprehensible to modern social scientists, who are accustomed to case studies or aggregate data.

Data for the study of children and their relationship to families in historical documents, particularly those in pre-industrial societies, are found in records that are largely judicial in nature: inquests into homicides or accidental deaths, court cases about property and inheritances, marriage contracts, care of orphans, and so on. This essay explains a new technique for analyzing such scattered evidence. The variety of existing evidence is presented in traditional analytical arguments, including quantitative data when possible as well as laws regarding families and court case evidence about particular applications of the laws. Finally, a composite biography serves as an additional tool of analysis that brings evidence together in ways that create informed understandings of persons in their historical circumstances. The present essay uses as an example a young girl born to an unmarried mother and a father who was a London citizen and who provided her with an inheritance. She therefore goes through all of the experiences an orphan would, but she has the added problem of legal bastardy.

LIFE COURSE ANALYSIS

Among sociologists and psychologists dealing with analysis of historical data, life course analysis has been particularly fruitful. Elder's (1974) early, well-known study explored the life experiences of a cohort of children in Oakland, California who grew up in the Great Depression. Elder wrote eloquently about the use of history and the advantages of life course analysis in a variety of publications. His recent publications (Elder, 1994; Elder, Modell, and Parke, 1993) provide a current review of the scholarship on historical studies using life-course analysis. Hareven (1978, 1982) also has been an advocate for the use of life-course analysis.

Life-course analysis has been done in a variety of ways, including longitudinal analysis of census returns, cohort analysis, and the study of each life stage. This analytical approach, however, has flaws. Census materials, which have been widely used for life-course studies, artificially lock analysis into slices of society taken every ten years. Cohort analysis (a variant of life course), while excellent for looking at the long-term behavior patterns of generations, can limit an understanding of family relationships and can obscure how definitions and behaviors change over time. Most of these studies are done through aggregate data derived from census samples or from questionnaires, tests, and interviews.

Many preindustrial societies including Japan, China, Europe and four-teenth- and fifteenth-century England present a number of challenges to traditional life-course analysis since ages are seldom given and censuses were not taken. The sources are in some ways richer for detail, but do not usually allow for continuous tracking of cohort groups or compilation of aggregate data. Researchers, therefore, must reconstruct each life stage from a variety of sources, many of which require qualitative data analysis. Because the qualitative data are themselves gleaned from so many varied types of sources, both literary and legal, the composite biography, as I shall demonstrate, has advantages as one tool for presenting a coherent picture of a life stage as opposed to life course analysis.

QUALITATIVE DATA AND COMPOSITE BIOGRAPHIES

As with all qualitative data, the interpretive problems are challenging. While researchers attempt to be aware of their own perspectives that might bias their interpretations of qualitative data, writing about the Middle Ages means that researchers must also be aware of the interpretative baggage that *readers* will bring to the discussion of anything related to that time period. For instance, both the general public and some professional histo-rians have regarded the Middle Ages as a retrograde period in which all that is horrible happened. Popular culture uses as a term of insult that "x behavior is truly medieval" or "social conditions are medieval," implying that we moderns have outgrown such behavior; we have evolved beyond the Middle Ages. Since we value children, for instance, popular culture is ready to assume that children were abused or childhood did not exist in the Middle Ages.

The tendency to collapse all aspects of the past into one distant period encourages such views. Thus, in folk belief, a gloomy, Dickensian por-trayal of nineteenth-century conditions of child labor in factories is pro-jected back to create an image of "medieval" childhood. This gross histor-ical anachronism moves the Industrial Revolution and factories back five hundred years to a period when factories did not exist.

Modern historians such as Ariès (1962) and Stone (1977) adopted the same folkloric prejudices. Their views have gained prominence, creeping into modern textbooks on family and childrearing and thereby becoming ensconced as orthodoxy. Briefly stated, they argued that our concept of childhood and adolescence only emerged at the earliest in 1500; that the Middle Ages was a period dominated by extended families rather than the more modern nuclear ones; and that parents did not love their children and treated them as little adults, dressing them in adult clothing and sending them out to work in the adult world. Neither of these historians seriously researched the medieval evidence and, as their female critics have pointed out, neither of them spent time with children (Hanawalt, 1977).

DOCUMENTING MEDIEVAL FAMILY LIFE

The second challenge for reconstructing the childhood experience in the Middle Ages arises from the documents of the period: their scanty preservation and the problems of interpreting those that survive. It is this second problem that will be the subject of this essay. The paper will discuss the types of documentation, their pitfalls, and the sorts of information that one may reliably glean from them. Although only medieval documents will be considered here, the interpretive problems exist in one form or another in using all historical documentary evidence and pose similar problems even with modern case records. How accurate are these records? Whose side or whose biases do these documents represent? What interpretive tools can the researcher use to validate a qualitative analysis of a case history or court record?

Since diaries, letters, and expressions of individual experiences (other than religious ones) do not exist for the Middle Ages, most of the documentation was generated for official purposes rather than with the view of providing information on life course. There are both advantages and disadvantages to working from court records and contracts. The information that they contain tends to be relatively straightforward recounting of events that are occurring in the life of a child or children rather than being highly emotional documents that lend insight into subjective sides of family life. The register of London orphans and their inheritance, for instance, is mostly informational.

Some of the records, however, such as the specific case analyzed below, are one-sided: they are individual bills to the mayor to have him decide a case or they are petitions to the king's chancellor to hear a case of some individual misfortune. Such evidence is in the category of special pleading and needs a counter-balance. Although the opposing side may also have some independent input into the matter, the strong emotional appeal, for example, of a mother seeking custody of her daughter, may dominate interpretations. It is necessary to move beyond the emotive appeals and place appeals within a context. An interpretation of the general context makes the subjective aspects of medieval family life more understandable.

A COMPOSITE BIOGRAPHY

In this section, I explain how I constructed a composite biography in order to demonstrate the vulnerability of a young orphan girl and compare her situation with the legal provisions and the social realities that pertained to orphans, bastards, and females in London. In my recent book, *Growing Up in Medieval London* (Hanawalt, 1993), I used traditional historical data analysis while adding portraits and short biographies of children at each life stage. The approach that I used was to form a quantitative and qualitative context for a case on which I had more complete information than on other cases. I constructed the case from a variety of types of evidence including wills, court cases, coroners' inquests, petitions for equity hearings from the Chancellor, proceedings of the court of orphans, church court records, and literary sources such as poems and advice books.

The methodological treatment of this evidence varied from researching legal provisions for orphaned children to statistically analyzing the laws' application; and observation of the physical arrangements for orphans and children in general. The final, composite biographies are as historically accurate as possible and the general, contextual materials were woven in to make a complete picture centering on one child's experience. The function of the composite biographies, methodologically, was to bring together the disparate pieces of historical data into an understandable case history. The composite biography provides an immediate sense of the experience that otherwise would be represented in more abstract terms.

The composite biography described here is that of Alison, the illegitimate child and heiress of John Rayner, citizen and cornmonger of London. The case was initially brought through a private bill to the mayor's court by Margaret, the mother of Alison and mistress of John Rayner. Margaret stated that as a servant in Rayner's house she had conceived the child, and Rayner had recognized the child as his. Indeed, Rayner left Alison a substantial bequest: 110 marks of silver, mazers, two pieces of silver with covers, one "note" with foot and cover of silver gilt, and 18 silver spoons. She was to be apprenticed to learn a useful craft. In addition, he had left Margaret and Alison a house to be jointly held by them for their lives.

Alison's bequest had been turned over to the mayor as was the custom for an orphan of a London citizen. Margaret assumed that she would be made guardian of the child and the property. Instead, she complained that "one John Bryan, fishmonger, came before [the mayor] and begged to have the goods and chattels delivered into his wardship until the majority of Alison together with her body." As a servant, she was powerless to oppose the decision. She was not a citizen and could not find substantial male citizens to stand surety for her daughter's property. She might have hoped for custody of the child if not her inheritance, and she did remain in close contact with her daughter as her testimony indicates. Within a few years, Bryan paid off Margaret's inheritance, which was a small amount. Margaret, however, had heard rumors that Bryan's fortune was faltering and that to pay off his apprentice, Richard Franceys, he had offered a marriage with Alison, giving him authority over Alison's goods. Margaret claimed that this marriage had been clandestinely arranged without the mayor's permission. In fact, the record indicates that Bryan had bought permission from the mayor to marry Alison.[1]

FORMING A CONTEXT

Forming a context for this rather full court case required a knowledge of London laws relating to bastardy, care of orphans, the position of servants, and the ways in which marriages were contracted. On the whole, London law was remarkably mindful of the welfare of citizens' children and the necessary legal protections of their persons and their well-being. While hardly a welfare state, the city enacted and administered legal protection for its young citizens and their inheritances.

Bastardy was, of course, a fairly common problem in a commercial city that had its share of businessmen away from home and a large, unmarried population of young men acting as servants, apprentices, soldiers, sailors, and general loafers. In addition, the vulnerable position of women household servants frequently reduced them to roles of concubines to the masters. London law recognized the problem of illegitimacy and tried to arrive at an equitable solution for at least the recognized bastards, as Alison was. Illegitimate children could not inherit the chief estate of their fathers, but they could inherit movable goods and could have life use of the property, just as Alison did.

London law also protected the orphaned children of London citizens by insisting that the orphans be placed under the guardianship of the mayor. Citizenship was limited to those born in London, completing apprenticeship there, or buying citizenship rights. That meant that when a citizen died, the children and their inheritance would be taken into the mayor's court. The mayor then granted the wardship of the children and inheritance to responsible parties who had to provide surety for the care of the children and goods; that is, they had to find four citizens who would guarantee the payment of the inheritance and intervene on behalf of orphans if need arose.

The mayor was charged with supervising the protection of the persons, property, and marriages of the children. Control over marriages insured that the children were not married below their station or that the guardians did not seek the wardship only to gain control of the inheritance through marriage with their own children.

The law was applied and as a consequence we know much about the provisions for 1,731 of London's orphans. In about 50 percent of the cases the mother or the mother and her new husband became guardians. The law stipulated that someone who would not stand to inherit should the child die was an appropriate guardian. Londoners obviously suspected the worst of human nature and removed the temptation to murder orphans from potential heirs to their fortunes. Since wives could not inherit their husbands' property, mothers were both a good legal and practical choice. In Alison's case, her father was a citizen, but her mother was a servant not married to the father. The more usual practice, therefore, was suspended.

The value of Alison's inheritance was high and Bryan was anxious to have the use of it. Even though the law required that he return 12d. for every pound of her inheritance when she reached the age of majority (sixteen if she married and twenty-one if she were not yet married), he had the use of a substantial sum of money to invest for a number of years (Hanawalt, 1993, pp. 87-107).

Alison's age was not given, but the quantitative analysis of those cases in which age and inheritance can be determined gives us some idea of the age and wealth of the orphans. The average age of a child entering wardship was seven to nine so that a guardian would have a substantial number of years to use the child's inheritance in business investments.

In my composite biography, I made Alison seven years old so that discussion of her marriage would begin at 12 when she should have been going into an apprenticeship, but was instead being considered for marriage. The average wealth of the orphans rose substantially over the fourteenth and fifteenth centuries. When Alison appeared in the records the wealth in cash averaged £416. In cash alone, Alison had in excess of £73 pounds and had, in addition, a number of gold and silver objects and use of a piece of real estate. Her estate was modest by comparison to the average, but still substantial enough to make her a good marriage prospect (Hanawalt, 1993, p. 224).

The provision that Alison become an apprentice, which Margaret mentioned in her bill, would be appropriate for a young woman who was illegitimate and not of the most desirable fortune in the marriage market.

Women entered into apprenticeship at the age of 12 to 14 and usually learned crafts such as dressmaker, embroiderer, or silkmaker. The term of apprenticeship varied from a few years to seven for women. A parental investment in an apprenticeship, including a down payment to the master and perhaps something toward room and board, was considered as part of the dowry that a young woman required in order to marry. Learning a skill craft, which as a married woman she could practice at home, would permit her to make an ongoing contribution to the household economy (Hanawalt, 1993, p. 143). Rayner had thought through his provisions for his bastard daughter by giving her a modest capital and goods toward marriage and also envisioning a useful craft to accompany it.

ARRANGED MARRIAGES IN THE MIDDLE AGES

Arranged marriages were common in the Middle Ages even among people with small amounts of property. The custom prevailed that the parents or friends of the couple would make arrangements involving both some degree of compatibility and certainly mutual financial obligations. The custom was a dowry from the wife—usually in terms of property that included, as Alison's did, valuable household items and cash—and a dower from the husband. The dower was a contractual obligation providing the widow a third of the husband's real estate for her life use, but not for her inheritance.

Margaret discovered that her non-marriage entitled her to very little out of a substantial estate and that the half interest in the house was worth only 40s. when the settlement was made. In the case of orphans, the mayor controlled the marriage, but he could grant out the right to marry the orphan for a fee. Usually the fee was calculated as a portion of the bride's estate. In Alison's case it was 20s.

Margaret's position as a servant/concubine was not enviable, but not atypical. On the whole, Rayner treated her rather well, if not as well as she seemed to have hoped. Female household servants in all periods have had an ambiguous relationship to the heads of households. On the one hand, heads of households were responsible for their well-being and their moral behavior. On the other hand, he was something of the Biblical patriarch among the women folk of his household. A business man who did not wish to remarry or who had a wife elsewhere often entered into a concubinage relationship with a servant. While wills indicated that they were usually generous to their bastard children, sometimes even having the legitimate children ensure the payments to the bastards, servant women usually gained less in wills than did the children born from liasons with heads of households.

Margaret was probably not alone in feeling bitterness at the separation from her child and the relatively poor position in which she found herself upon her master's death. Margaret was a persistent woman and put her complaints into a written form to the mayor; others would not have told their story so boldly.

Finally, the material environment in which the case unfolded is of importance in understanding childhood and the experiences of Alison. London was a city of parishes and political wards. For women and children, and even for many men, these were the small worlds within which they lived and spent most of their time. Craftsmen and merchants tended to cluster together in different wards and parishes with the butchers outside the city walls, the cornmongers around St. Paul in the west, and the fishmongers by the river and toward the east. The interior of the houses is also important for a child's development and, fortunately, a few inventories of houses of men of varying wealth were preserved in order better to execute their wills. These describe cradles and beds for children and give their furnishings and their locations throughout the houses including in the servants' room (P. R. O. Prob2/11, 98).

With this context in mind, I return to the composite that I drew of Margaret, Alison, and the Bryans. In addition to the narrative as laid out in Margaret's bill and in the license given Bryan to marry off Alison, I incorporated materials gained from other types of evidence and other cases. Alison's early life until the age of seven is pictured as a secure one in a house, smelling sweetly of grains, near St. Paul. Her mother is considerably younger than the elderly Rayner, but she is treated as a household manager rather than as either servant or wife. Alison slept in a cradle in her parent's bed chamber during the first few years of her life.

The change in Allison's life was abrupt when her father died. Her mother took her to the Guildhall where mayor gave control of her person and inheritance to the Bryans, who were complete strangers. Bryan the fishmonger's house was in a different quarter of the city and always smelled of stale fish. Since her mother stayed in close contact with her, I presumed that she initially moved into Bryans' house as an ordinary servant while Alison continued to stay in her chamber in a small child's bed. When Bryan bought out Margaret's inheritance, I posit that Margaret was forced to move to lodgings and become a beer seller on a nearby street. She spoke with her daughter frequently, and she knew the street gossip about Bryan's finances and the rumor that he proposed to pay off his apprentice by arranging Alison's marriage and turning over her dowry. She warned her daughter, now 12 years old, not to be enticed into a marriage.

VALID MARRIAGES IN THE MIDDLE AGES

For a marriage to be valid in the Middle Ages, the couple needed only to agree mutually that it was of their free will. This agreement was a binding contract. I suggest that Alison may have been tricked into giving her consent. The scene is a celebration to which the priest is invited and at which a roast rather than fish is served. Richard Franceys, who was an apprentice in his late teens in the household, was present with his family. Alison had known Richard since she moved into the house and always regarded him as a benevolent big brother.

That the relations between the children of a household and apprentices could be amicable appears in many other cases. When the Bryans asked her at the feast if she wanted to marry him, she had replied that she liked him but she would have to consult her mother. The Bryans assured her that Richard had to complete his apprenticeship, and she had to wait until she was sixteen to marry: they were only talking about whether or not she liked Richard enough to marry him. She said she did, and Richard presented her with a gold ring. Such a loose agreement was a valid marriage contract. The story concludes with Margaret bringing a bill to the mayor's court complaining of being cheated out of the wardship of her daughter, management of her inheritance, and the disposition of her daughter's marriage. The mayor upheld Bryan (Hanawalt, 1993, 97-100).

ADVANTAGES OF COMPOSITE BIOGRAPHIES

The advantage of composite biographies was two-fold in the study of childhood in medieval London. Because the study undertook to argue against both a prevailing folklore and a scholarly tradition about childhood in the Middle Ages, a presentation of evidence in a clearly narrative form permitted non-specialist readers, including students, to grasp quickly the essence of a variety of childhood experiences. If the statistics were not memorable to the non-specialist, hopefully, the stories would linger and influence perceptions about medieval childhood.

Second, the composites permitted an interplay between the other data about children and female servants within the context of one case. While still remaining Margaret's story, the legal provisions for orphans, the manipulations of the legal guardians, the feelings of mother and child, the position of female servants, and marriage arrangements could also be explored.

While the use of composite biographies may be found in other disciplines (Kirshenblatt-Gimblett, 1989), they can be regarded with suspicion. Historians, like journalists, tend to hold to a strict line of "only the facts." Thus, the journalist who won a Pulitzer prize for her story about a slum child ended in disgrace when it was revealed to be a composite and not a real person.

ETHICAL ISSUES

The ethical issues that the use of composites raises are important. A modern use of a composite, for instance, might be advisable when the anonymity of the person must be maintained or when a typical example will make the point clearer about a particular type of case. The caution with the method is that it must be as close to an accurate portrayal as is possible. Only the surrounding data, the context of the case as I have called it, will make this a convincing methodological tool. Finally, the composite must be clearly labelled as such or the charge of falsification can legitimately be made.

NOTE

1. Margaret's complaint appeared in the mayor's court original bills in the Corporation of London Record Office, MC1/1/62. An original bill is a complaint, not a final judgment, but most of the narrative comes from her bill. The case, told officially from Bryan's side, however, appears in another type of mayor's court and was recorded in Letter Book H, pp. 10-12 in which we learn that the executors quickly settled her claims to inheritance from Rayner, and Bryan paid 20s. to secure the right to marry off Alison. A note about monetary values will help give some perspective: a loaf of bread cost 1d. and an unskilled day laborer was paid 4d. a day.

REFERENCES

Ariès, P. (1962). *Centuries of childhood: A social history of the family.* Trans. Robert Baldick. London: Vintage.
Corporation of London Record Office. Mayor's Court, Original Bills MC1,2,3.
Elder, G. H., Jr. (1974). *Children of the Great Depression: Social change in life experiences.* Chicago: University of Chicago Press.
Elder, G. H., Jr. (1994). Time, human agency, and social change: Perspectives on the life course. *Social Psychology Quarterly, 57,* 4-15.
Elder, G. H., Jr., John Modell, & Ross Parke (Eds.). (1993). *Children in time and*

place: Developmental and historical insights. New York: Cambridge University Press.

Hanawalt, B. A. (1977). Childrearing among the lower classes of late medieval England. *Journal of Interdisciplinary History, 8*, 1-22.

Hanawalt, B. A. (1993). *Growing up in medieval London. The experience of childhood in history*. New York: Oxford University Press.

Hareven, T. K. (1982). *Family time and industrial time*. New York: Cambridge University Press.

Hareven, T. K. (1978). *Transitions: The family and the life course in historical perspective*. New York: Academic.

Kirshenblatt-Gimblett, B. (1989). Authoring lives. *Journal of Folklore Research, 26*, 123-149.

Public Record Office. Probate: Prob2.

Sharpe, R. R. (Ed.) (1899-1912). *Calendar of letter books of the city of London, A-L (1275-1497)*. London: John Edward Francis.

Stone, L. (1977). *The family, sex and marriage in England 1500-1800*. New York: Harper and Row.

Family Worlds and Qualitative Family Research: Emergence and Prospects of Whole-Family Methodology

Gerald Handel

SUMMARY. This article elaborates upon the importance of whole-family methodologies for family studies. Drawing upon *Family Worlds*, a seminal work in whole-family methodology, this essay shows by example and analysis the capacity of this approach to deepen and broaden understandings of diverse family experiences. Not only does whole-family methodology contribute to theory development, but it also has the capacity to help researchers construct the rich, complex, and sometimes fragmented experiences of "post-modern" families. *[Article copies available for a fee from The Haworth Document Delivery Service: 1-800-342-9678. E-mail address: getinfo@haworth.com]*

KEYWORDS. Whole-family methodologies, Symbolic interractionism, Family interviewing, Family process and interaction, Chicago School of Sociology

Gerald Handel is Professor, The City College and The Graduate School, City University of New York. Address correspondence to: 3 Gilmore Court, Scarsdale, NY 10583-1421.

This article is a revised version of a paper presented at the annual meeting, Speech Communication Association, New Orleans, 1994.

[Haworth co-indexing entry note]: "*Family Worlds* and Qualitative Family Research: Emergence and Prospects of Whole-Family Methodology." Handel, Gerald. Co-published simultaneously in *Marriage & Family Review* (The Haworth Press, Inc.) Vol. 24, No. 3/4, 1996, pp. 335-348; and: *The Methods and Methodologies of Qualitative Family Research* (ed: Marvin B. Sussman, and Jane F. Gilgun) The Haworth Press, Inc., 1996, pp. 335-348. Single or multiple copies of this article are available for a fee from The Haworth Document Delivery Service [1-800-342-9678, 9:00 a.m. - 5:00 p.m. (EST). E-mail address: getinfo@haworth.com].

335

Family Worlds, by Robert D. Hess and Gerald Handel, made distinctive contributions to the methodology of family studies and to theoretical understanding of family relationships and interaction. The purpose of this paper is to summarize those contributions, to describe the background from which the work arose, and to suggest some current implications The book was published by The University of Chicago Press in 1959 and in a paperback edition with a new preface in 1974. It was in print for 30 years and sold a total of 10,535 copies.[1] That is not a sensational sales figure but it is a respectable number of copies for a scholarly book. Its longevity is more noteworthy, and perhaps has not yet ended. In 1992, although the publisher had no copies left to sell, a royalty was paid; a Kinko copy center had paid a fee to reproduce the entire book. In May 1995, University Press of America reissued the paperback edition.

These nitty-gritty details testify, in a somewhat objective way, that *Family Worlds* had something to say that was of more than transitory interest; an invitation from the Speech Communication Association to speak about the work at its 1994 Annual Meeting is an additional affirmation, as is the opportunity to publish the discussion in this volume. I welcome these opportunities because I believe that the book's contributions are not obsolete despite the considerable changes that have taken place in the family institution in the 35 years since publication. Further, since the book includes five detailed family case studies, the book now acquires an added value as a contribution to the documentary history of American family life.

Let me first briefly summarize the book's contents. Then I will turn to a discussion of how the work was done and will conclude with brief comments regarding its main contributions and implications.

A SUMMARY OF FAMILY WORLDS

One of the two readers of the book manuscript for the publisher was Reuben Hill, a leading family sociologist. An excerpt from his review was quoted on the dust jacket: "[*Family Worlds*] breaks new ground in the social psychology of the family." That is a good concise statement of what the book is about. I recall that when we were doing the work I asked W. Lloyd Warner, a senior colleague, what we should call the kind of work that Hess and I were doing. Was it social psychology? That's what it seemed to me, but I had never read anything called social psychology of the family nor even heard or seen the expression until Reuben Hill's comment confirmed my notion. For what we were trying to do was to understand, describe, and analyze how families function. The opening chapter of the book presents the rudiments of a new theory of how families operate, how they construct and constitute the worlds they make for themselves. We understood full well that families are shaped by the society in which they live, but that was not our focus. Our focus was at the microsocial level of family relationships and interaction. Our opening sentence takes cognizance that families operate in a wider social context, but we wanted to analyze not the context but the construction of family life within it.

We had no precedents, no models for the work we were doing. The field of family therapy did not exist; it was just starting up at about the same time. Departments of family studies, fairly widespread today, were not even on the horizon, nor was there at that time a concept of family communication. Sociologists studied problems such as divorce and family breakup, but their major interest was on the ways in which family structure reflects the broader social structure and on how it changes as social structure changes. Psychologists did a little work on mother-child relationships, but it was not a major interest; indeed, it is only in the last few years that they even mention families in other than therapeutic contexts.

We studied 33 two-parent families of northwest European ancestry. Each family had either two or three children between the ages of 6 and 18. Each member of the family was interviewed at least once. In addition, each member told stories to Thematic Apperception Test (TAT) pictures and completed incomplete sentences. Each parent wrote a paragraph on the topic "The kind of person I would like my child to be." Each child wrote or spoke a few sentences on the topic "The person I would like to be like."

The first chapter of *Family Worlds* is based on the analysis of all this material. It formulates five processes of family functioning. The first and most general is that every family must work out a pattern of separateness and connectedness. We take as fundamental that every person is both connected to the other family members and is also a separate individual. We do not assume that families necessarily achieve a pattern that is enduring or that satisfies all the members, but rather that patterns are provisionally established while the process is a basic one that is ongoing.

The second process we called the family's effort to establish a satisfactory congruence of images through the exchange of suitable testimony. We argue that each member of a family develops an image of what each other member of the family is like, as well as a self-image and an image of himself or herself in relation to each of the others. One's image of a person defines that person for oneself as an object of one's own actions. The members of a family are likely to have somewhat varying images of any given member whose own self-image may also diverge from any or all of the images held by the others. By word and deed, family members try to establish a satisfactory congruence of images among themselves, a process that is not, as we know, always successful.

The third process that we formulated we called the establishment of a family theme. By this we meant that families tend to have some central locus of concern that has a shaping effect on family relationships and interactions. That is not to say that everything that goes on in a family is related to a single issue. That would be an oversimplification. But families do seem each to have a central concern reflected in members' thoughts, feelings, communications, and actions.

A fourth process that we introduced is the process of establishing family boundaries. A family maps its domain of acceptable and desirable experience. It seeks to screen out unwelcome experiences and strives to incorporate those aspects of the culture and the world that it values.

Finally, families must deal with the basic biosocial issues–age and sex/gender. While families do, of course, draw on larger cultural understandings of these issues, those understandings are not uniform and every family must construct its own understandings of the meanings of particular ages and the meanings of sex and gender and must deal with the problems that arise from intrafamilial differences in these meanings.

This is a brief summary of five processes that are more complex than these few sentences can convey. Following the chapter that presents them, the book proceeds to five chapters devoted to detailed analytic case studies of about 40 pages each. These are followed by a comparative chapter and a methodological appendix. The concluding chapter compared the five families in terms of the family processes that were expounded in the opening chapter. It also added some elaboration. For example, we looked at the families in terms of how they differed in their members' mutual regulation of behavior. We addressed these questions: How do parents exercise authority? How much room do they leave for negotiation with their children? How do children influence their parents? The methodological appendix described the background of the study and how we found the families to study. It also described the research procedures, including the topics covered in the interview guide, the use of the TAT pictures, and the 55 sentence beginnings that were to be completed by each parent and the 44 to be completed by each child.

With this brief exposition of the book's contents, let me turn now to a discussion of the background of the study and how the work was done.

WHY AND HOW WE STUDIED FAMILY WORLDS

Researchers come to the study of families from many perspectives and with many interests. At the risk of oversimplification, I would propose that those interests mostly fall into two broad categories. Most people who study families have a primary interest either in the marriage relationship or in the parent-child relationship. One or the other of these is the point of departure, although the end product may be broader. Robert Hess and I both came to this project with a primary interest in the parent-child relationship. This much said, what follows will largely be my personal account. Robert Hess died in 1993. If he were alive he might approach this topic differently. While I will sometimes refer to the work that *we* did, I will also present thoughts that I had or now have. It is, of course, not possible to recapture exactly the thoughts of 40 years ago. But I think my basic perspective has not changed significantly. Let me state it here in five propositions that constitute the methodological assumptions of the study. Although I could not have stated them as clearly 40 years ago, in one way or another they were in my mind as I entered into the work.

1. Childhood experience is consequential for a person's life course.
2. Children's experience of family life is a fundamental component of childhood experience.
3. Inasmuch as families are groups of members, children's experience of family life can only be understood by studying the whole family as a group of members.
4. Studying the family as a group means studying it as a symbolic order and as a socio-emotional order.
5. The symbolic and socio-emotional order of the family are manifested through face-to-face communication among the family members and in individually produced statements by family members such as responses to interviewer questions, stories told to TAT pictures, and written statements.

Obtaining data from each member of each family is the major methodological innovation of our study. That was a departure from prevailing practice, and it remains rare today. How did we come to do this? There are two major parts to an answer, an institutional part and an intellectual part. Let me take them in order.

Hess and I both did our graduate work in the Committee on Human Development, an interdepartmental degree-granting committee at The University of Chicago. The focus of this Committee was on the biological, psychological, and social factors influencing the development of the human person. Students took courses in a variety of departments, some of whose faculty were members of the Committee and some were not. There was no dominating point of view or doctrine. A great variety of theoretical outlooks was taught, and there was a great deal of methodological openness. Every student was individually responsible for working out his or her own integration of the very diverse material studied. The theoretical and methodological openness of the Committee was an important institutional factor facilitating our research, which Hess and I carried out as junior staff members after we had finished our graduate work.

Chicago School of Sociology

Like all universities, Chicago taught the logic of experimental method and the logic of statistical method. A distinguishing feature, I believe, was the tradition and heritage of what is known as "the Chicago School" in sociology. The term is somewhat misleading in suggesting an explicit doctrine. As scholars of "the Chicago School" have pointed out, a variety of work has been subsumed under this label (Bulmer, 1984; Faris, 1967). But this tradition did value qualitative work–fieldwork, qualitative interviewing, case studies. It emphasized the value of studying communities as functioning units and the importance of obtaining whatever kind of information about the subject could be obtained, whether it was amenable to statistical analysis or not. The progenitors of this kind of work were W. I. Thomas and Robert E. Park. Thomas also contributed a celebrated concept that influenced our formulation, the concept of "definition of the situation."

Another aspect of the Chicago School derives from George Herbert Mead, a philosopher who taught a social psychology course in the sociology department. Mead produced an influential theory of how children are socialized, part of a larger theory of human nature and of how society functions. Although Thomas, Park, and Mead were long gone, some of their students were influential members of the faculty. Also, Ernest W. Burgess, who had been a younger collaborator of Park and was still teaching at Chicago, was a family sociologist who, in 1926, had published an article with the suggestive title, "The Family as a Unity of Interacting Personalities" (Burgess, 1926). That title leads me to the intellectual part of my answer.

Although I did not study directly with Burgess, I encountered his concept of the family as a unity of interacting personalities in a family course and probably in one or more other courses. Yet I encountered no research based on this concept. In fact, the study of families as functioning groups did not exist, even though Charles Horton Cooley, a University of Michigan sociologist whose ideas link him to Mead's wing of the Chicago School, had in 1909 characterized families as primary groups, that is, the basic groups in which human nature is formed (Cooley, 1909). Psychologists studied parent-child relations, which in those days meant almost exclusively mother-child relations, and sociologists studied marriage. The actual study of family life was thus divided into these two parts which were mostly located in two different disciplines. Yet here were significant scholars such as Cooley and Burgess pointing to the fact that families live as groups. When Hess and I began our work, children mostly grew up in households with two parents, so that marital interaction, parent-child interaction, and sibling interaction were all happening concurrently and inter-relatedly in the same household. We believed that our interest in parent-child relations needed to be pursued in the whole family context, not as the segregated mother-child type of study that it had been up to that point.

Social Class and Family Life

In addition to the ideas of Thomas, Mead, Cooley, and Burgess, there were other intellectual sources that contributed to our work. Hess and I had both studied with W. Lloyd Warner and were now junior colleagues of his. Warner emphasized the importance of social class differences in American society, and from his work and the work of his colleagues such as Allison Davis and Robert J. Havighurst, we learned to be attentive to and think about social class differences in family life. In selecting our families for study, we purposely sought and obtained families from upper-middle, lower-middle, and working-class statuses. But I was also interested in understanding differences among families at any particular class level, and this required taking a family, rather than a social class, as the unit of analysis. Finally, among the various other suggestive ideas that contributed to our thinking I want specifically to mention the concept of group climate that had been introduced by University of Iowa social psychologists Kurt Lewin, Ronald Lippitt, and Ralph K. White. In the late 1930s they had studied experimentally three different types of leadership of boys club groups, each of which produced a different group climate. They called these "democratic," "authoritarian," and "laissez-faire" (Lewin, Lippitt and White, 1939; Lippitt and White, 1943). Their work focused our awareness that families, too, have different climates emotionally and socially, and it became part of our goal to find a way to capture those differences. We did not adopt their classification, because we did not assume that their categories were what would turn out to be most important in families. Rather, we worked inductively to try to develop our own understanding. Our concept of family theme captures the notion, and the titles of our five case study chapters characterize the climates of those particular families. We did not make any attempt to create a presumptively general or exhaustive classification.

WHAT FAMILY WORLDS *CONTRIBUTES*

Members of a family who inhabit a shared household over an extended period of time develop a group life that influences the individual life of each member. As George Herbert Mead pointed out, every member of a group has a distinctive position in and perspective on the group (Mead, 1934). This idea had not been applied to research on families, although Burgess probably had drawn on it when he conceptualized the family as a unity of interacting personalities. Mead's concept of individual perspectives in a group and Burgess's concept both carry the unmistakable implication that to understand a family, one must take account of the perspective of every member of the family.[2]

Then one must proceed to try to understand how those various perspectives encounter each other in interaction. Each child has his or her own perspective that cannot be discovered by asking either or both parents about it. Our case studies document this point clearly. While building on concepts formulated by Thomas, Cooley, Mead, Burgess, Warner, Lewin, Lippitt, White, and others, *Family Worlds* made a research advance in carrying out studies of families in which each member's perspective was studied–fathers as well as mothers, children as well as adults. Each member had the opportunity to communicate his or her family reality as he or she defined it. The researchers had the task of trying to understand how these various definitions meshed with or conflicted with each other. This methodological innovation required us to think about families as groups of members, which led to the theoretical formulation of family processes that was described in the summary of the book's contents.

We studied each family as a unit, as a functioning whole, as a case. In each case we tried to understand the meanings of each family member to all the other members, as well as the meanings that members were jointly creating. Because we saw families as groups creating meanings, and the research task as trying to understand those meanings and how they are generated, this kind of family research is essentially qualitative in nature. If it is possible to do quantitative research taking account of multiple members' perspectives, including those of young children, I am not familiar with such work. Most family research is not family research but research on one of the component relationships in a family. Either there is little recognition that families are groups whose members have individual perspectives on their family membership, or that approach is disregarded because it is not amenable to quantification and statistical analysis. To the extent that the latter perspective prevails, research in the field is being driven by a preference for certain methods rather than by the questions that merit attention. In my judgment, research questions should have priority;

methods adopted should be those appropriate for the questions. Questions should not be restrictively tailored to fit methods.

Theoretical Advances

Our methodology has made possible and has led to certain theoretical advances that are incorporated in the five family processes that we formulated. Let me expand briefly on some of their implications.

1. A family produces individuals as well as relationships. (I call your attention to the fact that society has an interest in the kinds of individuals that a family produces as well as in certain aspects of the relationships that it produces and that produce the family.) That individuality or separateness and that relatedness or connectedness are constitutive of family interaction in all its aspects, including communication and non-communication. With this formulation we have combined a social psychological or microsocial perspective with a child development and human development perspective into a single framework. This brings into focus the fact that a child develops into a person in its family not simply as part of a mother-child relationship but as a participant in a multi-personal web of interaction.[3]

2. We further specify the nature of that interaction when we say that life in a family can be regarded as the family's effort to attain a satisfactory congruence of images through the exchange of suitable testimony. This formulation builds upon and extends George Herbert Mead's concept of human action but in a way that is particular to families. Our formulation takes account of the fact that every member of a family has a particular kind of interest in every other member of the family so that each is endeavoring to communicate those several interests, while also receiving communications of interest that are often not compatible or congruent. Every member of a family is pulling and pushing and being pushed and pulled by the other members, each, in the process, forming a self-image and images of the others who are likewise forming their images of all. And all this effort is communicated in words and demonstrated in actions that are interpreted by the several others as to their appropriateness and desirability.

3. Family interaction as I have just described it creates a family group life, and that group life is not all over the map but tends to have a certain focus, and we called that focus a family theme. The concept of family theme is a way of trying to get a purchase on the corporate character of a family's life, but we went beyond this and stated that each family generates its own local culture, a proposition illustrated in our case studies. We were the first, I believe, to apply the culture concept to the individual

family level of organization. Previously, the concept had been used only at the macrosocial level.

4. A family does not construct its own culture out of whole cloth. It draws selectively on the culture of the wider society. There are things going on in society that families like and want to participate in, to bring into the home, and there are things that they do not like and want to screen out. And we introduced the concept of family boundaries to conceptualize this effort of families to regulate the interactions and communications coming into the family from the world outside the family.

5. Finally, we considered that age and sex are aspects of the human condition that shape family life but they are not aspects that can be considered as self-evident in their implications. Rather, we argued that each family must develop its own interpretations, its own meanings for these aspects of the human condition. Families may draw on meanings in the wider culture, but those meanings are far from uniform in a complex society and thus there are many meanings to sort out and to choose from.

In sum, we conceptualize families as complex active agents in constructing their own family life, and we conceptualize each family member, each child as well as each adult, as an agent whose actions contribute to shaping that family's interdependent life together–and apart. *Family Worlds* has influenced the work of family researchers in a variety of fields. In 1965, Salvador Minuchin wrote to this author: "Dear Dr. Handel: I read with interest your book, co-authored with Dr. Hess, *Family Worlds*, and it has been instrumental in the development of some of my ideas while working on our project for the disadvantaged child. . . . I would very much appreciate receiving some more copies of your excellent article 'Psychological Study of Whole Families' " (Minuchin, 1965). In 1994, L. Edna Rogers noted: "The influence of the family dimensions laid out by Hess and Handel has provided a foundation for most later models— for example, Kantor and Lehr's model of family processes, Fitzpatrick's typologies based in turn on Kantor and Lehr's work, David Reiss's dimensions of family, aspects of Minuchin's, and Lidz's work in the clinical area" (Rogers, 1994). Rosenblatt and Fischer have written: "Many influential case studies of families were published in the early volumes of *Family Process*. Books by Hess and Handel (1959) and by Handel (1967) were also influential, drawing the connections among case approaches in psychology, family therapy, and anthropology. The family case approach has been and still is central to the development of family systems theory, and family systems theory has been a key to inspiring qualitative studies of families as systems" (Rosenblatt and Fischer, 1993, p. 169).

Whitchurch and Constantine (1993) wrote: "Hess and Handel published the first in-depth empirical study of the family as a system. Their focus on the family as a 'psychosocial organization' marks a milestone in the development of family systems theory research that has been too often overlooked in recent years. Hess and Handel's *Family Worlds* is at the interface between systems and symbolic interactionist theories of family interaction" (p. 340). After summarizing the five processes of family functioning formulated in *Family Worlds*, LaRossa and Reitzes (1993) state: "Noteworthy is the fact that these five processes, which were delineated over 30 years ago and which are based on symbolic interactionism, have stood the test of time and in one form or another may be found in some of the most influential writings on the family. For example, the first definition—establishing a pattern of separateness and connectedness—is one dimension of the 'circumplex model' of family life (see Olson, 1989)" (p. 150).

In addition to this theoretical influence on later researchers the methodology has been explicitly applied in such varied empirical studies as those of families in which the husband/father has suffered a heart attack (Speedling, 1982); the impact of husband/father's work on family functioning (Piotrkowski, 1979); and the influence of family interaction on the school performance of poor black children (Clark, 1983). Thus, researchers working on a variety of problems have seen that utilizing a whole-family methodology results in insights and understanding less likely to be gained by other methodologies because the problem being studied involves multiple family members and is embedded in their construction of their social world. While not all problems lend themselves to this methodology, many more could be. (For additional discussion, see Handel, 1994, pp. 76-79.)

The family institution has changed greatly in the 35 years since *Family Worlds* was published. In 1991, only 26% of the 94 million households in the United States consisted of two parents and their own biological children age 18 or under (U.S. Bureau of the Census, 1992). While this is greatly reduced from the percentage of families with that composition when Hess and I began our work, it is still a very significant number. Further, our methodology is not restricted to families of that composition. It is as applicable to stepfamilies, single-parent families, and indeed families of any composition. While modifications in research procedure would have to be made for families of particular composition, the logic of the methodology is not restricted to two-parent, first-marriage families. A study of single parent families would either require inclusion of non-custodial parents living in separate households or would be restricted to the co-residential family members, depending on the research problem and/or available resources. Similarly, a study of step-families might be restricted to the co-resident parent, step-parent and children or it might include the non-resident parents, a goal that would be particularly important in shared custody situations. One way in which whole-family methodology can be used in studying contemporary families is exemplified in Judith Stacey's valuable ethnography of two "postmodern" families (Stacey, 1990).

No One Person Speaks for a Family

No member of any family is a sufficient source of information for that family. A family constructs its life from the multiple perspectives of its members, and an adequate understanding requires that those perspectives be obtained from their multiple sources. How this principle is implemented in particular projects will depend on the nature of the project. Infants cannot, obviously, be interviewed, and they cannot be said to have a perspective. But to study how a couple begins to socialize their newborn baby requires not only interviewing each parent about their feelings, hopes, perceptions, and aspirations for their child but also observing the infant alone and with each parent in various situations.[4] In families that have experienced multiple divorces or terminated cohabitations an adequate understanding may depend upon how thoroughly the researcher wishes or is able to pursue the multiple sequential partners, scattered in location.

In a front-page story dramatizing such families, *The New York Times* presented an account of a woman who married, had two children, divorced, had a live-in boyfriend for three years, kicked him out, moved with her children into the home of a divorced man whom she intended to marry, and departed with her children when that relationship did not work out (Chira, 1995). To understand how the children were shaped by their family life would require interviewing not only them and their mother, but their father, the mother's subsequent live-in boyfriend, and her subsequent co-residential husband-to-be, whose disciplinary style clashed with that of the children's mother. All three residential arrangements and all three men are part of the family experience of the children of this mother, and we need to know their input not only as recounted by the mother and the children but from the perspectives of the men who participated sequentially as members of this family.

Limited resources may make such research projects rare, but the first resource required is a researcher's recognition of the importance of such research, and the second resource necessary is a commitment to undertake the work. After that, a supportive research environment and, finally, funding are necessary.

Hess and I undertook the study that resulted in *Family Worlds* because we perceived a glaring disjunction between the writings of such theorists as Cooley, Mead, and Burgess, who adumbrated a logic of whole-family methodology, and the prevailing practice of studying child development in the restricted framework of mother-child relationships. Later researchers such as Piotrkowski (1979) and Speedling (1982) have illustrated how whole-family methodology can be utilized in problem areas other than child development and socialization, and Stacey (1990) has shown how it can be employed in studies of contemporary families whose membership is both shifting and is extended beyond that of the nuclear family. Each of these studies is innovative, even as it incorporates aspects of extant methodologies. Sufficient work has now been done to show how whole-family methodology can be adapted to diverse problems and situations and to demonstrate its value. If new generations of researchers recognize its value, they will continue to innovate and continue to close gaps left by their predecessors.

NOTES

1. In addition, a German translation, *Familienwelten*, was published in 1975 (Dusseldorf: Padagogischer Verlag Schwann) and was in print for 10 years.

2. Perspective may be defined as "The values, beliefs, attitudes, and meanings that provide the framework and point of view from which an individual views a situation. A perspective consists of assumptions that are usually not consciously defined, but which influence what the individual perceives and how he interprets his perceptions" (Theodorson & Theodorson, 1969).

3. Sibling relationships, for example, are not constructed only by the children, although they may be the primary actors.

4. For a more extended discussion of this example, see Handel (1994).

REFERENCES

Bulmer, M. (1984). *The Chicago school of sociology.* Chicago: The University of Chicago Press.

Burgess, E. W. (1926). "The family as a unity of interacting personalities," *Family, 7*, 3-9.

Chira, S. (1995). Struggling to find stability when divorce is a pattern. *The New York Times*, March 19, 1995, p. 1.

Clark, R. M. (1983). *Family life and school achievement.* Chicago: The University of Chicago Press.

Cooley, C. H. (1909). *Social organization.* New York: Scribner.

Faris, R. E. L. (1967). *Chicago sociology —1920-1932.* San Francisco: Chandler.

Handel, G. (1965). Psychological study of whole families. *Psychological Bulletin, 63*, 19-41.

Handel, G. (Ed.) (1967). *The psychosocial interior of the family*. Chicago: Aldine.

Handel, G. (1986). Beyond sibling rivalry: An empirically grounded theory of sibling relationships. In P. A. Adler and P. Adler (Eds.), *Sociological Studies of Child Development*, vol.1, Greenwich, CT: JAI.

Handel, G. (1991). Case study in family research. In J. R. Feagin, A. M. Orum, and G. Sjoberg (Eds.), *A case for the case study* (pp. 244-268). Chapel Hill: University of North Carolina Press.

Handel, G. (1994). Qualitative study of whole families in a time of great change. In G. Handel & G. G. Whitchurch (Eds.), *The psychosocial interior of the family*, 4th ed. (pp. 69-85). New York: Aldine de Gruyter.

Hess, R. D. and Handel, G. (1959). *Family Worlds*. Chicago: The University of Chicago Press.

LaRossa, R. & Reitzes, D. (1993). Symbolic interactionism and family studies. In P. G. Boss, W. J. Doherty, R. LaRossa, W. R. Schumm, & S. K. Steinmetz (Eds.), *Sourcebook of family theories and methods* (pp. 135-163). New York: Plenum.

Lewin, K., R. Lippitt, & R. K. White (1939). Patterns of aggressive behavior in experimentally created social climates. *Journal of Social Psychology, 10*, 271-299.

Lippitt, R., and R. K. White. (1943). The social climate of children's groups. In R. G. Barker, J. S. Kounin, & H. F. Wright (eds.), *Child Behavior and Development* (pp. 485-508). New York: McGraw-Hill.

Mead, George Herbert (1934). *Mind, self and society*. Chicago: The University of Chicago Press.

Minuchin, S. (1965). Personal communication, March 26, 1965.

Olson, D. (1989). Circumplex model and family health. In C. N. Ramsey, Jr. (Ed.), *Family systems in medicine*. New York: Guilford.

Piotrkowski, C. (1979). *Work and the family system*. New York: The Free Press.

Rogers, L. E. (1994). *Family worlds*. Talk presented to Commission on Family Communication, annual meeting, Speech Communication Association, New Orleans, LA, Nov. 19, 1994.

Rosenblatt, P. & Fischer, L. R. (1993). Qualitative family research. In P. G. Boss, W. J. Doherty, R. LaRossa, W. R. Schumm, & S. K. Steinmetz (Eds.), *Sourcebook of family theories and methods* (pp. 167-177). New York: Plenum.

Speedling, E. J. (1982). *Heart attack. The family response at home and in the hospital*. New York and London: Tavistock.

Stacey, J. (1990). *Brave new families*. New York: Basic.

Theodorson, G. & Theodorson, A. K. (1969). *A modern dictionary of sociology*. New York: Crowell.

Whitchurch, G. G & Constantine, L. (1993). Systems theory. In P. G. Boss, W. J. Doherty, R. LaRossa, W. R. Schumm, & S. K. Steinmetz (Eds.), *Sourcebook of family theories and methods* (pp. 325-352). New York: Plenum.

U.S. Bureau of the Census (1992). *Current Population Reports*, Series P 20 No. 458. *Household and Family Characteristics: 1991*. Washington: DC: U.S. Government Printing Office.

Narrative Accounts, Generative Fathering, and Family Life Education

David C. Dollahite
Alan J. Hawkins
Sean E. Brotherson

SUMMARY. This article suggests that theory and story can be effectively linked in interpretive family life education programs and illustrates this potential by discussing how personal narrative accounts of fathers' encounters with their children can be used to understand and encourage good fathering (herein referred to as *generative fathering*). The article (a) presents a theory of how fathers change and the implications of this theory for the use of fathers' narrative accounts in interpretive family life education, (b) briefly discusses the concept of generative fathering and presents a conceptual framework for understanding and encouraging generative fathering,

David C. Dollahite and Alan J. Hawkins are Assistant Professors, Family Sciences, Brigham Young University, Provo, UT 84602-5525. Sean E. Brotherson is a doctoral student, Human Development and Family Studies, Oregon State University, Corvallis, OR 97331-5102.

The authors are grateful to Jennifer Call, Bing Dao, Marty Erickson, Kathy Froerer, Sandra Jensen, Rachelle Knight, Warren Price, and Qing Zeng for assistance in interviewing fathers. The authors also appreciate the helpful comments on previous drafts by Ralph LaRossa, Rob Palkovitz, Wes Burr, Jane Gilgun, and two anonymous reviewers.

This is a revision of a paper presented at the 1994 Theory Construction and Research Methods Workshop of the National Council on Family Relations in Minneapolis, MN, November 9, 1994.

[Haworth co-indexing entry note]: "Narrative Accounts, Generative Fathering, and Family Life Education." Dollahite, David C., Alan J. Hawkins, and Sean E. Brotherson. Co-published simultaneously in *Marriage & Family Review* (The Haworth Press, Inc.) Vol. 24, No. 3/4, 1996, pp. 349-368; and: *The Methods and Methodologies of Qualitative Family Research* (ed: Marvin B. Sussman, and Jane F. Gilgun) The Haworth Press, Inc., 1996, pp. 349-368. Single or multiple copies of this article are available for a fee from The Haworth Document Delivery Service [1-800-342-9678, 9:00 a.m. - 5:00 p.m. (EST). E-mail address: getinfo@haworth.com].

349

and (c) illustrates the potential utility of narrative accounts in encouraging generative fathering in family life education with accounts collected from fathers. Although the method applied herein is not, in the strictest sense, qualitative research, it illustrates how qualitative methodology can be applied to family life education. *[Article copies available for a fee from The Haworth Document Delivery Service: 1-800-342-9678. E-mail address: getinfo@haworth.com]*

KEYWORDS. Fathering, Generative fathering, Family life education, Narratives of change

Family scholars and practitioners can benefit from efforts to link methods of scholarly inquiry with methods of educational practice. Qualitative methods may be particularly helpful in bridging the gap between research and intervention. In this paper we suggest that one type of qualitative approach, personal narrative accounts, may be especially helpful in family life education. The stories people tell about their own experiences, along with the meanings they attach to those stories, constitute what we call *narrative accounts*. We draw upon our theories of fathering and a collection of narrative accounts we have gathered to illustrate this approach. Thus, this article describes an emerging qualitative method that has the potential both to advance knowledge *and* to encourage change. Therefore, although the method applied herein is not, in the strictest sense, qualitative research, it illustrates how qualitative methodology can be applied to family life education. It demonstrates how theory, method, and practice can relate to each other effectively by showing the way our theories of generative fathering and father change can be woven together with narrative accounts to encourage good fathering in family life education.

We discuss issues of fathering, the interpretive paradigm in family life education, our theory of how fathers change, and the implications of this theory for the use of narrative accounts in interpretive family life education. Next, we briefly present our conceptual framework for understanding and encouraging generative fathering. Then we illustrate the use of narrative accounts in promoting generative fathering with accounts collected from fathers of children with disabilities. We conclude with some implications for family life educators.

THE NEED TO UNDERSTAND AND ENCOURAGE
GOOD FATHERING

Fatherhood recently became one of the most significant social issues in America (Blankenhorn, 1995) and an important conceptual and empirical domain in American social science (Gerson, 1993; Hood, 1993; Marsiglio, 1995; Snarey, 1993). Recent research has provided us with important information on fathers and fathering in general, and the importance of emotional and physical nurturance and support in particular (Snarey, 1993). Yet, much remains to be discovered about these interactions and the contributions that fathers make to children's development and well-being. Some scholars are suggesting that family scholarship has tended to unduly emphasize fathers' deficits (Doherty, 1991; Hawkins & Dollahite, 1994; Hawkins & Dollahite, in press). Despite the research that demonstrates men are capable caregivers to their children and important to their children's development (Biller, 1993), fathers are usually painted with broad strokes as uncaring, uncommitted, uninvolved, and unmotivated to change (see Blankenhorn, 1995). While these terms tragically describe some fathers, they are inaccurate for many others (Brotherson, 1995).

Little research has provided examples of good fathering or investigated specifically *how to help* fathers better connect with and care for their children. Family life educators will benefit from concrete images of fathers caring for and connecting to their children. Narrative accounts can fill a void in the scholarly and applied work on good fathering. They illustrate ways that fathers connect with and care for their children and suggest the personal meanings, feelings, and motivations embedded in these paternal actions.

Our personal and professional task as scholar-practitioners is to work both to understand and encourage *generative fathering* (Snarey, 1993), which is *fathering that responds to and actively seeks to meet the needs of one's children across the life cycle and in different circumstances.* To do this we have embarked on a project that involves listening to stories of how and why fathers connect with and care for their children. We want to use these narrative accounts (a) to understand what fathers are doing to connect with and care for children in families, and (b) to encourage fathers to learn and apply principles of generative fathering. We believe the use of personal narrative accounts holds promise as a way to encourage generative fathering.

USING NARRATIVE ACCOUNTS OF FATHERING IN FAMILY LIFE EDUCATION

Narrative accounts of father-child interaction can be usefully employed in family life education. For some it may be unclear what relevance a collection of narrative accounts may have for the family life educator whose mission is to facilitate healthy change in families (Arcus, 1990).

Most family life education consists of defined programs of activity and instruction from family "experts" who impart information and practices established by behavioral scientists as promoting individual and family well-being. The assumptions are that general laws of human and family behavior exist and are discoverable, and that these laws when taught will be a catalyst for positive change (Morgaine, 1992).

Increasingly, however, scholars and educators in a post-modern era are questioning the universal application of this instrumental/technical paradigm (Braybrooke, 1987; Morgaine, 1992), and are exploring alternative paradigms. Making the use of narrative accounts central to family life education fits well with one of those emerging alternative paradigms—the interpretive paradigm, founded on the human need to understand self and others (Braybrooke, 1987).

In educational settings where the interpretive paradigm is central, reflection on the meanings of every day life is a critical learning and motivational tool. As participants come to see the meanings that underlie human actions they are better able to understand their own problems and challenges and take appropriate actions to improve. Reflection on one's own experiences is most common in this kind of educational activity, but meanings and understanding can come from the narrative accounts of others, as well.

Narrative accounts are less didactic than scientific "facts" and invite listeners/readers to reflect on the meaning of the stories for themselves, with the frequent result of greater personal understanding and motivation for action, drawing from them answers that best meet their unique situations. Because men in classroom and group settings are sometimes reluctant to share personal experiences, a ready collection of narrative accounts of generative fathering may be especially well suited to educational programs for men.

A THEORY OF HOW FATHERS CHANGE
AND HOW NARRATIVE ACCOUNTS
COULD BE USED IN FAMILY LIFE EDUCATION

The possibility that men often learn and grow in ways different from women suggests the value of alternative methods to help them accomplish positive growth. In this section we provide a more detailed discussion of our theory of change; that is, how men (in general) and fathers (in particular) change and grow as well as our thoughts about how narrative accounts can help facilitate growth toward generative fathering. These ideas flow from our experience as family life educators and therapists and from the findings of the literature on change in relation to narrative.

There is a growing body of literature in the social and behavioral sciences on the narrative approach to understanding people and helping people "story" their lives in more healing and useful ways (Brotherson, 1995; Day, 1991; Dollahite, Hawkins, Brotherson, & Jensen, 1994; Josselson & Lieblich, 1993; Hawkins, Dollahite, Jensen, & Brotherson, 1994; Kotre, 1984; Mair, 1988; Martin, Hagestad, & Diedrick, 1988; McAdams, 1985; Palus, 1993; Parry & Doan, 1994; Polkinghorne, 1988; Riessman, 1993; White & Epston, 1990). For example, Palus (1993) found that lasting transformative experiences in adulthood are narrative in nature and are incorporated into the "life story" of the person, and McAdams (1985) found that identity is formed and changed in a "life story." Since people "live in narrative," using their own and other people's narrative accounts is a powerful way to encourage change in important areas of life (White & Epston, 1990).

The literature suggests that for psychosocial change to be deep, meaningful, and lasting, it must involve *affective, behavioral, cognitive,* and *ethical* dimensions (Mahoney, 1991). Narrative accounts of generative fathering can be particularly helpful in facilitating men's growth toward generative fathering since they typically include and facilitate all four of these dimensions. Stories tend to influence people so powerfully because they prompt reflection (cognitive), touch hearts (affective), provoke moral examination (ethical), and provide a model for action (behavioral).

Cognitive Dimension of Change

A key component of growth for fathers, and men in general, seems to be the process of cognitive appraisal and absorption. We believe that in order to prompt positive change practitioners must do more than provide simple formulaic solutions and suggestions. Many fathers will not move toward change if their creative instincts are not engaged; they want the opportunity for problem solving and talking initiative. Narratives are inherently interesting, drawing a person in. Stories at once take us from the comfort zone of our own lived experience and place us in a different setting–encouraging us to see things from other perspectives. A story illustrates a possibility on which fathers can build to find their own creative solutions in the fathering experience. The chance to think creatively and feel a sense of ownership in the solutions can encourage fathers to pursue them even at substantial personal cost. They expand their abilities as caregivers and find validation through the rewards of parenting.

As fathers search for answers to how to connect with and care for their children at different developmental periods, they may not find the answers they need in their own past experience. Some are new fathers and even experienced fathers continually face new situations; divorced fathers, step-fathers, adolescent fathers, and others cannot always rely on their own lived experiences for guidance. Stories from other fathers can help fill in the gaps.

Affective Dimension of Change

Narrative accounts naturally draw an individual into an emotional inter-action. Fathers sometimes need a strong stimulus to cause them to feel the need for change. In reaching people emotionally, stories can act as the spark often necessary to trigger personal transformation.

The messages found in narrative accounts are also less likely to be rejected since stories can bypass the cognitive defenses that may lead to the rejection of others' prescription of behavior. This aspect of story can help in working with those fathers who argue with theories and data or who manifest other forms of "resistance" to other, more rational-empiri-cal educational approaches. If a person's heart is touched, he may be more likely to move towards behavioral change. The transformative potential of narrative perhaps can be summed up best by a Hasidic proverb: "Give people a fact or an idea and you enlighten their minds; tell them a story and you touch their souls" (Chinen, 1992, p. 2).

Ethical Dimension of Change

It is important to respect most fathers' underlying desire to improve and connect meaningfully with their children. Narrative accounts reinforce this desire and help them to identify with others who have articulated their regard for good fathering.

Because stories are both descriptive and potentially prescriptive, indi-viduals can choose to interpret a story in a way that will meaningfully address their own experience as well as their ethical commitments. Narra-tive accounts are much more complex than a laundry list of things to do and yet much more accessible than most forms of social science informa-tion. They allow a person to identify what is most meaningful to him or her in a personal way and provide a vehicle for ethical reflection. Stories are "teaching mirrors" in the sense that each person comes to a story from his or her own perspective and takes from the story a unique message. Thus, family life educators can use narrative accounts to encourage ethical reflection without sounding preachy.

Behavioral Dimension of Change

Cognitive, affective, and ethical insight in fathers can take place dramatically, but in regard to fathering behavior, incremental change is likely, with gradual revising and re-formulating behavior in the process of daily activities. Many men resist quick transformation, seeing it as inconsistent with their self-image. Stories do not demand immediate change. They allow time to consider inner reactions privately and to formulate a comfortable response. A person who is slow to change can read or hear a story, remember it, digest it, and take time to apply it personally in a way that fits this need.

In relationship to behavioral changes, many fathers like to refer to a pattern, a blueprint, or model of thought and action. Story offers a model for consideration. It can be adapted by a father to the needs and desires of his own family situation.

Any effort to promote positive change in fathers to help them become more generative must recognize the wide variety of factors that influence fathers in their parenting experiences. Not only is there a broad variety of fathers in terms of cultural, ethnic, socioeconomic, and religious backgrounds, but fathers also have a variety of life experiences and live in varied circumstances. The value of narrative in reaching such a great variety of fathers lies in the fact that narrative itself is responsive to tremendous varieties of individual experience. Any number of people can read the same story and each come away with something that is personally meaningful, but ultimately different from what each of the others experienced. Because brief narratives can be numerous enough to represent many socio-cultural circumstances and problems and solutions, the use of narrative accounts may be a particularly effective way to help a variety of fathers change behaviorally (see Lovrien, in Johnson & Palm, 1992, p. 146-151).

A CONCEPTUAL MODEL OF FATHERING AS GENERATIVE WORK

This section presents our conceptual framework for understanding and encouraging generative fathering. Space only permits a very brief discussion of our ideas about fathering here; for a more complete discussion of the model see Dollahite, Hawkins and Brotherson (in press).

Generativity is the process of reaching out beyond the self to nurture those who are younger, helping to connect generations (Erikson, 1963, 1982). We refer to this caring activity when done by fathers as "generative fathering" (Snarey, 1993). While our use of the term *generative* derives from Erikson's and Snarey's developmental work, it also has a broader meaning for us.

We conceptualize generative fathering as ethical-stewardship-development-relationship *work*. We use Bellah et al.'s (1985) meaning of work as a *calling*, rather than as a job or career. With this meaning, "work constitutes a practical ideal of activity and character that makes a person's work morally inseparable from his or her life" (p. 66).

The central concepts in our model are the responsibilities of generative work and the corresponding capabilities that fathers generally bring to this generative work. We identify eight fundamental responsibilities and capabilities which, as a heuristic for assisting practitioners and fathers, begin with the same letter. We suggest that generative fathering involves the call and capacity to:

commit–to bind oneself in a relationship of obligation to a child.

choose–to make decisions in day-to-day life that meet the needs of children.

create–to meet a child's material needs through work that produces and/or procures resources the child needs for healthy development.

consecrate–to dedicate a major portion of one's time, talents, resources, and energies, to the well-being of the next generation in a way which often involves sacrifice.

care–to provide for children what they need at the time.

change–to change and adapt the care given as children grow and as the father matures in his ability to respond to need.

connect–to form healthy lasting attachments with a child (and the child's mother).

communicate–to relate with children by sharing meaning with them both verbally and non-verbally.

There are, of course, many other important elements to good fathering and we make no claim that the concepts discussed above include all of the most important things that good fathers do. We do think that, together, these eight ideas represent critical dimensions of good fathering. Brotherson (1995) recently tested this theory using narrative accounts and found support for these concepts in the stories fathers tell about their relationships with their children.

METHOD

Narrative accounts seemed particularly appropriate to both learn about and encourage good fathering given the advantages of qualitative research mentioned by Miles and Huberman (1994), including natural setting, local groundedness, richness and holism of data, flexibility, emphasis on meaning, and usefulness for hypothesis development and testing.

We have been involved in an ongoing project to collect personal narrative accounts that promote generative fathering. For this study, we sought particularly fathers who had experienced special challenges in their nurturing and caring, and who might therefore be more likely to provide narrative accounts that motivate, inspire, teach, and encourage other fathers. Snarey (1993) found that fathers who had come close to losing their children experienced what he called "generativity chill" in which there is a heightened emphasis on fathering. Thus, we focused on fathers with at least one child with some type of disability or special need.

Sample and Procedure

Participants in this study consisted of 25 married fathers living in central Utah, most with at least one disabled child. Most were involved in a local support program for such families. Participants were mainly white, middle-SES fathers in their late twenties to late thirties, usually with two or three children. Participants included one African-American father and one Chinese father (in the U.S. as a student).

Questions were developed, pre-tested and refined. Interviews were conducted by the authors and a small group of trained student interviewers who participated in a research seminar on fathering. The research interviews were then conducted from late 1993 to early 1995 in the homes of participants in one to two-hour sessions. All of the interviews were tape-recorded and then transcribed to capture the nuances of the participants' own language.

Participants were told about the nature of the research and were specifically asked to tell stories and provide the personal meanings they found in those stories. The participants were asked open-ended interview questions about their relationship with their own fathers and with their children, and the personal meaning of these experiences to them. Most fathers were able to tell a number of meaningful stories, some said they had difficulty recalling specific experiences with their fathers, and some only provided descriptive statements about their relationships with their father and/or their children. The interviews were conducted in the spirit of being students of those fathers participating in the study, consistent with Josselson's and Lieblich's (1993) ideal of "listening to people talk in their own terms about what had been significant in their lives" (p. ix).

The fathers agreed to participate in order to further research into fathering and were not offered any monetary compensation, but at the end of the interview participants were told that they would receive a tape-recording and transcript of the interview in appreciation for their involvement.

Analyses

The research design was interpretive, intended to provide both description and interpretation by both the researchers and the fathers themselves. After the stories were collected, the fathers' narrative accounts were read and explored for themes about how fathers acted to care for children and how they understood the caring experience from their own perspective. Second, the fathers' narrative accounts were analyzed in order to test whether the concepts in a model of generative fathering are present in fathers' lived experience. Finally, the narratives were evaluated relative to our theory of change.

Reflexivity. The issue of reflexivity in qualitative research recognizes that a researcher acts from a subjective, interpretive position in the research process (Hammersley & Atkinson, 1983; Riessman, 1993). Similarly, individual interpretation by the participant is inseparable from his narrative presentation of life events (Widdershoven, 1993). Our role as scholar-practitioners, as understood in this study, was not to objectively separate ourselves from the stories and participants, but rather to be intimately involved in collecting, relating to, and seeking to understand the narrative accounts (including interpretations) given to us by respondent fathers in order to provide narrative accounts that could be used by educators. By explicitly recognizing this reflexive position as researchers, we have sought to account for and minimize the effect of our biases, but we realize that our efforts to interpret fathers' narrative experiences are subjective and so strive for "believability, not certitude, for enlargement of understanding rather than control" (Stivers, 1993, p. 424).

Insights gained from studying the narratives were used to connect with our theory about fathers' caring experience and how men change. Making such connections can increase the potential scholarly and educational value of research that uses narrative; Josselson and Lieblich (1993) said,

"Story cannot stand alone but must be linked to some theoretical context or previous knowledge" (p. xii). The collection of research narratives and the development of a conceptual model was an interactive process (Taylor & Bogdan, 1984). The narratives gathered in the research provided the richness of detail and contextual experience necessary to enrich our theory of change and to give examples for family life education involving fathers.

Overall, a number of themes emerged from the analyses of the narrative accounts that fathers provided, including (a) preparing children to deal with difficulties, (b) balancing occupational and fathering work, (c) competence in responding to childrens' needs, (d) making commitments to meet children's needs, and (e) sacrificing for children. For more detailed information about procedures and analyses, see Brotherson (1995).

ILLUSTRATIONS OF THE USE OF NARRATIVE ACCOUNTS TO ENCOURAGE GENERATIVE FATHERING

The five narrative accounts presented below provide both story (what happened) and the narrator's interpretive meaning. The interpretive meanings are highlighted in italics. Along with each story, we will briefly discuss some of the elements of our theory of generative fathering (change, commitment, care, etc.), and suggest ways the story relates to the elements of change in our theory (cognitive, affective, ethical, behavioral) that can be used in family life education. The interpretive approach calls for emphasis on activities that encourage exploration of personal meaning. Thus we provide the conceptual articulation only as *a* possible meaning, not as *the* meaning. However, we believe that many men do appreciate having some additional frameworks for meaning beyond their own personal perceptions; therefore, we suggest that family life educators can benefit from the theoretical implications of the narratives we provide. In the interest of space, the discussion of each story will usually focus on only two or three of the eight elements of generative fathering and one or two of the four dimensions of change. Since the interpretative approach is to focus on meaning and self-reflection in family life education, questions raised by the narrative accounts that could be posed to members of a group or classroom will be suggested. We also suggest some questions meant to encourage storytelling by fathers and family life educators.

In offering examples of narratives linked to theory, we note several qualifications. First, our purpose is not to provide a detailed presentation of our empirical results, but rather to illustrate how narrative accounts collected by family scholars can be used in family life education. Second, it is not easy to match narrative accounts with discrete topics and themes because stories are often multi-thematic. Third, we recognize that our use of a story to illustrate a specific idea may not make the same point for every father listening; different people can react to or interpret the same story differently. Fourth, the stories we selected for this article were not the most dramatic or moving stories in our collection. Rather, we chose fairly prosaic, simple, and commonplace stories because we thought most fathers would be able to relate to them. Fifth, these stories are not designed to entertain or provide the kind of humorous anecdotes that many successful educators employ, but rather to encourage reflection and discussion. Finally, we realize that readers may develop different and equally valid interpretations for these stories in family life education; we merely illustrate possibilities.

Narrative Account 1

> The most painful experience I've had with Jil (not her real name) was when she was about three or four. We were living in a neighborhood where kids would tell her that they could not play with her because she did not have a white face. They would spit on her even though I was standing there, because she was black. *That hurt. . . . It was painful for me because I thought I had marched, been spit on, kicked, beat up, jailed, called all kinds of names in the 1960s, and through the civil rights movement so that this should not be happening. Particularly with neighbors that we go to church with. If it was said to me, that would be fine, but not to my kids, not to my wife. I learned that I had to prepare my kids to deal with all kinds of people, no matter where they are. Also, to understand that it's not their problem and they shouldn't take the other person's problem, who is bigoted or narrow-minded, away from them and put it on themselves.*

Theory. Generative fathering involves preparing children to deal with a variety of difficulties and challenges. The father's *care* for his daughter is evident. He realized he had not prepared her adequately for the challenges of living in a racist society. He recognized a need to *change* and *committed* himself to greater diligence in terms of helping his daughter be able to dismiss bigoted words and actions as reflections on her self-worth. His caring and change may supply more supportive conditions for his daughter's social development and self-concept.

Education. This story particularly illustrates the *cognitive* and *behavioral* dimensions of change and suggests at least these questions: Have I done enough to prepare my children for the difficulties they will encounter in their unique circumstances? What more can I do to teach my children about the world and how to face its challenges? A storytelling question would be: Have you had an experience in which you tried to help your child through a particularly challenging situation?

Narrative Account 2

> I drove a truck for a while *and I think that contributed to our being distant.* Lisa felt like she didn't have a daddy. I came home and told her to clean something up and she said, "You can't tell me what to do. You're not my daddy." *That ripped me apart. I don't think it was really meant, but it hurt.* I stopped driving a truck really fast and brought myself back home. *She was more or less saying, "You should be home."*

Theory. Generative fathering involves careful (and often difficult) balancing of occupational and fathering work, an issue that surfaces repeatedly in our narratives. This father's *commitment* to being there for his daughter and an honest (but painful) *communication* between them encouraged him to make a difficult *choice* to alter his work situation (at the expense of greater income). His daughter's words were powerful in influencing his subsequent decision to be home more to strengthen his *connection* to his daughter.

Education. In an economy where too often fathers have been required to sacrifice their family lives to employment demands, stories that model putting families first can help others to cultivate such commitments and actions in their own lives. This story has a powerful *affective* dimension ("You're not my daddy anymore") and poses an important *ethical* dilemma since most fathers will not be in a position to simply change jobs that easily. Questions that could be posed include: Have you ever had your child question your love by suggesting that if you cared you would be there more? How can you help your child know that you care for them when you can't be there as much as you would like?

Narrative Account 3

> I think Michael was probably about two and . . . Karen was working and I was home when I wasn't in class. One day Karen needed to go into work and Michael was sick. His fever just kept on getting higher and higher. It was really scary because he was thrashing around the floor and was really uncomfortable. I called the doctor and was a little bit nervous about the whole thing. He had a fever of about 105

degrees and was just burning up. I took care of him and put him in the bathtub in lukewarm water, brought the fever down, and I remember that Michael just wanted to be held. I remember that I just held him all night long. He didn't want anybody else to hold him. *I felt pretty close to him at that time.*

Theory. Father-child relationships are strengthened when fathers competently respond to a child's needs. This father's response to his son's critical health need avoided a potentially serious situation. After the health concern was resolved, his son desired further *connection*, wanting to be held all night long for comfort. This facilitated their attachment to each other. Although few words were expressed, the father's love and *commitment* to his son were clearly *communicated*. Although we often associate caring for sick or injured children with maternal care, this account shows other fathers ways to strengthen their relationships with their own children.

Education. To use this story, an educator could focus on the meaning of caring for children when they are ill, injured, or otherwise experiencing frightening difficulties. The story can initiate discussion about *behavioral* competence: How can I become a more competent parent given the various problems, issues, dilemmas, and choices that will face my child? The story has an *affective* dimension since the father experienced both fear for his child and emotional closeness because of the experience. Possible questions include: How have you dealt with the fears you have about your child and his/her future? Have you had times where you did not feel competent to care for your child?

Narrative Account 4

They give it back. As much as you give your parents, they find ways to give it back. Seven years ago I was in a partnership in construction and it went sour. The company got into a bad situation and, without going into a lot of detail, the bottom line was that I left. All I had known was construction for five or six years, I didn't know anything else, and construction was gone. Basically what ended up happening is that I ended up losing a home from it, was unemployed and didn't have money. *I learned from my family that they are survivors. You face situations. Nothing is ever critical. There's always a tomorrow. You're not going to die, etc. Yes, it might be important or a sticky situation, but you'll face it and tomorrow you'll go on.* For the first time in my life, I didn't feel like there was a tomorrow. I had no money. I had bill collectors coming to the door. When it really got to me was when I realized that I didn't have enough money to buy a loaf of bread to feed my wife and my one child at the time. *When you are put into situations like that, you lose all self-confidence and all feelings of self-worth. You're just devastated and you really feel like you're not worth anything. . . .* My father could sense that something was wrong. They didn't know how bad it was and they didn't know what the situation really was, but they just showed up with some groceries. They acted as if "We don't know what you need, but we have some extra and here it is." *It's probably one of the few times that I've cried in front of my father.*

Theory. Generative fathering involves providing help when your children (even adult children) need you. An aware father sensed his son's difficult financial situation. But because his son would have difficulty asking for help, he *creatively* responded by showing up with the needed groceries without being asked. The father's actions demonstrated his care for his son. This narrative account reminds us that providing sustenance and *consecrating* one's material resources to one's children does not end when children leave home.

Education. This story could help in initiating discussion about fathers' past and present relationship with their own fathers. A *cognitive* dimension to this story is that, although most fathers find adolescent children may not want as much active father involvement, adult children still sometimes need and want their fathers to be there for them. The *affective* dimension of the story ("One of the few times I cried in front of my father") opens the possibility for discussion of emotional expression with one's children and father. Questions that could be asked include: How do you find your relationship with your own father changing over the years? How do you feel about the expression of emotion with your father/children? A storytelling question is: Can you relate a time when meaningful emotion was expressed between you and your father or you and your child?

Narrative Account 5

The last account was related by a Chinese man studying at a university in the U.S.:

It was wintertime and I had to walk to the school every morning. I wasn't old enough to ride any bicycles and there wasn't any bus or anything, so I had to walk to school and it was usually about a forty-five minute walk. . . . In the wintertime, very early in the morning, my father would always walk me to school and make sure that I was okay on the road. . . . Usually we went there early in the morning and tried to get to school by the time it was light, which means that we had to wake up before it was light. We had to carry a lot of our rice and other things to the school so that we had something to eat. My father would never let me carry those things, he would always carry those things for me. Sometimes in the early winter, when it was very cold and there was a lot of strong wind, we didn't have money to buy me a new hat and so he would put his hat, which he had from years ago, on me. It was too big for my head, but he himself used a cold towel. There was no heat in the house, of course, unlike America, and so in the morning that towel was frozen. It was frozen solid. But he would wrap that towel around his ears because of the wind in the winter. *I will never forget that. In fact, I have an ambition to write a lot of those experiences so that my children will be able to learn from my parents. . . . [W]hen you are nurtured and cared for then you are the one to transform that love to the next generation.*

Theory. Generative fathering calls for regular and sometimes profound sacrifice. Sacrifices can bind the generations and serve as an example for the future father. The father in this narrative account was unable to provide for his family as many material resources as he would have liked. Still, this illustrated *consecration* of a father's time and endurance of discomfort as he walked his son to school to ensure his safety. He gave his son his good hat to protect him against the bitter wind during those long walks, and wrapped a frozen towel around his head. This story leaves a potent image of paternal caring. The narrator mentions that the example of his father is so important that he plans explicitly to pass it on to his children in written form.

Education. The *ethical* and *affective* dimensions of this story will likely cause listeners to remember specific sacrifices their fathers made for them (or failed to make) and can therefore lead to a good discussion of the practical meaning of paternal commitment. A possible question to follow the telling of this story would be: What are the most meaningful sacrifices your father made for you and that you make for your child? The image of the father walking with his son each day suggests the question: How can we "walk side by side" with our children and show our support and care?

DISCUSSION

Narrative accounts like these can be used in educational settings to teach men about good fathering and strengthen their resolve to do likewise. We encourage family life educators who work with fathers to use narrative accounts of generative fathering in their programs. A skilled educator can determine the challenges and concerns faced by fathers in his or her group or class and present narrative accounts that may help fathers better understand the reasons behind their challenges and concerns, stimulate thinking about creative responses, and motivate greater effort. To assist educators in this effort, we are undertaking a project to create a repository of narrative accounts of good fathering in challenging circumstances that can assist family life educators to offer programs more responsive to the varying needs and situations of individuals and families. Ultimately, this bank of narratives will come from families in many different situations and structures, with diverse cultural, racial, ethnic, religious, and socioeconomic backgrounds, encountering a variety of circumstances.

We have collected narrative accounts from 14 Canadian Chippewa fathers and are now gathering stories from fathers in New Zealand (including Maori men) and from U.S. fathers who have experienced marriage disruption, including some who have remarried. We are creating a home page on the World Wide Web (Internet) where narrative accounts of generative fathering in challenging circumstances will be available. Furthermore, fathers can add their own stories. We will use this home page to create a world-wide community of fathers and to conduct research and to provide virtual family life education.

The use of narrative provides an effective way to improve family life education, by integrating theory, story, meaning, and personal expression. Narrative accounts can help educators integrate the interpretive paradigm into their family life education programs, which Morgaine (1992) argues, will make their efforts more effective in helping individuals and families change. Family scholars and family life educators should work together in these efforts to link theories and methods in ways that provide more meaningful and helpful family life education.

REFERENCES

Arcus, M. (1990). The nature of family life education. In National Council on Family Relations, *Family life education's curriculum guidelines.* Minneapolis, MN: Author.

Bellah, R. N., Madsen, R., Sullivan, W. M., Swidler, A., & Tipton, S. M. (1985).

Habits of the heart: Individualism and commitment in American life. New York: Harper & Row.

Biller, H. B. (1993). *Fathers and families: Paternal factors in child development.* Westport, CT: Auburn House.

Blankenhorn, D. (1995). *Fatherless America: Confronting our most urgent social problem.* New York: Basic.

Braybrooke, D. (1987). *Philosophy of science.* Englewood Cliffs, NJ: Prentice Hall.

Brotherson, S. E. (1995). *Using fathers' narrative accounts to refine a conceptual model of generative fathering.* Unpublished master's thesis, Brigham Young University, Provo, UT.

Chinen, A. (1992). *Once upon a midlife.* New York: Putnam.

Day, J. M. (1991). Narrative, psychology, and moral education. *American Psychologist, 46,* 167-168.

Doherty, W. J. (1991). Beyond reactivity and the deficit model of manhood: A commentary on articles by Napier, Pittman, and Gottman. *Journal of Marital and Family Therapy, 17,* 29-32.

Dollahite, D. C., Hawkins, A. J., & Brotherson, S. E. (in press, 1997). Fatherwork: A conceptual ethic of fathering as generative work. Pp. 17-35 in A. J. Hawkins & D. C. Dollahite (Eds.), *Generative fathering: Beyond deficit perspectives.* Thousand Oaks, CA: Sage Publications.

Dollahite, D. C., Hawkins, A. J., Brotherson, S. E., & Jensen, S. R. (1994, November). Using father's narrative accounts to encourage generative fathering. Paper presented in a "Special Symposium on the Issue of Fathering" at the Theory Construction and Research Methodology Pre-conference Workshop of the National Council on Family Relations, Minneapolis, MN.

Erikson, E. H. (1982). *Identity and the life cycle.* New York: W. W. Norton.

Erikson, E. H. (1963). *Childhood and society* (2nd ed.). New York: Norton.

Gerson, K. (1993). *No man's land: Men's changing commitments to family and work.* New York: Basic.

Giorgi, A. (1975). Convergence and divergence of qualitative and quantitative methods in psychology. In Giorgi, A., Fischer, C., & Murray, E. (Eds.), *Duquesne Studies in Phenomenological Psychology,* Vol. 2, pp. 72-79, Pittsburgh, PA: Duquesne University Press.

Hammersley, M., & Atkinson, P. (1983). *Ethnography: Principles in practice.* New York: Tavistock.

Hawkins, A. J., & Dollahite (in press, 1997). Beyond the role inadequacy perspective of fathering. Pp. 3-16 in A. J. Hawkins & D. C. Dollahite (Eds.), *Generative fathering: Beyond deficit perspectives.* Thousand Oaks, CA: Sage Publications.

Hawkins, A. J., & Dollahite, D. C. (1994). Essay-book review of *No Man's Land: Men's Changing Commitments to Family and Work.* Kathleen Gerson. New York: Basic. 1993; *Men, Work, and Family.* Jane C. Hood (Ed.). Newbury Park, CA: Sage. 1993; *American Manhood: Transformations in Masculinity from the Revolution to the Modern Era.* E. Anthony Rotundo. New York:

Basic. 1993; *Growing Up Male: The Psychology of Masculinity.* B. Mark Schoenberg. Westport, CT: Bergin & Garvey. 1993; *How Fathers Care for the Next Generation: A Four Decade Study.* John Snarey. Cambridge, MA: Harvard University. 1993. In *Journal of Marriage and the Family, 56*(3), 772-776.

Hawkins, A. J., Dollahite, D. C., Jensen, S. R., & Brotherson, S. E. (1994). Transformative narratives: Using personal narratives to help fathers connect with and nurture their children. Presented at the "Men in Families" Pre-Conference of the NCFR Annual Conference, November 8, 1994, Minneapolis, MN.

Hood, J. C. (1993). *Men, work, and family.* Volume 4 in Research on Men and Masculinities Series. Newbury Park, CA: Sage.

Johnson, L., & Palm, G. (1992). What men want to know about parenting. Pp. 129-156 in The Minnesota Fathering Alliance's *Working with fathers: Methods and perspectives.* Stillwater, MN: nu ink.

Josselson, R. J., & Lieblich, A. (1993). *The narrative study of lives (vol. 1).* Newbury Park, CA: Sage.

Kotre, J. (1984). *Outliving the self: Generativity and the interpretation of lives.* Baltimore: John Hopkins University Press.

Mahoney, M. J. (1991). *Human change processes: The scientific foundations of psychotherapy.* Delran, NJ: Basic.

Mair, M. (1988). Psychology as storytelling. *International Journal of Person Construct Psychology, 1,* 125-137.

Marsiglio, W. (1995). *Fatherhood: Contemporary theory, research, and social policy.* Vol. 7 in Research on Men and Masculinities Series. Thousand Oaks, CA: Sage.

Martin, P., Hagestad, G. O., & Diedrick, P. (1988). Family stories: Events (temporarily) remembered. *Journal of Marriage and the Family, 50,* 533-541.

McAdams, D. P. (1985). *Power, intimacy, and the life story: Personological inquiries into identity.* Homewood, IL: Dorsey.

Miles, M. B., & Huberman, A. M. (1994). *Qualitative data analysis.* Thousand Oaks, CA: Sage.

Morgaine, C. A. (1992). Alternative paradigms for helping families change themselves. *Family relations, 41,* 12-17.

Palus, C. J. (1993). Transformative experiences of adulthood: A new look at the seasons of life. In J. Demick, K. Bursik, & R. DiBiase (Eds.) *Parental Development* (pp. 39-58). Hillsdale, NJ: Erlbaum.

Parry, A., & Doan, R. E. (1994). *Story re-visions: Narrative therapy in the postmodern world.* New York: Guilford.

Polkinghorne, D. E. (1988). *Narrative knowing and the human sciences.* Albany: State University of New York Press.

Riessman, C. K. (1993). *Narrative Analysis.* Qualitative Research Methods Series #30. Newbury Park, CA: Sage.

Snarey, J. (1993). *How fathers care for the next generation: A four-decade study.* Cambridge, MA: Harvard University Press.

Stivers, C. (1993). Reflections on the role of personal narrative in social science. *Signs: Journal of Women in Culture and Society, 18*(2), 408-425.

Taylor, S. J., & Bogdan, R. (1984). Introduction to qualitative research methods, (2nd Ed.). New York: Wiley.

White, M., & Epston, D. (1990). *Narrative means to therapeutic ends.* New York: W.W. Norton.

Widdershoven, G. A. M. (1993). The story of life. Hermeneutic perspectives on the relationship between narrative and life history. *The Narrative Study of Lives, 1,* 1-20.

Money, Marriage and the Computer

Supriya Singh

SUMMARY. In this paper, I describe how I used the computer to develop a grounded theory of the social meaning of money and information. In doing this, I take up Bryman and Burgess's (1994) challenge for qualitative researchers to "articulate as fully as possible the processes associated with data analysis" (p. 224). This account is written in the active voice using the personal pronoun, for I am acknowledging agency (Van Maanen, 1979, p. 249) in the transformation of data to theory. *[Article copies available for a fee from The Haworth Document Delivery Service: 1-800-342-9678. E-mail address: getinfo@ haworth.com]*

KEYWORDS. Social meaning of money, Grounded theory, Money and marriage, Qualitative data analysis

THE STUDY

This paper is based on an empirical study of money in banking and marriage. I collected data through open-ended interviews with 37 persons from 21 households in a middle-income Melbourne suburb I call Woodville, between June 1991 and February 1992. They were randomly selected from the suburb's polling list. The majority were married, Anglo-

---

Supriya Singh is Senior Research Fellow, Centre for International Research on Communication and Information Technologies (CIRCIT), 13th Floor, 300 Flinders Street, Melbourne, Victoria 3000, Australia.
This article is based on the author's (1994) dissertation.

[Haworth co-indexing entry note]: "Money, Marriage and the Computer." Singh, Supriya. Co-published simultaneously in *Marriage & Family Review* (The Haworth Press, Inc.) Vol. 24, No. 3/4, 1996, pp. 369-398; and: *The Methods and Methodologies of Qualitative Family Research* (ed: Marvin B. Sussman, and Jane F. Gilgun) The Haworth Press, Inc., 1996, pp. 369-398. Single or multiple copies of this article are available for a fee from The Haworth Document Delivery Service [1-800-342-9678, 9:00 a.m. - 5:00 p.m. (EST). E-mail address: getinfo@haworth.com].

Celtic, Australian-born, with an annual household income of more than $A50,000. I compared their use of banks with the banking patterns of 188 non-English-speaking background (NESB) persons with literacy difficulties, from an adjacent region I call Dreampark. These persons came from more than 33 countries of origin, with most having an annual household income of less than $11,000. They were studied, using a quantitative survey, between November 1991 and April 1992.

In the study I contribute to a social theory of money and information by analyzing how people construct the meaning of money in the different contexts of marriage and banking. Married couples construct the meaning of money in marriage by using the joint bank account to channel *ritual information.* It stresses the *jointness* of marriage where money is shared and pooled, while blocking questions of power and equality, which make money nebulous rather than calculable. In personal retail banking, persons seek to separate different kinds of money according to source, control and use. Hence persons do not always seek information about interest rates. This leads to an understanding of how *marriage* money is different from *banking money* and how both differ from the ideal type of *market money.* It is summarized in Figure 1. I also empirically demonstrate the relationship of the economic and non-economic aspects of social and cultural life, by describing how changes in banking technology have influenced the way couples manage and control money in marriage.

FIGURE 1. Characteristics of marriage money, banking money and market money among middle-income, Anglo-Celtic couples in Australia

A Joint Personal Private	B Nebulous Cooperative Domestic
C Calculable Contractual	D Public Individual Impersonal

AB = MARRIAGE MONEY
AC = BANKING MONEY
CD = MARKET MONEY

In this paper, I confine myself to retracing the development of one of the central concepts of the grounded theory of money and information. I detail how I analyzed the data to arrive at an understanding of marriage money. This also illustrates how I came to appreciate the role of the joint banking account as a conveyer of ritual information. I base this analysis mainly on the qualitative data from Woodville. This is because the study focuses on marriage money among middle-income Anglo-Celtic married couples in Australia. The Dreampark quantitative data was more central to developing the concept of banking money.

In order to recapture the analytic process, in the first section, I discuss how the central themes of money and information emerged. In the second, I concentrate on how I used the computer to shape the concept of marriage money.

EMERGENCE OF CENTRAL THEMES

In this section, I attempt to clarify the muddy process by which the initial research question changed and the new themes were recognized. This process was influenced by prior theory, the data, discussions with my supervisors and personal experience. The final push, however, came because of the analytical procedures required for the computer analysis and the actual writing of the thesis. So money and information emerged as central themes of the study, when I was writing the first draft of the thesis.

The Changing Question:
The Influence of Prior Theory and Personal Experience

The study began with the question: How has deregulation changed the relationship of banks and consumers in Australia since 1983? From my previous study of banking in Australia and Malaysia (Singh, 1984, 1989, 1991) and my involvement in the Australian consumer movement, I was aware there was little study of banking from the consumers' perspective. However, pilot interviews with 11 persons questioned the assumptions behind the original question. Firstly, I had accepted bankers' and regulators' statements that deregulation was the most important change in banking in this century. Persons I interviewed seldom mentioned deregulation until I brought it up. Secondly, they didn't always think they had changed the way they banked. When they felt they had changed, they did not trace it to deregulation. This was jolting as bankers talked of little else in 1989 and 1990. Those interviewed spoke of the importance of life-stage changes such as whether a woman was in paid work or not; having children; buying a house and paying off the mortgage. Thirdly, I had assumed there was a relationship between banks and consumers. This was shattered when one of the men stressed he did not feel he had a "relationship" with the bank, for the bank did not treat him as an individual, even after he had been a customer for 30 years.

So at the end of the pilot interviews, I widened the question to: How have consumers changed the way they bank because of changes in banking and family? As it became clear that the marital unit was the financial unit in terms of banking, the question was further refined to: How do married couples in Australia bank? This question, however, did not wholly encompass the patterns in the data of the pilot interviews and the early open-ended interviews. As my supervisor, Lyn Richards–whose forte is Australian family studies–pointed out, I was asking about changes in banking, but they were talking of the way they handled money in their marriage. Ray Jureidini, my second supervisor–an economic sociologist– had at the beginning of the thesis tried to direct me to the sociological study of money. I, however, continued to maintain that my thesis was about consumers' use of banks. Responding to their feedback, I reluctantly added a few questions to probe persons' attitude to money and how they dealt with it in their marriage. It remained, however, a study of banking. It was not till I started writing up the thesis in May 1993, a year after data collection was completed, that money became a central theme of the thesis. The role of information in the construction of the meaning of money emerged only in the process of testing the theory, mid-way through the second draft of the thesis.

Had I conducted theoretical sampling at this stage–that is, sampling in "search for validity of findings" (Finch & Mason, 1990, p. 28)–I would have explored the way the meaning of money is constructed in different social contexts. One obvious scenario would have been to contrast the Woodville married couples with recently separated or divorced couples on the one hand and de facto couples on the other. Other options would have been to study middle-income couples with lower-income couples; Australian Anglo-Celtic couples with non-Anglo-Celtic couples; couples in Australia with those in India; couples that differed in lifestage, education and occupation; couples where the woman earns as much or more than the man; couples where the wife is not in paid work. The list goes on. Each of these theoretically would have tested and expanded the theory of money and information in different directions.

There is little mention in the methodological literature of the critical effect of timing on theoretical sampling. I started a comparative study in

Dreampark, six months after the pilot interviews in Woodville. At the time, the emphasis of the study was still on changes in banking and deregulation. So the Dreampark study was designed to answer questions on how non-English-speaking background persons with literacy and numeracy difficulties—as opposed to middle-income Anglo-Celtic persons— use the banking system.

Looking back at the missed opportunities to consciously probe money and information in banking and marriage, I realize that prior theory and fear drove my initial analysis. I was reluctant to let go the gains that came from my expertise on banking, for I wanted to complete my thesis rapidly. I did not want to plunge into the relatively unexplored field of Australian marriage and money. I feared the study would be aborted for I would be intruding on the very private domain of marriage and money. This would be further complicated because as an Indian-born Malaysian, I was even more a stranger to their world.

I also resisted the changed focus, because I did not want to reflect on money in my own marriage. It was dangerous territory for it threatened to unmask some of the troubling compromises in my marriage, centering round trust, money, power and equality. The fear was justified. After months spent listening to persons talk about money in their marriage, and sharing my own perceptions, I could not evade similar questions in my own life. This hastened the end of my marriage. It, however, sensitized me to seeing how marriage money is transformed in divorce. What was joint became individual. Trust was replaced by the need for evidence. The nebulous nature of "our money" in marriage was transformed to the precise calculation of individual money. This transformation alerted me to the distinguishing characteristics of money in marriage. So I started focusing on analyzing money in marriage and money in banking through consumers' use of banks.

I had recognized the importance of information to patterns of banking from the very start. This came from the consumer movement's push for more disclosure in banking and my work at an interdisciplinary research centre on communication and information technologies. But the concept of ritual information, that is the ritual blocking of questions as a way of constructing meaning, emerged only in the second draft of the thesis. Three things contributed to it, nearly simultaneously. The first was recognizing my reluctance to ask questions about money, equality and power in my own marriage. The second was that the persons interviewed had also not addressed the questions on power and equality in their marriage. I asked them about money, power and equality and they had talked of jointness in banking. A computer text search for "power" and "equality" confirmed this vividly. This moved the emphasis from information as a means to more profitable banking to ritual information as a way of constructing the social meaning of money.

Though personal experience helped me recognize the importance of the themes of money and information in marriage and banking in the data, this in itself was not sufficient to displace banking from the centre of the study. The confidence to say that money and information were the key areas of investigation in marriage and banking was a result of a multipronged process of memoing, coding and indexing the data for a computer-aided grounded study. It was also crucially driven by the need to write up the data and make sense of it.

Grounded Theory, Codes and Memos

I started out trying to conduct a grounded study of Australian consumers' use of banks, in the manner of Glaser and Strauss (1967), that is "the discovery of theory from data" (p. 1). It was a grounded theory study in the sense that I did not set out to test a theory. As Strauss and Corbin (1990) describe the process, I began "with an area of study and what is relevant to that area is allowed to emerge" (p. 23). However, the emergence of theory from data was different in process and sequence from that described by Glazer and Strauss and also from that described by Miles and Huberman (1984).

I started out trying to follow Glazer and Strauss's coding methods in August and September 1991. I attached codes to text to make retrieval possible. I also tried to do open coding for theory generation. This meant the text had to be coded sentence by sentence (Glaser, 1978, p. 16), line by line or even word by word to open up the inquiry (Strauss, 1987, p. 29). According to Strauss and Corbin (1990) open coding involves "the use of questioning; analysis of a single word, phrase, or sentence; the flip-flop procedure; the making of comparisons, both close-in and far-out; and waving the red flag. All it takes is practice, the more the better, and creative imagination" (p. 95).

Following this method, I asked a battery of questions about words and phrases. For instance, when Robyn (not her real name), a middle-aged professional woman, between the ages of 35 and 44 years, in full-time paid work, earning between $18,000 to $21,000, said she did not know her gross household income, I asked myself: What was interesting about that? Why was I interested in it? What further questions or images did it raise? She said

> I know what happens to my money which goes straight to the bank to pay the mortgage. So I depend on him to give me some housekeeping.

In the context of a joint account what does it say about the distinction between "my" money and "our money?" Is it possible to think of money as joint and not know the household income? How does dependence go with jointness? Housekeeping and jointness? This minute analysis generated four codes on jointness and another two codes on information. I then subjected the codes to a series of questions in the coding paradigm investigating causal conditions, context, action/interactional strategies and consequences (Strauss, 1987, pp. 27-28; Strauss & Corbin, 1990, pp. 114-115). It is this kind of questioning that is supposed to produce new categories which then get merged into core categories and new theory.

Though ways of coding are not meant to be prescriptive, the detailed manual approach (Richards & Richards, 1991b, p. 42) sets standards that are hard to ignore at the early stages of a study. This attempt at open coding was productive, but it effectively froze coding for weeks as I faced the nearly impossible task of analyzing the text in detail when I was unsure of the central themes of the study. I didn't know a better way, but I feared that in this dismembering of the interview, the context and meaning would be lost. Not sure of what I was doing, and only knowing that this detailed questioning of data so early in the analysis was not working, I continually asked, Am I doing it right (Gilgun, 1992, p. 27)?

The early stages of analysis were traumatic, for I was also trying to keep to the sequence set by Miles and Huberman. They say, "One simple rule of thumb is this: Always code the previous set of field notes before the next trip to the site" (Miles & Huberman, 1984, p. 64). They set an impossible standard for a study conducted by an unfunded single researcher. Not being able to meet this standard ground the study to a halt for months. It was only the need to move on to the questionnaires for the Dreampark study and the looming deadlines that got me back to interviewing in Woodville.

Some of the difficulties related to the particularities of the data collection process and the available resources. As I had written batches of 20 to 30 letters asking for interviews, I had a number of interviews booked one after the other. These were nearly always in the evening. It was not possible to transcribe and code one interview before going on to the next, even when recognizing the possible benefits of having coding and data collection go side by side. The reality of the situation was that two-thirds of the interviews were transcribed and coded only in early 1993—nearly a year after data collection—when I received a departmental grant to have the interviews transcribed.

The second hurdle was that textual coding is solitary work and tedious in the early stages when directions are unclear. It was hard to shift in a stop start fashion from data collection to textual coding, for it requires a different mind set and rhythm. Interviewing is stimulating for you listen to someone tell of her or his life and perceptions. Interviewing involves you in trying to follow another person making sense of his or her life. Detailed textual coding meant moving from the broad picture to carve up the interview into small segments. It was hard to do this early on, and yet keep in mind the emerging themes of the study. This proved particularly difficult for me, as my introduction to open coding and qualitative computing happened at the same time. Both require an investment of massive amounts of time and effort, with little immediate result.

It was for these reasons, that the preliminary analysis, for me, was driven by sequential and thematic memos, rather than codes. The broad sweep of the memos was in tune with the rhythm of data collection, for both deal with the whole interview or questionnaire session. I wrote up the field notes to capture the flavor of the interview or questionnaire session and to do a round-up of what appeared to be the most significant aspects of the data. Memos were what index cards and the fieldwork journal are in participant observation. The word processor and its filing abilities enabled me to write up the notes as sequential memos tied to a particular case and as thematic memos under what I saw as the important themes of the study at the time. Transcription of the interviews, by again throwing me into the data, yielded yet more memos.

Memos as Broad Codes

The distinction between memos and codes is artificial, for memos are broad codes. Both are analytical exercises. Both flag a particular issue, say it is important and this is the way it fits into the central question of the study. Both are bridges between the collection and analysis of data. The difference is that memos are attached to field cases, concepts and themes, whereas coding—as traditionally used in qualitative analysis—is attached to units of text.

After the troubled start, what worked for me was to memo and code the interview very broadly. It was later reassuring to read Glaser's changed view of open coding in 1992. He says open coding is a way of "forcing" theory from the data. Instead of the detailed questioning of data, he says, "The requisite conceptual skills for doing grounded theory are to absorb the data as data, to be able to step back or distance oneself from it, and then to abstractly conceptualize the data" (p. 11).

These memos and broad codes became the building blocks of the coding index I used with NUD•IST (Non-numerical Unstructured Data Indexing Searching and Theorizing), a computer program for the analysis of qualitative data. The detailed analysis of the retrieved text came later through further indexing and text searching via the computer.

Qualitative Computing

The use of computers redefines the way qualitative data is analyzed. At the most obvious level, the computer lightens paperwork, and increases expectations of precision when dealing with large bodies of qualitative data. But at a more fundamental level, it allows the researcher to muddle through. Just as the word processor makes it easier to write down half-baked thoughts for future refinement, qualitative computing encourages memoing and coding to enable the central themes and concepts to emerge. It is possible to change the coding framework without having to physically recode the qualitative data. The researcher can take repeated swipes at different bits of data, depending on the level of analysis. These character-istics of qualitative computing support grounded theory, for it is possible to feel one's way to the concepts and theory that best fit the data.

Even more important is the fact that the computer generates information on this muddling through process, identifying what happened and what did not happen. It is this "informating" (Zuboff, 1988, p. 9) aspect of computer analysis that allows for a rigorous and precise description of the generation of concepts and the testing of theory.

I was, however, ill prepared to cope with the way computers change the analytic process. Writing on qualitative computing was then still very much at the "brochure" stage where the creators are setting out their wares, describing functions and possibilities. It is still rare to find any reflection of how computer methods change qualitative research (Richards & Richards, 1991b). However, computer programs for qualitative analysis were established enough so that the decision to be made was not whether to use computers or not, but which program to use for analysis.

The decision to use NUD•IST rather than any other computer program was partially an act of faith. I was competent at word processing, but I did not have the expertise to comparatively evaluate all the different computer programs for qualitative data and I was unable to anticipate my needs and possible problems. Lyn Richards, my supervisor, was co-developer of the program and had used it effectively in *Nobody's Home* (1990). Research teams at the university were using it for two large projects. Because it was being marketed by my university, I felt I would have help when I needed it. So my experience of qualitative computing was intimately bound up with my experience of NUD•IST and the process of doing grounded theory.

Needed: Time and Energy

Having done word processing, I took the automating function for ꞬꞱꜵꙇꞇꞃꙇ I had not analyzed qualitative data using a cut-copy-file basis, so I could not confirm Lyn and Tom Richards' remark how one of the bene-fits of NUD•IST was "an extraordinary lightening of clerical loads" (1994, p. 155). To me, it seemed that learning how to use NUD•IST needed an investment of huge amounts of time and energy. Moreover in 1991, the version I used was a mainframe prototype. The downside of using a program still in the developmental stage was that it seemed that just as the mechanics of the program became manageable, the newer version with its manual appeared.

At the beginning, I was most comforted by two characteristics of NUD-•IST. Firstly, it did not require a near final coding index at the beginning of the study. This was important for I was conscious that my question had changed and that the framework would most likely continue to change. With NUD•IST, I could add, delete, copy and move text and codes. Sec-ondly, it was possible to retrieve text in context hence allaying my fear that the end result of the code and retrieve exercise would be disembodied text (T. Richards and L. Richards, 1994).

These two aspects complemented the grounded theory approach. They, however, changed the coding process. I no longer asked whether I was coding for retrieval or coding for grounded theory. They were no longer incompatible, but came into play at different phases of the analysis (Rich-ards & Richards, 1994). Coding for retrieval came first. Using codes as labels to retrieve text was, at one level, treating qualitative data like quanti-tative data, just putting it in different piles. Once there was a workable index in place, and the text was in retrievable chunks, it was possible to play with the data using NUD•IST's text-search and index system search-ing functions to build more interpretive codes to test and verify hypothe-ses. This was more like the open coding described by Strauss and Corbin, where coding is creative, theory-building and fun.

Changing Indices and Retrieving Text

The abilities to change the index and retrieve text in context were impor-tant for starting the analysis. They also became critical to the emergence of the central themes and the generation and testing of grounded theory.

The tree-structured index. NUD•IST allows for a tree-structured index of any size or complexity. The nodes in the index can be continually altered and restructured (T. Richards and L. Richards, 1994). The program permits multiple coding of any unit of text. This is one of its strengths, but in the beginning, like open coding, it seemed to open up a bottomless pit of computer processing.

Two things happened in tandem before any progress was made. The first was to code broadly so that the data was reduced in bulk. The second step was to simplify the index. The breakthrough was to realize that NUD•IST was a tool that allowed for possibilities, but that all the possibilities did not have to be grasped simultaneously. It was comforting to read later that this was one possible approach, that is, index generally to reindex later as theory is built and verified (Richards & Richards, 1991b).

Shaping the index was a theoretical process, for the index was the conceptual map of the study. As Figure 2 depicts, the change in the main categories of the index documented the change in the central themes of the study. As the question shifted, so did the index. It was like a throbbing bellows. The index started off in mid-1991 as an articulated version of the prior theory. Hence the major categories related to changes in the banking environment and consumers' patterns of banking. After the first few interviews, "partnership" was added as a category. The next major shift came in May 1993, when I embarked on a major writing exercise. This was like a stocktaking exercise to see where I was, where the gaps were and what directions needed to be pursued. It produced a detailed table of contents which visually revealed that money was a major theme of the study and led to a major reorganization of the index. It was an interactive process, in that the index in turn helped to further elaborate the table of contents. By

FIGURE 2. The changing shape of the index: Top level categories at three stages

November 1992	May 1993	March 1995
Base data	Base data	Base data
Billing environment		SPSS
Consumers & financial institutions	Consumers & banks	Consumers & banks
Transaction systems	Transaction systems	Transaction systems
Banking Information	Banking information	Information
Social differences & banking	Social differences & banking	Social differences
Partnership	Partnership	Partnership
Method	Method	Method
	Money	Money
	Nature of account	Nature of account

March 1995, "information" and "social differences" shook loose of banking, to relate to money and marriage. Figure 2 shows the top level categories, under which finer subcategories were explored and organized, at three different stages.

The process of adding, deleting, moving, amalgamating codes was time-consuming for even with NUD•IST, it was like moving a lumbering elephant. A balance had to be struck between getting my arms around the complexity of the data and yet keeping the structure of the indexing system in my head. This reorganization was theory producing, for it focused attention on why a code should exist and how it related to the central question of the study.

At times, it was like peeling an onion, discarding some of the outer skin, to reveal the core. The problem was to determine what to do with the outer skin, for this outer skin may become important at a later date, and the residual may become central. As Mills (1959) said, major themes of a work are recognized because "they keep insisting upon being dragged into all sorts of topics . . . " (p. 216).

This happened with the major themes of my study, for codes for information and money kept coming up in different sections of the index. In November 1992, midway through analysis, money appeared in the sections on "base data" (categories that index the whole document), "consumers and banks" the "transaction systems," along different nodes of "social differences and banking" and partnership. Information was at the centre of "banking information," but it was also a sub-category under "banking environment," "consumers and banks," "transaction systems," "social differences and banking" and "partnership." The only way to cut through some of the duplication, was to give them major categories of their own, reorganize the index and recognize that they were at the centre of the study.

Writing as Analysis

Writing allowed me to assess how the categories fitted together in a whole. This was essential, for at the beginning, when the index was developing, it was creative, traumatic and theory producing. Towards the end of the study when the categories seemed to fit, there was an element of danger, for the coding became mechanical. It was hard then to distinguish between the repetition of themes and personal saturation. In this sense, writing worked for me the way Richardson (1994) described it, as "a *method of inquiry*, a way of finding out about yourself and your topic" (p. 516).

Writing the thesis revealed the inadequacy of my prior theory. At the draft stage of the thesis it had become clear that the thesis was about money and information in marriage and banking. So the old framework which revolved round competition and the profit maximizer model of the consumer was inadequate. But this in itself did not produce theory.

Connecting the Analysis with Prior Theory and Research

The shift in the question had been so great, that while collecting data, memoing, coding and even when I was indexing, there was little prior theory with which I could relate. There has been little study of money and information in sociology (Balnaves, 1993; Collins, 1979, p. 190; Smelt, 1980, p. 204; Tilly, 1988; Turner, 1986, p. 110). This is especially true for the study of money within marriage (Bailey & Lown, 1992; Blumstein & Schwartz, 1983; Pahl, 1989; Zelizer, 1989, 1994). Money is especially invisible in studies where women are the central focus (Rabow, Charness, Aguilar & Toomajian, 1992, p. 191, Hartsock, 1983). Money is not an organizing topic in Australian feminist historiography despite the fact that the economic dependence of women is a major theme (Alford, 1984; Dixson, 1984; Grimshaw, Lake, McGrath & Quartly, 1994; Summers, 1975, 1994), nor of Australian community studies (Bryson & Thompson, 1972; Bryson & Wearing, 1985; Dempsey, 1992; Poiner, 1990; Richards, 1985, 1990).

In this relative theoretical and empirical vacuum, the work of Viviana Zelizer in economic sociology connected best with my data (Zelizer, 1979, 1985, 1988, 1989). She holds there are multiple monies, each influenced by patterns of social relations and meaning in different social contexts. Money not only shapes social values and relations but is itself shaped by them. Brenda Dervin's "sense-making" approach to information as a user construct from library science and information studies (Dervin, 1977, 1989, 1992; Dervin & Dewdney, 1986; Dervin & Nilan, 1986) fitted in well with the users' perspective in my study of banking. This differed from the more traditional approach in banking of information as a commodity ready to be accessed. Their separate approaches to money and information led me to ask questions of the data that I had not anticipated when I was collecting it.

I had asked persons how much information they had about their banking accounts and their sources of information. I had not asked them how they made sense of that information and what made them seek that information. I did not set out to take them back step by step through the informing and decision-making process. This meant that the quantitative data from the Dreampark survey could not be reinterpreted. But when I retrieved the qualitative data on information and banking in Woodville, I found that though I had not asked the specific question, persons had told the story in this way for banking situations that had been most meaningful to them. But these gaps needed to be recognized.

The same kind of gaps were present for data on marriage money and banking money in the Dreampark data. I had not asked in Dreampark how people define money in marriage and money in banking. In Woodville, I had asked persons about their attitudes to money in marriage; whether they fight over money; how they manage it; control it; monitor it; how they are informed about it. But I was operating with the traditional sociological concept of market money rather than Zelizer's theory of multiple monies. So I did not ask them whether they thought money in marriage was different from money in banking. Thus there were no quick answers in the data. The interview transcripts were also not coded in this way. This is why the concepts of marriage money and banking money which are central to the theory of money and information do not appear in the index. The concepts of marriage money and banking money had to be constructed.

In the second part of this paper, I will describe how I used node searching, node building, matrices and text retrieval within the node–attributes of NUD•IST–to develop and test the concept of marriage money. This placed qualitative computing at the centre of the process of theory building and verification.

DEVELOPING THE CONCEPT OF MARRIAGE MONEY

There were three steps in the development of the concept of marriage money. The first was to discover that marriage was the most important boundary of domestic money among middle-income Anglo-Celtic married couples in Australia. The second was to explore the characteristics of marriage money, and the third was to retrace the process by which people construct the meaning of money. This in turn led to the concept of ritual information. In this part of the paper I describe how the computer influenced the shape of the concept of marriage money in particular and gave birth to that of ritual information.

Marriage Money

The marital boundary of domestic money is so much taken for granted in Australia, that none of the persons interviewed remarked on it. But this was one of the first characteristics of domestic money I noticed, for ideologically in India, it is the family, variously defined, that is the financial unit. The notion of privacy in money in India is also more broadly defined.

Anthropological studies confirm that marriage is not always the most important marker of domestic money in all cultures. Women in many parts of Asia and Africa are excluded from the main means of production by ritual taboos (Afshar & Agarwal, 1989, pp. 2-7; Ram, 1991; Stirrat, 1989). In India, gender ideology, cultural norms and practices often make it difficult for women to have access to land (Agarwal, 1989, p. 71). There are also explicit expectations that money will flow from the marital unit to the wider kin group (Ewen, 1985, pp. 104-105; Stivens, 1987, pp. 100-101; Thorogood, 1987, pp. 27-29). Money is also not always private to the marital couple. Ram's (1991) study of Mukuvvar women in a fishing community in South India shows that often kin and neighbors know more about the loans and debts of the household than the husband (p. 147).

More Connections

It was my cultural history and anthropological studies in Asia and Africa that made me keep exclaiming about marriage as marking the most important boundary of domestic money. I followed this perception by investigating the text that related to the joint account, the flow of money and privacy about money. In order to do this, I first built new collective nodes, so that I would have a broad sweep of the data relating to the theme. That is, I would use the program's ability to "collect" and retrieve text at a higher level in NUD•IST's tree-structured index, rather than confine myself to a particular sub-sub-node. This was partly because I did not always trust the finer coding I had done when marriage money was not a central concept.

As Figure 3 illustrates, when I was investigating the marital joint account as an indication of the boundary of domestic money, I had the

FIGURE 3. Retrieving collected nodes

(10 3)	/nature of account/jointness
(10 3 1)	/nature of account/jointness/definition
(10 3 2)	/nature of account/jointness/couple only
(10 3 3)	/nature of account/jointness/couple and children
(10 3 4)	/nature of account/jointness/income
(10 3 5)	/nature of account/jointness/joint accounts
(10 3 5 1)	/nature of account/jointness/joint accounts/ritual
(10 3 6)	/nature of account/jointness/married before
(10 3 7)	/nature of account/jointness/separation
(10 3 90)	/nature of account/jointness/joint account-collect

option of retrieving text coded at node (10 3 5) together with its sub-node (10 3 5 1). Instead I went further up the tree and built a collective node at (10 3 90) and called it "nature of account/jointness/joint account-collect." This helped me have the text coded along all the nodes under (10 3) and lessened the chances of my having missed connections.

It was this broadly retrieved text that I then investigated closely, seeking patterns and testing for deviant cases. At this stage, to discover broad patterns in the data, I used matrices. Unlike Miles and Huberman (1984), these matrices were not used to display data in the final report, but became an intermediate stage for further theory building. The matrices were especially useful for building typologies of money management and control, and the kinds of joint accounts.

The Marital Unit as the Financial Unit

This analysis of the joint account revealed that the marital unit, rather than the family or the household, was the financial unit in Dreampark and Woodville. In Woodville, 88 per cent of the married couples had joint accounts. There was not a single instance where married persons had joint accounts with parents, siblings or adult children. When the children were young, the mother most often had a trustee account together with the child. But once the child grew up, the children's money and the parents' money ceased to be joint. The joint account was not confined to the middle-income Anglo-Celtic married couples in Australia, for the Dreampark data showed that 71 per cent of married persons in Dreampark also had a joint account. In Dreampark, there were two cases, where a recent single migrant had a joint account with his brother and a single woman had an account with her mother. In both cases, however, the persons were single. In the joint account, money formally belongs to the couple just as the marital home belongs to the couple. The marital boundary of domestic money was further confirmed by the data on the flow of money and the privacy of money.

The flow of money. To analyze the flow of money in Woodville, I first built a collective node for money/flow which incorporated the general node of money/flow and its sub-node of money/flow/inheritance. This brought up eight cases which were coded under this collective node. As Figure 4 illustrates, I summarized the data by case number to reveal the patterns. The cases showed that money did not generally flow outside the marital unit to parents or grown-up children. When it did flow outside the marital unit, it went from parents to children, as in the case of Rose, Ian and Ingrid, Kris and Korn, and Peter. None of the persons interviewed in Woodville spoke of helping their parents financially. Moreover, some

FIGURE 4. Money flow

1-3	Rose, 74, a pensioner, gave her children money when she sold her house to move to a nurse's retirement unit.
3-1	Annie, 35-44, a housewife talks of the gift obligations and reciprocity obligations that follow from being part of an Italian family.
4-2	Barry, 35-44, realizes that his mother is having a difficult time coping. The help he gives is not financial but 'Just with time, telephone calls, getting over there, doing some house maintenance and just doing what we can . . . trying to keep mum up to date with what services are available.'
4-3	Betsy, 81, Barry's mother thinks the financial achievement is to have the house paid off so that they can manage on their own, without looking to their children for help. Proud that she 'didn't ask anybody for anything . . . they've never had to do anything.'
9-1	Gale, 45-54, whose husband is unemployed, says her employed sons who stay with them do not contribute enough towards their board. But Gale does not know how to ask them. She herself used to give money to her mother when she was living with her. Feel maybe it is their turn to give us a hand. For when they were out of work, they helped them.
11-1& 11-2	Ian and Ingrid, both retired, have given their children money.
14-2& 14-3	Kris and Korn, both retired, have given their children money.
17-2	Peter, 78, has also helped his children out.

parents, like Betsy, felt it was important that they have not had to call on their children for financial help.

Marriage money is private. The boundary of marriage money was maintained by the fact that money was intensely private for all the middle-income Anglo-Celtic couples I studied in Woodville. It was as if the privacy of money drew a circle round the couple, excluding children, parents, siblings and friends. It was a matter of "minding your own business," a phrase two people used. Ian, 72, a retired air force officer, went further and said talking money was "a bit like talking to your children about where babies came from." He said he would go as far as asking his children if the bank was good or not, "but nothing more than that." This privacy about money goes across generations, for it is true for Ian, 72, as for Keith in his 40s.

Summarizing the data by cases in the retrieved text enabled me to discover that not a single one of the 37 had talked of their financial affairs with their children, though two were prepared to advise their children on money if asked sometime in the future. Only four said they had or would discuss money with their parents. And all four were women. One woman said she spoke of money to her sister. She was unusual, for money is not often talked about even with brothers and sisters.

Money was nearly wholly out of bounds as a subject for discussion with friends. In Woodville, only two of the 37 persons said they would discuss money with their friends. Privacy about money extends to salaries and even to finding out how much friends paid for a house or received for it. The privacy about money did not speak of a lack of interest in money. It was just that the marital boundary of domestic money was so strong, that persons sought this information through a roundabout manner from others in the know, keeping an eye on what the others could afford. Keith said he and his parents kept an eye on each others' financial status through seemingly casual conversation. He said,

> Just in passing I might mention to my parents, you know, how are things going? Are you doing all right with your pensions? Or they might say how are you going? Are you meeting your mortgage repayments?

This building of collective nodes and examination of the retrieved text dealing with the joint account, flow of money and privacy helped confirm that marriage marks domestic money in a very significant way among middle-income Anglo-Celtic married couples in Australia.

The marital joint account excluded other adults in the household and the family. Little money flowed from the marital unit to parents, grown up children or other members of the wider kin group. Having established that the marital unit was the domestic financial unit, the next step was to explore the different characteristics of marriage money.

Characteristics of Marriage Money

The joint account and the importance of privacy relating to money signalled that "jointness" and "privacy" were important features of marriage money among middle-income Anglo-Celtic couples in Australia. I was conscious of not universalizing this for marriage money, for the "separate pot" system of money management is more common in the world than the "common purse" (Blumberg, 1991, p. 122, Papohunda, 1988).

Persons interviewed in Woodville did not talk of the "jointness" or "separateness" of marriage in conceptual terms. These terms were used mainly with the joint bank account, for that was the most frequent expression of the jointness of marriage money. In order to unpack the different meanings of "jointness" in marriage money, I first retrieved all the text relating to the collective nodes relating to money/management, money/ flow, money/spending, money/control, partnership/information, partner- ship/decision making, partnership/ideas, nature of account/personal, nature of account/business, nature of account/jointness, nature of account/separate- ness. Summarizing the data, it became clear that when talking of jointness, persons were speaking of "pooling," "trust," "commitment," doing things "together" and "sharing." I investigated these further through text searches of the collective nodes previously identified.

It was possible to delve deeper, to ask whether "jointness" meant the same things to men and women. In order to do this, the critical functions of NUD•IST that I used were text search and index system searching. I had learnt of the importance of narrowing enquiry by searching the index system, early in the analysis. When I attempted a general retrieval of text with the term "money," I was alarmed to find that nearly the complete interviews came spilling out of the printer. To avoid this, I then used the index system creating a "union" of nodes relating to jointness and "inter- secting" the resulting node with the node titled "base data/gender/ women." This created a new node indexing only the data I wanted—where women had been coded as discussing the jointness issues. I did the same for men. When I searched the text retrieved under each new node, I was able to say what men and women thought about jointness, and how many thought of it in a specified way. This allowed me to be precise about the number of cases that fitted the theory, so that the results could then be checked against cases that did not fit. This was not just a matter of convert- ing "soft" qualitative data to "hard" results, but it helped test theory precisely (Richards & Richards, 1991a, p. 10).

Dimensions of jointness. Pooling resources and sharing expenses was seen by many persons studied in Woodville as an essential characteristic of marriage. It was variously interpreted. Thirteen persons (5 women and 8 men) of the 37 spoke of "pooling" their money or having a "pool" of funds. Pooling of money can exist in different forms. Money can be wholly or partially pooled. It does not presuppose two equal streams of income. It usually starts when there are two incomes at marriage, but continues even when there is only one income. Then pooling shifts from being the combining of income, to a "pool" of money for joint use. These variations under the umbrella of pooling allowed the provider and mother- hood ideologies to coexist with that of the companionate marriage.

One of the consequences of pooling is that individually earned money becomes joint money and in the process it becomes nebulous. It moves the emphasis from earning to the joint spending of money. It masks who contributed what amount and who spent what amount.

The joint account also led to discussions of trust. All six persons who spoke of trust in marriage money spoke of trust as being essential to marriage. The trust comes first. They trust their partner, so they trust him or her with their money. While more women spoke of trust–four women compared with two men–the men were equally definite that trust was the basis of their marriage, and that money in marriage was based on this trust.

Togetherness was not a major expressed dimension of jointness. Only one woman, Beth, 41, spoke of marriage in terms of togetherness. The theme of doing things "together" is most often within the context of managing and deciding about money "together" or pooling it "together." Women spoke of it more than men in both contexts in that six women and three men talked about deciding together, whereas five women and two men used it for accounts being pooled or joint "together."

Though more women than men spoke of "togetherness" and "trust," they used them in much the same way. However, men and women spoke of "sharing" and "commitment" in remarkably different ways. It was a measure of the gap between the companionate ideology of marriage and the expressed reality of marriage, that "sharing" did not come up often when persons spoke of their marriage or more particularly of money in marriage. Only two persons–both men–spoke of sharing as being essential to marriage. Looking further into their case studies, one notes that both controlled the money in their marriages and made the major financial decisions.

Women spoke of sharing in the sense of sharing costs. Ingrid, an older woman in her mid to late 60s, talked of "sharing" the cost of a microwave with her husband and how that became their Christmas present to each other. Robyn, a middle-aged woman, spoke of sharing as in sharing expenses. She said, "I wouldn't mind if the bill came in and we both put in our share." Kris, an older woman, also used sharing in the same sense of dividing up the costs.

Sharing, if it came with the connotation of equal shares, was in this sense the opposite of pooling. Pooling of income did not necessarily translate to the concept of sharing of income, in the sense that the husband owned 50 per cent and the wife owned 50 per cent or whatever the proportion decided. Pooling in an essential way worked by denying shares, by making the individual collective. Though pooling was often popularly seen as sharing, the latter concept had the assumption that parts of the pie would belong to one person and other parts would belong to the other. However, pooling assumed the whole pie could only be eaten together.

Commitment was assumed to be essential to marriage. It was, however, not spoken of much when persons in Woodville talked of jointness in marriage. Maybe it was so much taken for granted that it was not verbalized. But when people did speak of "commitment," it came through as one of the main gender differences in the way men and women saw jointness in marriage money.

For the men in Woodville, jointness in money went together with "commitment" in the sense of a financial commitment to meet the bills. Five men spoke of "commitment" solely in this way. Women did not speak of commitment at all, despite the fact that I brought it up at least twice with women. The consciousness of financial commitment was absent in the way the women spoke of joint money.

NUD•IST text and index system searching allowed me to state that the joint account fixes the meaning of jointness in marriage money by focusing on "trust," "pooling," "sharing," "commitment" and "togetherness." This was further tested by examining the cases where the couple did not have a joint account. These cases showed that jointness was not always expressed in the joint account. In three cases, where the main savings were in one person's name, this spoke of a greater trust than having a joint account. The joint account also did not necessarily mean that all the income was pooled. But the absence of total pooling in two cases, did not mean that they did not feel the "trust," "commitment," "togetherness" and "sharing" of marriage money. Though the joint account was the most common expression of the jointness of marriage money, this was not necessarily so.

In order to explore the meanings of money in marriage, it was important to discover what was not being said. This was salutary especially with qualitative data where the most colorful cases stick in mind. To give a simple example, I thought there was a difference in my interviewing of men and women, and that I had interviewed the women in the kitchen and the men in the lounge. One particular case stuck in mind, where I interviewed the woman on two separate occasions—as the interview was incomplete the first time—and both times we sat round a table next to the kitchen. When I went in the evening to interview the husband, we sat in the living room.

Thinking it would give context to the section on the open-ended interview, I retrieved the codes that related to "interviewing." I discovered to my amazement that only in one case—the case I remembered—did this happen. In all the other cases, I interviewed both husband and wife in the same place—20 in the living room and 16 in the meals area.

Marriage money was not equal. The text search mechanism was equally effective when it came to defining what was not being said when people spoke of money in marriage. Following the Western feminist ideology of marriage as an equal partnership, I had assumed that equality was an important dimension of jointness. A text search revealed that the assumption was so strong that I was introducing it into the interviews. However, the surprise was that persons in Woodville were not talking of equality when they spoke of jointness in marriage. It was also not what they spoke of when they talked of money in marriage, despite the fact that money can be precisely measured.

A text search helped discover that only three of the 37 mentioned "equality" and that, too, only once. Two of them talked of equality, when their money management styles were characterized by inequality. Lily, earning less than $7,300 a year from part-time paid work spoke about the ideology of equality. But she was the only one among the persons studied in Woodville who does not own a house jointly with her husband, and whose husband controls the bulk of their savings through his personal account. Roland, a businessman, spoke of equality as a process, associating equality with sharing, seeing the joint account as "one of the equalizing factors." But instead of equality meaning an equal share in terms of money and expenses, for him the joint account equalized the situation, because it rendered the different contributions less visible. He said if the emphasis was on a 50-50 sharing of expenses, then marriage would be more like a business. It would lead to constant "arguments about percentage contributions," and money would be an arena of possible conflict. So the way to deal with it was to "chuck it in the bucket," to render the different contributions less visible. What is interesting, though, is that what he saw as equality, his wife saw as control.

It was only in one case where equality referred to quantum of money. This was Cathy, a childless woman who held an executive position in a financial institution. She was speaking of the way she and her husband pool some income and keep some apart. At first, when he was earning more, they thought that equal sums of money in the pooled account was the way to go. Now that she is earning more, they have moved to an equal percentage of their pay in the pooled account.

Bypassing the issues of "power" and "control." The questions about "power" and "control" were more difficult to ask. I started my thesis seeing money as an idiom of power which was closely related to gender. The gender inequalities in the income earned, the division of labor in the home, the influence of the patriarchal ideology were clear. However, issues of "power" and "control" were bypassed when the subject was money. This was despite the fact that I often directed the interview to a discussion of power and control.

The concept of "power" came up in only two of the 37 cases, except when I introduced it in another eight cases. When I asked persons point blank whether money was a symbol of power in their relationship, only Kris, 68, said yes. She was also the only person who chose to have separate accounts for most of her 45 years of marriage.

In Woodville, 29 of the 37 persons talked of "control." But when I searched through the qualitative data, I found that in 18 of the 29 cases, the discussion was primarily in answer to my question. In the 11 cases where the concept came up independently or was a substantive issue, seven persons spoke of it in terms of "control over money" compared to four who spoke of control exercised by one partner over another. The images of control over money are those related to the idea of money as flow: controlling where it went, keeping it under control, damming it. The idea was to control the flow of money; keep a tight rein on the mortgage; control spending.

Money as an instrument of control in marriage was talked about only in the negative, to show how the person speaking did not have control. Persons in Woodville talked of not controlling access and the use of money; not controlling information. If they had done that, they would be seen as having power, something which was ideologically not permissible in an egalitarian partnership.

Ritual Information: Constructing the Meaning of Marriage Money

The silence about power and money was so potent, that by the time I had coded the data, I, too, was tiptoeing round the issue of money, gender and power, in the same way as my respondents were. Despite all the sociological literature on power and marriage and the central place of patriarchy in feminist analysis, I found myself writing of jointness as the central theme, sidestepping the issue of power. Only when my supervisor pointed out this obvious turnaround did I face up to the way power like equality was being redefined as jointness in middle-income Anglo-Celtic marriage in Australia.

Power, like the notion of equality, was too troubling a dimension to be articulated in most Western marriages espousing an egalitarian partnership. Not only had the couples blocked the information which may have demonstrated the way money related to power in marriage, but I had been a willing collaborator. Questions of power were troubling in a personal sense because they shone the torchlight on the power games in my own two marriages, and how I, too, had been in patriarchal marriages while espousing an egalitarian ideology. Dependence was couched within an egalitarian ideology, blocking questions and information about the power of patriarchy. It also allowed for the presumption of equality without equal responsibility.

It was this analysis using textual search that led to the emergence of the concept of ritual information, the cultural markers which block information, channelling it into more socially acceptable directions. Ritual information converted marriage money into something nebulous rather than calculable. And it was the joint account which was the instrument for blocking culturally undesirable information.

The joint account was a ritual that channelled information. It fixed the meaning of jointness and blocked information that might challenge this fixed meaning. It helped "negotiate" (Richards, 1990) and reconcile conflicting ideologies—those of the egalitarian companionate marriage and the gendered ideologies of motherhood and of the male provider. It also bridged the gap between the presumption of equality in a companionate marriage and the reality of the unequal incomes of the partners.

The joint account was effective because it deflected questions about contribution, liabilities and expenditure, when the marriage was current. When the marriage dissolved, it was the questions that were blocked during marriage—the quantum of the financial contribution; the value of the non-financial contribution—which emerged as central to the financial arrangements at divorce.

The joint account, by emphasizing that money was pooled and shared together in marriage, emphasized the cooperative dimensions of marriage money. This prevented precise, open documentation and evidence of how much was contributed and spent by the husband and wife. This blocking of information was an important part of the ritual information conveyed by the joint account.

The joint account's role in blocking questions of power and control, was dramatically borne out in the exceptional cases when power and control were talked of. Kris, 68, spoke of power and connected it to her and her husband's decision to have separate accounts and now independently controlled joint accounts. She said, "We decided we don't control each other's money." Cathy, 32, a finance executive, was the other person who spent a substantial part of the interview speaking of her need to control money. She was the only woman in the Woodville sample who earned more than her husband.

These two women were also the only ones who had purposively chosen the joint account for instrumental reasons. Both Cathy and Kris were and had been financially independent during their marriage. Both kept control of part of their earnings for discretionary expenditure. They were unusual in this study, because both recognized they have a need to spend on themselves, and value their ability to do it without question. Cathy, however, differed from Kris, in that she was the only person who talked of joint money in terms of quantum—how much should be joint and how much should be separate. Cathy and her husband, Cowley, had gone behind the general concept of "sharing" to ask: How much is my share? This had been a matter for discussion and negotiation. Cathy was also the only one who talked of implications of motherhood on her control of money.

By not asking questions about contribution, liabilities and expenditure, when the marriage was current, the joint account deflected attention away from the financial dependence of most of the wives. In Woodville, in all except one case, where both were employed, the husband earned more than the wife. Of the 15 women under 60 years of age, only six earned more than $14,500 a year and only three of them earned more than the average weekly earnings of $22,885 (Australian Bureau of Statistics, 1994). Half the women in part-time paid work earned less than $7,300 a year.

The presumption of equality in the companionate marriage needed to survive this discrepancy in income. This was particularly difficult, for the norms of success and self-worth in the market were in the idiom of market money. Women, like men, ranked non-financial contribution to the marriage as less important than the financial contribution (Funder, 1986).

The strategies used in the ritual of the joint account to bridge the gap between the ideology of egalitarianism and the reality of unequal incomes are similar in many respects to those used to live with the unequal sharing of housework (Bittman & Lovejoy, 1994). A powerful blocking tool was the privacy of marriage money. This contributed to a lack of "monetary realism" (Rabow et al., 1992).

Monetary Implications of Transitions

The monetary implications of the transition to marriage and then from marriage to parenthood are seldom discussed. That was why Cathy stood out in the sample, for she discussed what having children could do to her control over money. Despite publicity about the rising divorce percentages, none of the persons interviewed in Woodville admitted to thinking about the financial implications of separation and divorce.

Another important strategy was to redefine equality in marriage as jointness. An equally effective way to avoid seeing money and power as linked was to present money as not being meaningful. This was done by persons who controlled the money in their marriage and those who did not. The importance of money was further reduced by minimizing personal wants, or seeing personal wants satisfied in collective expenditure. Both men and women talked of spending money in a collective way in Woodville.

DISCUSSION

In this paper I have described how the research process was essentially a process of muddling through from initial questions influenced by prior theory and personal history ultimately to a grounded theory which fit the data. It was not smooth and linear where a methodological rule book helped generate one insight followed by another in logical sequence. Instead, it was a muddy process as the initial research questions changed and new themes fought for recognition. I needed to go back to the record of computer analysis to recognize these processes.

What surprised me most was the tenacity with which prior theory and personal history drove the analysis. It was this information about the research process that enabled me to keep checking how I was shaping the analysis. Through the computer I was able to list precisely what was in the data. But I was also able to document what was not in the data when I thought it was. It was humbling to record the missed opportunities and the resulting gaps in the data. But it was precisely this realization which was most productive for theory generation.

Qualitative computing became central to the analytic process, not only because it allowed me to muddle through but because it permitted pro-cesses I could not have otherwise attempted. As the wordprocessor allows one to continually refine a paper, qualitative computing, as I experienced it, enabled me to keep modifying my conceptual framework and checking it against the data, without having to physically recode.

It was critical in this analytic process that the tree-structured index allowed constant visualizing of my conceptual framework. This helped reveal the central themes as I saw them. It also illustrated how long I was not willing to recognize them. This in turn led me to question why I had not seen them earlier, and helped change the questions.

The computer also offered tools to investigate the data precisely, through building nodes and text searching. This enabled me to keep refin-ing my questions to investigate the way women thought of jointness in marriage money and how different this was from the men. This may have been possible by more laborious manual methods. However, it also thrust before me the fact that there were questions neither the men nor women wanted to address. For me this documenting of what was not in the data, of how the theory did not fit, was what made qualitative computing central to the transformation of data to theory.

REFERENCES

Afshar, H., & Agarwal B. (Eds). (1989). *Women, poverty and ideology in Asia: Contradictory pressures, uneasy resolutions.* London: Macmillan.

Agarwal, B. (1989). Women, land and ideology in India. In H. Afshar & B. Agarwal (Eds.), *Women, poverty and ideology in Asia: Contradictory pressures, uneasy resolutions* (pp. 70-98). London: Macmillan.

Alford, K. (1984). *Production or reproduction? An economic history of women in Australia, 1788–1850.* Melbourne: Oxford University Press.

Australian Bureau of Statistics. (1994). *Average weekly earnings: States and Australia, November 1993.* (Catalogue No. 6302.0). Canberra: Australian Government Publishing Service.

Balnaves, M. (1993). The sociology of information. *The Australian & New Zealand Journal of Sociology, 29*(1), 93-111.

Bailey, W. C., & Lown, J. (1992). Counting the coins: A Cross cultural evaluation of the money beliefs and behaviors scale. In V. A. Haldeman (Ed.), *Proceedings: 38th Annual Conference of the American Council on Consumer Interests* (pp. 111-116). Columbia, MO: American Council on Consumer Interests.

Bittman, M., & Lovejoy, F. (1994). Domestic power: Negotiating an unequal division of labour within a framework of equality. *The Australian & New Zealand Journal of Sociology, 29*(3), 302-321.

Blumberg, R. L. (1991). Income under female versus male control: Hypotheses from a theory of gender stratification and data from the third world. In R. L. Blumberg (Ed.), *Gender, family, and economy: The triple overlap* (pp. 97-127). Newbury Park, CA: Sage Publications.

Blumstein, P., & Schwartz, P. (1983). *American couples: Money, work, sex.* New York: Pocket Books.

Bryman, A., & Burgess, R. G. (1994). Reflections on qualitative data analysis. In Bryman, A. & Burgess, R. G. (Eds.), *Analyzing qualitative data* (pp. 216-226). London: Routledge.

Bryson, L., & Thompson, F. (1972). *An Australian newtown: Life and leadership in a working-class suburb.* Maimsbury, Vic.: Penguin.

Bryson, L., & Wearing, B. (1985). Australian community studies–a feminist critique. *Australian and New Zealand Journal of Sociology, 21*(3), 349-366.

Collins, R. (1979). Review essay: *The Bankers*, by Martin Mayer. *American Journal of Sociology, 85*(1), 190-194.

Dempsey, K. (1992). *A man's town: Inequality between women and men in rural Australia.* Melbourne: Oxford University Press.

Dervin, B. (1977). Useful theory for librarianship: Communication, not information. *Drexel Library Quarterly, 13*(3), 16-32.

Dervin, B. (1983). Information as a user construct: The relevance of perceived information needs to synthesis and interpretation. In S. A. Ward & L. J. Reed (Eds.), *Knowledge structure and use: implications for synthesis and interpretation* (pp. 153-183). Philadelphia, PA: University Press.

Dervin, B. (1989). Users as research inventions: How research categories perpetuate inequities. *Journal of Communication, 39*(3), 216-232.

Dervin, B. (1992). From the mind's eye of the user: The Sense-making qualitative-quantitative methodology. In J. D. Glazier & R. R. Powell (Eds.), *Qualitative research in information management* (pp. 61-84). Englewood, CO: Libraries Unlimited

Dervin, B., & Dewdney, P. (1986). Neutral questioning: A new approach to the reference interview. *RQ, 25*(4), 506-513.

Dervin, B., & Nilan, M. (1986). Information needs and uses. In M. E. Williams (Ed.), *Annual Review of Information Science and Technology* (Vol. 21) (pp. 5-33). Medford, NJ: Knowledge Industry Publications for the American Society for Information Science.

Dixson, M. (1984). *The real Matilda: Woman and identity in Australia, 1788 to the present* (rev. ed. originally published 1976). Ringwood, Victoria: Penguin.

Ewen, E. (1985). *Immigrant women in the land of dollars: Life and culture on the Lower East Side 1890-1925.* New York: Monthly Review Press.

Finch, J., & Mason, J. (1990). *Studies in qualitative methodology* (Vol. 2). Greenwhich: JAI Press.

Funder, K. (1986). His and her divorce. In P. McDonald (Ed.), *Settling up: Property and income distribution on divorce in Australia* (pp. 224-240). Sydney: Prentice-Hall of Australia.

Gilgun, J. F. (1992). Definitions, methodologies, and methods in qualitative family research. In J. F. Gilgun, K. Daly, & Handel, G. (Eds.), *Qualitative methods in family research* (pp. 22-39). Newbury Park: Sage Publications.

Glaser, B. G. (1978). *Theoretical sensitivity: Advances in the methodology of grounded theory.* Mill Valley, CA: Sociology Press.

Glaser, B. G. (1992). *Basics of grounded theory analysis: Emergence vs Forcing.* Mill Valley, CA: Sociology Press.

Glaser, B. G., & Strauss, A. L. (1967). *The discovery of grounded theory: Strategies for qualitative research.* Chicago: Aldine.

Grimshaw, P., Lake, M., McGrath, A., & Quartly, M. (1994). *Creating a nation.* Melbourne: McPhee Gribble.

Hartsock, N. C. M. (1983). *Money, sex and power: Toward a feminist historical materialism.* Boston: Northeastern University Press.

Miles, M. B., & Huberman, A. M. (1984). *Qualitative data analysis: A Sourcebook of new methods.* Beverly Hills, CA: Sage Publications.

Mills, C. W. (1959). *The sociological imagination.* New York: Grove Press.

Pahl, J. (1989). *Money and marriage.* London: Macmillan.

Papohunda, E. R. (1988). The nonpooling household: a challenge to theory. In D. Dwyer & J. Bruce (Eds.), *A home divided: Women and income in the Third World* (pp. 143-154). Stanford, CA: Stanford University Press.

Poiner, G. (1990). *The good old rule: Gender and other power relationships in a rural community.* Sydney: Sydney University Press.

Rabow, J., Charness, M., Aguilar, A. E., & Toomajian, J. (1992). Women and money: Cultural contrasts. In P. A. Adler & P. Adler (Ed.), *Sociological studies of child development* Vol. 5 (pp. 191-219). Greenwich, CT: JAI Press.

Ram, K. (1991). *Mukkuvar women: Gender, hegemony and capitalistic transformation in a South Indian fishing community.* Sydney: Allen and Unwin.

Richards, L. (1985). Australian family studies: On the cutting edge of Family Sociology. *Contemporary Sociology, 14*, 11-14.

Richards, L. (1990). *Nobody's home: Dreams and realities in a new suburb.* Melbourne: Oxford University Press.

Richards, L., & Richards, T. (1991a, March). *"Hard" results from "soft" data? Computing and qualitative analysis.* Paper delivered to British Sociological Association, Annual Conference, Manchester.

Richards, L., & Richards, T. (1991b). The transformation of qualitative method: Computational paradigms and research processes. In N. G. Fielding & R. M. Lee (Eds.), *Using computers in qualitative research* (pp. 38-53). London: Sage Publications.

Richards, L., & Richards, T. (1994). From filing cabinet to computer. In Bryman & R. W. Burgess (Eds.), *Analyzing qualitative data* (pp. 146-172). London: Routledge.

Richards, T., & Richards, L. (1994). Using computers in qualitative analysis. In N.K. Denzin & Y. S. Lincoln, (Eds.), *Handbook of qualitative research* (pp. 445-462). London: Sage Publications.

Richardson, L. (1994). Writing: A method of inquiry. In N. K. Denzin & Y. S. Lincoln (Eds.), *Handbook of qualitative research* (pp. 516-529). London: Sage Publications.

Singh, S. (1984). *Bank Negara Malaysia: The first 25 years 1959-1984.* Kuala Lumpur: Bank Negara Malaysia.

Singh, S. (1989). *Banking on the margin.* Collingwood, Vic: Australian Financial Counselling and Credit Reform Association.

Singh, S. (1991). *The bankers: Australia's leading bankers talk about banking today.* North Sydney, N.S.W.: Allen & Unwin Australia.

Singh, S. (1994). *Marriage, money and information: Australian consumers' use of banks.* Unpublished doctoral dissertation, Department of Sociology and Anthropology, La Trabe University, Victoria, AU.

Smelt, S. (1980). Money's place in society. *British Journal of Sociology, 31*(2), 204-223.

Stirrat, R. L. (1989). Money, men and women. In J. Parry & M. Bloch (Eds.), *Money and the morality of exchange* (pp. 94-116). Cambridge: Cambridge University Press.

Stivens, M. (1987). Industrialisation: the case of Rembau, Negeri Sembilan, Malaysia. In H. Afshar (Ed.), *Women, state & Ideology: Studies from Africa and Asia* (pp. 89-110). London: Macmillan.

Strauss, A. L. (1987). *Qualitative analysis for social scientists.* Cambridge: Cambridge University Press.

Strauss, A., & Corbin, J. (1990). *Basics of qualitative research: Grounded theory procedures and techniques.* Newbury Park, CA: Sage Publications.

Summers, A. (1975). *Damned whores and God's police: The colonization of women in Australia.* Ringwood, Vic: Penguin.

Summers, A. (1994). *Damned whores and God's police* (rev. ed.). Ringwood, Vic.: Penguin.

Thorogood, N. (1987). Race, class and gender: the politics of housework. In J. Brannen & O. Wilson (Eds.), *Give and take in families* (pp. 18-41). London: Allen & Unwin.

Tilly, C. (1988). Review essays. *Sociological Forum, 3*(4), 613-614.

Turner, B. S. (1986). Simmel, rationalisation and the sociology of money. *The Sociological Review, 34*(1), 93-114.

Van Maanen, J. (Ed.). (1979). Epilogue: Qualitative methods reclaimed. In J. Van Maanen (Ed.), *Qualitative methodology* (pp. 247-268). Newbury Park, CA: Sage Publications.

Zelizer, V. (1979). *Morals and markets: The development of life insurance in the United States.* New York: Columbia University Press.

Zelizer, V. (1985). *Pricing the priceless child: The changing social value of children.* New York: Basic Books.

Zelizer, V. (1988). Beyond the polemics on the market: Establishing a theoretical and empirical agenda. *Sociological Forum* 3 (Fall): 614-634.

Zelizer, V. (1989). The social meaning of money: "Special monies." *American Journal of Sociology, 95*(2), 342-377.

Zuboff, S. (1988). *In the age of the smart machine: The future of work and power.* New York: Basic Books.

Reflexivity and Qualitative Family Research: Insider's Perspectives in Bereaving the Loss of a Child

Elizabeth B. Farnsworth

SUMMARY. The author uses her experiences with death and bereavement to select her research problem and to become a sensitive collaborator and listener with others who had the same experience of the loss of a loved one. From deep listening and opening of her heart to colleagues she began the integration of personal, empirical, theoretical, practical and spiritual knowledge into her research. A reconceptualization of maternal bereavement occurred. It is an open, fluid, dialectical process of change. *[Article copies available for a fee from The Haworth Document Delivery Service: 1-800-342-9678. E-mail address: getinfo@haworth.com]*

KEYWORDS. Researchers' experience, Child's death, Stories, Qualitative research, Feminist theory, Feminist research

Elizabeth B. Farnsworth is a therapist in private practice and Adjunct Assistant Professor, Central Virginia Community College, Lynchburg, VA 24502. Address correspondence to: Elizabeth B. Farnsworth, P. O. Box 1103, Forest, VA 24551.

The author gratefully acknowledges the helpful comments of Jane F. Gilgun and two anonymous reviewers.

This article is developed from the author's (1994) dissertation.

[Haworth co-indexing entry note]: "Reflexivity and Qualitative Family Research: Insider's Perspectives in Bereaving the Loss of a Child." Farnsworth, Elizabeth B. Co-published simultaneously in *Marriage & Family Review* (The Haworth Press, Inc.) Vol. 24, No. 3/4, 1996, pp. 399-415; and: *The Methods and Methodologies of Qualitative Family Research* (ed: Marvin B. Sussman, and Jane F. Gilgun) The Haworth Press, Inc., 1996, pp. 399-415. Single or multiple copies of this article are available for a fee from The Haworth Document Delivery Service [1-800-342-9678, 9:00 a.m. - 5:00 p.m. (EST). E-mail address: getinfo@haworth.com].

Contemporary qualitative researchers have noted that the private lives of researchers influence the process and products of research (Allen, 1994; Daly, 1992; Fonow & Cook, 1991; Krieger, 1991; Marks, 1994; Stanley & Wise, 1991). Research is a matter of selective perception. As Marks (1994) said, "What we select and what we attend to rests on who we are and what we are becoming" (p. 166). Allen (1994) discussed the fusion of personal, theoretical, empirical, and political in her work as a *process* that has guided her beyond traditional family theory toward postmodernist thought–a consciousness of pluralism and change in individual and family experience (Baber & Allen, 1992).

Daly (1992) suggested that the personal experiences of researchers are "essential parts of the research process, and they demand not just acknowledgment, but conscious and deliberate inclusion" (p. 109). How can the self be brought into research processes in ways that are conscious and deliberate, yet nonoppressive to research participants? Can we come closer to the lived realities of individuals and families by acknowledging our personal experiences as scholars and members of families?

In this paper, I present one perspective on these questions based on my dissertation research–a qualitative study of mothers who were bereaved of a young child between birth and two and one-half years of age (Farnsworth, 1994). The research emphasized mothers' stories and perceptions of change following the death of a child. Feminist and family stress theory guided this research. An expanded discussion of the research is the subject of another paper (Farnsworth & Allen, 1994, unpublished manuscript). The current paper focuses on the ways self was integrated into the study.

Drawing upon my own personal experience as a bereaved mother guided me in honoring the complexity of the death of a child in the mothers' ongoing lives, to listen attentively and quietly, to know when to probe, and when to reflect upon their words in ways that connected our similar, yet unique experiences. The decision to draw consciously and deliberately upon reflexivity departs from traditional social science assumptions of researcher as expert and authority on the experiences of others (Belenky, Clinchy, Goldberger, & Tarule, 1986). Reflexivity invites participants into the research process by encouraging them to take the lead as conversationalists and authors of their own stories with the researcher becoming a respectful, guiding co-learner. By "drawing out" the stories of others in this way, the nuances of the meanings of experience can evolve and be understood by others.

As a bereaved mother who was also a doctoral student, I initiated my graduate study with a personal interest in bereavement and found numerous opportunities to delve into various aspects of the topic for course projects. When I began my dissertation research, it seemed comfortable and honest to reveal to potential participants that I was also a bereaved mother and therefore had personal as well as academic interests in the topic. Knowing of our common ground at the time of initial contact seemed to facilitate the process of forging connections with one other (Belenky et al., 1986). During the course of the interviews, the mothers revealed that they felt relieved to share their feelings and perspectives with someone who was also a bereaved mother and that they would have been cautious about going into as much detail with someone who might not understand. All of the participants discussed experiences with others in their social systems that had, in some way, marginalized their experiences. From these experiences, they had learned to be cautious in sharing their perspectives with others.

However, insider status is not a panacea in conducting research. While it can help "to unravel the experience of the other" (Daly, 1992, p. 110), it may simultaneously present challenges to the conduct of research. Use of personal information must be drawn upon selectively in a manner that facilitates the interviews with participants. The goal of research studies, after all, is to understand participants, and all that goes on in interviews must serve that goal. Far from presenting a fully articulated perspective in this paper, I recognize that my own awareness of the self in qualitative research is emergent. This paper represents a step in my own process of fusing personal, theoretical, empirical, and political knowledge.

CONCEPTUAL FRAMEWORKS

Two perspectives, feminism and the contextual model of family stress, provided conceptual undergirding for my research with a sample of 10 mothers who had been bereaved at least two years prior to the initiation of the study. The purpose of selecting a sample of mothers removed two years from the losses was to move away from a study of symptoms and move toward a study of process and change in bereavement experiences.

Feminism

A feminist perspective provided an orientation in which the mothers' stories, experiences of change, and messages to others in the social system were highlighted. Feminist scholars critique aspects of traditional social science that records conditions of devaluation of women and systematically ignores alternative possibilities (Westkott, 1979). A sociology *for* women places women and their concerns in the center of analysis with the goal of emancipation from oppressive conditions (Westkott, 1979). According to Acker, Barry and Esseveld (1991), an emancipatory social science "would provide women with understandings of how their every-day worlds, their trials and troubles, were and are generated by the larger social structure" (p. 135). In short, feminism illuminates the personal perspectives of both researchers and researched, places these experiences within particular sociohistorical contexts, and fosters understanding and connection between researchers and researched.

Allen (1994) has found that a feminist perspective has freed her to ask more inclusive questions in the conduct of research and to see previously obscured realities in her own life and the lives of her research participants. As I worked, I, too, began to see the influence of stereotypical ideology in my own life and to recognize the value of telling one's own stories rather than having those stories told from the perspectives of others. It is as though the act of telling and naming our experiences serves to change consciousness of ourselves and our experiences.

Feminism and Qualitative Methodology

A feminist conceptual perspective coupled with qualitative methodology were useful and appropriate in my research to address the sensitive nature of maternal bereavement. Experiences of growth and marginalization became visible as women's actual voices and perspectives were revealed in the research. Feminism, as a world view, has changed my consciousness of myself and the social constraints and opportunities surrounding my experiences and simultaneously increased my tolerance and respect for the experiences of others. It has fueled my desire to practice and write in ways which are accessible to others.

As I read Allen's (1994) words regarding the influence of feminism in her research, I continued to reflect upon my own project while remaining open to other questions and other realities in my work. For example, one complex truth in my own life is that the death of a child, while painful, has also presented unique opportunities for me to grow and change; yet this is a perspective that has evolved over time for me. As an insider, I recall the enormous sense of loss, pain, and anger I felt during the early months of my bereavement.

Drawing upon personal knowledge, I felt that the issue of growth and change in bereaved mothers is an issue to be approached with care and sensitivity by researchers. A feminist perspective leaves open many possibilities and has expanded my consciousness of process, complexity, and dialectics in bereavement and pointed me to fluidity in the bereavement of myself and others. This fluidity contrasted noticeably with the assumptions in the literature that the symptomatology of depression and somatic complaints change little over time (Cleiren, 1993). This recognition, in and of itself, was an important benefit of the study for myself and others— bereavement, while painful, is not a life sentence to psychopathology. Drawing upon my own bereavement experiences led me to review the literature with a personally informed consciousness. Maturing in my own bereavement, I am no longer sensitive about acknowledging the tremendous positive impact of the life *and* death of my infant son; yet I also acknowledge that the pain surrounding this loss emerges and revisits from time to time unlike other deaths I have experienced. Feminist ideology freed me to think about these complex, dialectical issues in lived experience (Stacey, 1990).

Feminist Perspectives on Motherhood

Feminist perspectives on motherhood illuminate standard sociological assumptions about gender in families and essentialist imperatives for women (Baber & Allen, 1992). A traditional family consists of a heterosexual legal marriage, an instrumental male breadwinner, an expressive female homemaker, and the presence of biological children (Cheal, 1991; Scanzoni, Polonko, Teachman, & Thompson, 1989). Within this model, motherhood is assumed to be a natural role for women (Andersen, 1993). Central to the ideology of a "good mother" is the preservation of the life of a child (Ruddick, 1989). The death of a child, thus situated, is often accompanied by blame and/or pathologizing on the part of the social system and the belief in mothers that they have failed in their natural "roles" (Andersen, 1993; Dally, 1982).

Thus, motherhood became visible to me as a social construction involving both pain and pleasure (Ruddick, 1989). I became conscious of the possible diversities of potential respondents along age, race, class, sexual orientation, and functional status junctures. Feminism frees scholars and research participants alike to place their experiences within a social context and to rethink traditional views about women in families (Baber & Allen, 1992). In my study, I took seriously the plurality in women's experience.

Family Stress

A second conceptual perspective guided my thinking in the research— the contextual model of family stress (Walker, 1985). This model supported an examination of the perspectives of individuals in families regarding the impact of stressful circumstances. The death of a child is assumed to be stressful for parents (Cleiren, 1993; Gilbert, 1989; Schiff, 1977). Stress is assumed to have a rippling effect on multiple interdependent levels of the social system–the individual, the dyad, family and social contexts, community and cultural levels of analysis (Walker, 1985). Mothers are not only reactive; they are also *active* and influence the social system within which they are situated. The contextual model of family stress was consistent with a feminist perspective, because a range of possible experiences was central to the perspective.

Assessing my experiences from a contextual lens enabled me to acknowledge my own embeddedness within a particular socio-historical context. To increase my consciousness about my own and others' contextual experiences, I read excerpts of letters and diaries of bereaved mothers of diverse historical contexts. Reading the words of Puritan and colonial women (Dally, 1982; Rosenblatt, 1983) and homesteader women (Stewart, 1913) dialectically brought me closer to myself–I felt freer to acknowledge my own experience as one in a stream of historical circumstances, not superior, not inferior, but nonetheless significant and appropriate to reflect upon as I carried out my research.

In summary, feminist and contextual conceptual perspectives emphasize diversity of experience and the voices of researcher and researched. Qualitative methodology in which the voices and perspectives of individuals are visible (Acker et al., 1991; Gilgun, 1992; Rosenblatt & Fischer, 1993) was an appropriate methodological choice which augmented the conceptual perspectives guiding the study, illuminated the phenomenon under investigation, and allowed my personal exposure to the phenomenon to inform the research.

METHOD

Qualitative research "is defined as processes used to make sense of data that are represented by words or pictures and not by numbers" (Gilgun, 1992, p. 24). There is a great deal of variability in qualitative research and theories but common to almost all approaches is "a focus on meanings and other subjectivities in or about families" (Rosenblatt & Fischer, 1993, p. 168). In contrast to "an arm's length methodology like a mailed questionnaire, qualitative family research closely involves the researcher with participants and data" (Daly, 1992, p. 9). While feminist scholars do not advocate a singular methodological approach to research (Harding, 1987: Jayaratne & Stewart, 1991; Peplau & Conrad, 1989; Reinharz, 1992; Thompson, 1992; Walker, 1985), qualitative methodology is consistent with feminist and other perspectives that emphasize the experiences and perspectives of research participants, the social construction of knowledge, and the place of researchers in the investigation.

I conducted in-depth qualitative interviews, desiring an open-ended format based on relationships between researcher and researched and that allowed participants to generate their own stories, words, and images. Each participant was interviewed twice for a total of about 5 hours. Each interview was audiotaped and transcribed verbatim. The participants also shared poems, writings, photographs, and other mementos of the deceased child. One mother, for example, painted a rich, vivid picture of her child's funeral with her words and photographs as she pointed out the location on the family's farm where her 3-month old son is buried:

> [W]e lined it [coffin] with a blanket . . . I knew instinctively that the more we could do ourselves, the better off we would be. . . . we had a private burial with just the immediate family and the grandparents. . . . We buried him in the family graveyard, which is up here [on the hill near the house]. The service, we planned that ourselves. (Marie)

As Marie spoke, I had a sense of being present during her baby's funeral. I felt a reverence and respect for her experience as revealed and elaborated through this choice of methodology. Her knowledge surrounding her family's autonomous decisions regarding the funeral was apparent to me as I listened. Reflexivity in the conduct of research involves talking, listening, and sharing experiences that build connections and shared understanding between participants and researcher. In the process, participants are empowered to fully participate by sharing in-depth information about their lives which is handled respectfully by the researcher. Qualitative methodology allows the researcher flexibility to get close to the social life of participants and to experience a part of their reality. My understanding of Marie's knowledge and strength was deepened as *she* guided me to understand what was significant about her baby's funeral.

Qualitative methodology provides opportunities to build nonhierarchical relationships with participants and to access "privileged information [with] a heavy responsibility to present it respectfully in written reports" (Rosenblatt & Fischer, 1993, p. 167). This choice of methodology allowed the meanings and experiences of the respondents to be visible in the document. The diversities of families were also apparent to me as I connected with mothers of diverse ages, races, classes, and family structures.

The conceptual perspectives guiding my research and the choice of qualitative methodology provided fertile ground for me to articulate my own subjectivity in the conduct of the study. Who am I as the researcher? What interest and perspectives do I bring to the topic under investigation? How can the self be inserted into the process? Personal narratives were a way of entering the study and revealing my personal exposure to the topic. These reflections about my own experiences freed me to be more attentive to and respectful of the stories of the participants without overwhelming the study with my own perspectives.

PERSONAL NARRATIVES

One way consciously and deliberately to insert the self into the research processes is to begin to clarify one's own experience and perspectives on the phenomenon under study (Krieger, 1991). With the support and encouragement of my doctoral advisor, Dr. Katherine R. Allen, I began my own personal narrative at the proposal stage of my research. She introduced me to Krieger's (1991) work which provided a model as I made this transition to articulate my own experience in the research journey. Having been influenced by traditional ideas about researcher objectivity, I was hesitant to do this initially. I also drew upon Dr. Allen's classroom teaching–a model of reflexivity in which the personal experiences of instructors and students are acknowledged and taken seriously in the learning process (Allen, 1988). Such connections served to increase the consciousness of instructors and learners and prepare all participants for their own reflexive journeys. This was a powerful, positive model in thinking about my future interactions with research participants.

As I continue to reflect upon my own journey as a student, I am conscious that these classroom activities and the construction of personal narratives under the supervision of a feminist scholar empowered me to connect in a new way with *my own* story, my own lived experience, prior to entering the homes of others to do my research. Dialectically, this connection freed me from my own opinions and perspectives enabling me to enter the research arena conscious, yet unencumbered, by my own history. I began my narrative as follows:

> I entered my doctoral program in 1990 with a story to tell, an experience which continues to influence my life over time, and, perhaps, a search for comprehension of a seemingly incomprehensible experience. Frequently, I have "left out" the personal, because it seemed trivial and inappropriate in academia; but as I have read and studied, I have located epistemological, theoretical, and methodological underpinnings which bring me back to what I know well, the lived

experience as a source of knowledge, a foundation for the creation of social science.

As I continued to write my narrative, it became more revealing of my personal experience surrounding my child's death:

> In 1985, my second child, Thomas, who had Down Syndrome, died at the age of 7 months. He had spent the last 6 weeks of his life in a university medical center undergoing and recovering from open heart surgery. The weeks were long and hard, as we watched him improve, only to slowly slip away. I cried rivers of tears at his bedside, as I gradually came to embrace the inevitable, my powerlessness as his mother to kiss the wounds and heal them.

As I reflected upon my writing, I became conscious of knowledge that might help me understand and conceptualize the meanings of research participants. For example, I recognized that my own child died following a lengthy illness. This brought to my attention that a sudden, unexpected death is a diversity in maternal bereavement. Deaths from Sudden Infant Death Syndrome (SIDS) and accidents, for example, could be expected to lead to variations in mothers' experiences of bereavement.

Another theme I became aware of in my personal narrative was the use of the word "we." Who experiences the bereavement? Is there a partner, a dyadic context, with whom bereavement and responsibilities for surviving siblings are shared? Do these relationships provide buffers or additional obstacles for mothers? The experiences of bereaved single mothers, for example, do not occur in the same social context. Some mothers experience the death of a child in the context of limited social support and financial resources, and the data bore out this variation. Such contexts became clear to me as I reflected upon and analyzed my own personal narratives, went into the field, and collected data. One participant said of her experience:

> There are a lot of women that are losing children that have no one. You have to [work], you have no choice, not unless you just want to wallow and lose everything. . . . I feel like I am a better mother than I was before this happened. . . . You have a tendency to take a lot for granted. (Val)

Writing my narrative and then entering the field challenged my personal sense of powerlessness as a bereaved mother; there was something else, a sense of agency and action, an awareness of the social context within which contemporary mothers experience bereavement:

I did more than cry. I became an activist, resisting those who said that bereaved mothers are passive and need to "get on" with their lives. Perhaps "getting on" with one's life after the death of a child involves change for mothers—in priorities, values, and behaviors.

This increase in awareness led me to recognize and articulate more complex possibilities in bereaved mothers' experiences than those traditionally captured in the literature. Standard assumptions of depression and somatic complaints were revealed to be only a slice of a more complex picture of growth and change in mothers who lose a child to death. This awareness contributed to the product of the study by directing my attention to numerous possibilities in the lives of the mothers.

The process of writing my stories and perspectives empowered me to connect more deeply with my own experience in a social system which simultaneously idealizes and blames mothers for the outcomes of children (Ruddick, 1989). Coming to terms with my own sense of powerlessness in this way seemed to transform and continues to transform my experience of bereavement and the sense of loss of control. Somehow the incomprehensible has become comprehensible as I became part of, listened to and resonated with previously unheard experiences of women. Reflexive activities empowered me and enabled me to acknowledge personal experience and interest in the topic under investigation (Baber, 1994). Beyond acknowledgement has come a sense of making visible that which has been invisible and conducting research which has the potential to empower myself and others.

Becoming more conscious of the attitudes and biases I brought to the project freed me to listen more attentively and nonjudgmentally to the similar and diverse experiences of others. By honoring self-knowledge, I felt prepared to enter the field with care for the experiences of others, with renewed energy and ability to listen to the nuances of each respondent's story, and respect for the advantages of consulting and listening to the self as a researcher (Thompson, 1992).

I felt changed in this process, and I continue to benefit from self-awareness, reflexivity (Fonow & Cook, 1991), and consciousness of contextual circumstances (Walker, 1985). I believe I have learned to think more inclusively, and less painfully, about diversity of experience—my own and others. These attitudes and values now travel with me in my research, my classroom teaching, and my practice of therapy. In taking self-knowledge seriously, I have learned to listen more attentively and less reactively. In research, teaching, and therapy, these perspectives seem to bring me closer and respectfully to the experiences of others.

Reflexive Practices and Participants

I conducted two in-depth interviews with each of 10 research partici-pants. While the interviews began with an open-ended interview guide to obtain mothers' perspectives of their experiences and changes on multiple levels of the social system, they emerged as conversations between women with a similar lived experience that is socially taboo in late twen-tieth-century America (Stinson, Lasker, Lohmann, & Toedter, 1992). When a child dies, the natural order is defied, leaving mothers in an ambiguous social position—mothers without the physical presence of the child who died. The conceptual perspectives guiding the study focused my attention to the circumstances of women in a cultural context which often disadvantages and distorts their experiences (Andersen, 1993; Baber & Allen, 1992; Westkott, 1979).

As I studied the literature, it became apparent to me that women's experiences as creative actors following the death of a child were invisible in many studies. Their voices and actual experiences were often obscured, and their experiences were portrayed in terms of symptoms (Cleiren, 1993). I attempted to place women in the center of the study. Doing so guided me to listen to mothers' stories and increased my consciousness of change in their lives following the death of a child. The data indicated that the mothers redefined themselves. In their work settings and in their fami-lies, they experienced increased empathy. In addition, they took more full advantage of opportunities to teach and help others. They started bereave-ment support groups; they assisted other women through the labor and delivery of stillborn children; they became patient advocates in hospitals. Others became more conscious of the needs of living children and partners and discussed "pulling together" as a family. Reflexivity—processes of talking, listening, and sharing during the study—enabled the research par-ticipants to become authors of their own stories and to teach me what was important to them. As a result, findings were articulated which might have otherwise been invisible. Drawing upon the complexity of my own experi-ence enabled me to listen attentively for meanings, perspectives, and change.

While the purpose of this paper is not to provide an articulation of the data from this study, two excerpts illustrate the complexities of change in mothers following a child's death:

> I have finished nursing school, and I do work in labor and delivery; and I've had a lot of dead babies to deal with. But what's always been real dear to me has been life, in general, the birthing in general, and I always looked forward to having that first delivery that I would

> get to do. And my first delivery was a stillborn. And I didn't antici-
> pate that. It was in the middle of the night, and the doctor was on his
> way. . . . I knew inside that I was gonna have to . . . then I had to just
> remind myself that, who better to deliver this baby than me? . . . With
> all the courage I could muster, I did an excellent delivery. . . . that
> was really hard, and yet, who better than me? I didn't think it was
> weird to touch and kiss that baby. (Beth)

> I think it's made me more compassionate. . . . I never thought I could
> deal with anybody who had disabilities like that, you know, retarded;
> and because of him, I got involved with [the early intervention
> program] as a special needs facilitator and found out it's something I
> like and I am good at. (Terry)

Again and again, there was evidence in the data of positive change in mothers who had experienced the death of a child. Reflecting on their experiences in a supportive context seemed to allow them to illuminate themselves as creative actors and, hopefully, to take these reflections into their lives in a more deliberate fashion. Their experiences were far more complex than symptoms. The qualitative research design emphasized their words allowing complex changes to be articulated, not lost, in the process.

Attempting to reduce hierarchy (Oakley, 1981) in the research process, I acted as conversational guide, not an expert on the participants' experiences. How do these practices affect participants? The data suggested that bereaved mothers were comfortable sharing their experiences with an "insider" and that they are hesitant to share the range of their experiences with others who may not be sensitive to the topic:

> It was easy for me to talk with you. I wouldn't have told you half of
> what I told you if you came in here . . . somebody else might have
> been horrified . . . but I thought you would probably understand that.
> I wouldn't have opened up as much, there's no way. (Jill)

> This is the first time that I have really told this whole story. You
> don't go up to people that you meet now, you don't even tell them,
> you know, you don't have many people that you can talk to about it.
> (Jan)

> I was anticipating that I was going to be depressed [from the inter-
> views], but I wasn't. . . . it was real easy to talk with you. (Terry)

> I've never met you before, but I'm comfortable with you. . . . [but] I
> was amazed. . . . I am totally in shock about how powerful the

experience is. . . . It shook me a little bit, but it renewed where I am coming from, where I want to go, and my practices [as a labor and delivery nurse]. (Beth)

It's been a positive thing. . . . It helped me to talk to you about it. . . . talking to you about it was different, because you and I both know what it's like. (Wendy)

These data provide evidence that drawing upon personal experience in qualitative research and revealing it to research participants constructs a bridge between women similarly situated and fosters the development of participants as authors of their own stories. Yet, the topic was sensitive and painful at times for both myself and the participants. Tears were shared as mothers constructed their memories. Qualitative research is labor-intensive, and I was generally very fatigued following the interviews. It was important to manage my own feelings and to be conscious of the ethics of my practices during all phases of the investigation.

Ethical Issues

The sensitive nature of the research called for special attention to ethical issues. When research involves a sensitive area, self-interest can be oppressive to research participants, unless researchers reflexively manage their own responses and experiences. My doctoral advisor, through our collaboration, helped me to maintain this delicate balance by guiding me to write personal narratives and to discuss the study with her at length. These activities freed me to focus on the participants' words and their needs during the study, not my own. It was important to keep my own subjectivity separate from the subjectivities of the participants.

In addition, interpretations must be faithful to the data (Gilgun, 1992). Again, my advisor provided valuable feedback on my conceptualizations of the data; our conversations and collaborations throughout the investigation helped me to think theoretically about the data and to see linkages and differences in participants' bereavement experiences. For example, some mothers found bereavement support groups helpful as they adjusted to the death of a child; others did not. This highlighted the importance of listening attentively to participants and understanding varying needs and perceptions of support. It is important to allow similarities and differences to be visible in the data, and qualitative methodology is useful in achieving such elaboration of diversity.

I also informed the women prior to the interviews that discussions regarding a child's death may be difficult and that it was acceptable for them to interrupt or stop an interview at any time. Because informed consent is problematic in qualitative research due to the emergent nature of the study (Daly, 1992), I informed them that they were free to ask me to delete any material from the transcript data that they felt was too sensitive to be included in the written document. I shared the results of the study with the women and asked for their feedback (Acker et al., 1991).

One woman asked me to add a sentence which clarified two items related to family support and the importance of spirituality in her bereavement experience. In this way, participants had some control over the presentation of their experiences; but ultimately, I was the author of the document.

Finally, giving something back to participants is important in qualitative research (Daly, 1992). I presented each mother with a wrapped gift at the conclusion of the final interview in appreciation of her time and energy during the research. I also provided information about bereavement books and materials and a list of support groups and counselors if participants felt additional assistance was needed. The delicate balance here is between wanting to share knowledge and experience and not assuming an all-knowing attitude. Insider's knowledge is helpful in deciding "the kinds of things to say, how to say them, and when to bring them up in the course of the interview" (Daly, 1992, p. 109).

Yet, there are limits to "insider's" understandings of the experiences of others; healthy skepticism about my understandings guided me to draw upon gentle probes and open-ended questions to double-check my perspectives with the participants.

Drawing upon my own experiences guided me to understand that participants are giving a tremendous investment of time and energy to divulge sensitive material. An overarching framework of support, empathy, and respect toward the participants guided the phases of the research.

DISCUSSION

The conscious use of self in the process of research allowed my personal interest in the topic to be visible and guided me toward understanding and respecting the experiences of others. Reflexivity enabled me to become more conscious of my own experiences as a bereaved mother and then to put these experiences aside in order to listen with care and attention to the research participants. In turn, their perspectives helped me to continue to explore, to reflect upon my own bereavement and to respect further my own experiences.

These processes were complex and often painful, but they helped me begin to integrate personal, theoretical, empirical, and political knowledge in my research. Feminist and contextual perspectives broadened my consciousness of diversities of women's experiences and enabled me to consult and listen to myself during all phases of the investigation (Thompson, 1992). My own journey was facilitated by my feminist mentor and advisor who was connected and dedicated to our collaboration. The choice of qualitative methodology supported my attention to process and allowed the actual words and experiences of participants to be visible in the study. These conscious, deliberate choices also helped me to draw upon self-knowledge and enabled me to connect meaningfully with the participants. In my ongoing life and work, I continue to reflect upon our conversations and to reconceptualize maternal bereavement as an open, fluid, dialectical process of change.

REFERENCES

Acker, J., Barry, K., & Esseveld J. (1991). Objectivity and truth: Problems in doing feminist research. In M. M. Fonow & J. A. Cook (Eds.), *Beyond methodology: Feminist scholarship as lived research* (pp. 133-153). Indianapolis: Indiana University Press.

Allen, K. R. (1994). Feminist reflections on lifelong single women. In D. L. Sollie & L. A. Leslie (Eds.), *Gender, families, and close relationships: Feminist research journeys* (pp. 97-119). Thousand Oaks, CA: Sage.

Allen, K. R. (1988). Integrating a feminist perspective into family studies courses. *Family Relations, 37,* 29-35.

Andersen, M. L. (1993). *Thinking about women: Sociological perspectives on sex and gender* (3rd ed). New York: Macmillan.

Baber, K. M. (1994). Studying women's sexualities: Feminist transformations. In D. L. Sollie & L. A. Leslie (Eds.), *Gender, families, and close relationships: Feminist research journeys* (pp. 97-119). Thousand Oaks, CA: Sage.

Baber, K. M., & Allen, K. R. (1992). *Women and families: Feminist reconstructions.* New York: Guilford.

Belenky, M. F., Clinchy, B. M., Goldberger, N. R., & Tarule, J. (1986). *Women's ways of knowing.* New York: Basic.

Cheal, D. (1991). *Family and the state of theory.* Toronto: University of Toronto Press.

Cleiren, M. P. H. D. (1993). *Bereavement and adaptation: A comparative study of the aftermath of death.* Philadelphia: Hemisphere.

Daly, K. (1992). Parenthood as problematic: Insider interviews with couples seeking to adopt. In J. F. Gilgun, K. Daly, & G. Handel (Eds.), *Qualitative methods in family research* (pp. 103-125). Newbury Park, CA: Sage.

Dally, A. (1982). *Inventing motherhood: The consequences of an ideal.* New York: Schocken.

Farnsworth, E. B. (1994). *Reflexive conversations with bereaved mothers: A feminist and contextual perspective.* Unpublished doctoral dissertation, Virginia Polytechnic Institute and State University, Blacksburg, VA.

Farnsworth, E, B,, & Allen, K, R, (1994), *Reflexive conversations with bereaved mothers.* Unpublished manuscript.

Fonow, M. M., & Cook, J. A. (1991). Back to the future: A look at the second wave of feminist epistemology and methodology. In M. M. Fonow & J. A. Cook (Eds.), *Beyond methodology: Feminist scholarship as lived research* (pp. 1-15). Bloomington: Indiana University Press.

Gilbert, K. R. (1989). Interactive grief and coping in the marital dyad. *Death Studies, 13*, 605-626.

Gilgun, J. F. (1992). Definitions, methodologies, and methods in qualitative family research. In J. F. Gilgun, K. Daly, & G. Handel (Eds.), *Qualitative methods in family research* (pp. 22-39). Newbury Park, CA: Sage.

Harding, S. (1987). Introduction. Is there a feminist method? In S. Harding (Ed.), *Feminism and methodology: Social science issues* (pp. 1-14). Bloomington: Indiana University Press.

Jayaratne, T. E., & Stewart, A. J. (1991). Quantitative and qualitative methods in the social sciences: Current feminist issues and practical strategies. In M. M. Fonow & Krieger, S. (1991), *Social science and the self: Personal essays on an art form.* New Brunswick, NJ: Rutgers University Press.

Marks, S. R. (1994). Studying workplace intimacy: Havens at work. In D. L. Sollie & L. A. Leslie (Eds.), *Gender, families, and close relationships: Feminist research journeys* (pp. 145-168). Thousand Oaks, CA: Sage.

Oakley, A. (1981). Interviewing women: A contradiction in terms. In H. Roberts (Ed.), *Doing feminist research* (pp. 30-61). London: Routledge & Kegan Paul.

Peplau, L. A., & Conrad, E. (1989). Beyond nonsexist research: The perils of feminist methods in psychology. *Psychology of Women Quarterly, 13*, 381-402.

Reinharz, S. (1992). *Feminist methods in social research.* New York: Oxford University Press.

Rosenblatt, P. C. (1983). *Bitter, bitter tears: Nineteenth century diarists and twentieth century grief theories.* Minneapolis: University of Minnesota Press.

Rosenblatt, P. C., & Fischer, L. R. (1993). Qualitative family research. In P. G. Boss, W. J. Doherty, R. LaRossa, W. R. Schumm, & S. K. Steinmetz (Eds.), *Sourcebook of family theories and methods: A contextual approach* (pp. 167-177). New York: Plenum.

Ruddick, S. (1989). *Maternal thinking: Toward a politics of peace.* New York: Ballantine.

Scanzoni, J., Polonko, K., Teachman, J., & Thompson, L. (1989). *The sexual bond: Rethinking families and close relationships.* Newbury Park, CA: Sage.

Schiff, H. S. (1977). *The bereaved parent.* New York: Penguin.

Stacey, J. (1990). *Brave new families: Stories of domestic upheaval in late twentieth century America.* New York: Basic.

Stanley, L., & Wise, S. (1991). Feminist research, feminist consciousness, and experiences of sexism. In M. M. Fonow & J. A. Cook (Eds.), *Beyond methodology: Feminist scholarship as lived research* (pp. 265-283). Bloomington: Indiana University Press.

Stewart, E. P. (1913). *Letters of a woman homesteader.* Boston: The Atlantic Monthly Company.

Stinson, K. M., Lasker, J. N., Lohmann, J., & Toedter, L. J. (1992). Parents' grief following pregnancy loss: A comparison of mothers and fathers. *Family Relations, 41*, 218-223.

Thompson, L. (1992). Feminist methodology for family studies. *Journal of Marriage and the Family, 54*, 3-18.

Walker, A. J. (1985). Reconceptualizing family stress. *Journal of Marriage and the Family, 47*, 827-837.

Westkott, M. (1979). Feminist criticism of the social sciences. *Harvard Educational Review, 49*, 422-430.

Index

Page numbers followed by "t" indicate tables.

interviews
  with community members, 303
  conversation guides for, 104
  elder role models study,
    130-132
  ethnographic, 57-87
  family, 308-309,317-318,
    335-347
  gender and power issues in
    marriage, 89-104
  informal, 303
  post-retirement women's work
    study, 170-171
  resources for, 266-267
  service provider, 309-310
  transcription of, 318
justice principles in child support,
  203-216
  coding by pattern matching,
    204-207
  modified analytic induction,
    207-215,210t-211t
  theoretical sampling from text,
    204
key informants, 306-307
low-income family ethnographic
  study
  data analysis, 311-315
  data collection, 307-311
  multiplicity of, 302-303
  pragmatic approach to study,
    300-301
  pre-fieldwork, 303-304
  purposive sampling, 304-307
  research design, 301-302
marriage money study
  coding process changes, 378
  connecting analysis with
    theory and research, 381-382
  grounded theory and methods,
    374-376
  index changes and text
    retrieval, 378-380,379t
  memos as broad codes,
    376-377

  prior theory and personal
    experience, 372-374
  qualitative computing, 377
  writing as analysis, 380-381
narrative accounts, 357-360
  analyses, 358-359
  sample and procedure,
    357-358
photo-journals, 310
post-retirement women's work
  study, 169-174
  data analysis, 171-173,172t
  data gathering, 169-171
reflexivity study of marital
  decision making, 90-93
researcher reflections, 310-311
resource maps, 310
site selection, 304-305
windshield surveys, 303
Middle years, of family life cycle,
  19-21
(University of) Minnesota, 1-5,9-40,
  123-164,193-222,223-239,
  323-334
Moments of truth, 29-31
Money
  African-American adolescent
    women's perceptions,
    115-116
  Bahamian folk tales about, 71-72
  and marriage, 369-398. *See also*
    Marriage money
  social meaning of, 369-398. *See*
    also Marriage money
Money issues, xxi
  in women's work, 177-179
Motherhood, 18-19
  feminist perspectives on, 403
Mothers, African-American
  adolescent women's
  perceptions, 116-118
Mourning, 399-415. *See also*
  Bereavement

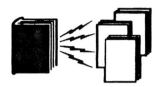

Haworth
DOCUMENT DELIVERY
SERVICE

This valuable service provides a single-article order form for any article from a Haworth journal.

- *Time Saving:* No running around from library to library to find a specific article.
- *Cost Effective:* All costs are kept down to a minimum.
- *Fast Delivery:* Choose from several options, including same-day FAX.
- *No Copyright Hassles:* You will be supplied by the original publisher.
- *Easy Payment:* Choose from several easy payment methods.

Open Accounts Welcome for ...
- Library Interlibrary Loan Departments
- Library Network/Consortia Wishing to Provide Single-Article Services
- Indexing/Abstracting Services with Single Article Provision Services
- Document Provision Brokers and Freelance Information Service Providers

---

MAIL or *FAX* THIS ENTIRE ORDER FORM TO:

Haworth Document Delivery Service
The Haworth Press, Inc.
10 Alice Street
Binghamton, NY 13904-1580

or FAX: 1-800-895-0582
or CALL: 1-800-342-9678
9am-5pm EST

PLEASE SEND ME PHOTOCOPIES OF THE FOLLOWING SINGLE ARTICLES:

1) Journal Title: _____
   Vol/Issue/Year: _____ Starting & Ending Pages: _____
   Article Title: _____
   _____

2) Journal Title: _____
   Vol/Issue/Year: _____ Starting & Ending Pages: _____
   Article Title: _____
   _____

3) Journal Title: _____
   Vol/Issue/Year: _____ Starting & Ending Pages: _____
   Article Title: _____
   _____

4) Journal Title: _____
   Vol/Issue/Year: _____ Starting & Ending Pages: _____
   Article Title: _____
   _____

(See other side for Costs and Payment Information)

COSTS: Please figure your cost to order quality copies of an article.

1. Set-up charge per article: $8.00
   ($8.00 × number of separate articles) _____

2. Photocopying charge for each article:

   1-10 pages: $1.00 _____

   11-19 pages: $3.00 _____

   20-29 pages: $5.00 _____

   30+ pages: $2.00/10 pages _____

3. Flexicover (optional): $2.00/article _____

4. Postage & Handling: US: $1.00 for the first article/

   $.50 each additional article _____

   Federal Express: $25.00 _____

   Outside US: $2.00 for first article/
   $.50 each additional article _____

5. Same-day FAX service: $.35 per page _____

GRAND TOTAL: _____

METHOD OF PAYMENT: (please check one)

❑ Check enclosed ❑ Please ship and bill. PO # _____
   (sorry we can ship and bill to bookstores only! All others must pre-pay)

❑ Charge to my credit card: ❑ Visa; ❑ MasterCard; ❑ Discover;
   ❑ American Express;

Account Number: _____ Expiration date: _____

Signature: ✗ _____

Name: _____ Institution: _____

Address: _____

_____

City: _____ State: _____ Zip: _____

Phone Number: _____ FAX Number: _____

MAIL or *FAX* THIS ENTIRE ORDER FORM TO:

Haworth Document Delivery Service	**or FAX:** 1-800-895-0582
The Haworth Press, Inc.	**or CALL:** 1-800-342-9678
10 Alice Street	9am-5pm EST)
Binghamton, NY 13904-1580	